Orders of Ex

Orders
of Exclusion

*Great Powers and the Strategic
Sources of Foundational Rules
in International Relations*

———◆———

KYLE M. LASCURETTES

OXFORD
UNIVERSITY PRESS

OXFORD
UNIVERSITY PRESS

Oxford University Press is a department of the University of Oxford. It furthers the University's objective of excellence in research, scholarship, and education by publishing worldwide. Oxford is a registered trade mark of Oxford University Press in the UK and certain other countries.

Published in the United States of America by Oxford University Press
198 Madison Avenue, New York, NY 10016, United States of America.

Library of Congress Cataloging-in-Publication Data
Names: Lascurettes, Kyle M., author.
Title: Orders of exclusion : great powers and the strategic sources of foundational rules in international relations / Kyle M. Lascurettes.
Description: New York, NY : Oxford University Press, [2020] |
Includes bibliographical references and index.
Identifiers: LCCN 2019045488 (print) | LCCN 2019045489 (ebook) |
ISBN 9780190068547 (hardback) | ISBN 9780190068554 (paperback) |
ISBN 9780190068578 (epub) | ISBN 9780190068585 (online)
Subjects: LCSH: Great powers. | International organization. |
Balance of power. | International relations—Philosophy.
Classification: LCC JZ1310.L37 2020 (print) | LCC JZ1310 (ebook) |
DDC 327.1/12—dc23
LC record available at https://lccn.loc.gov/2019045488
LC ebook record available at https://lccn.loc.gov/2019045489

1 3 5 7 9 8 6 4 2

Paperback printed by LSC Communications, United States of America
Hardback printed by Bridgeport National Bindery, Inc., United States of America

To my parents, Janet and Tod, for everything

Contents

Acknowledgments

IT SOUNDS CLICHÉ, I know, but living and working in the Pacific Northwest for the past five years has taught me that writing a book is a lot like climbing one of the Cascades Volcanoes: you can't even fathom what you're attempting to do at the start, you shake your head in resignation and vow to quit on countless occasions in the middle, and you only end up making it with the encouragement—and, where necessary, some motivational kicks to the butt—from a lot of obnoxiously friendly and infinitely helpful people around you. Here's hoping the book doesn't go the way of Mount St. Helens in 1980, however.

My intellectual journey began at St. Lawrence University in Upstate New York, where I only ended up in an international relations course after I couldn't get into a class about Neanderthals. I thank Karl Schonberg for letting me into his Intro IR class, and more importantly for inspiring an unexpected passion for international affairs in his engaging classes and seminars. Other professors at St. Lawrence were instrumental in helping a shy kid from the sticks come out of his shell, and are a testament to what a wonderful liberal arts education can do. Thanks especially to Tom Berger, Fred Exoo, Kerry Grant, and Ansil Ramsay.

This project was born at the University of Virginia, a wonderful place for graduate training in international relations, and where I happened to luck into the world's greatest dissertation committee. All four committee members have been instrumental in the long journey culminating in this book. My biggest debt is to Jeff Legro, who was so much more than an adviser and committee chair. Without Jeff's guidance and uncanny knack for knowing when my delicate psyche needed affirmation more than criticism, there never would have been a dissertation, a doctorate, or a career in the academy. At every stage of the long process from initial idea to book, Jeff's trenchant advice for framing the argument and keeping my primary targets in sight was invaluable in pulling me back from my many attempts to wander off path. Never has reading page after page of comments like "UGH" in the margins of my written work meant so much.

Dale Copeland is the best classroom teacher I've had the pleasure of learning from. His enthusiasm for IR theory was infectious from the first day of class, instantly making me excited to immerse myself in a world I barely understood at that time. He also taught me through his own scholarship how argument-based research projects can be just as provocative and powerful as question-based ones. And while I'm not sure that anyone will be able to fully drag realist theory into the twenty-first century, Dale is without a doubt realism's best hope.

The initial idea for this project came during a seminar on hegemony taught by John Owen, who provided wonderfully helpful feedback at all of its subsequent stages. He possesses a gift for somehow always packaging cutting and incisive critique in the gentlest and most encouraging language possible. While I was knee-deep in the weeds of dissertating, the release of John's masterful book on ideological conflicts also provided a fortuitous reminder of what the best scholarship in our field can illuminate. It is one of my very favorite IR books and remains a pleasure to teach and to reread.

Mel Leffler is a model scholar and my professorial idol in all things, from research and writing to teaching and mentorship. Simply put, he phones *nothing* in, including the traditionally minimal duties of a dissertation committee's "outside" reader. His incisive and detailed comments throughout this journey made the historical chapters of the dissertation—and now the book—so much richer and better.

I also had an unusually close, supportive, and rambunctious graduate cohort at UVA who made me better and happier in all things. Whoever says that graduate school is all work and no fun simply didn't do it right, and like we did, at Virginia. For all their curricular and extracurricular contributions, I thank Hilde Restad, Emily Charnock, Nadim (the Dream) Khoury, Molly Scudder, Anne Peters, Claire Timperley, Allison and Dave Novitsky, Susan Brewer, Tom Moriarty, Ryan Pevnick, James Patterson, Will Umphres, Greta and Ben Snyder, Sarah and Patrick Bradshaw, Sarah and Dave Kaczor, Lauren and Andy Miller, Emily Pears, Emily Sydnor, Justin Peck, Zuri Linetsky, Jen Silva, and Bethany Blalock. I am especially grateful to Kyle Haynes, Kate Sanger, and Brandon Yoder, good friends but also excellent colleagues, for our many impromptu IR workshops in Charlottesville. This meant that they routinely brutalized early iterations of the book's arguments from the comfort of my living room, all while consuming the pizza and beer I had purchased for them. Thanks a lot, guys.

Work on my dissertation was supported at UVA by the Gallatin Fund and, especially, by the Miller Center for Public Affairs. I thank Brian Balogh, James Graham Wilson, Mike Greco, Amber Lautiger, and Anne Mulligan for making my residency at the Miller Center so productive and enjoyable. And I owe a special thanks to John Ikenberry for serving as my outside mentor during that fellowship year. I can't think of many giants in our field who would so encourage a young scholar whose work directly targets their own, but John did so happily and helpfully.

The project matured during a two-year interlude in Washington, DC. At the George Washington University, I thank Charlie Glaser for welcoming me into an outstanding IR security community at the Elliot School, and Alex Downes, Eric Grynaviski, Julia MacDonald, Harris Mylonas, Josh Shifrinson, and Rachel Stein for helpful comments on my work or otherwise stimulating conversations during my time at GW. A subsequent year at Georgetown University's Mortara Center was especially productive, made possible by a grant secured by the Peace Research Institute Frankfurt (PRIF) and Charles Kupchan. I thank Charlie for his mentorship, and am also appreciative of the advice and support I received while at Georgetown from Kate McNamara, David Edelstein, Keir Lieber, Rebecca Friedman Lissner, Oriana Mastro, John McNeill, Halley Lisuk, and Moira Todd.

Many other teachers and colleagues have helped along the way and at various conferences and workshops over the years, even if they don't remember how, or even who exactly I am (hint: BIG HAIR). They include Mike Beckley, Josh Botts, Sarah Bush, Jonathan Caverley, Seth Center, Erica Chenoweth, Mike Cohen, Dan Deudney, Gary Goertz, Seva Gunitsky, Brendan Green, Will Hitchcock, David Lake, Mark Lawrence, Dan Lindley, Tim Luecke, Allen Lynch, Rich Maass, James McAllister, Sid Milkis, Evan Montgomery, Stacie Pettyjohn, Jonathan Renshon, David Rowe, Herman Mark Schwartz, Todd Sechser, Michael Joseph Smith, David Waldner, and Bill Wohlforth.

Lewis & Clark College has been a wonderful place to begin my professional career and finish this project. I thank my colleagues in the International Affairs department—Elizabeth Bennett, Cyrus Partovi, Heather Smith-Cannoy, Laura Vinson, and especially Bob Mandel—for their support, advice, and encouragement. As the book was taking shape, I had the opportunity to teach several versions of a seminar on Global Order for incredibly talented and imaginative Lewis & Clark students who sharpened my thinking on some of its most important components. Though they are too numerous to name individually, some special standouts included Sophia Freuden, Caroline Gray, Hannah Luzadder, Shamil Magomedov, Miranda Mora, Sam Perszyk, Hannah Stoddard, Marissa Valdez, and Dina Yazdani. And thanks especially to Drake MacFarlane, who was not only an outstanding student in the first iteration of that course but also provided invaluable research assistance on many aspects of the project.

At Oxford University Press, I thank my editor, Dave McBride, for being enthusiastic about the project from the beginning and for making each stage of the process since then painless and even enjoyable. Thanks also to Holly Mitchell, Shalini Balakrishnan, and Debbie Ruel for their help in bringing the book to press as well as in saving me from some embarrassing mistakes. Parts of chapter 5 appeared in an earlier form in "The Concert of Europe and Great-Power Governance Today: What Can the Order of 19th-Century Europe Teach Policymakers about International Order in the 21st Century?" *RAND National Defense Research Institute/ISDP Report* (January 2017). I thank the RAND Corporation for permission to use that material here, and am also grateful to Michael Mazarr and Miranda Priebe for inviting me to contribute to their larger project on Building a Sustainable International Order.

Throughout the arduous process of book writing and rewriting, wonderful friends and family have been critical to maintaining my sanity. In Portland, this included Maryann Bylander, Iris Maria Chávez, Meredith Davison, Whitney DeBree, Tara Ericksen, Sarah and Ben Gaskins, Erin Mckalip, Margaret Metz, Scott Permar and Jordan Culberson, Emily and Adam Peter, Rachel Ratner, Lexie Rhodes, Meg and Tony Rulli, Mary Warrington and Marc Whitehead, Olivia and Nick Young, as well as all my Mazamas peeps for dragging me up those mountains. I also thank Noodles and Rhubarb—both dogs—for each helping me get across the finish line on two crucial but stubborn empirical chapters. For years, I pledged that I was going to get "substantial work" done on the book while spending holidays with my Martinez family in Denver. I never did, but nonetheless very much appreciate all of the opportunities for fun and R&R they provided in Colorado. Finally, and at those rare moments when I was feeling a bit too confident about my work or myself, the daily and never-ending chain of derogatory text messages from lifelong friends in Upstate New York—Kevin Crumb, Jim Parker, Zac Wasielewski, and Chad Knutti—always managed to appropriately humble me once again.

This book is dedicated to my parents, Janet and Tod Lascurettes. They won't be familiar with much that is in it, but it wouldn't have been possible without their unyielding support and unconditional love. They also improved this acknowledgments section, the part of a book I always look to for a window into the author's life. Without receiving a bit of my mom's warmth and enthusiasm for everyone around her, I certainly wouldn't have so many great people to thank for making life beyond these pages so worth living. And without inheriting a bit of my dad's irreverence, I definitely wouldn't have the audacity (or poor sense) to be cracking bad jokes in the opening pages of my first scholarly monograph. Oops.

KML
Portland, Oregon

I

Power Politics and International Order

IN RECENT DECADES, foreign policymakers in the United States have increasingly focused on America's ability to shape something called "international order." The administration of Barack Obama prioritized this concept to such an extent that they characterized order building as one of the four most important pillars of American's grand strategy in both of their *National Security Strategy* (NSS) blueprints.[1] "We have to shape an international order that can meet the challenges of our generation," President Obama himself emphasized to the graduating West Point cadets in his 2010 commencement address.

To outside observers, it might sound strange to hear the leader of the most powerful country on earth speaking favorably about tying his country even tighter into a constraining web of global commitments. Yet in an age when many believe that America's hegemonic power in global affairs is on the wane, a prevailing view in both policy and academic circles since the end of the Cold War has been that a pivot to "international order" is a winning proposition for the United States of America. So this argument goes, order is that rare subject area in which a bipartisan generation of American elites did their homework after the Second World War, making farsighted investments in an international architecture that would prove both advantageous and enduring. Back at West Point again in 2014, Obama lauded this monumental achievement: "After World War II, America had the wisdom to shape institutions to keep the peace and support human progress—from NATO and the United Nations, to the World Bank and IMF." This order, Obama confidently declared, has "been a force multiplier—reducing the need for unilateral American action, and increased restraint among other nations."

Behind these sentiments rested a common assumption about the architecture that outlasted the Cold War and then grew even stronger in its wake: compared to systems of the past, *this* arrangement, the American-led liberal international order of the postwar era, has been the most inclusive, the most universally benefi-cial, and therefore the most popular and just order the world has ever seen. To the extent that US leaders can tie their country's fate to this system, the United States of America will remain at the summit of global politics in perpetuity.

Indicative of this optimism have been forecasts about the United States' rela-tionship with rising powers like China or resurgent powers like Russia. Even as others are increasingly able to challenge America's *power* on the world stage, these optimists say, American *influence* will remain paramount as the dynamics of lib-eral order trump the dynamics of power politics. Liberal order is a rising tide that lifts all boats. As a consequence, other states—even those that are seen as America's fiercest competitors—will have little incentive to fundamentally trans-form an arrangement that continues to serve their interests so well. "Although the United States' position in the global system is changing, the liberal inter-national order is alive and well," writes the political scientist John Ikenberry, a leading advocate of this optimistic perspective. "The struggle over international order today is not about fundamental principles. China and other emerging great powers do not want to contest the basic rules and principles of the liberal inter-national order; they wish to gain more authority and leadership within it."[2] As a result, *this* great power transition, unlike others in the past, will be both more peaceful—without war—and less transformative—without fundamental revi-sions to the rules of the system.

Unfortunately, however, events of the last five years have demonstrated that all is not well with the liberal international order. Even during the Obama years, the global architecture lauded by elites, academics, and the president himself was beginning to show significant wear and tear. As civil war raged on in Syria and another transnational jihadist network ravaged the larger region, the great powers of the United Nations Security Council remained deadlocked not only about the Middle East but over a broader approach for addressing global flash-points that more and more frequently blurred the lines between domestic and international issues. China increasingly picked fights with its regional neighbors over disputed territories and rights at sea, often appearing disinterested in abid-ing by international law. Russia, meanwhile, reverted to viewing global dynamics through a Cold War lens, forcibly annexing territory from Ukraine, fomenting unrest and insecurity in a number of former Soviet domains along its borders, and attempting to meddle in America's electoral processes.

While Obama claimed in his 2014 speech that "it has been our willingness to work through multilateral channels that kept the world on our side," defections from both the Western cooperative and Western domestic model have become more the rule than the exception. Other rising powers like Brazil, India, and

South Africa surprisingly but vocally backed Russia in its regional aggression,[3] as did resurgent right-wing nationalist movements across Europe.[4] Empowered by the backlash to a refugee crisis that has tested the European Union's unity, these groups scored a dramatic first blow against this edifice in their stunning victory in the United Kingdom's Brexit referendum in 2016. As the United States and its traditional allies scrambled to respond to such challenges, the central Asian autocracies deepened economic, energy, and security ties with each other at the West's expense while developing states across Africa and Latin America have increasingly turned toward China for both aid and ideological inspiration.[5] *The Economist* warned that Russian and Chinese assertiveness have "driven a tank over the existing world order," while a prominent *Washington Post* columnist lamented that "global disorder seems a more distinct possibility than it has since the 1930s."[6]

All of this took place even before the rise of Donald Trump. Yet more than any other development, his 2016 victory has awoken many observers to the surprising fragility of the liberal international order.[7] "Around the world and here at home," Senator John McCain warned shortly before his passing, recent developments have contributed to "the erosion of that order and the institutions that protect it—and we cannot act soon enough to reverse this trajectory."[8]

The Trump administration does not appear interested in this course of action. While the Obama team framed international order as a central component of American strength, President Trump's NSS doesn't even mention the term. If anything, the Trump team seems to deride the very idea of order, declaring that "there is no arc of history that ensures that America's free political and economic system will automatically prevail." When it comes to the international organizations central to liberal order, Trump argues that "all institutions are not equal," and that "the United States will prioritize its efforts in those organizations that serve American interests."[9] As Walter Russell Mead has put it, "for the first time in 70 years, the American people have elected a president who disparages the policies, ideas, and institutions at the heart of postwar U.S. foreign policy."[10] "America's choice" in the 2016 election, argues Francis Fukuyama, "signifies a switching of sides from the liberal internationalist camp, to the populist nationalist one."[11]

If the American-constructed order is meant to be so durable and popular both around the world and within the United States itself, it isn't possible to make sense of these profound disruptions. I do not try to do so. Instead, this book tells a different tale about the trajectory of order in world politics, one that calls into question not only the optimistic narrative about today's order but also the rationale for why throughout history great powers have constructed new orders in the first place. In particular, it develops an alternative theory for what powerful states seek to achieve through order and why they have sought to defend or advance such different order visions across space and time. In brief, I contend that the origins and evolution of the contemporary order follow a long pattern of power-ful states engaging in order building not to be benevolent and inclusive, as the optimists have claimed, but instead to *exclude* particular actors and entities in world politics. The origins of international orders, I will argue, are to be found in the logic of competition and exclusion.

The order optimists—often today called *liberal internationalists* for the kind of order principles they champion—posit that the contemporary order is excep-tional in part because it had exceptional origins compared to orders of the past. By contrast, I aim to illuminate the striking continuities between the origins of past and present orders.

History is replete with instances of order architects constructing new systems to weaken, leave out, or hold back perceived rivals and competitors. For instance, the birth of the modern states system in Europe came about when it did only because the victors of the Thirty Years' War wanted to shatter the universalist authority claims of their religious and imperial adversaries, a feat they achieved by championing sovereign statehood (chapter 4). The conservative vanquishers of Napoleon in the nineteenth century created the so-called Concert of Europe in order to stamp out transnational liberal movements and forestall the rise of another revolutionary liberal state (chapter 5). And while Woodrow Wilson's vision for a new postwar order after the First World War was heavily couched in peaceful and progressive rhetoric, it was in fact heavily influenced by a fierce and conservative opposition to the Bolshevik Revolution in Russia and a correspond-ing fear of radicalism catching fire around the world (chapter 6).

Though the debate over order is one of significant interest to political sci-entists and historians, its importance extends beyond academia. The stakes are high for future generations. While great power competition is an endemic fea-ture of international affairs, the nature and character of world politics more generally will hinge on whether that competition continues within the circum-scribed boundaries of the existing order or instead explodes into an existen-tial battle between competing visions of contrary orders. If the inclusive logic emphasized by liberal internationalists stands up to scrutiny, US policymak-ers would do well to double down on the most open and mutually beneficial elements of this order. Yet if the excluding logic advanced in this book has purchase, then influential powers like the United States and China will find it difficult to defy the patterns of adversarial order building I argue have been pervasive throughout history.

Understanding how international orders have been formed—and why lead-ing states have sought to create, change, or destroy them—is thus crucial for understanding the trajectories of both American grand strategy and world poli-tics more generally in the twenty-first century. Yet because the debate over today's international order is only one aspect of an emerging research program on political order more generally, I step back in the next section to take stock of this program. I then sketch out the broad contours of my argument, situate it within existing theories of international relations (IR), and outline the rest of the book's structure and content.

1.1 What Are International Orders?

The term *international order* is invoked frequently these days, but the systematic study of international order is still in its infancy. While almost all scholars of politics are in some way interested in political order, the vast majority have focused on domestic order, or order within polities. This is especially true in the field of comparative politics. Comparative scholars have generated important insights regarding the sources of state formation and political and economic development. One could therefore expect scholarship on *international* order to draw upon some of this rich literature's key insights. Unfortunately, studies of order at the international level have thus far done so only sparingly, weakening both the conceptualization of international order as well as explanations for its origins.[12]

Conceptualizations of order at the domestic level have focused on particular types of rules and institutions. Max Weber famously drew distinctions between different kinds of political authority, favoring a rational-legal pathway that would produce stable, impartial institutions.[13] In Samuel Huntington's classic treatise, order "depends upon the strength of the political organizations and procedures in the society. That strength, in turn, depends upon the scope of support for the organizations and procedures and their level of institutionalization."[14] And in Fukuyama's update to Huntington, order refers to the confluence of three sets of domestic institutions: a semi-autonomous and effective state apparatus, the rule of law, and some mechanisms of accountability to a broader population.[15]

These conceptions of order at the domestic level say little about the content of such institutions and rules, leaving broad space for the vastly different forms order can take. Order in world politics, by contrast, has too often been associated with specific and desirable outcomes like peace and harmony between states. According to the late IR theorist Hedley Bull, for example, "international order" implies three normatively positive things about relations between states: that people will be relatively secure against violence; "that promises, once made, will be kept"; and that "the possession of things will remain stable to some degree."[16] Others have been even more explicit in associating order with positive normative content. In one such study, Yuen Foong Khong argued that at the international level, order is most widely construed in terms of its normative substance, as the condition of "peace" or the absence of general war. As an introductory textbook on international relations put it, "Order is when relationships between states are stable, predictable, controlled and not characterized by violence, turbulence or chaos."[17]

It is tempting yet faulty, I posit, to adopt this line of reasoning. The American-led order of the postwar era may indeed possess a variety of attributes deemed desirable, at least from a Western vantage point. But if the very definition of order is now synonymous with other positive attributes, the concept itself becomes useless for describing ordered systems of prior centuries. For if *all* orders have been peaceful or at least broadly desirable, it makes little sense to devote resources toward changing them—as leaders have often done throughout history—or to talk about "a just and sustainable international order"—as the Obama administration often did.[18]

Instead, I argue that it is more useful to think of order simply as *actors of a system regularly observing common rules*. More specifically, an ordered system is one where a common set of rules is observed by a majority of that system's polities. These rules, or "order principles," come in two types: those that govern external behavior and relations between polities—behavior rules—and those that govern internal behavior and dictate the kinds of units allowed full recognition and rights in world politics—membership rules.

Behavior rules can correspond to if and when it is appropriate for actors to use military force or intervene in others' internal affairs, or what kinds of international economic policies are encouraged or discouraged, for example. Membership rules involve minimum standards that actors must meet to be considered full participants of the order. For the last few centuries, issues of membership have most often involved ideological attributes, promoting socialist or capitalist or democratic or authoritarian domestic institutions, for instance. Order principles of either type may or may not be codified in official international agreements, but they nonetheless have tangible implications for foreign policy behaviors and national identities.

Aside from providing conceptual separation, a principal advantage of this rule-based conception of international order is that it is normatively neutral. The content of order principles can vary widely and point in normatively good *or* normatively bad directions. Particular order principles have created between polities violent conflict, economic and social inequality, and instances of gross injustice. In other words, characterizing an international system as "ordered" says very little about whether that system should be considered a positive or negative development for human relations.

1.2 What Are the Sources of International Orders?

As with its conceptualization, prominent *explanations* for where international orders come from tend to uniformly focus on normatively positive developments. This again contrasts with the study of domestic order, which affords a greater causal role for conflict and power-based explanations. Comparative political scholarship on state formation serves as a telling example. While this literature is in many ways diverse, it is united by an underlying assumption that power and conflict have been integral to the formation of strong nation-states. Time and again scholars have invoked Charles Tilly's famous dictum that "war made the state, and the state made war" to elucidate new understandings of the relationship between conflict and order formation within states.[19] Even when it is only part of a larger causal story, scholarship on domestic development broadly accepts the existence of an important connection between competition and order.[20]

Existing explanations for international order look banal by comparison. Where we observe order at the international level, these explanations suggest, polities must have cooperatively banded together to overcome the most pernicious effects of anarchy, competition, and war that often plague world politics. Since international order is normatively positive, the story of its development must be equally positive. Social constructivist scholarship on international order in particular has often embraced this approach to order formation.

This book adopts a different starting point for explaining order's origins. To put it plainly, I seek to account for where international order comes from by looking not for broad consensus among many actors, as social constructivists often do, but to the order preferences of the most powerful actors in world politics. No matter the era, some actors are always better positioned than others to enact their preferences over the larger system. This is not to say that dominant actors are always successful at getting the orders they prefer. Nevertheless, we can still observe that when orders have experienced important transformations throughout history, they have most often done so in ways that mirror the preferences of the most dominant actors. In sum, this is a book about hegemonic preferences for international order.

1.2.1 A New Argument

This is not the first study to trace the causes of major systemic changes to the interests of the great powers. A central assumption of Robert Gilpin's *War and Change in World Politics*, for example, is that "the behaviors rewarded and punished by the system will coincide, at least initially, with the interests of the most powerful members of that social system."[21] Ikenberry has similarly argued that the "struggle over order has tended to be, first and foremost, a struggle over how leading states can best provide security for themselves."[22]

This study's greatest departure from prior works comes not from its focus on dominant actors, but from the pride of place it affords to competition and conflict in the production of international order. Whereas prior studies have focused on the consensus-driven origins of orders, I argue that the propelling motivation for foundational rule building at important historical junctures has most often been exclusionary, not inclusive. My core contention is that dominant actors pursue fundamental changes to order only when they perceive a major new threat on the horizon, a threat to their security or to their enduring primacy. When these actors seek to enact fundamentally new order principles, they do so for the purpose of targeting this perceived threat, be it a powerful state, a contrary alliance, or a foreboding ideological movement. The goal of order building, then, is weakening, opposing, and above all excluding that threatening entity from amassing further influence in world politics.

Take the Utrecht peace settlement of the early eighteenth century as example. The settlement is remembered for instituting two major changes to European order after the War of the Spanish Succession: the legitimization of states seeking a "balance of power" on the continent, and the delegitimization of rulers using dynastic (family) connections to redraw Europe's borders. In conventional accounts, the Utrecht negotiators agreed that these consensus principles were necessary for lasting peace. Analysis of the actual negotiations reveals a different story. It shows the war's most powerful victor, Great Britain, using the settlement to address its continuing fear of the powerful and ambitious ruler of France, King Louis XIV. By outlawing interstate dynastic claims, British leaders abruptly dismembered Louis's easiest path to expanding French influence across Europe. And through popularizing the idea of a legitimate balance of power, they instantly erected a barrier against the Sun King's well-known ambition for French hegemony over the continent. Not coincidentally, then, each new order rule deprived France of some aspect of the power deemed so threatening to British elites. It was the nature of the dominant actor's perceived adversary, not some consensus forged through cooperative understanding, that conditioned the changes to Europe's order. Far from falling outside the bounds of traditional statecraft, order building has been, to paraphrase Clausewitz, the continuation of power politics by other means.

Students of IR will quickly notice the commonalities between the core of my argument and realism, long the dominant school of thought in IR theory. Realist scholars typically focus more on the paramount role of power in world politics and less on the things like norms, institutions, and rules that are often associated with international order. Contemporary realists (or neorealists) are so skeptical of order that they often either deny its existence or simply ignore the concept altogether.[23] However, for a prior generation of realists—those who are today called classical realists—the story I tell here will make more sense. Behind the curtain of international order, classical realists argued, is the familiar backdrop of great power competition for influence. Notable scholars writing in this tradition have at least loosely highlighted a relationship between powerful states' strategic interests and the resulting system of rules in world politics. As E. H. Carr famously put it, "'international order' and 'international solidarity' will always be slogans of those who feel strong enough to impose them on others."[24] At its core, my argument fits within this tradition.

While generally indebted to the realist perspective, this book's primary argument—which I call *ordering-to-exclude theory*—also corrects for significant weaknesses and ambiguities in realism in at least three important respects. First, *all* types of realist theories would have difficulties explaining the focus of this study, the order preferences of great powers. For neorealists, great powers should simply never bother with order in the first place. But because of this, neorealism cannot account for any scenario in which we observe actors devoting significant attention toward changing the rules of order.

Classical realism has more to say on the subject, yet remains flawed in one crucial respect: while it can tell us which actors will be most capable of shaping order to serve their interests, it tells us virtually nothing about what those interests will be. In practice, the simple prediction that actors prefer orders that serve their interests is unhelpful and unfalsifiable, as it tells us nothing about what interests those actors will prioritize. Lacking sound deductive reasoning, classical realists fall back on post hoc and case-specific claims.[25] Yet without a more general theory of order preferences, they cannot account for why dominant actors have advocated for vastly different visions of order across time and space even when they have faced similar structural incentives. My argument provides such a theory.

A second distinctive quality of my argument involves the scope and conceptualization of international threats. To be sure, the heart of my argument is compatible with realism, as traditional measures of state power remain an important component of threat perceptions in the grand narrative of order building. This core logic of the theory is captured in the boxed-in portion of Figure 1.1.

Yet ordering-to-exclude theory also features a broader conceptualization of threats than realists have typically recognized. In particular, I argue that dominant actors have often felt threatened at least as much by contrary *ideologies*—ideas about how best to organize domestic societies—as they have by other traditionally powerful *states*, and yet still do so for very rational and materialist reasons. As I seek to show, many of the most consequential order changes in history began as responses to threatening transnational ideological movements, such as radical liberalism in the nineteenth century or revolutionary socialism in the twentieth.

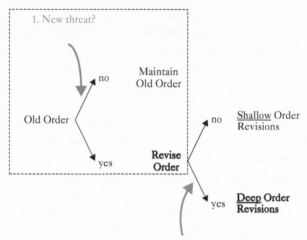

FIGURE 1.1 When will dominant actors revise international order?

I contend that it is when they believe they are facing multidimensional adversaries—those wielding not only formidable military might but also formidable ideological appeal to a broad international audience—that dominant actors are most apt to advocate for the deepest, most penetrating changes to order (Figure 1.1). Deep changes involve recasting not only behavior rules but also rules of membership, digging down within polities to control their domestic relations as much as their international ones. It was thus no coincidence that the statesmen of Europe created the very first order with explicit membership principles immediately following the unprecedented upheaval caused by the system's first truly ideological threat, Revolutionary France. Manipulating the rules of states' behavior remained important but was not by itself enough to forestall revolutionary contagion and upheaval from *within* societies, an entirely new kind of threat at that time.

Finally, my argument takes more seriously than realism the political power of ideas. Realists typically either deny or ignore any such power. In contrast, I offer a logic under which leaders assume, quite rationally, that they can strategically employ the ideas behind new order principles to inflict very real harm against adversarial actors or movements. In so doing, ordering-to-exclude theory adds to a growing body of work demonstrating how actors often strategically manipulate collective ideas to advance their own self-interests. Yet it also goes beyond previous work by demonstrating precisely *how* abstract principles can be used by some actors to disadvantage others. In chapter 3, I identify a number of pathways through which dominant powers have often used the principles of order to target, weaken, delegitimize, and exclude other actors and entities. Doing so helps illuminate some of the precise processes through which order building can be a rational strategy available to prudent leaders, a claim almost never advanced in realist scholarship.

1.2.2 The Argument and International Relations Theory

More generally, ordering-to-exclude theory both embraces and rejects elements of the major paradigms in IR theory. It embraces the basic thesis of social constructivism that ideational phenomena related to international order are worth studying (the outcome), but often parts ways with constructivist explanations for how those phenomena come about (the cause) by focusing on dominant actors and their reactions to the strategic environment around them, a point I develop in more detail in chapters 2 and 3. Conversely, it faults realism for ignoring this kind of outcome—international order—while employing a causal logic broadly but not entirely consistent with realist propositions. Neither realism nor constructivism can offer a complete explanation for dominant-actor order preferences, the former because it does not take order seriously, the latter because it does not recognize dominant actors' crucial role in producing order.[26] For these reasons, I do not systematically engage with either perspective throughout the book's case investigations.

Instead, I assess ordering-to-exclude theory against three more viable explanations that are broadly consistent with the liberal paradigm of IR theory. First, powerful states could seek to advance order principles designed to increase the longevity of their preponderance by making their leadership more acceptable to the other, smaller actors of the international system ("binding"). Second, great powers might prefer order changes that bring important elements of the international system more in line with their own domestic institutions, beliefs, or ideologies ("exporting"). Third, dominant powers could seek to advance a vision of international order designed to address and prevent the reemergence of some notable problem or past catastrophe in their history ("learning").

Not coincidentally, each of these arguments also contains an element of liberal internationalist optimism pervasive in existing narratives about the American order-building project. Ikenberry has argued for a version of the first: in the wake of the Second World War, American leaders created an institutionalized order to "lock in" their favorable international position while reassuring allies of their benevolence. On the second, many in the US policymaking community frequently advance the view that the American-led order has been a natural outward projection of America's liberal values and democratic institutions. And on the third, historians in particular often point to the failure of the League of Nations and the onset of the Great Depression as the catalysts for producing an order explicitly designed to respond to and overcome those calamities.

These perspectives also all reach a common verdict on the American order-building experience: it has been exceptional, it has been uniquely inclusive, and it should engender optimism about the future. It is *exceptional* because the United States was motivated to build it for reasons distinct from the motives behind order-building projects in the past. It is also uniquely *inclusive*, forged out of a desire to make the system as open and accommodating to outsiders as possible. And precisely because of its exceptional origins and inclusive attributes, the continued endurance of this order engenders an *optimism* about the future of world politics and America's role in it. If there is purchase to any of these hypotheses, we could gain more confidence in the claim that the American order-building project really does represent a significant break from the past.

1.3   The Order of This Book

The ultimate aim of the book is to uncover patterns of order building from the advent of the modern states system to the present. It is macro-historical in scope and comparative-historical in method. Because order preferences are difficult to quantify, statistical analysis is inappropriate for this endeavor. Instead, I employ two important tools of qualitative analysis—congruence testing and process tracing—to test competing motives for order building across time and space. I discuss these methods in more detail in chapter 3.

In selecting cases, I have focused on periods when dominant actors have had *order change opportunities*. These are special moments in history when particular polities possessed both an abundance of material capability and some special recognized right to rewrite the foundational rules of world politics. In practice, I focus on order change opportunities created by major shocks to the international system. I say more about two distinct types of shock, as well as the specific criteria for case selection, in chapter 2. For now, Table 1.1 lists the nine historical moments that constitute the empirical core of the book.

Chapter 2 addresses issues of conceptualization and case selection, while chapter 3 grapples with theoretical explanation and method. In chapter 2, I make a case for characterizing order as a set of observed rules, defend an approach for explaining order that focuses on the preferences of dominant actors, and then use both to justify the cases listed in Table 1.1. Readers most interested in my central argument—ordering-to-exclude theory—might want to skip directly to chapter 3, the book's theoretical core, where I develop the core thesis and establish its corresponding hypotheses. Chapter 3 also generates hypotheses for the

Table 1.1 The Cases

Years	Formative Events	Dominant Actors
1648	Treaties of Westphalia after the Thirty Years' War	France, Sweden
1713	Treaties of Utrecht after the War of the Spanish Succession	Great Britain
1763	Treaty of Paris after the Seven Years' War	Great Britain
1814–1818	Congresses / Treaties of Chaumont, Vienna, Paris (2), and Aix-La-Chapelle after the French Revolutionary and Napoleonic Wars	United Kingdom (UK), Austria, Russia
1848	Aftermath of revolutions across Europe	UK
1856	Congress / Treaty of Paris after the Crimean War	UK, France
1919	Paris Peace Conference / Treaty of Versailles after World War I	United States (US), UK, France
1945–1949	Bretton Woods (1944), Brussels (1948), and Washington (1949) conferences / agreements after World War II	US
1989–1990	Malta (1989) and Washington (1990) conferences / agreements after breakup of the Soviet Empire in Europe	US

alternative arguments and details the methods of analysis I employ for the subsequent historical comparisons.

Those case studies are the focus of chapters 4 through 8. Chapter 4 tackles important instances of European order building in the early modern era, while chapter 5 focuses on the rise and demise of the Concert of Europe order in the nineteenth century. Together, these chapters seek to demonstrate the *breadth* of the theory through a sweeping overview of European power politics from an order-building perspective.

Chapters 6 through 8 focus on the twentieth century and, predominantly, on the United States of America. Chapter 6 aims to demonstrate the *depth* of the argument, or its ability to account for the precise details of a case for which we have an abundance of evidence: US President Woodrow Wilson's vision for order at the end of the First World War. Chapters 7 and 8 assess the origins and evolution of today's system, the liberal international order created after the Second World War. Chapter 7 seeks to disentangle the complexity of the American order-building project in the 1940s, while chapter 8 explores the extraordinary developments in the late 1980s that created an opportunity for American leaders to create a new world order at the end of the Cold War. I conclude by discussing my findings and their implications for future order-building endeavors in chapter 9, focusing in particular on the dynamics of order construction and contestation in the midst of the coming Sino-American power transition.

2

Reordering International Order

THIS CHAPTER HAS three objectives: conceptual brush clearing, conceptual rebuilding, and linking this rebuilt conception to an empirical agenda for the rest of book. First, it surveys the existing conceptions of order in IR scholarship and identifies some problems inherent in each. Specifically, I present a two-step process of conceptualization to help clarify and streamline the debate over how best to define and think about international order. The first step establishes a baseline definition for what pattern of behavior constitutes a state of order. I posit that an ordered system is one that incentivizes units to engage in equilibrium-perpetuating behavior. The second step focuses on the content of an order that produces this pattern of behavior. When it comes to international order, I argue, the dominant IR paradigms actually agree on the first step. Their disagreements come over the second step, the content that produces equilibrium-perpetuating behavior.

Second, I detail a new, synthetic conceptualization of order that stands on the shoulders of prior approaches but seeks to avoid their shortcomings. I argue that order is best conceptualized not as particular material, institutional, or normative environments but instead as the presence of a set of *observed rules* in world politics. Third, I return to the primary empirical focus of this book, dominant-actor preferences for international order. After justifying this focus, I more precisely define dominant actors and moments of order change opportunity. I then use these definitions to identify the set of historical cases that are the focus of chapters 4 through 8.

2.1 Laying the Groundwork

The task of finding common conceptual ground necessarily begins with defining some basic but important terms. First, the terms *unit* and *polity* denote a basic and discrete political conglomerate that has at least nominal separation between its domestic system and the international system. These terms are preferable to *state* because a general conceptualization of order should remain applicable to international systems that are not populated by sovereign nation-states.

Second, a *system* exists when two or more units have enough contact and interaction with one another that they "have sufficient impact on one another's decisions, [causing] them to behave—at least in some measure—as parts of a whole."[1] The "whole" in a system is not always simply reducible to the preferences and behaviors of individual units. As Robert Jervis has put it, "we are dealing with a system when (a) a set of units or elements is interconnected so that changes in some elements of their relations produce changes in other parts of the system, and (b) the entire system exhibits properties and behaviors that are different from those of the parts."[2] "System" is therefore synonymous with some basic level of interdependence. The presence of a system is a necessary but insufficient condition for *order*, a term that has most often been used to denote something beyond simple interdependence. Thus, we need a basic-level definition for order itself.

2.1.1 Step 1 of 2: Defining Order

The basic level of a concept is the "top of the pyramid," its general essence, what it most broadly and fundamentally means.[3] "Democracy" implies political contestation through elections, for instance, while "war" denotes some sort of material conflict. I posit that a basic-level definition of order should point only to general systemic patterns, leaving sufficient space for more specific behaviors and outcomes like war, peace, or cooperation toward a common goal. I thus offer a basic-level definition that aims to capture how scholars working from distinct IR perspectives frequently seem to think about the concept: *order is a pattern of equilibrium-perpetuating behavior among the units of a system*. That is, in an ordered system units behave in ways that reproduce the status quo. Status quo perpetuation may come about through individual unit behaviors or through the aggregation of a multitude of unit actions collectively. Put another way, while unit behavior may be more cooperative and coordinated in an ordered system, it need not be, so long as the aggregate result is perpetuation of the status quo across the system.

It follows that while the presence of order might lead to normatively desirable things like peace or justice, it need not necessarily do so. Orders could be premised on normatively undesirable conditions, including rigid inequalities, intense competition, or even violence. Behaviors that are undesirable can and often do take place within ordered systems. As Donald Black has observed, behavior that is labeled "criminal" in modern societies actually often serves as a form of social control and conflict management in traditional societies, ones without a strong role for the rule of law.[4] The same can be said of the modern international system, where the rule of law is heavily contested at best.[5] Yet in an ordered system, even antagonistic behaviors are patterned, and the aggregation of conflicts is circumscribed enough to perpetuate the status quo.[6] "Order does not prevent war, but regulates it and keeps it within bounds," writes Richard Ned Lebow. And while it might be true that "justice is best served by an ordered world" where behavior is patterned and predictable, order even in this case would be at best a necessary but insufficient requirement for justice throughout the system.[7]

Since this definition of order does not hinge on peace, violence, or specific normative content, these things also cannot be used to define the negative pole of the concept "disorder." Disorder cannot simply be synonymous with war and violence, or enmity and injustice. Instead, the term denotes only a lack of external constraint on the units of a system, allowing them to act in ways that, collectively, work to disturb or alter the systemic status quo. As with order, "disorder does not entail specific behaviors; its set of possible actualizations is infinite."[8]

In sum, at the basic level, *order* refers only to a system where units exist and behave in ways that reinforce equilibrium. If this definition sounds incomplete or even tautological, it is, at least without more conceptual information. Different IR paradigms contend that very different kinds of things make up the environment that ensures equilibrium in the first place. This is the secondary level of the conceptualization process.

2.1.2 Step 2 of 2: Conceptualizing Order

It is at the secondary level where IR theories fundamentally disagree over international order. I focus here on the three most prominent approaches to order in the IR literature: neorealism, institutionalism, and systemic constructivism.

To hear realist scholars describe it, a persistent and fundamental tenet of world politics has always been the distinct lack of order.[9] Yet upon closer inspection, realists often do have a conceptualization of order, even as many realist scholars are hesitant to label it as such. Realists look for order and account for its variation by examining a particular consequence of anarchy—namely, the fact that the system's units must assess one another according to their relative power. In an ordered system, the material environment dictates *either* that it is in no major actor's interest to fundamentally upset or seek to overturn the status quo, *or* that no actor that attempts to do so will be successful. Actors recognize—or else painfully come to realize—that the material costs of seeking major systemic change outweigh the material benefits. The term *material environment* most often refers to the distribution of capabilities (or relative power) among the units of a system. More specifically, many realists focus on *polarity*, or the number of great powers in the system, as the foremost measure of the distribution of capabilities.[10] The dynamics of an order will be fundamentally different if there is only one great power (unipolarity) versus two (bipolarity) versus more than two (multipolarity).[11]

From a second perspective, the content of order isn't the material environment constituted by the distribution of power but the degree of institutionalization in world politics. Order in this view is the proliferation of formal networks of interaction between actors, or the institutionalization of inter-unit exchanges. As one prominent scholar has put it, "the relation between international institutions and order is a relatively simple one. The entire point of institutions is to embody norms and rules, and thus to induce more certainty and predictability in patterns of international interactions."[12] Institutionalist scholars argue that institutions produce equilibrium-perpetuating behavior among units because they fulfill the purposes for which they were created. Self-interested actors create institutions for utility maximization, which becomes more possible because institutions perform services such as increasing actors' routine interactions with and information about one another, monitor compliance with agreements, and identify and punish defecting actors. Once these mutual benefits become manifest, units will recognize these benefits, work to preserve the institutions that make them possible, and perhaps even seek greater institutionalization across the system. Effectively institutionalized systems are ordered, whereas systems without effective institutions are not. An ideal constitutional order, John Ikenberry argues, is one containing numerous entrenched institutions that set "binding and authoritative limits on the exercise of power" and are hard for even the most powerful actors to manipulate. More order exists in the institutionalized environment with strong checks on the unilateral use of power, as well as when there is broad acceptance of institutionalization by many units over many issue areas. Less order presumes either fewer institutions, less agreement among them, or less effectiveness in them.[13]

Focusing not on material or institutional environments but on normative (or ideational) ones, constructivists equate order with a stable social structure that exists above the units of a system and conditions their interests, behaviors, and identities. Order is constituted by a common set of norms over fundamental issues in international politics. Common ideas shared by units across a system form the normative environment, also sometimes described as "shared understandings," "collective knowledge," "collective identity," or "world culture."[14] This environment then acts back upon the agents, influencing their interests, behaviors, and identities.[15] Constructivists often argue that the modern international system is remarkable not for the disparities it produces but for the considerable uniformities in beliefs and behaviors across actors regardless of their disparate circumstances.[16] These similarities serve as evidence of a powerful social structure bearing down upon units, driving them toward behaviors and identities that feed back into and reproduce that structure. It is this uniformity and consensus that perpetuates the status quo, as the reproduction of behavior dictated by the normative environment acts as a strengthening mechanism back upon that environment.[17]--

While each of these conceptualizations has its strengths, together they all share a common conceptual flaw: each presupposes a particular set of causes for the origins of order, or what causes order to break out or break down in the first place. As a result, they often talk past each other because each focuses on its preferred set of explanatory variables. Realists quite clearly presuppose materialist causes for order, for example. For if order is simply the distribution of material power, as they imply, only factors that affect that distribution will bring about changes to it. This is important because many scholars share with neorealists a belief in international structuralism yet disagree with realists that material power is the most important aspect of order. But if we were to accept the realist *conception* of order, it would be impossible to deny that material *causes* of the type that realists focus upon—military spending, economic growth, the distribution of technology, and so forth—are the principal factors that dictate order. Once winning the order conceptualization debate, realists would automatically also win the debate over order's causes.

On the surface, institutionalism appears to do better than realism in separating the concept of order from its causes. Yet institutionalists are also self-professed functionalists, arguing that the institutions that constitute order are created in the first place to fulfill the very functions they perform.[18] Thus by definition they presuppose particular causes for order, limiting the potential explanatory factors to either (a) the rational self-interests of the units that create the institutions, or (b) the structural conditions—such as increasing interdependence and "issue density"—that condition the units' rational self-interests.[19] Nearly as much as with realism, institutionalism's conception of order therefore comes with a privileged set of causes.

Constructivists also clearly presuppose particular ideational causes for order. By definition they begin their analysis by blurring the boundary between causes and outcomes, as actors' ideas and interactions create the very normative environment that acts back upon them. This poses challenges for any analysis conducted from a constructivist perspective. Yet it becomes even more problematic when it comes to conceptualizing order, since it means that constructivists begin by assuming genuine agreement on and internalization of the norms that make up order.[20] Even if we were to accept that collective ideas are important to order, it does not necessarily follow that these ideas must be internalized by the units of a system. As I argue in the following section, one can accept aspects of the constructivist conception—that order is constituted by social components—without embracing the accompanying assumption about true internalization.

2.2 A Synthetic Conception of Order

Each of these approaches thus focuses on its own preferred kinds of causal forces for explaining order's origins. This obscures the fact that at the most basic level, they all agree in some sense on what order really is: a pattern that results in fixed and stable interactions among the units of a system. Yet by studying order only through the lenses of their preexisting frameworks, they do not bring us much closer to understanding precisely how—and if—order actually matters in world politics in a way that makes it distinct from power, institutions, or ideas.

In this section, I detail an alternative secondary-level conception of order. I start from the same basic-level definition; but rather than focus on the distribution of power, formal institutions, or normative structures, I draw attention to the importance of rules in world politics. More specifically, I conceptualize order as equilibrium perpetuation constituted by the presence of a set of *observed rules* among the units of a system. I explain in subsection 2.2.1 what I mean by rules and discuss why they can help overcome the pitfalls in prior order conceptions. The point is not to replace power, institutions, or norms with yet another category but instead to focus the substance of order on something that each of the paradigms can ultimately accept without betraying their foundational assumptions.

2.2.1 Equilibrium through Observed Rules

Rules refer to system-wide standards of behavior and of membership that are clear and definitive. According to Hedley Bull, rules "are general imperative principles which require or authorize prescribed classes of persons or groups to behave in prescribed ways."[21] While they may have the status of codified international law or customary precedent, they can instead come about without formal agreement or even direct negotiation. *Observed* rules are those that are both widely recognized and widely practiced.

I contend that it is only when rules are both recognized and practiced— that is, when they are observed—that they are sufficient for producing order. If rules are practiced but not recognized as such, they may simply correspond with behaviors that have already been adopted regardless of rules. We do not need laws prohibiting citizens from giving away all of their property to the point of poverty, for instance, just as states do not require treaties prohibiting their use of nuclear weapons to annihilate their own cities. If such rules existed, they would be redundant. Behaviors would appear broadly consistent with them, but not *because* actors recognized the rules as such.[22]

Likewise, rules that are recognized but not frequently practiced are also insufficient. Actors could pay lip service to all kinds of rules without ever actually complying with any of them.[23] Instead, "a rule, to be effective in society, must be obeyed to some degree, and must be reckoned as a factor in the calculations of those to whom it applies, even those who elect to violate it."[24] As two legal scholars have put it, "When explicit rules are unrelated to how states and other international actors actually behave, fidelity is destroyed."[25] In international relations, units can and often do violate rules, but violations should not be widespread and should often trigger some kind of backlash or punishment against the offender.[26]

The principal advantage of this conception is that observed rules remain neutral in regards to order's origins in ways that other secondary-level conceptions do not.[27] This offers the benefit of not privileging any one type of explanation for how order comes about, what keeps it functioning, or "what makes the world hang together" as John Ruggie famously put it.[28] At some times and places, order might be the product of interaction and internalization processes emphasized by constructivists. At others, it might be brought about by the types of utility-maximizing calculations and strategic bargains highlighted by institutionalists, or by the threats and coercive bargains that are the focus of realists.

This approach also allows order the potential to be observed separately from the distribution of power, the extent of formal institutionalization, and the degree of socialization in the international system. The presence or degree of order (as observed rules) might then be poised to compete with these other factors as an important systemic cause of big events or behaviors in world politics. Alternatively, the degree of order may complement analyses employing these other factors. We might ask, for instance, whether a set of observed rules—an order—becomes more entrenched and stable when rules become valued for their own sake apart from strategic considerations,[29] or when they are more often codified in durable international organizations,[30] or under an asymmetrical and unipolar distribution of power.[31]

Figure 2.1 illustrates the observed-rules conception of international order, employing Goertz's framework of a multilevel concept. At the far left is the basic-level definition, order as equilibrium-perpetuating behavior. In the conception I have introduced here, the presence of observed rules constitutes the secondary level, in place of the material, institutional, or normative environments emphasized by other approaches. Goertz's additional "indicator" level here serves two purposes. Most importantly, it provides the specific, observable measures that signify the presence of the basic concept itself. Second, because most indicators

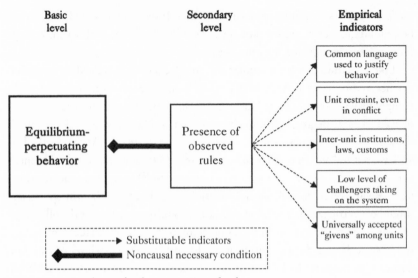

FIGURE 2.1 An observed-rules conception of order.

are substitutable—that is, they need not all be present to indicate the existence of secondary-level concepts—they provide a "natural way to incorporate historical and cultural diversity into a larger theoretical framework."[32] In other words, not all of the empirical indicators listed in Figure 2.1 must be present for order to exist.

These indicators identify empirically observable phenomena that correlate with the existence of observed rules. On the positive side, the presence of certain factors—such as a common justificatory vocabulary for explaining and defending unit actions—often indicates the presence of order. Though I noted earlier that formal institutions are not necessary for order, their presence is often indicative of order. On the negative side, the absence of certain factors also indicates the existence of order. These factors include all-out conflict with no signs of restraint and high rates of units attempting to fundamentally "take on" and overturn the status quo. When such factors are absent, it is more likely that some degree of order exists.

2.2.2 Behavior and Membership Rules

These observed rules (or order principles) can be further reduced to two general types, arguably the most basic types of rules any social system can have: those that govern external behavior and relations between units (behavior rules), and those that govern internal behavior and dictate relations within units (membership rules).[33] *Behavior rules* regulate interactions between units. They often pertain to issues such as the use of force; the legitimate means for system maintenance tasks such as peacekeeping missions; whether certain units are afforded special privileges relative to others; or whether inter-unit relations are characterized by ad hoc or institutionalized interactions. All orders must contain at least some observed rules of behavior. These rules set the parameters for both the legitimate goals actors can seek and the legitimate actions they can take to accomplish them.

In practice, behavior principles have less to say about what types of political entities "count," thus taking the existence of some basic and recognized unit types as given. Instead, they prescribe and proscribe types and patterns of unit behavior on the international stage. For instance, the Treaty of Utrecht *prescribed* upholding or advancing a "balance of power" as a legitimate goal of units' foreign policies. At the same time, it also *proscribed* units from invoking international dynastic ties to amass territory outside of their recognized boundaries (chapter 4).

There is room for almost limitless kinds of actions and issues within behavior rules, including violence and, perhaps, even war. The outbreak of war need not necessarily mean that order has broken down, so long as a relevant number of important actors continue to observe common rules. This will preclude most major wars since, as we will see later in the chapter, these conflicts by definition will involve many of the most important actors of the system fighting against each other. Yet even among major conflicts, not all wars have necessarily coincided with order breakdown. For instance, both the Dutch War of Louis XIV (1672–1678) and the War of the League of Augsburg (1688–1697) were major wars yet not order-destroying events. Even though both involved most of Europe's great powers, those actors were not fighting over or attempting to fundamentally revise the order principles governing their relations that had been established at Westphalia in 1648 (see chapter 4). Nor were they trying to completely wipe their adversaries off the map. The French Revolutionary and Napoleonic Wars (1789–1815), by contrast, were major wars that also signified order contestation and breakdown (chapter 5). The major actors—namely, Revolutionary France and its conservative great power adversaries—sought either to totally destroy each other or at the least topple and replace one another's regimes. More importantly, these conflicts involved fundamental contestation over both how units behaved in their relations with one another—or the order's behavior rules—as well as what units looked like internally, or its rules of membership.

Membership rules define who or what is seen as an acceptable member of a system, and refer to particular internal attributes of units. Over space and time, principles of membership have frequently encompassed issues such as the political structure of the regime; the stability and coercive power of the regime; the nature of domestic economic transactions; and the capacity or willingness of the regime to uphold basic human rights. The particular categories and criteria for membership have varied over time. Membership issues in the nineteenth century centered around political regime type (liberal vs. monarchical regimes), while throughout the Cold War the fundamental cleavage often involved economic institutions as much as political ones (free-market capitalist vs. state-led communist). Unlike behavior rules, a developed conception of membership rules is not strictly necessary for order.[34] In other words, orders have existed in history without clearly defined principles of membership.[35] Yet membership rules are essential for the *study* of order both because so many orders do observe them and because those that do are often fundamentally different from those that do not.

When a polity meets an order's membership requirements, it is afforded whatever privileges and protections are set forth in that order's behavior rules. Recognition through official diplomatic missions is a part of membership. Yet there is often more to membership than formal recognition. If there are protections against certain types of conquest in an order's behavior rules, for instance, members will be protected from such encroachments, no matter how small or weak they may be.[36] Those that do not meet the criteria for inclusion, by contrast, will be left to fend for themselves.

Orders with membership principles thus become exclusive clubs for members that to at least some extent discriminate against non-members. As individuals we all reap the benefits of belonging to certain clubs while simultaneously recognizing (and perhaps lamenting) that we remain non-members of others. For example, AAA members are entitled to certain privileges—such as reduced hotel rates—and certain protections—including speedy roadside assistance—not available to non-members. Likewise, the victors of the Napoleonic Wars established a rule that only conservative or "traditional" regimes would be considered members in the new post-1815 order. As a result, while the great powers acted to preserve the autonomy of conservative monarchies facing the prospect of conquest, these same powers ignored or even supported similar conquests in polities with liberal regimes. Because liberal regimes were not considered order members, they did not qualify for the protections afforded by that order's behavior rules (chapter 5).

All orders possess principles of behavior, but not all contain corresponding rules of membership. We can thus make a basic differentiation between two kinds of orders, one with membership rules and one without. I use the dimension of *order depth* to describe whether the principles of an order govern unit interaction only or also penetrate into domestic relations.[37] Orders are *shallow* when their principles address unit interaction but not membership. By contrast, *deep* orders contain both behavior and membership rules. The settlement of 1815 was a watershed moment in history from this perspective, as it marked the first time that states enacted a deep international order premised in part on explicit principles of membership. All system-wide international orders since that time have been deep ones, containing definitive principles of interaction as well as of membership.

In sum, the observed rules that constitute an international order—its order principles—come in two types: those governing unit interaction and those designating which units are partial or full members of that order. Table 2.1 highlights some of the most major rules changes (or, in the case of 1919, attempted rules changes that were adopted but soon after cast aside) in the western conception of order from the seventeenth through the twentieth centuries.

Table 2.1 Major Rule Changes in the Western Conception of Order

Era	Behavior Rules	Membership Rules
Post-1648	1: Enhanced autonomy for territorially bounded polities	X
Post-1713	1: Delegitimating transnational dynastic claims 2: Legitimating "balance of power" as a desirable end / state objective	X
Post-1814	1: Great powers (GPs) designated special status 2: Defend territorial-political status quo through multilateral consensus 3: System management through regular GP meetings	To anti-liberal, monarchic regimes
Post-1919	1: Institutionalized dispute resolution mechanisms 2: Abolition of inter-unit war initiation 3: Gradual transition from imperial system to colonial mandates system	To orderly and nominally democratic regimes
Post-1945	1: Multilateral cooperation to enhance economic openness, standardization, and stability 2: True collective security through mutual guarantees 3: Establishment of a security community with porous borders	To social welfare–enhancing and liberal democratic regimes
Post-1989	1: Problems previously considered domestic now identified as international, legitimating more frequent intervention into units' internal affairs	[More expansive advocacy of the above]

Some of these rule changes were only implicitly recognized in formal legal documents. These include the behavioral changes set forth in the 1713 Utrecht Treaty discussed earlier (chapter 4). Others were more explicitly codified in treaties or formal organizations. The order changes proposed after the world wars, for instance, were formally established in charters like the League of Nations Covenant, the IMF Articles of Agreement, and the North Atlantic Treaty. Some—like the rule establishing something akin to territorial sovereignty after the Thirty Years' War—have more clearly been internalized by actors of the system. By contrast, one could argue that the order principle prescribing economic openness, stability, and standardization after World War II has been less internalized and is followed by many actors more for strategic and instrumental reasons than for normative ones. Yet whether formalized or not, internalized or not, all of these rules have been observed by a plurality of the units within the system at a given time. Conceptualizing order as observed rules allows us to encompass this diversity.

2.3 Order's Origins and Reordering Moments across History
2.3.1 Two Approaches to Order's Origins

Observed rules make up and constitute international order. Yet where do orders come from? From the outset, we can distinguish between two broad approaches for explaining order's origins: horizontal consensus and vertical imposition.

The first type of explanation begins from the premise that order is the product of a broad agreement or understanding, or what we can call a *horizontal consensus* between polities. Social constructivist scholarship has often embraced this horizontal consensus approach to order formation, though the precise mechanisms vary across accounts. Some constructivists look for order as a product of multilateral agreement attained at the famous peace conferences following major wars throughout history.[38] Others focus more on the domestic origins of order principles, positing that new developments within polities often aggregate up into revolutionary changes at the international level between polities.[39] Whatever the causal pathway, constructivists most often explain order by looking to the origins of actors' cooperation, convergence, or consensus over new order principles.

Horizontal consensus accounts often effectively describe the processes through which orders change. They are typically weak, however, on actual explanation. Consensus-focused constructivists typically fail to explain why consensus breaks out at some postwar conferences but not at others. Similarly, accounts emphasizing domestic forces aggregating up often fail to explicate the processes that connect unit-level changes to changes in actors' order preferences at the international level. Horizontal consensus accounts also often ignore the effects of material factors on order, such as the unequal power that exists between polities. This is in part a byproduct of the fact that constructivist studies often come with a well-documented bias of privileging explanations and outcomes that are normatively progressive.[40] Yet because power and competition are even more pernicious elements of world politics than domestic ones, their absence in explanations for international order is especially glaring. In focusing on cooperation, convergence, and consensus, however, horizontal consensus accounts often simply gloss over these possibilities.

This oversight is the starting point for an alternative perspective, what we can call the *vertical imposition* approach to order. From this perspective, the focus should be not on consensus between many actors but instead on the preferences of the most dominant actors in the system. The foundational assumption of the vertical imposition approach is that only the most powerful actors are ever in a position to potentially affect significant order change. As some prominent realist practitioners of this perspective have reminded us, often missing from the conventional narrative on order is "the fact that hegemonic great powers are agents with disproportionate material wherewithal for shaping their social environment."[41] Yet while many realists will be sympathetic to this approach, it is not the exclusive purview of realism alone. Prominent liberals like Ikenberry clearly embrace the perspective.[42] And while many constructivists adopt the horizontal consensus approach, others argue instead that "it is great powers that are responsible for defining what counts as legitimate behavior in international politics," as one constructivist has recently put it.[43] In sum, scholars from a variety of disparate perspectives already embrace the starting assumption that order principles are most frequently imposed by superiors, not negotiated among equals.

This book also adopts the vertical imposition approach.[44] I thus focus on explaining dominant-actor order preferences, treating this as the most critical link to order's origins across history. Yet what particular kinds of moments are most ripe for studying dominant-actor order preferences? And how should we select particularly important case studies from these types of moments? I take up each of these questions in turn in the following two subsections.

2.3.2 The Universe of Cases

From the outset, we must take care to identify cases not by looking only for instances where dominant actors preferred order change. Selecting on the dependent variable in this way could mask larger causes that separate order change moments from order continuity moments or distort the true causal effects of the competing hypotheses assessed in this study.[45] Instead, I focus on moments when dominant actors have an *order change opportunity*. In these periods, actors have a unique and rare window to attempt significant changes to the rules of order. In other words, they have the capacity to impose significant order changes whether or not they ultimately choose to do so. A positive byproduct of adopting this approach is that it generates a universe that includes negative cases, moments of opportunity where actors ultimately chose order continuity. Yet it also raises additional questions of clarification and measurement: First, who counts as a "dominant actor"? Second, when are such "moments of opportunity" most likely to emerge?

Dominant actors are *great powers*, a term I use to refer to those who possess both formidable material power and some social recognition from others of their dominant status.[46] To change the rules of order, actors must be great powers (GPs). Yet not every GP has been able to change order, and even the most dominant of powers have often only been able to successfully pursue such changes in particular circumstances. These are moments of order change opportunity. In these moments, particular great powers find themselves with both: (a) an unusual preponderance of power compared with power distributions in more normal times (preponderant capacity); and (b) some recognized right to revisit and perhaps even revise social facts—such as the foundational rules of international order—that were previously considered settled (preponderant legitimacy).

In practice, moments of preponderant capacity and legitimacy emerge after momentous shocks to the international system. In identifying such moments, I focus on enabling shocks of two types: (a) *major war*; and (b) *the sudden death of another great power*. Major wars are military conflicts that involve most or all of the system's great powers fighting at full or near-full intensity.[47] For conflicts to be considered major wars, they must either: (a) result in at least one million great power battle deaths; or (b) involve a majority of the system's great powers *and* result in at least one hundred thousand great power battle deaths.[48] Defined along these lines, Table 2.2 summarizes all instances of major war in the modern international system.

The second type of shock is sudden great power death, modern instances of which are summarized in Table 2.3. The "sudden" aspect disqualifies cases of gradual decline from GP status, such as Spain, Sweden, and the Dutch Republic in the eighteenth century. Likewise, "death" necessarily implies permanence, thus excluding cases that were quickly reversed, like the Nazi occupation of France. Great power deaths come in two forms, either of which can cause significant systemic disturbances: (a) the sudden death of great power *states*; or (b) the sudden death of great power *regimes* within states.

Table 2.2 Major Wars, 1600–2000

Years	Event	Great Powers (GP)	GP Battle Deaths	GP Side 1 (Victors)	GP Side 2 (Losers)
1648	Thirty Years' War	6 of 6	2,071,000	France, Sweden, Dutch Republic, England	Spain, Austrian Habsburgs
1672–1678	Dutch War of Louis XIV	6 of 6	342,000	France, England, Sweden	Dutch Republic, Spain, Austrian Habsburgs
1688–1697	War of the League of Augsburg	5 of 6	680,000	France	Austrian Habsburgs, Dutch Republic, England, Spain
1701–1713	War of the Spanish Succession	5 of 6	1,251,000	Great Britain, Austrian Habsburgs, Dutch Republic	France (Spain)
1739–1748	War of the Austrian Succession	4 of 4	359,000	Austrian Habsburgs, Great Britain	France, Prussia
1755–1763	Seven Years' War	5 of 5	992,000	Great Britain, Prussia	France, Russia, Austrian Habsburgs
1792–1815	French Revolutionary and Napoleonic Wars	5 of 5	2,532,000	UK, Russia, Austria, Prussia	France
1853–1856	Crimean War	4 of 5	217,000	UK, France, Austria	Russia
1914–1919	World War I	7 of 7	7,734,300	US, UK, France, Japan, Russia	Germany, Austria-Hungary
1939–1945	World War II	6 of 6	12,948,300	US, UK, France, USSR	Germany, Japan

Sources: Jack Levy, War in the Modern Great Power System, 1475–1975 (Lexington: University Press of Kentucky, 1983), 75, 88-91; A. F. K. Organski and Jacek Kugler, The War Ledger (Chicago: University of Chicago Press, 1980); Karen A. Rasler and William R. Thompson, Great Powers and Global Struggle, 1490–1990 (Lexington: University Press of Kentucky, 1994).

Table 2.3 Sudden Great Power Deaths, 1600–2000

Years	Event	Regime Death	State Death
1688	Glorious Revolution	England's absolute monarchy	X
1789–1815	French Revolution(s), Bourbon Restoration	Bourbon dynasty and various French regimes (6)	X
1830	July Revolution	Bourbon Restoration (France)	X
1848	Liberal revolution, birth of Second Republic	July Monarchy (France)	X
1848	Metternich resigns, some liberal reforms	Austria (partial)	X
1870	Liberal revolution, overthrow of Napoleon III	Second French Empire	X
1917	February and October (Bolshevik) revolutions	Romanov dynasty and Russian Provisional Government	X
1918	German revolution, abdication of Wilhelm II	German Empire	X
1918	Dissolution of the Dual Monarchy	X	Austria-Hungary
1933	Hitler becomes Chancellor, Reichstag passes Enabling Act	Weimar Republic (Germany)	X
1945	Defeat, occupation, and division of Germany	Third Reich	Germany
1945	Defeat and occupation of Japan	Empire of Japan	X
1989–1991	Breakup of Soviet Empire in Europe, dissolution of USSR, fall of Soviet Russia	Russian Soviet Federative Socialist Republic	USSR

Source: Derived in part from data presented in Tanisha M. Fazal, *State Death: The Politics and Geography of Conquest, Occupation, and Annexation* (Princeton: Princeton University Press, 2007), Appendix B.

State deaths typically occur through conquest or dissolution. As great powers by definition possess formidable capabilities, GP state deaths are, unsurprisingly, rare. The only great power state deaths in the modern age have been the dissolution of Austria-Hungary at the end of the First World War, the division of Germany between 1945 and 1990, and the dissolution of the Soviet Empire in Eastern Europe and then the USSR itself between 1989 and 1991. Great power *regime* deaths have been more frequent. These typically occur through internal revolution from below or coup d'état from above. The notion of "regime death" implies not simply regime change, but wholesale regime type replacement. This typically involves changes of both leadership and political institutions. A prototypical case of regime death is France throughout its revolutionary era in the late eighteenth century, though France again experienced regime deaths in 1830, 1848, and 1870.[49] GP regime deaths have often coincided with major wars, though some, such as Britain's "Glorious" Revolution and the fall of the German Weimar Republic, occurred in relative isolation from other shocks.

Both types of shock—major war and sudden great power death—present unique opportunities for dominant actors to pursue international order changes, and for both material and ideational reasons. Materially, victory in major war or the sudden collapse of another power offer dominant actors at least a brief period of elevated material superiority. Until others are able to get back on their feet, or new vacuums of power are filled, dominant actors will have even greater capacity to exercise fundamental change.

Realists and rationalists would typically stop here. And yet it is important to acknowledge that these kinds of shock often do more than simply amplify the material influence of dominant actors. If we look at the normative side of these moments, both types of shock also open up a window of legitimacy for dominant actors to pursue significant changes. This is true because of what we know about collective trauma and the social impact of traumatic events. Such events dislodge settled expectations and ways of thinking—including the collective faith that had been placed in an existing set of order principles—and give privileged actors a window of opportunity to build anew. As William Walldorf has recently observed, "the collective, event-driven search for answers opens space for social agents, or carrier groups, to explain what is happening through . . . new master narratives." And it makes sense that in international relations, these "effective carrier groups" would be those already-powerful actors that have emerged from the traumatic events even more empowered and influential.[50]

To be clear, I am not arguing that international order can *only* experience changes at the hands of dominant powers or in these unique moments of opportunity. One could easily posit, for instance, that the most recent order change highlighted in Table 2.1—whereby developments within states that had previously been treated as domestic problems are now often identified as international ones, legitimating more frequent interventions in others' internal affairs—is one that has taken place outside of the kinds of moments of order change opportunity that are the focus of this study. And yet I focus on these kinds of moments due to the simple empirical fact that the most major changes to order across history have coincided with the preferences of the most dominant actors when they have found themselves in the midst of these special moments of opportunity.

2.3.3 Winnowing the Universe of Cases

As Tables 2.2 and 2.3 indicate, focusing on periods following these two types of shock provides a sizable number of order change opportunity cases. To make selecting among them more manageable, I follow others in separating the modern international system into three discrete eras. The first is the era of absolutist states before the dawn of mass participatory politics. It lasted from roughly 1648— the approximate advent of the modern system—to the outbreak of the French Revolution in 1789. The second era began in the wake of the destructive wars produced by France's revolutionary transformation. It was characterized most of all by the concert of great powers that helped maintain stability across Europe for much of the nineteenth century. The third era began with the First World War and lasted until the end of the Cold War. Above all, it was characterized by the primacy of the first hegemonic actor in history to be a full liberal democracy, the United States of America.

Within each of these three historical eras, I select three cases of order change opportunity for study. The clearest candidates are those where both types of shock coincide: (a) 1814–1818, (b) 1919, and (c) 1945–1949. Including the periods following the most destructive of the major wars—those involving every great power and resulting in at least one million GP battle deaths— yields two more cases: the peace settlements of (d) 1648 and (e) 1713 following the Thirty Years' and Spanish Succession Wars, respectively. Two additional periods stand out in Table 2.3 for the confluence of multiple GP deaths at once: the revolutionary wave that engulfed Europe in (f) 1848, and the death of the Soviet Empire, the Soviet Union and the communist regime in Russia in (g) 1989–1991.

I have now identified seven cases, three from the twentieth century and two each from the absolutist and concert eras. It is not difficult to identify the next most disruptive shock in each of those two earlier eras. After the Thirty Years' and Spanish Succession conflicts, the Seven Years' War was the most destructive conflict of the absolutist age. I thus also examine its aftermath in (h) 1763. Finally, the

Table 2.4 Opportunities for Order Change: The Cases

Years	Systemic Shocks	Resulting Events	Dominant Actors
1648	Thirty Years' War	Treaties of Westphalia	France, Sweden
1713	War of the Spanish Succession	Treaties of Utrecht	Great Britain
1763	Seven Years' War	Treaty of Paris	Great Britain
1814 -1818	Regime death in France / Revolutionary and Napoleonic Wars	Congresses / Treaties of Chaumont, Vienna, Paris (2), and Aix-La-Chapelle	UK, Austria, Russia
1848	Regime deaths in France, Austria (partial)	(No formal settlements)	UK
1856	Crimean War	Congress / Treaty of Paris	UK, France
1919	Regime deaths in Germany and Russia / Austria-Hungary state death / World War I	Paris Peace Conference / Treaty of Versailles	US, UK, France
1945–1949	Regime deaths in Germany and Japan / Germany State death / World War II	Bretton Woods (1944), Brussels (1948), and Washington (1949) conferences/agreements	US
1989–1990	Death of Soviet Empire in Europe / USSR state death / regime death in Russia	Malta (1989) and Washington (1990) conferences/agreements	US

Crimean War stands out as the only systemic conflict of the concert era involving more than two great powers, making its settlement in (i) 1856 a worthy candidate for analysis. These nine cases form the basis for the empirical investigations in chapters 4 through 8, and are summarized in Table 2.4.

In this chapter, I have argued that international orders as sets of observed rules can be categorized by the content of their order principles (that is, their specific behavior and membership rules) and the depth of those principles (that is, whether or not they include rules of membership). I defended a vertical imposition approach focused on dominant-actor preferences to explain where international orders come from. Finally, I established case selection criteria and identified the particular moments of order change opportunity that will occupy the empirical component of this study.

Yet assuming that powerful actors enjoy a particularly high degree of influence in shaping orders, where do their ideas come from? And when precisely will they seek or forgo revolutionary changes to order? These are the motivating questions for chapter 3.

3

A Theory of Exclusion

IN THE LAST chapter I made a case for explaining international order's origins by focusing on dominant actors' preferences. Yet just because many great powers expend resources to reshape order doesn't mean that all do so, or do so similarly. History has shown that the dynamics of order building are multifaceted and complex. Why do powerful states seek to enact major changes to foundational order rules? In moments of flux and opportunity, certain actors have sought radical changes in order principles, while at other times actors with similar opportunities have chosen to forego revolutionary order upheavals. Explaining such discrepancies is the focus of this chapter.

In particular, I detail a number of novel hypotheses for dominant-actor order preferences, all of them centered around a new explanation for why powerful states advance particular order principle changes when and as they do. In brief, I argue that actors seek to enact order principles to target and weaken entities they believe threaten their future security and enduring primacy. The larger and more immediate the threat, the more likely dominant actors are to pursue significant change to foundational order principles. Overall, the theory I develop aims to account for both *when* dominant actors will attempt significant reorderings and, in these moments, *what* exactly they will prefer to replace existing order principles with.

The chapter is structured as follows: First, I detail the core logic of this new explanation— ordering-to-exclude theory—before developing important extensions of the argument. Second, I introduce three alternative explanations for dominant-actor order preferences and deduce testable hypotheses for each. Finally, I discuss the research methods that inform the subsequent empirical chapters and set the stage for the case studies to come.

3.1 Ordering to Exclude: A New Theory

In this section, I detail a logic of order building by exclusion. After first laying out the basic argument, I elaborate on the logic behind the dominant actor order-building strategies it describes. I then refine the argument to pinpoint more specific hypotheses intended to help explain more variation throughout history.

3.1.1 A First Cut: Ordering against Threats

I begin with a basic proposition: dominant actors seek to reorder the international system out of a desire to inflict harm upon a threatening force or entity. In other words, they erect new orders in the interest of weakening, opposing, ostracizing, and above all excluding those entities they perceive as most threatening. Such a strategy entails enacting order principles that preclude the possibility of the threatening entity amassing enough power or influence to disrupt the existing system or challenge for control of it. This involves new order rules that can not only inflict harm on the threatening entity but also ones that could ingratiate other actors to the dominant actor(s) in the interest of ostracizing the threatening entity.

Figure 3.1 captures the core logic of the argument: at moments of opportunity, the presence of a formidable threat will induce dominant actors to transform order rules out of a desire to target and weaken that threat. Hypotheses 1A and 1B disaggregate this logic into two testable propositions. First, when dominant actors perceive a major new threat on the horizon, we should observe a significant attempt to reshape the system's order principles to weaken that threat in some notable way. This is reflected in hypothesis 1A:

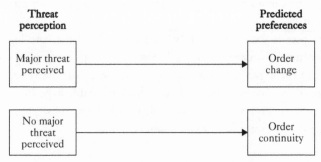

FIGURE 3.1 The Argument (I): dominant-actor order preferences at moments of opportunity.

Hypothesis 1A ("Excluding"): *Dominant actors will advocate new order principles when they perceive a major new threat on the horizon and will do so for the purpose of targeting and weakening that threatening entity.*

This hypothesis is weakened if dominant actors do not advocate new order principles in the face of major perceived threats, or if evidence indicates they were not primarily motivated by a desire to target perceived threats.

Second, the content of these new order principles—that is, the new behavior or membership rules proposed by the dominant actor(s)—should advance opposite or opposing values for some dominant trait or characteristic behavior of the threatening entity. For example, if regime type is a particularly salient issue, we would expect the dominant actor to advocate rules that stigmatize the threatening entity's domestic political institutions in some way. This is reflected in hypothesis 1B:

Hypothesis 1B ("Excluding"): *The content of the new order principles advocated by dominant actor(s) will be antithetical to some significant characteristic(s) or pattern(s) of behavior distinct to the threat. The characteristics/behaviors in question will also be attributes that distinguish the threat from the dominant actor and will possibly also separate the threat from third-party actors coveted as potential allies.*

This hypothesis is weakened if the content of the principles advocated complements rather than conflicts with salient characteristic(s) or pattern(s) of behavior of the threat, or if the characteristic/behavior in question is one that the threat and the dominant actor share in common.

While hypothesis 1A highlights the initial motivation for reordering, hypothesis 1B focuses on the specific content of the reordering. Which content issue areas will be most salient is dependent on historical context. Without case-specific historical details, it is difficult to know when one type of issue—economic regime type versus political regime type versus international behavior over sovereignty, multilateralism, institutions, or the use of force, to name but a few examples—will be the primary focus in a given reordering moment. Moreover, actor perceptions of salient similarities and differences are often contested and in flux. "What constitutes cultural commonality is admittedly open to political and social construction," observes Charles Kupchan. "Through political and social change as well as shifts in discourse, cultural others can become kin, and kin can become cultural others."[1] Commonality and difference, in other words, are open to social construction. We can generally posit, however, that the issues most likely to be salient are those in which the dominant actor perceives the threatening entity to be most dangerous to its interests. For instance, the victors of the Thirty Years' War focused on combating transnational claims to authority rooted in Christianity because it was through these religious ties that their greatest threats—the Habsburgs, Holy Roman Empire, and Catholic Church—would be able to amass the power necessary to threaten their security and challenge their primacy.

What exactly counts as a threat? More specifically, at what threshold does a threatening entity trigger an order-building response? Threat perception is a topic of considerable debate in international relations. While prominent neorealists like Waltz and Mearsheimer have focused on material capabilities alone to calculate threat, others have posited that additional factors are critical to threat perceptions. These include an actor's offensive weapons capability,[2] its intentions,[3] its projected future capabilities,[4] or some combination of these things.[5]

I do not intend to resolve the threat perception debate here. Instead, ordering-to-exclude theory works from a simple threat proposition: *Dominant actors will view as threatening any entity that could realistically jeopardize their security or their primacy in the near future.*

Simply put, dominant actors value their regional or international primacy because of the benefits they accrue from it.[6] Aside from simply enhancing an actor's security, primacy can be valuable for at least three additional reasons.[7] First, by virtue of being any subordinate actor's most important bilateral relationship, primacy maximizes a dominant actor's freedom of action vis-à-vis all other actors and thus gives that actor greater bargaining power in bilateral and multilateral interactions.[8] Second, primacy affords dominant actors much greater certainty about their international environment and thus allows them to maximize their prospects for positive future outcomes, none perhaps more important than their continuing economic growth and prosperity.[9] Third, primacy gives dominant actors agenda-setting powers over more fine-grained rules, norms, and institutions that do not rise to the importance of foundational order principles yet are still crucial for governing particular bilateral and/or multilateral relationships.

On this last point in particular, capitalizing on agenda-setting powers is a utility-maximization strategy that has often been recognized even by scholars of disparate theoretical perspectives. "The power to write rules has been long recognized as an awesome power," writes David Lake, a rationalist, "and it may be one of the most important benefits of being in authority."[10] Realists Brooks and Wohlforth have similarly argued that "seeking changes in the nonterritorial element of the system exists as a strategy that the leading state can pursue as an alternative to relying on military force to pursue territorial aggrandizement."[11] Intelligently employing agenda-setting powers over what is considered legitimate will also, at the least, allow dominant actors to preserve the status quo without the constant threat or use of force and, at the most, might even be necessary for maintaining long-term primacy and broader systemic stability. "Without at least tacit acceptance of power's legitimacy," writes Martha Finnemore, a constructivist, "the wheels of international social life get derailed. Material force alone remains to impose order, and order creation or maintenance by that means is difficult, even under unipolarity."[12]

To refine the core proposition of ordering-to-exclude theory, then, we should expect dominant actors to attempt significant order changes when they perceive on the horizon an entity that could imperil their security or undermine or challenge their dominance.[13] *Undermining* dominance involves threatening the dominant actor's immediate security or significantly degrading its capabilities in a way that would hinder its ability to maintain primacy. *Challenging* dominance entails actually competing with the dominant actor for international or regional primacy and all the benefits that primacy confers.

Ordering-to-exclude theory predicts that in the presence of these types of threatening entities, dominant actors will seek to use any opportunity they may have to reshape order principles for the purpose of targeting, weakening, and possibly even destroying those entities. I will have more to say on threat perceptions when I refine the theory in section 3.1.3.

3.1.2 How Orders Can Exclude

The preceding discussion has focused on *why* rational actors might use the process of order construction to their advantage. Here I highlight *how* they are often able to do this. This component of ordering-to-exclude theory contributes to a growing literature highlighting the strategic use of ideational content to advance one's self-interests while harming those of competitors. Scholars have shown how such principles have been used strategically, for example, by secular rulers attempting to curtail the authority of the Catholic Church in the medieval and early modern eras;[14] by political or ethnic groups to achieve their favored outcome in territorial disputes;[15] by rising powers to prevent the formation of counterbalancing coalitions against them;[16] by minority groups looking to receive citizenship rights from governments otherwise predisposed not to grant them;[17] by smaller states looking to manipulate institutional norms in ways that empower the weak against the strong;[18] and by actors of all sorts attempting to justify their defense or abuse of the principle of sovereignty.[19]

I focus in this section on elucidating three causal pathways in particular. It is through these pathways, I contend, that abstract order principles can translate into tangible material rewards for those actors employing them and tangible costs for those entities targeted by them. These pathways are illustrated in Figure 3.2. In the empirical chapters to come, I refer to each of them and describe how they have been employed to combat perceived threats throughout history. While I describe these pathways as separate here, the case studies will reveal that they sometimes—perhaps even often—overlap with one another. In sum, these are the tangible ways through which new rules of order are employed to weaken threatening entities.

First, dominant actors can advocate behavior or membership rules that they share in common with other actors who they hope to unite in the larger cause of opposing the threatening entity (Pathway #1: "Commonalities for Contrast" in Figure 3.2). The adoption of such rules subsequently increases the likelihood that these actors will both recognize that entity's threatening nature and unite with the dominant actor in opposing it. This might at times involve the use of inducements or even indirect coercion, as dominant actors find ways to pressure less powerful, would-be allies to embrace the ways in which they are strategically framing an issue against a threat. The great power victors of the Napoleonic Wars, for instance, erected an order premised on preventing the emergence of liberal regimes across the continent, even though many of the smaller polities that signed onto the relevant accords had previously feared only a powerful France, not all liberal governments and revolutions more generally (chapter 5).

At other times, the process could involve genuine socialization, as the dominant actor uses a new rule to make more salient to coveted allies the similarities they share in common and their corresponding differences with the threatening entity. For example, Daniel Nexon has shown how the leaders of the Protestant Reformation used its ideas to mobilize previously disparate actors by creating

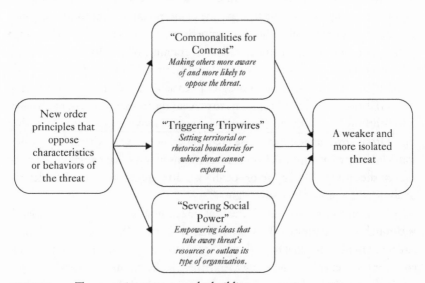

FIGURE 3.2 The strategic returns to order building.

"networks of co-confessionalists that transcended local and social cleavages," cleavages that had long been used by dynastic rulers to prevent precisely this kind of mobilization against them.[20] Regardless of the precise circumstances and degree of socialization involved, pathway #1 highlights a process through which dominant actors use order principles to convince their audience "that the challenger is a significant threat, one worth bearing the cost of containment or confrontation" or whatever else may be necessary to oppose it.[21]

Second, by invoking particular ideas to establish an order with recognizable members and boundaries, dominant actors can use new order principles to limit a threatening entity's opportunities to expand its geographic, political, or ideological reach (Pathway #2: "Triggering Tripwires"). In a way, this pathway becomes a deterrence mechanism under which dominant actors can use rules to draw red lines they then credibly commit to defend.[22] At the height of the Cold War, for instance, American statesmen sought to use new order principles to integrate key states into their sphere in a way that would demonstrate to the USSR both that they could not join and that pressuring those states already admitted would by definition be seen as an affront to the order itself (chapter 7). If the first pathway makes clearer the content along which a dominant actor will link itself to others to oppose a threat, the second pathway establishes the precise boundaries of the order for the threatening entity.

These boundaries can be physical and material, yet need not be either. Threatening entities can also run up against rhetorical or ontological boundaries. Rhetorically, one actor can trap another into or against a particular course of action by using its own past statements against it in a way that limits its subsequent possible actions.[23] One can also strategically invoke principles so important to the threat that to contradict them would jeopardize its "ontological security," the self-perception it must preserve to survive.[24] At the end of the Cold War, for instance, the United States was able to secure Soviet acquiescence to a reunified Germany joining the NATO alliance by using Soviet leader Mikhail Gorbachev's past statements about self-determination against him. Gorbachev was left with the choice of backing down or invalidating the entire premise of Soviet "new thinking" that had been the rationale behind his leadership and the leeway he had been given to pursue transformative change in the international system. He was thus left not only unable to challenge the existing liberal order but also unable to prevent its expansion (chapter 8).

In a third and final pathway, actors can advance new order principles to sever the social sources of the threatening entity's power, unity, and coherence, precluding forms of organization that would enable that entity to best harness its resources (Pathway #3: "Severing Social Power"). Examples of using ideas to undercut adversaries in this way abound throughout history. Rodney Bruce Hall has shown how medieval kings were able to transform their initially dubious authority claims into widely accepted positions by using dominant religious ideas to delegitimize the very existence of rival factions within their borders, effectively halting other actors from forming rival social organizations in the first place.[25] Similarly, the secular state victors of the Thirty Years' War sought to fragment the transnational ties from which their adversaries derived their power. They did so by advancing norms of autonomy for the hundreds of principalities within Germany, a move that shattered the transnational religious claims that had allowed their competitors to rule over much of Europe for centuries (chapter 4). Rather than simply limiting the threat's ability to expand its influence in particular directions (pathway #2), in this pathway the new rules of order are used to reconstitute what that threatening force actually *is*, typically by rendering it far weaker and less influential than it had been in its prior form.

In sum, the strategy of ordering to exclude—that is, advancing a particular set of new order principles for the purpose of targeting a threatening force or entity—offers dominant actors tangible strategic benefits.[26] Rather than the antithesis of strategic action, it actually often fits well within the realm of Machiavellian diplomacy and *realpolitik* thinking. It offers dominant actors a comparatively cost-effective strategy for hedging against long-term threats. This makes it an attractive option even before such actors resort to more traditional, expensive, and provocative options—including external balancing and preventive war—that realists have most often focused upon. "Strong actors prefer to exercise social control through the use of legitimate institutions than through direct coercion," argues Ian Hurd, "because it generally carries lower social costs."[27] Using honey is, where possible, more prudent than employing vinegar, and doing so will always be less provocative than resorting to overt balancing or militarized conflict. This is especially apt to be true in instances where the likelihood of the threatening entity's rise is high for the future, but the dominant actor's costs for pursuing a reordering strategy are low in the present.[28]

If employed prudently, ordering to exclude can thus afford dominant actors the luxury of containing and combatting threatening entities to their security and primacy "on the cheap." This is not to say that such a strategy is costless, however, and I return to a discussion of its costs potentially outweighing its benefits in section 3.1.4.

3.1.3 A Second Cut: Two Types of Threats

Earlier I posited that dominant actors will view as threatening any entity that could realistically jeopardize their security or undermine or challenge their primacy. Still, even threats fitting these criteria can come in very different shapes and sizes. In this section, I therefore refine ordering-to-exclude theory by positing that the very type of threat dominant actors face can also affect the precise kinds of order changes they advocate.

More specifically, we can differentiate between two broad types of threats germane to international order building. First, dominant actors often identify other states with powerful militaries—or what I will call *state power threats*—as their greatest adversaries. Realists in particular have argued that state leaders focus primarily on the material threats that other states can pose. In so doing, they disregard threatening states' unit-level characteristics such as ideology, leadership, or economic structure.[29] From this perspective, dominant actors will focus upon the largest rising states in the system as the threatening entities most likely to jeopardize their primacy and endanger their security.

In particular, we can identify two developments that will make a state or group of states threatening enough to trigger a reordering response. First, projected trends in relative power favoring a rising state will make that state particularly threatening to a dominant actor.[30] Second, polities that possess sizable or especially destructive offensive military capabilities—or have plans or the realistic potential to develop or acquire them—will also appear sufficiently threatening to trigger a reordering response.[31] This is true not only because they could use their increased power/offensive capability against the dominant actor (jeopardizing security) but also because they could use these capabilities to coerce other actors into abandoning the dominant actor and banding together with them instead (jeopardizing primacy).

In spite of what many realists would have us believe, however, raw military power is not the only type of threat that matters in international relations.[32] Throughout history, state elites have often focused as much on threats of another type, those posed by contrary ideological movements—or what I will call *ideological power threats*. The term *ideology* denotes a polity's organization at the domestic level—which in different contexts could refer to regime type, economic structure, or what it means to be a citizen—as well as elite beliefs over and preferences for these things.[33] These attributes might at first appear divorced from the topic of international threats and threat perceptions. Yet as a burgeoning literature on ideology and international security has shown, ideological movements can very quickly pose dire material threats in much the same way that powerful states can.

In particular, contrary ideologies can come to materially inflict costs on even the most dominant of actors, and in at least two ways. First, dominant actors can rationally come to fear that the success abroad of an ideology contrary to their own might imperil the stability of their domestic system at home, not to mention those of their allies. Because of fears associated with these ideological "demonstration effects"—or what Mark Haas describes as the "fact that political developments in one state can inspire similar ones in others"—dominant actors will seek to weaken groups embracing contrary ideologies both at home and abroad.[34] The success of any contrary ideological movement abroad is threatening because it increases the likelihood of subsequent conversion or subversion in others. It was no coincidence that the Bolshevik Revolution in Russia in 1917, as weak as it initially was, triggered the First Red Scare all the way across the Atlantic in the United States, for example. The perpetrators of any revolution are always at least implicitly issuing a challenge to internationally accepted norms as much as they are to local ones. Though they understandably focus at first on local issues, all revolutions have "started with a presumption that the boundaries between states are invalid, that sovereignty defined as non-interference is an ideology of the oppressors," writes Fred Halliday. It therefore should not be surprising that revolutionary regimes and movements typically "do seek to export revolution by arms, political support, and ideological encouragement."[35] Major ideological events unleash forces that could reach a dominant actor's shores very quickly, often faster than an adversary's military could.

Second, dominant actors can also come to fear contrary ideological movements for their potential to create antagonistic international alliances. Ideologies tend to link and sometimes even ally polities that otherwise have little in common. Even currently dominant states and their rational leaders must take this possibility seriously. While these leaders might recognize that *they* would never make decisions out of ideological conviction, they must still allow that elites *elsewhere* could be prone to ideologically driven decision-making.[36] And when elites start behaving ideologically, there is a higher likelihood that alliances will cease forming according to the dictates of balance-of-power theory. Instead, international alignments become more erratic and unpredictable. Even dominant actors with sizable power advantages can rationally come to fear for ideologically motivated encirclement, as the Habsburgs did at the height of the Protestant Reformation in Europe, for instance. Ideologically charged periods put even the most powerful actors on alert. What made the Soviet threat so potent to US elites throughout the Cold War, one can argue for example, wasn't the raw power of the formal USSR—which consistently paled in comparison to American might—but instead the power that Soviet leaders could harness in ideological alliance with their fellow communist and socialist regimes across the world.

Still, what makes a particular ideological movement so threatening that it will trigger a dominant actor pursuing a significant reordering strategy in response? I posit that two interrelated conditions must exist for an ideological movement to trigger this kind of countervailing strategy. First, the contrary ideology must have the potential for universal appeal in the international or regional system in question.[37] Ideologies premised upon scope conditions that cannot be met by a large percentage of a system's polities are unlikely to fulfill this criterion. Fitting here are those premised upon a particular gender, racial, religious, or cultural hierarchy. In these ideologies, membership in the favored group is predetermined by biology or genealogy, leaving the potential for joining this privileged group an outright impossibility for many. Islamism may be a viable ideology in the Middle Eastern system, for instance, yet observers rightly question whether it is truly a global ideological competitor to liberalism today in the way state socialism was in the twentieth century. By definition Islamism either potentially alienates (women in Western societies) or outright excludes (non-Muslims) wide swaths of humanity from full participation in any community that adopts its core maxims.

Second, evidence must exist that the ideology either has or could soon have a significant state power sponsor. When an ideology grabs hold of a significant polity, it demonstrates to other actors in the system that it is viable enough to attract important adherents, perhaps enough to one day become the foundational premise for an international order of its own. Without evidence that it can capture a notable state, new ideologies will often be treated as fringe movements.[38] For instance, the anarchist movements across Europe in nineteenth century did not constitute a major threat to the dominant actors of the time since, as disruptive as they often were, there was little fear that they could capture a significant state. Anarchism's sister movement, communism, only became truly threatening once it contributed to the overthrow of the czarist government in Russia in 1917. "Significance" here denotes a state's possession of either (a) great material power or (b) great importance for reasons other than material power—its geographic location, vital resources, or even historical significance, for instance. For reasons having to do with geography and historical significance, for example, the fate of Turkey is today often seen as an ideological litmus test for the future of competing ideological movements in the Middle East and North Africa.

In sum, state power and ideological power constitute two distinct types of threats that dominant actors may face. Distinguishing between them is particularly important for international order, I argue, because it affects the *type* of reordering strategy wary dominant actors will pursue to combat them. When the threat is state-centered and non-ideological—that is, when the threat isn't menacing for ideological reasons—it is viewed as conventional. Statesmen can locate the threat's emanating source, easily identify its leaders, and will have a good idea of what its expansion would look like (traditional coercion and conquest). Facing this kind of threat, a dominant actor will adopt a "shallow" reordering strategy focused on order principles of behavior but not membership. This is true because the threatening entity is menacing due to its potential international behaviors, not its domestic or transnational ones, thus rendering issues of membership irrelevant for combatting it. Dominant actors will only advance new principles that they believe are necessary for opposing the threatening entity. This is the case because advocating new rules above and beyond this purpose might unnecessarily tie a dominant actor's own hands in the future (a point I develop in section 3.1.4).

When the threat has an ideological component—and the ideology has universal appeal and significant state sponsorship—however, dominant actors will view it as uncontained, unpredictable, and above all unconventional. Ideologies typically have no clear capital or single "return address," possess multiple leaders across numerous polities, and can expand in a number of different ways, often more quickly and less predictably than through conquest (fomenting revolutions or subversion from below, for example). A dominant actor nervous about this type of threat will favor a "deep" reordering strategy premised on revising order principles of behavior *and* membership. Solidarity over domestic (membership) characteristics becomes critical when addressing ideological power threats, since the threatening entity now has the ability to expand within polities in addition to spreading across them. Because both types of expansion are possible when dealing with ideological threats, dominant actors will have to manipulate both types of order principles to successfully combat them.

Overall, these more fine-grained arguments are summarized in hypothesis 1C:

> *Hypothesis 1C* ("Excluding"): *Dominant actors will advocate* <u>deep</u> *order changes—involving rules of behavior and membership—when facing ideological power threats. When facing state power threats, however, they will favor only* <u>shallow</u> *changes limited to behavior rules.*
>
> This hypothesis is weakened if dominant actors propose major changes in membership rules when the threat is non-ideological, or if they only seek changes in behavior rules in the presence of ideological threats.

Figure 3.3 depicts the refined causal logic and illustrates the two most important claims of ordering-to-exclude theory. First, it is the presence of a major threat that determines when dominant actors will prefer major changes to international order. Second, it is the type of threat that determines the depth of the order changes dominant actors will pursue in attempt to combat that threat.

3.1.4 Explaining Order Continuity

None of the preceding discussion is meant to imply, however, that pursuing order transformations is costless, or that dominant actors constantly go searching for

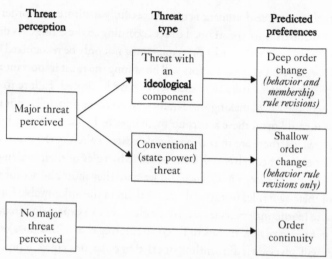

FIGURE 3.3 The Argument (II): dominant-actor order preferences at moments of opportunity.

monsters to destroy where none exist. To the contrary, when they do *not* perceive major new threats on the horizon, ordering-to-exclude theory predicts that dominant actors will forego revisions to international order. This is the case because even successful instances of order building are costly. Dominant actors must invest time and resources recruiting others to accept new order principles. Attempting to sell a set of principles to a skeptical international audience requires dominant actors to spend social and political capital, not dissimilar to how the American president must spend capital to advance his legislative agenda to a divided and parochial Congress.

In addition to building the requisite international support, building support at the domestic level—support that is necessary for marshaling the resources required to enact major order changes—also becomes more difficult in the absence of a clear international threat. "The absence of a unifying existential threat makes it harder for policymakers to mobilize societal resources for foreign policy goals that do not pose a clear and present danger to national survival," argues Yoav Gortzak in reference to dominant actors and international order enforcement. "On the other hand, it also opens up the foreign policy sphere to competing interest groups that seek to harness the capabilities of the state for their own purposes" that have little to do with order.[39] Even for hegemonic powers, order management is only one facet of foreign relations, and one that can be subordinated to others deemed more pressing in a particular moment or era.

Furthermore, once dominant actors successfully institute new order principles, they themselves are constrained to act according to these rules. As discussed
in chapter 2, to be effective order principles must not only be recognized but also
regularly practiced. Dominant actors will be among the most important rule followers, particularly for rules they themselves have instituted. Failure to comply
with rules of their own making will fatally weaken these principles, not to mention that it could open these actors up to charges of hypocrisy.[40] In addition to
tangible rewards, there are thus also tangible costs to altering the rules of order.
Dominant actors themselves will have to abide by rules of their making if they
want those rules to carry significance and weight. They must also accept the possibility of their own rules being used against them in the unknowable future.[41]

Because reordering strategies are not costless, we can expect dominant actors
that do not perceive new threats to forgo attempting them. This does not mean
that they will advocate a dismantling of existing order principles, a process that
would also be taxing and costly. Instead, we can expect them to actively or passively
advocate continuity in the order. This expectation is reflected in hypothesis 1D:

> Hypothesis 1D ("Excluding"): *Dominant actors will not attempt major revi-
> sions to order principles when they perceive no major or new threat on the
> horizon, or where the immediacy of such a threat is perceived to be low.*
>
> This hypothesis is weakened if dominant actors advocate major changes
> to order principles when they do not perceive significant or new threats.

While it may at first look like the simple inverse of hypothesis 1A, proposition 1D is a crucial component of ordering-to-exclude theory. It predicts that
even dominant actors with tremendous opportunities to reshape order will often
choose to uphold continuity in the existing order instead. Being able to account
for order continuity is as important as order change, and four out of the nine
cases assessed in the chapters to come depict instances of order change opportunity where I argue that dominant actors ultimately preferred and then advocated
for order continuity over order change.

3.2 Alternative Motives: Liberal IR Theory and Order Preferences

Once caricatured as more of a normative than a positive and causal approach
to world politics, IR liberalism is now recognized as a discrete paradigm with
a coherent—if still internally diverse—research agenda. Different scholars have
succeeded in taking different aspects of the liberal agenda to construct causal

theories of foreign policy behavior.[42] While IR liberalism still defies a simple definition, its practitioners hold certain maxims in common. First, international anarchy does not always produce a state of war. Second, different polities act differently, often because of their different domestic-level properties or ideological beliefs. Third, polities in the international system have basic goals that often go beyond a simple preoccupation with security.[43] Particular strains of IR liberalism are also well suited for generating powerful hypotheses for dominant-actor order preferences. In this section, I introduce three such arguments that serve as the principal alternatives to ordering-to-exclude theory for the rest of the book.

These are certainly not the only possible motivations one could examine for explaining dominant-actor behavior more generally, or in the case studies.[44] Moreover, they have not been chosen simply because they can be closely associated with liberal theory. I focus on these three in particular, however, because together they represent a balance between the most prominent existing explanations for dominant-actor order preferences (in the case of binding and exporting) and, at least on the surface, the most logically intuitive explanations within many of the historical cases (in the case of exporting and learning).

3.2.1 Binding

One group of liberals—often called neoliberals or neoliberal institutionalists— focuses less on sub-national preferences and domestic institutions and more on the special properties of international institutions. These liberals argue that even if we assume that states are strategically minded actors—the assumption of realists and rationalists—they often still find greater utility in creating international institutions or operating within existing ones than in "going it alone." And this is a good thing, neoliberals argue, because institutional interaction typically leaves all parties better off than they would have been in the absence of institutions.[45]

In the context of international order, John Ikenberry's prominent work fits most closely with this perspective.[46] Ikenberry argues that after major wars, dominant actors often attempt to preserve their favorable position in the international system by binding both themselves and the weaker actors that populate the system to an institutional order. These institutions serve to restrain the dominant actor from acting unilaterally while also giving smaller actors more say in the order's governance than they would have in a system based on power alone. The rationale for dominant actors doing this, Ikenberry argues, is that it makes their dominance appear less threatening and more desirable, thus decreasing the likelihood for widespread dissatisfaction that could culminate in attempts to balance against or overthrow it. Championing such a system also allows dominant actors to "lock in" a favorable order and ensures that they will continue to exercise leadership within it even as their own material power inevitably declines in the future.

While Ikenberry implies that the merits of this strategy should be evident to *all* rational actors, numerous structural factors have made the pursuit of this strategy and, especially, success in pursuing it, increasingly prevalent through history. Specifically, "postwar states are most likely to seek an institutional bargain when democratic states face each other in highly asymmetrical power relations: that is, when a newly powerful state is most concerned with establishing an order that does not require a continuous power struggle . . . and when the type of states that are party to the settlement are most able to establish institutions that are credible and binding" because they are democracies.[47] In other words, this strategy should be most prevalent (and most successful) the more materially dominant the dominant actor is and the more democratic the polities populating the system are. Overall, I refer to this hypothesis simply as "Binding":

> *Hypothesis 2* ("Binding"): *Dominant actors will advocate order principles that will make their leadership more acceptable and legitimate to weaker actors in the system, often because it "binds" the dominant actor's coercive power in ways that make it less threatening to others.*
>
> This hypothesis is weakened if dominant actors advocate order principles that do not bind their ability to exercise their preponderant power, or if evidence indicates that their preferences were not primarily motivated by a desire to legitimize their leadership to weaker actors.

Binding may overlap with the excluding motive that is at the heart of ordering-to-exclude theory to the extent that we observe dominant actors rallying weaker entities to their cause, and into their order.[48] Yet the motives for doing so will be fundamentally distinct between the theories. If binding is correct, they will behave in this way for the purpose of constructing the most legitimate order—that is, the most universally accepted—as is possible. If excluding has more purchase, we should only witness dominant actors rallying weaker ones for the purpose of combatting and excluding a larger perceived threat (pathway #1 of ordering-to-exclude theory).

3.2.2   Exporting

Other liberal IR theorists argue that the determinants of states' actions come not from systemic factors, but instead from domestically derived attributes. In other words, what states want is determined at the domestic level—within them—rather than at the international level between them.[49] All else equal, a state with democratic and capitalist domestic institutions should prefer to see democratic and capitalist values spread across the international system, for example.

Ideas consistent with this strand of liberalism are often invoked to explain actor preferences for the future of international order.[50] While diplomatic historians of the United States often implicitly embrace these types of arguments,[51] political scientists have employed them as well. Charles Kupchan argues that "the norms informing hegemonic orders are often derivative of the metropole's own domestic order," while Colin Dueck posits that domestic cultural traditions are necessary to explain fundamental changes in the American grand strategic approach to order.[52] Mark Haas has argued that domestic "ideological distance" between states will condition their relations with one another, while John Owen's work aims to show how, when, and why rulers are likely to incorporate the foreign promotion of their own domestic institutions into their preferences for international order changes.[53]

From this perspective, great powers should thus prefer order principles that bring important elements of the international system more in line with their domestic systems. I refer to these kinds of arguments as "Exporting." The strongest version of this hypothesis predicts that dominant actors directly translate salient domestic attributes, values, or traditions into preferences for order at the international level:

> *Hypothesis 3A* ("Strong Exporting"): *Dominant actors will advocate order principles that are most similar to their domestic institutions and ideological preferences.*
>
> This hypothesis is weakened if dominant actors advocate order principles that do not match or are in conflict with their domestic preferences and characteristics, or if evidence indicates that their preferences were not motivated primarily by a desire to externalize internal/domestic processes.

Yet a weaker version of exporting might also be useful here, one that embraces the more general liberal hypothesis that domestic competition to capture control of the policymaking process within a state often influences that state's foreign relations. From this perspective, to explain a dominant actor's order preferences we should look to the battles that are taking place between competing domestic factions within a dominant state:

> *Hypothesis 3B* ("Weak Exporting"): *Dominant actors will advocate order principles that emerge as the outcome of domestic political battles between competing factions vying for control of the policymaking process.*

This hypothesis is weakened if dominant actors advocate order principles that do not reflect the conflicts or outcomes of domestic political battles, or if evidence indicates that their preferences were insulated from domestic political processes of any sort.

Either form of the exporting motive will be distinct from ordering-to-exclude theory in the level of analysis that is causally driving dominant-actor order preferences. Exporting predicts that the causes will be found at the unit level (internal attributes), while excluding expects to find them at the international level (external threats).

3.2.3   Learning

The final alternative, learning, has not always been associated with liberal IR theory, nor has it been explicitly applied to dominant-actor preferences for order. Nonetheless, it emerges as a powerful motive in many historical accounts of the cases examined ahead, and centers around a highly plausible general premise: actors are often preoccupied with preventing the reoccurrence of traumatic events in their past. In postwar periods, this motive will often manifest itself as a desire to punish the perpetrator of the recently concluded war, though it could also include a more general focus on averting that war's perceived causes or its most pernicious effects. For instance, many accounts of American order preferences after World War II highlight a desire to avert the kinds of closed economic blocs of the 1930s that US elites believed were a primary cause of the war.[54]

In political science scholarship, scholars studying how actors learn from history have concluded that humans draw upon their experiences in recent formative events when planning for the future.[55] Some of these arguments might appear closer to psychological than liberal approaches to international relations. Yet the concepts of learning from the past and, especially, the ability of humanity to overcome its most destructive inclinations over time, are at the core of IR liberalism.[56] I do not adjudicate between these disparate approaches, instead posing a broader formative events hypothesis that I simply call "Learning":

Hypothesis 4 ("Learning"): *Dominant actors will advocate order principles that they believe will best address the most recent negative formative event in their history, typically by preventing it from reemerging again in the future.*

This hypothesis is weakened if dominant actors advocate order principles that do not correspond with the most recent negative formative event in their history, or if evidence indicates that their preferences were not motivated primarily by past history.

The predictions of the learning hypothesis and ordering-to-exclude theory may overlap in instances where a dominant actor fears an entity it perceives as a present or future threat (the focus of excluding) but that has also been threatening to it in the recent past (the prediction of learning). The differences between them will therefore become evident by examining underlying motives. Learning predicts that dominant actors will simply look backward, consumed as they are with righting past wrongs or preventing past calamities from reoccurring. Ordering-to-exclude theory, by contrast, expects to find dominant actors worrying about threatening entities in the present and immediate future, regardless of their relationship with those entities in the past. The difference, in short, is about whether dominant actors are more prone to looking backward or forward in critical moments of order change opportunity.

3.3 *Methods of Assessment*

Excluding hypotheses 1A and 1B represent the core propositions of ordering-to-exclude theory most in competition with the alternative arguments, while hypotheses 1C and 1D represent refinements and extensions of the core argument. In this section, I detail the methods I employ for across- and within-case analysis in the empirical chapters to come.

To ensure uniformity of comparison, each case study focuses on identifying the dominant actors of the system, determining their preferences for changes to behavior and membership order principles, and exploring the factors that led them to adopt such preferences.[57] More specifically, each case analysis is similarly structured to address a common set of questions:

Order Preferences: What major new order rules or changes to existing rules do dominant actors prefer and advocate? If preferences exist for order changes, do they come in the form of behavior rules, membership rules, or both?

Threats and Motives: What major threats, if any, do dominant actors perceive and identify on the horizon? How well do threat perceptions align with and account for those actors' order preferences in the ways hypothesized by ordering-to-exclude theory?

Alternatives: How well does each of the alternative motives perform in accounting for those same order preferences?

Measuring the dependent variable of interest—dominant-actor order preferences—is no simple task. The very presence of such rules, not to mention actor preferences for them, are much harder to observe than, say, military capability. In settled times, both order rules and actor preferences for order rules are often so entrenched in the day-to-day conduct of international relations that they can be imperceptible. Fortunately, the cases of order change opportunity I examine are by definition *not* at settled times. Moments of upheaval and change produce better observation opportunities for hard-to-observe phenomena than periods of stasis and continuity.[58] It is in these moments of order change opportunity that the relevant decision-making agents will openly question principles they have taken as given in settled times.[59]

In measuring preferences for order in these critical moments, my research questions focus on dominant-actor intent. First, what does the historical record suggest the relevant agents advocated? Second, what can this record tell us about the reasoning that brought them to these preferences? Where possible, I use primary source documents to reconstruct order preferences. Many of the case periods I investigate resulted in treaties or other settlement documents. Major diplomatic conferences also often produced a wealth of documentary evidence. Yet where the documentary record paints an incomplete portrait or one subject to multiple interpretations, I also make extensive use of secondary historical sources.

To evaluate the relative utility of the competing hypotheses, I employ both cross-case comparison and within-case analysis. Within each case investigation, I use both *congruence testing* and *process tracing* to eliminate potential explanations.[60] Step one utilizes congruence testing. As George and Bennett describe it, "the essential characteristic of the congruence method is that the investigator begins with a theory and then attempts to assess its ability to explain or predict the outcome in a particular case."[61] With this in mind, I conduct congruence tests within each case for each competing hypothesis. I do this by (a) establishing what order preference(s) would be compatible with each of the four competing explanations given the value taken by each argument's independent variable(s); followed by (b) eliminating the explanations that do not accurately predict the observed order preferences for that case.

Congruence testing is an important first step. But especially for those cases in which multiple competing hypotheses pass the congruence testing hurdle, investigating actor motives becomes a crucial second step. This is where process tracing comes in. After congruence tests, I unpack the events and processes between the remaining theories' independent variables and those observed order preferences to assess actor motives. For this study in particular, process tracing serves two important purposes. First, it reveals whether the relevant causal factors are logically and sequentially connected to the observed order preferences in the way the corresponding theory hypothesizes.

Second, process tracing illuminates which causal forces were most important to the relevant elites actually making policy decisions at the time. Even though this is not an agent-driven investigation of order continuity and change, looking at the motives of the relevant agents remains a crucial method of inquiry for this study. David Lake has instructively described the importance of investigate agents' motives in this way:

> If policy makers were, in fact, concerned with such issues [those the corresponding theory identifies as important], it would not confirm the theory, but it would help establish the plausibility of the theory and reassure us that it was capturing something meaningful about the real world. The absence of such evidence would be even more revealing. [We should be] skeptical of any theory . . . that lacks individual-level support.[62]

Without employing this crucial second step, we risk identifying spurious correlations rather than true underlying causes. Process tracing, in sum, helps shed light on whether the relevant agents spoke, acted, and even thought—depending on the availability of personal diaries or correspondence—in the ways that the competing theories hypothesize.

In instances where dominant actors advocated multiple order changes, I test each theory for each rule change. I discuss the results of these tests in the aggregate at the end of chapters 5, 7, and 8 (summarizing my findings for the European, American, and end of the Cold War cases, respectively) and, especially, in concluding chapter 9. In the next chapter, I begin to assess the explanatory utility of ordering-to-exclude theory and the alternative motives by exploring the most critical opportunities for order change between 1600 and 1800, the so-called golden age of great power politics in Europe.

4

Order in the Age of Great Power Politics

THIS CHAPTER TESTS the applicability of the binding, exporting, learning, and excluding motives for dominant-actors' order preferences across more than one hundred years of European history. Beginning with the settlements of Westphalia in 1648, it assesses three moments of opportunity where the great powers of Europe could have plausibly sought significant changes to the principles of the European international system. In two of those moments—the Westphalian settlements of 1648 and the peace of Utrecht after the War of the Spanish Succession in 1713—they seized this opportunity, while in one—the negotiated end of the Seven Years' War in the early 1760s—they did not.

In a book about international order, it might at first seem puzzling to begin with these cases or to examine this historical era at all. Many of the most prominent prior studies of order, after all, do not begin until the nineteenth century and the Concert of Europe, or even the twentieth-century aftermath of the world wars. I of course examine those same important eras and cases in subsequent chapters. Yet if I can show that the dynamics of order building highlighted in the previous chapter were at work even earlier than those eras that are the most studied, it would lend even more plausibility to ordering-to-exclude theory.

This is indeed what I find in this chapter. I demonstrate that the logic of excluding most convincingly explains the dominant actors' preferences and actions in these critical early moments of the modern states system. When they perceived no major threat on the horizon—in 1763—dominant actors were content to focus on the particularities of settling the most recent war rather than attempting larger changes to order principles. But in the presence of major and new perceived threats, the dominant actors of 1648 and 1713 sought larger and more fundamental changes that went beyond the issue-specific conflicts of the day. Instead, they sought to fundamentally revise the rules of international order in ways that they believed would work against those threating forces and entities in a variety of creative ways. Overall, I aim to show in this chapter that exclusionary rule-writing has been a staple of great power politics since the advent of the modern states system circa 1648.

4.1 Visions of Order in 1648

The peace settlements reached in the nearby German towns of Münster and Osnabrück that ended the grueling Thirty Years' War in 1648 have come to be known jointly as the Peace of Westphalia. The great power victors of the war were Sweden and its even mightier ally, France. Allied with many of the Protestant German principalities of the Holy Roman Empire, France and Sweden eventually defeated a Habsburg-Catholic coalition led by the Austrian Habsburg Holy Roman Emperor—commanding a majority of the Catholic German principalities of the Empire—and King Philip IV of Spain, leader of the Spanish wing of the Habsburg dynasty, though also often with at least the tacit support of the papacy in Rome.

I argue here that the signature change to international order that French and Swedish leaders successfully advocated in the settlement provides strong support for the ordering-to-exclude theory detailed in the last chapter. In so doing, I split the difference between other IR treatments of the Westphalian settlement. On one side, constructivists like Daniel Philpott and Christian Reus-Smit argue that Westphalian outcomes were revolutionary for international order and that the actors promoting those outcomes did so with revolutionary intent.[1] On the opposite side, realists like Stephen Krasner posit that neither the outcomes of the settlement nor the motives behind them were revolutionary.[2]

I seek to show that the order revisions enacted at Westphalia were in significant ways revolutionary, and constituted a major change to the behavior rules of order as argued by the constructivists. Yet the motives behind these changes were strategic and relatively shortsighted—focused upon threats on the immediate horizon—rather than principled and farsighted, thus bolstering realist arguments about great power motivations at Westphalia. The victors of the Thirty Years' War may have instituted a new and revolutionary order principle, but I argue that they did so not out of some desire to fundamentally remake European relations but instead to discredit and weaken their principal adversaries.

The main issues at stake in the Thirty Years' War were the political autonomy of the individual principalities—or "estates"—of the Holy Roman Empire (HRE), the religious freedoms of political entities across the continent, and the legitimate scope of influence of the Habsburg Empire and Catholic Church in seventeenth-century Europe.[3] Though the precise origins of the war are difficult to disentangle, most scholarship agrees that the conflict erupted when the tinder of longstanding religious conflict between European Catholics and Protestants born out of Martin Luther's challenge to Catholicism in 1517 met the flame of a local intra-German conflict centered around the autonomy of the German estates relative to the Holy Roman Emperor.[4]

The spark that ignited this larger fire, the Bohemian rebellion that began in 1618, involved the religious toleration of Protestants in the predominantly Catholic HRE, an issue at the forefront of European politics for the century since the advent of the Protestant Reformation. A year before the Bohemian rebellion, the devoutly Catholic Archduke Ferdinand II—a polarizing figure who Protestants rightly feared would become the next Emperor—was named King-Designate of the important German territory of Bohemia, a development that incited the 1618 rebellion there. Under the guise of restoring order to Bohemia, Ferdinand seized the Imperial crown in 1619 and set about making an example out of the Bohemian Protestant agitators. Religious polarization in the Empire escalated throughout the 1620s, culminating in Ferdinand's call to reverse decades of Protestant territorial gains with the infamous Edict of Restitution in 1629.

Fearing this consolidation of Habsburg power in the name of Catholicism, France—itself preoccupied with a bruising series of Huguenot uprisings at home—subsidized Sweden to invade the HRE in 1630 to roll back Ferdinand's gains and halt his ambitions. Five years later, and in the midst of even greater Habsburg gains and increasing cooperation between its Spanish and Austrian (HRE) branches, France itself declared war on Spain and soon found itself fighting against the junior wing of the Habsburg dynasty in the HRE alongside Sweden.[5] As great power war raged on into the 1640s, the exhausted and encircled Ferdinand III—who had succeeded his father as emperor in 1637—decided to make peace with his principal adversaries, an endeavor that was finally achieved in the settlements of 1648. While Spain would continue to wage war against France for another decade, it was clearly out of its league without the aid of the HRE and finally sued for peace in 1659.

4.1.1 Order Preferences: Westphalia as Transformation

It is the 1648 settlements that are my focus here. The peace negotiations, which had begun in earnest in 1644, were from the start plagued with confusion and controversy.[6] There was no ceasefire on the battlefield, a fact that continuously marred negotiations as one side or the other would hold out on making concessions when they believed they held the advantage in battle.[7] There was also substantial disagreement about which entities were legitimate actors worthy of a place at the negotiation table. The bicameral nature of the conference came because of (a) the unwillingness of many Catholic actors to recognize the legitimacy of Protestant ones (and vice versa), as well as (b) disagreements between France and Sweden themselves over which held primacy over the other as the principal negotiator for their side. Thus, France and many of the Catholic principalities of the HRE negotiated at Münster, while Osnabrück was reserved for Sweden and many of the Protestant Germans. The Holy Roman Emperor had officials at both conferences, with his most important representative, Count Maximilian von Trauttmansdorff, traveling between the cities.[8] Because the towns were only thirty miles apart, France and Sweden also carefully coordinated their aims.[9] What today is referred to as the Westphalian settlement was thus actually two treaties: one between the Empire and Sweden, known as IPO (*Instrumentum Pacis Osnabrugense*), the other between the Empire and France, referred to as IPM (*Instrumentum Pacis Monasteriense*). Both were signed on October 24, 1648.[10]

No party got everything they wanted in the settlement. Yet French and Swedish representatives succeeded in enacting their most far-reaching objective at Westphalia: a new behavior rule to international order, represented in various aspects of the treaties, **delegitimating universalist claims to authority across all of Latin Christendom (Europe) in favor of the authority claims of local and territorially bounded actors (Westphalia rule #1).**

While Westphalia is often remembered for establishing religious tolerance and territorial sovereignty, much of the treaties' most important content focuses on the internal structure of the Holy Roman Empire. And even on these specific issues related to the HRE, scholars still disagree on the treaties' ultimate meaning and significance. The 1648 settlement *either* (a) significantly weakened the Holy Roman Emperor's claims to authority over the German principalities of the HRE;[11] *or* (b) reaffirmed the rights these principalities already had while more clearly delineating the limits of the Emperor's authority over them.[12]

Either way, the Westphalian peace settlement clearly rejected the open-ended authority claims the Habsburgs had long invoked through the Imperial title of Holy Roman Emperor—whether or not these universalist rights had actually existed before this time—and allowed the German polities that made up the HRE to engage in practices they likely would have been blocked from undertaking earlier.[13] Perhaps the most important component of the settlement in this regard was Article VIII of IPO, which "established and confirmed" the rights of "every elector, prince, and estate of the [Holy] Roman Empire . . . the free exercise of their territorial rights." IPM went on to specify that the principalities

shall enjoy without contradiction, the Right of Suffrage in all Deliberations touching the Affairs of the Empire; but above all, when the Business

in hand shall be the making or interpreting of Laws, the declaring of
Wars, imposing of Taxes, levying or quartering of Soldiers, erecting new
Fortifications in the Territorys of the States, or reinforcing old Garisons;
as also when a Peace of Alliance is to be concluded, and treated about,
or the like, none of these, or the like things shall be acted for the future,
without the Suffrage and Consent of the Free Assembly of all the States
of the Empire.[14]

Crucially, both treaties also specified that "each Imperial estate shall freely and
forever enjoy the right of making alliances with other estates or with foreigners
for its own preservation and security,"[15] a sovereign right of paramount importance. This left the aggrieved German principalities, especially the Protestant
ones, free to forge alliances with their liberators, France and Sweden, in the event
that they ever again felt their autonomy threatened. To the estates, these external
powers became the "guarantors of the new order within the Empire."[16]

Important to clarify is that the treaties did not create state sovereignty for
the estates as we understand that concept today. Their authority was still limited in a number of ways: they still could not make alliances against the Empire
and Emperor, for instance, and their powers in respect to religious liberties for
individuals within their borders were actually *limited* at Westphalia compared to
what had been granted at Augsburg in 1555.[17]

Yet in both intent and subsequent outcomes, the treaties were more than a
mere stepping stone on the path to a sovereign states system and were in fact
crucial to its emergence. The fate of Europe was intimately tied to the governance
of the HRE, the statesmen of Westphalia had determined, and the Empire would
only be made stable by either legally granting or explicitly codifying (depending
on one's interpretation) the rights of the principalities relative to the Emperor.
The treaties "attained their epochal significance because for the first time they
had succeeded by means of modern international law to make peace between
equal powers within Europe without creating a summit hierarchy—thus laying
the first foundations of the international law of treaties in the European order for
the next 150 years."[18] Above all, they signified a decisive turn from an age of "heteronomous" political order[19]—characterized by "the combination of hierarchy
and non-exclusive jurisdictions" among many different kinds of units—to something resembling an order of sovereign equality among similar units. Summing
up the significance of Westphalia, Reus-Smit has perhaps put it best:

The Westphalian settlement did not bring forth a fully formed sovereign
order. . . . But it was a critical moment in the transformation toward such
an order. In particular, it recognized the political agency and authority of

a range of new polities, and it granted these states legitimate powers that would come to be seen as the sole preserve of modern sovereign states.[20]

Yet why would the war's victors, France and Sweden, expend significant effort to promote such an order? This is the focus of the next section.

4.1.2 Threats and Motives

I submit that this revolutionary order change was one actively promoted by the victors of the Thirty Years' War to counter, cripple, and exclude the threatening entities that made universality claims to authority in Europe, namely the Habsburg Empire and the Catholic Church. I proceed by making five points: first, the threat itself was universalist forms of authority, the antithesis of territorial sovereignty; second, this threat was the stated reason for France and Sweden entering the Thirty Years' War in the first place; third, this threat was still clearly foremost on their minds at the Westphalian negotiations; fourth, the principal blueprint for the victors' aims at the peace conference explicitly called for a transformation of order above all; and fifth, various behaviors by Sweden and France in the negotiations demonstrate that their stated positions on the settlement were strategic rather than principled.

First, what Sweden and especially France feared in the early seventeenth century was not religious or ideological in nature but geopolitical: territorial and political encirclement by a hegemonic power with universalist claims to authority across all of Latin Christendom. These threats were manifest in two of the most traditionally powerful actors in Europe. The Catholic "Church and [Holy Roman] empire were universalist forms of organization," explains Hendrik Spruyt is his classic study of medieval polities. "By their very nature they could not admit any rival authority as legitimately equivalent. There could only be one church, since it was sanctioned by God. There could only be one empire, since it was the secular arm of the church."[21] There would be no sovereign equality among different actors as long as these entities were predominant. The Church could amass the political power of the papacy in Rome. But what was especially threatening was the extended Habsburg dynasty, which by the seventeenth century included the thrones of Spain, the HRE, and their allies, the predominantly Catholic German principalities of the HRE that dominated much of central Europe.

It was for this reason—fear of encirclement by an empire sustained by politically and territorially limitless claims to authority—that Sweden and then France ultimately entered the conflict, broadening what was ostensibly a German civil war into an epic great power struggle. In his war manifesto of 1630, Sweden's famed leader and gifted military commander Gustavus Adolphus focused on the fact "that the Spaniards and the House of Austria have been always intent upon a Universal Monarchy, or at least designed the conquest of the Christian states and provinces in the West, and particularly of the principalities and free towns in Germany, where that House has made such a progress. . . ."[22] Had he lived for the peace negotiations, his vision no doubt would have aligned with countering these threats.[23]

In France, King Louis XIII's chief minister, the cunning and powerful Armand Jean du Plessis, Cardinal de Richelieu, also claimed to be most concerned about the Emperor "making himself Germany's master, turning the empire into an absolute monarchy, and destroying the venerable laws of the Germanic *Respublica*."[24] Though Richelieu was consistently preoccupied with the threat emanating from the House of Habsburg throughout his tenure, this fear had not always focused him on the HRE, evidenced by his reluctance to directly involve France in Imperial affairs for years.[25] It was not until Ferdinand II began cracking down on the Protestant principalities while receiving more coordinated support from the Spanish Habsburgs and papacy that France came to fear for the looming hegemonic union of all these actors. It was only at this point, in 1635, when Richelieu finally brought France directly into war against the Habsburgs.[26]

Third, the Swedish and French representatives at Westphalia continued to voice these same fears as motivation in 1644–1645, demonstrating that the long experience of the war had not abated their perceptions of threat. "There was not a country under the sun in a better position to establish universal monarchy and absolute dominion in Europe, than Germany," wrote the Swedish negotiator Johan Adler Salvius. He warned that "if one potentate wielded absolute power in this realm, all the neighboring realms would have to apprehend being subjugated." The only relief would be France and Sweden choosing to "oppose this as much as is in their power; their security consists in the liberty of the German estates."[27] The French plenipotentiary Count d'Avaux agreed, writing to the German estates "that the House of Austria is plotting a monarchy that is to cover all Europe; that, as a foundation for this vast edifice, it is establishing supreme dominion over the Roman Empire, so to speak, the centre of Europe."[28] This fear would continue to dominate their negotiating positions up until the signing of the treaties in 1648.

Fourth, France's objectives in particular were modeled upon a peace directive written by Richelieu, the titan of French diplomacy throughout this era, in 1642. Even though the powerful cardinal died a year later, his protégé and successor, Cardinal Jules Mazarin, continued to rely on it and changed little from Richelieu's original intent.[29] That Richelieu's decades-long vision of a general peace for Europe (*"paix générale"*) was designed above all to prevent the realization of a universal monarchy (*"à la monarchie universelle"*) is beyond dispute. As one close analysis of his writings summarizes,

Richelieu interpreted Spain's ambitions as aiming to subject the smaller states of Christendom . . . to Spanish Habsburg interests. But the pope was also to be linked into the Spanish Habsburg system. And in so far as it was a platform for repelling more powerful opponents to such a usurpation of control—France, chiefly—the whole of Christendom would ultimately have to submit to this pretension to universal power and authority on the part of the Spanish-dominated house of Habsburg. This is the basic line of argument behind Richelieu's last drafts for the directives at the peace negotiations.[30]

Like all peace directives by the victorious side, Richelieu's called for *some* territorial acquisitions (or "satisfaction," to use the term of the day). Yet his instructions were most remarkable *not* for their territorial ambition but for their surprising modesty on this front. Instead, Richelieu made clear that France's ultimate goals were political rather than territorial, a position his successor Mazarin honored.[31] Historians of the era agree on this point. Klaus Malettke argues that Richelieu's directive displays "in all clarity that the cardinal did not pursue a definite and inflexible program of territorial acquisition," and was instead "primarily concerned with the realization of a politically strategic goal, namely the permanent opening of the borders surrounding France."[32] Croxton and Parker note how the language "repeatedly emphasized the security of the peace over the justice of specific territorial acquisitions." While the victors were intent on taking *some* Habsburg territory for their security, "neither Richelieu nor Sweden's chief minister, Axel Oxenstierna [after the death of Gustavus Adolphus] was confident that this measure alone would provide sufficient security."[33] Both powers achieved some territorial "satisfaction,"[34] but the heart of their objectives at Westphalia centered around intra-German affairs in the HRE.

Instead of focusing on territory, France and Sweden pursued their objectives primarily through changes to the Holy Roman Empire, demanding an overhaul in both its internal reorganization and its relationship with the rest of Europe. The overarching goal was to make it less unified—both as a branch of the Habsburg dynasty and as an empire unto itself—and thus far less threatening to the territorial integrity of independent European polities.

In so doing, they employed pathway #3 of ordering-to-exclude theory detailed in the last chapter, "severing the social power" of the threat by undercutting its authority structures. "Before multiple sovereign authorities could be recognized, the authority of pope and Emperor had to be undermined conceptually," writes Derek Croxton, "either by denying altogether the religious basis of secular authority, or that the Church's authority flowed through a single individual as opposed, for example, to a council of believers."[35] They accomplished this by advocating the major order change detailed in the prior section.

In practice, this meant empowering the rights of the German estates, the individual polities of the HRE that could serve as a check on the ambitions of the Emperor. That this was their objective was evident even from the beginning of the peace negotiations.[36] France held up the opening of the conferences by insisting, first, on the rights of representatives from the German estates to participate, and second, that the conference be a general and universal one, addressing all of the war's outstanding issues rather than one among many incomplete or contradictory negotiations and agreements.[37] After winning this right, and upon arriving in Münster in April of 1644, France's representatives immediately issued an open invitation to all the German estates—rather than just the ones allied with Sweden and France as had been the understanding—to particulate in the negotiations.[38]

What they ultimately accomplished in the final settlement, described in the prior section, was significant: codifying and in all likelihood increasing the rights of the German principalities relative to the Emperor. Worth noting is that the final settlement also advanced the victorious powers' goals of weakening the Empire by (a) allowing for future French or Swedish intervention in the HRE to defend their allies in the estates, and (b) prohibiting the HRE from lending material support to Spain in its continuing war with France.[39] The great power victors therefore most advanced their security not through their modest territorial gains, but instead by using the new order principle at the heart of the settlement to forever weaken the Emperor, sever the Spanish-Austrian Habsburg connection, and effectively undercut the religious cleavage the papacy had employed to intervene in Europe's affairs for more than a century.

The possibility remains, of course, that French and Swedish leaders might have been acting out of genuine belief in these ideals rather than according to geopolitical imperatives. Evidence does not support this position, however. Instead, undercutting the Emperor specifically and universalist forms of organization more generally was a strategic move rather than a principled one. This is the fifth and final point in support of ordering-to-exclude theory. Simply put, France and Sweden had no principled reason for demanding a far less centralized HRE.[40] Instead, this impulse came entirely from their security considerations. As a recent study of the HRE has concluded, strategy decisively beat out principle:

> The "German freedom" of the imperial Estates was formalized to prevent the emperor converting the Empire into a centralized state capable of threatening its neighbors. Immediate practical conditions shaped this more than theoretical considerations. The peace of Westphalia forbade Austria from assisting Spain, which remained at war with France

until 1659. . . . These efforts generally ran counter to the interests of the Habsburgs. . . .[41]

French hypocrisy was particularly acute throughout the negotiations. They fought hard for a "universal" conference that would settle all European matters together. This suited their interests as long as it linked them with their allies, Sweden and the Dutch Republic, in order to gain leverage in the negotiations and achieve the best possible settlement. Yet France also quickly abandoned this demand for universalism in favor of disjointed negotiations when it came to interacting with the Austrian and Spanish Habsburgs, a tactic designed to divide its adversaries.[42] French leaders claimed to act on principle in supporting the liberties of the German estates above all. Yet they attempted to close out these same actors in negotiations over their own territorial "satisfaction" when doing so suited French interests, and even went so far as to forcibly take territory away from estates they claimed to be defending (France's acquisition of Alsace serves as the most egregious example here, but certainly not the only one). Finally, both France and its ally Sweden professed to favor something akin to sovereign equality across Europe. Yet the two powers couldn't even agree to surrender supremacy claims *with one another* for long enough to hold a peace conference in one town rather than two.[43] These were, in sum, strategically motivated positions rather than genuinely held convictions.

In short, the great powers victorious in the Thirty Years' War promoted the revolutionary ideas in the Westphalian settlement not out of principle or a conscious desire to radically transform European order, but instead simply to weaken what they saw as their principal security threats and rivals for continental dominance: the Catholic Church, the Habsburg Empire, and the religious and historical foundations through which both actors claimed limitless authority over Latin Christendom. As Croxton and Parker summarize, "their watchwords were *liberty* and *balance*, their fear was universal monarchy, and their goal was security."[44] In that it forever blunted the Habsburg bid for mastery of Europe, Westphalia was enormously successful as an instance of ordering to exclude.

4.1.3 Alternatives

Ordering-to-exclude theory performs well in a theoretical vacuum, but is even more impressive relative to the alternative motives for dominant-actor order preferences detailed in chapter 3.

Binding

Some evidence for the binding thesis can be found in Richelieu's peace directive, a document that I have already argued served as the blueprint for France's objectives at Westphalia. Richelieu called for a form of collective security leagues—two in particular that would have been centered in Italy and Germany—to help enforce whatever peace principles were agreed to at Westphalia.[45] Had these leagues been implemented as a core component of the settlement, the binding motive could offer some explanatory purchase. The problem, of course, is that this was the most important part of Richelieu's directive that Mazarin entirely dropped by the time of the negotiations, as he reportedly had far less faith than Richelieu in the utility of such leagues to enhance French security.[46]

After Richelieu's death, Mazarin and his representatives made no discernible effort to forge a settlement that would either make French power more acceptable to other actors or "lock in" an institutionalized settlement preferable to actors across Europe. To the contrary, it was the remarkable lack of restraints erected against French power in the settlement that allowed the young boy who sat upon the throne at war's end, King Louis XIV, to ravage the continent over his lifetime. Even John Ikenberry agrees that the Westphalian settlement was used by the war's victors "to undermine or erode the religious universalism and hierarchical control of the Holy Roman Empire."[47]

Exporting

Exporting arguments take a number of forms for the Westphalian case, but also do not provide much explanatory guidance. The most straightforward version travels alongside the conventional view of the war as a religious struggle between Catholic and Protestant polities seeking to export their confessional beliefs onto others. The obvious problem with this interpretation is that major polities actually crossed religious lines. France stands out as the most glaring anomaly, definitively Catholic but allied with Protestants (most notably, Sweden) against the other Catholic powers of Europe. Had France followed its religious inclinations, it would have aligned itself with the pro-papist *dévots*, those in French society who wanted the King to side with Church and Emperor and engage in a vigorously pro-Catholic crusade across Europe. Instead, the French regime came to be dominated by the *politiques*, those who prioritized the French state—and a strong monarchy in particular—above transnational religious goals during the Reformation and French Wars of Religion. Richelieu's ascendance and implementation of *raison d'état* during the Thirty Years' War epitomized the power of the *politiques* over the *dévots*. His position as cardinal did not prevent him from viewing the Habsburgs' militant Catholicism as a political tool to justify their goal of hegemony, nor of seeing Protestants as allies.[48] "If the [Protestant] party is entirely ruined, the brunt of the power of the House of Austria will fall on France," he had once argued.[49]

France's ambivalence over religious issues carried into the negotiations. While Sweden might have at times preferred to remake parts of Europe in its Protestant image, its more powerful ally opposed entangling *any* part of the settlement in religious doctrine. At French insistence, religious grievances were not even discussed at their conference in Münster and were thus relegated to Osnabrück.[50] And in instructions sent to the French delegates in the peace negotiations, France's foreign minister Henri de Loménie de Brienne made clear how little interest France had in bringing religion into the settlement:

> On one point we concur with the Swedes, but not on the means. Weakening the excessive power of the House of Austria, establishing the liberty of the princes of the Empire; that has, indeed, been the aim of our union and of the war. But to reach it by strengthening the Protestants, by weakening the Catholics, that is what we do not concur with and, on the contrary, our goal must be to love. . . without distinction of religion.[51]

Quite clearly, then, confessional exporting wasn't a top priority for either power, but especially for the more powerful actor, Catholic France.

A more sophisticated variant of the exporting motive is potentially more illuminating. As two of the most "state-like" polities in Europe at the time, France and Sweden might have developed a vested interest in seeing their type of political organization become the standard across Europe. Both Philpott and Reus-Smit offer variants of this argument.[52] Philpott in particular presents compelling correlative evidence linking domestic crises of Protestantism within polities to those polities then advocating for something akin to sovereign statehood on the European stage.[53] In France, he highlights how the Huguenot wars led to the rise of the *politiques* of which Richelieu was a part, actors who then advocated for the overthrow of universalist forms of authority once they had captured power in France.

Philpott's account hinges on the fact that French leaders did not advocate for the total dismantling of Imperial or Habsburg authority earlier than they did, even though they had long recognized Habsburg Spain as a significant threat to French interests. He attributes this delay and subsequent policy shift in the Thirty Years' War to the rise of the *politiques*, which meant that finally "France's security interests could be entirely prioritized above the welfare of Christendom."[54] It was only when this domestic authority was consolidated under the *politiques* and vested in Richelieu that a revolutionary new foreign policy could be fully articulated and administered.

This account is plausible in a logical and correlative sense, allowing us to code exporting as passing the congruence hurdle for 1648. The problem is that there exists a much simpler explanation for the evolution in France's geopolitical strategy: while French leaders had feared Habsburg encirclement for decades, it wasn't until the 1630s that this threat moved from the theoretical to the actual. Richelieu had for years maneuvered to keep France out of costly conflict by taking efforts short of war to deal with the Habsburg threat. This ultimately changed not because of religion or French domestic politics, but because of France's rapidly deteriorating security environment in the 1630s. The crushing Imperial military victory at Nördlingen (1634), the Peace of Prague (1635), and increasing Imperial-Spanish cooperation throughout these years made France's fear of hegemonic Habsburg encirclement more real than ever before.[55] When Spain provocatively captured the strategically vital city of Trier—whose elector had become the most important foreign prince to put himself under France's protection in 1632—Richelieu had little choice but to finally declare war.[56] In sum, it was not France's changing domestic or religious environment but a much simpler condition that finally drove Richelieu's most fateful policy shift in 1635: the ultimate manifestation of his—and France's—most long-feared threat.

Two additional points against this variant of the exporting motive also support ordering-to-exclude theory. First, the settlement was much more a *negative* rejection of universal, limitless claims of authority than it was a *positive* proclamation of which units were to "count" in European politics. Though France and Sweden bitterly opposed the Emperor's universalist claims, they did not oppose the continued existence of other heteronomous forms of political organization.[57]

Second is a reiteration of a point made earlier: whatever autonomy was granted to the German states in the Westphalian settlement, it fell short of sovereignty as we now understand the term. Weakened as it was, the HRE continued to exist for another century and a half. Furthermore, the settlement did not grant total religious freedom to the principalities. Instead, it froze in place each territory's faith as it had been in 1624 while insisting on toleration for religious minorities.[58] While this was not sovereignty per se, it still achieved the victors' goal of legitimating the right to embrace the religious ideas of the Reformation against the wishes of Emperor and Pope. For all of these reasons, exporting fails the process tracing test for 1648.

Learning

Learning appears to be the most viable of the alternative motives for explaining dominant-actor preferences at Westphalia. If we accept at least basic elements of the conventional view of the Thirty Years' War as a religious conflict, the religious toleration principle promoted in the Westphalian settlement fits well with a learning explanation. The sheer destruction of the war made all sides amenable to a peace that would ensure no future conflicts between confession-based alliances. To this end, an order principle affording greater autonomy to polities over religion (among other things) was an ideal way to address the havoc wreaked by the Reformation for the century and a half prior to Westphalia. As a logical explanation linking cause to outcome, the learning thesis thus passes the congruence test criterion for Westphalia.

As argued earlier, however, the initial conflict, great power intervention, and principles advocated in the peace negotiations all had more to do with non-religious security issues than they did with religion. France's chief aims were to prevent Europe from being usurped by a single entity in general and to sever the traditional ties between the Empire and Spain in particular. While achieving this goal partly involved severing religious ties—the Pope's alliance with the Habsburgs and legitimation of the religious powers of the Emperor—it also involved weakening the Habsburg's universalist claims, claims that were not primarily based upon religion. And with this focus paramount, it was more about the insecurity the Habsburgs could still cause *in the future* that was most alarming, rather than damage they had already inflicted in the past. "France and Sweden's general strategic goals at Westphalia were . . . not so much rectification of specific wrongs as the prevention of future injustice on the part of the Habsburgs," argue two experts of the conflict and settlement. "Their peace negotiations were, therefore, unusually forward looking."[59] In all of the statements of Westphalian policymakers employed throughout this section, the focus of the relevant leaders was avoiding potential future chaos rather than addressing past grievances. Throughout the century, Habsburg hegemony had been a looming threat to be avoided, not a fully realized one to be rolled back. Learning, in sum, fails to clear the process tracing bar for Westphalia.

"Both in procedure and in outcome, the peace negotiations in Münster and Osnabrück constituted the first major political conference to be held by the European powers," argues Volker Gerhardt. "This was not a Church Council, nor an Imperial Diet, but a meeting of independent territorial and political entities, where, for the first time, relevant alliances were taken into account."[60] The settlement was revolutionary, and in this regard the skeptics are wrong. Yet in other respects they are on firmer ground. As Krasner has aptly put it, the principles at the heart of the Westphalian treaties actually just "reflected the short-term interests of the victorious powers, France and Sweden, rather than some overarching conceptualization of how the international system should be ordered."[61] The purpose of Westphalia was to discredit and exclude the entities most threatening to France and Sweden, namely the Habsburg Monarchy and the Catholic Church. Thus, the two goals of the treaties of Münster and Osnabrück that are often treated as distinct—domesticating confessional passions and containing hegemonic aspirations—were really one and the same.

Recognizing the damage it would do, the Pope attempted to use a Papal bull (*Zelo domus dei*) to declare the entire settlement null and void. Yet his protest fell on deaf ears across the continent, even with the actors ultimately opposed to the settlement, showing just how much the papacy's powers had already been weakened.[62] In that regard, Westphalia had done exactly what it was designed to do by the great power orderers most responsible for enacting it.

4.2 *Visions of Order in 1713*

Westphalia had satisfactorily dealt with two major causes of conflict in Europe, religious divisions and universalist authority claims. Yet one source of conflict that was left on the negotiation table—the fusion of disparate polities through dynastic ties—would soon rear its ugly head as the cause of the continent's next colossal struggle, the War of the Spanish Succession (1702–1713).[63] The war was waged by Great Britain and its allies to prevent the kingdoms of France and Spain from fusing under one ruler from the House of Bourbon. While British leaders opposed the unity of French and Spanish kingdoms for its own sake, the grown up and now supremely powerful King Louis XIV of France had tried for years, and ultimately in vain, to prevent a succession crisis for fear that it would trigger a counter-hegemonic balancing coalition against him.[64]

I demonstrate here that the war's principal victor, Britain, used the peace negotiations—culminating in the Treaty of Utrecht in 1713—to ensure that it would never face another such crisis again. Specifically, British leaders enacted order changes that would prohibit dynasts from making disruptive transnational territorial claims in the future, especially where such claims would threaten to upend the balance of power in Europe. Given that these were Britain's greatest perceived threats in the immediate postwar period, the case fits nicely with the expectations of ordering-to-exclude theory.

Europe's leaders had known since the ascent of Charles II to the Spanish throne in 1665 that the sickly ruler—whose illnesses were likely the result of centuries of Habsburg inbreeding—was unlikely to produce an heir or to live very long. This would end the long history of Habsburg Spanish rule and, due to the marriage of French King Louis XIV to Maria Theresa of Spain, likely install a Bourbon on the Spanish throne. With this knowledge, the French king had negotiated with King William III of England (and the Dutch Republic) to produce a succession agreement that would prevent the entirety of Spain from passing by default to a member of Louis's House of Bourbon, a development that actors recognized would be deeply destabilizing for the continent.

The issue was seemingly resolved with the First Partition Treaty of 1698, which promised the Spanish throne to Joseph Ferdinand of Bavaria—neither a

Habsburg nor a Bourbon—and mandated a division of the rest of the Spanish Empire in Europe between France and Austria. When Ferdinand's unexpected death the following year invalidated that statute, France and England negotiated a Second Partition Treaty. This agreement promised Spain to the Archduke Charles of Austria, the second son of Holy Roman Emperor Leopold I (and an Austrian Habsburg). Yet unlike the first treaty, this second agreement also declared that France, not Austria, would receive the bulk of Spanish territories in Italy. Both partition agreements, but especially the second, were deeply unpopular in Spain and thus contested by its sickly ruler, Charles II.

This was the uncertain state of affairs when Charles succumbed to his many illnesses soon thereafter, in 1700. Disregarding the partition treaties, his will recognized the Duke of Anjou, King Louis XIV's grandson, as his legitimate heir (thus making him Philip V of Spain). Louis reluctantly recognized his grandson's ascension to the Spanish throne, even while knowing it would likely bring war. Despite years of effort, Europe's leaders now faced the outcome they had long hoped to avoid, resulting in the devastating War of the Spanish Succession.[65]

By 1711, France was left soundly but not decisively defeated.[66] England (hereafter Great Britain, which it became after the 1707 Treaty of Union) led the settlement negotiations as the war's dominant victor. Technically, victory was also shared by the Austrian Habsburgs and the Dutch Republic, while France and most of Spain (those parts loyal to the Bourbons) were on the losing side. Spain was the indisputable loser of the conflict and the ensuing peace settlement. Though the Spanish crown refused to recognize the legitimacy of the settlement, it was unable to reverse its losses in the decades following, thus marking its decisive exit from the ranks of the great powers.[67] Unlike its Spanish ally, however, France was able to emerge from the conflict still a dominant force on the continent. In fact, her strong relationship with Britain gave France's leaders a more influential role in the peace process than that enjoyed by Britain's wartime allies. Those surprised by this development shouldn't have been. England had actually favored amicable relations with France before the war, a fact that its central role in the torturous negotiations to avoid the succession crisis attest to. Once it was clear who would win the war, British elites actually broke with their wartime allies to sue for a separate peace with Louis XIV, the preliminaries of which were achieved in London in 1711.[68]

4.2.1 Order Preferences

This bilateral agreement became the basis for the general settlement at the negotiations in Utrecht in 1712–1713.[69] The terms were concluded primarily by the two countries' acting foreign ministers, Colbert de Torcy and Viscount Bolingbroke (hereafter Torcy and Bolingbroke).[70] The most immediate and context-specific result of the settlement was that the Duke of Anjou, a Bourbon, would be allowed to keep the Spanish throne, but would have to forever renounce his Bourbon line's claim to the French crown.

Yet the agreement also recognized and responded to a more general peril for Europe—the fusion of French and Spanish power under one leader—and thus sought to prevent that possibility into the future. The heart of the settlement consisted of a discussion of general principles as well as the written renunciations of a number of important individuals: the Duke of Anjou (now Philip V of Spain) renouncing his family's rights to the French throne, and the Dukes of Berry and Orleans (Louis XIV's grandson and nephew, respectively) renouncing their lines' claims to the Spanish crown. Yet it is the general principles behind these specific agreements, and their implications for the European order, that I focus upon here.[71]

Order membership was not yet at issue in the settlement, and all the principal players were afforded the same rights at the negotiating table.[72] Instead, the Utrecht settlement added two important new behavior principles to the larger European order. **First, dynastic territorial claims across recognized state boundaries would no longer be treated as sacred entitlements of rulers predominant over all other principles (Utrecht rule #1).** This did not, strictly speaking, outlaw dynastic territorial claims. But it did stipulate that dynastic entitlements were no longer absolute, to be treated prior to all other considerations.[73] The result was that dynastic claims—and consequently, success at actually fulfilling such claims in practice—became much more circumscribed after Utrecht.[74] This was a sea change in the interstate politics of Europe.

Instead, such claims would now be subordinate to the second novel behavior principle advanced in the Utrecht negotiations: **maintaining or promoting a balance of power in Europe was now recognized as a legitimate end of state action (Utrecht rule #2).** In other words, acting in defense of a balance (or "equilibrium," as it was often called at the time) was now accepted as a legitimate motivation and justification for foreign policy.[75] The belief was that balance/equilibrium would help control the passions, envies and fears that actors recognized as leading causes of conflict in the prior century.[76]

Together, the confluence of these new rules resulted in agreement among the great powers on the clear subordination of dynastic claims to balance of power considerations. A passage from the Duke of Berry's renunciation epitomizes the interaction of these new order principles, and is worth quoting at length:

> All the powers of Europe finding themselves almost ruined on account of the present wars . . . [have] agreed, in the conferences and peace

negotiations being held with Great Britain, to establish an equilibrium, and political boundaries, between the kingdoms [whose] interests have been, and are still, the sad occasion of a bloody dispute; and to hold it for a fundamental maxim, in order to preserve this peace, that provision ought to be made that the forces of these kingdoms may not become formidable. . . .

For this purpose the King [Louis XIV] . . . and the King of Spain . . . have agreed and concluded with the Queen of Great Britain, that reciprocal renunciations shall be made by all the Princes, both present and to come, of the crown of France, and of that of Spain, of all rights which may appertain to each of them, to the succession of the one or of the other kingdom . . . by making an immovable balance to maintain the equilibrium, which is intended to be placed in Europe . . . to serve as an example for all such as may happen.[77]

While the Utrecht texts understandably referred most frequently to the specific succession crisis at hand, they also clearly stated that their provisions were to remain in force beyond the specific problems of the day. The Duke of Berry's renunciation noted that no member of the Austrian Habsburg family (in addition to his own Bourbon line) could claim the Spanish throne either, since that would similarly "destroy the equality that is establishing at present . . . which is the end that is proposed by this political equilibrium."[78] Britain likewise sought and received international recognition of the Hanover/Protestant line of succession at home, thus permanently delegitimating the claims of the Stuart/ Catholic descendants of James II to the English throne.[79] And the Duke of Orleans's renunciation made clear that the subordination of dynastic interests to a balance of power would now be a general principle extending beyond the immediate crisis.[80] In short, the settlement made clear that "no family was going to dominate European politics, and no settlement would be fashioned that provided any possible opportunity for a dynast again to seek 'universal monarchy.' "[81]

This subordination of dynastic right to the balance of power became a dominant maxim of European relations for the rest of the eighteenth century and continued to inform the post-Napoleonic order of the nineteenth century (chapter 5). Going forward, dynastic rights were far less frequently invoked or recognized as legitimate reasons for pursuing expansion or inciting conflict.[82] Meanwhile, invocations of the balance of power became significantly more common after 1713.[83] "It was now no longer sufficient to accept [a balance of power] as the . . . automatic result" of geography and state sovereignty, writes Matthew Anderson. Instead, "more and more it tended to be regarded not merely as a useful political device but as something with a moral value and justification of its own."[84] The order principle changes of the Utrecht settlement were thus clear and profound: as dynastic claims crumbled as a justification for state action, a new justification—the defense or promotion of a balance of power—was born from its ashes.[85]

4.2.2 Threats and Motives

The leaders of Great Britain drove the terms of the Utrecht settlement's most important components, and the advent of its two new order principles represent perhaps the most straightforward case of the ordering-to-exclude logic at work. Legitimating the balancing of power (rule #2) came in response to the novel nature of the French hegemonic threat. And delegitimating international dynastic claims (rule #1) would stamp out the recurrent threat of great power fusion through familial ties. True, one potential menace on this front was a very old one: the potential for Spanish and Austrian unification via Habsburg ties, the same dynastic link that had consumed France and Sweden both in and after Thirty Years' War.[86] Yet the biggest danger here by far was the prospect of Louis XIV's France linking up with *any* other power, of which Spain was the most likely candidate after Louis's marriage to Philip IV's eldest daughter in 1660. By using the settlement to rein in dynastic claims by rule, British leaders sought to cut off Louis's most direct path to achieving European preponderance, a tactic he had in fact already employed in the form of his expansive *réunions* policy in the decades prior to these events.

Starting first with the second rule change effectively advocated and implemented by Britain's statesmen—legitimating the balance of power—we would expect to see the corresponding threat of unprecedented preponderant power in need of being contained or rolled back. At first glance, British advocacy for this rule change might not seem to naturally or automatically follow from the logic of the theory. The threat of hegemony on the continent wasn't new, after all, as this is what the victors of the Thirty Years' War had feared a generation earlier. Additionally, British leaders were by this time well aware of their own country's rising power, thus making it plausible that they could soon be constrained by this anti-hegemonic rule of their own making.

What this line of reasoning neglects, however, was the unprecedented nature of the *French* hegemonic threat in particular, not only before the War of the Spanish Succession but also after its conclusion. Though statistics for the era are dubious, even the basic numbers available suggest that France's preponderance in the late seventeenth century was unprecedented (see Figures 4.1, 4.2 and 4.3). The nature of the French hegemonic threat was novel in size as these statistics

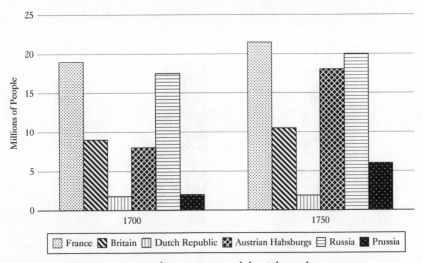

FIGURE 4.1 Great power population size around the eighteenth century.
Source: Paul Kennedy, *The Rise and Fall of the Great Powers* (New York: Vintage Books, 1987), 99.

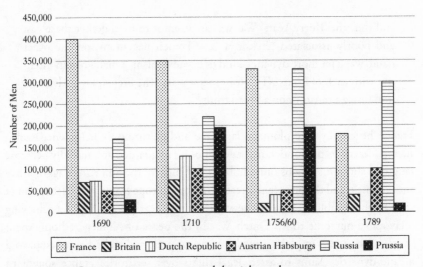

FIGURE 4.2 Great power army size around the eighteenth century.
Source: Paul Kennedy, *The Rise and Fall of the Great Powers* (New York: Vintage Books, 1987), 99.

suggest, but also in nature. As Charles Doran effectively differentiates between the threats looming over the statesmen at Westphalia and Utrecht,

the Spanish hegemony [during the Thirty Years' War] was defensive. It was implemented in an area which long had been under the Habsburg crowns,

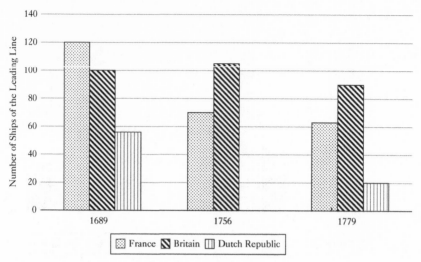

FIGURE 4.3 Great power navy size around the eighteenth century.
Source: Paul Kennedy, *The Rise and Fall of the Great Powers* (New York: Vintage Books, 1987), 99.

and thus the Thirty Years' War was an attempt to tie together these vast and poorly associated territories. The French hegemony, on the other hand, was a far more dynamic kind of expansionism, which grew in intensity with each of Louis XIV's four major wars. The French king advanced into foreign territory on a broad front.[87]

French hegemony in diplomacy, language and culture only heightened continental fears of its preponderance, as did Louis's unguarded and nakedly bellicose language about his expansionist ambitions.[88] Indeed, the Sun King's aggrandizement constituted the principal threat to the rest Europe from France's invasion of the Dutch Republic in 1672 all the way to Louis's death in 1715.[89] After achieving a favorable outcome to his Dutch War in the peace of Nijmegen, Louis spent much of the 1680s implementing his *réunions* policy whereby France employed arcane dynastic claims to assert legal rights over territories France sought to assimilate into its empire.[90] After a brief war with Spain, the Truce of Ratisbon legitimated most of Louis's *réunions* gains of the previous years. Still not content, he then invaded German territory in 1688, triggering a counterbalancing coalition and the War of the League of Augsburg (or Nine Years' War). Perhaps only England's unexpected entry into the league against Louis in 1689—a direct result of William (III) and Mary's (II) surprising accession to the English throne in the "glorious" revolution of the previous year—kept France from amassing even greater gains.[91] Louis may have finally been ready to moderate his ambitions after the more balanced Treaty of Ryswick ended the Nine Years' War 1697.[92] Yet it was precisely at this time that the looming Spanish succession crisis took center stage, connecting Britons' first fear—the Sun King's expansionist ambitions—with their second, great power aggrandizement through dynastic ties.

That British leaders greatly feared France's material preponderance coupled with Louis's notorious ambition is abundantly clear. Bolingbroke, secretary of war through much of the conflict and Britain's chief negotiator in the Utrecht talks, wrote extensively about the dangers of "Universal Monarchy," shorthand for French domination of Europe. After the Treaty of Ryswick, he noted, "it was plain that the confederates had failed in the first object of the grand alliance [the League of Augsburg plus England], that of reducing the power of France; by succeeding in which alone they could have been able to keep the second engagement, that of securing the succession of Spain to the house of Austria." Instead, "the pretensions of the House of Bourbon on the Spanish succession remained the same. Nothing had been done to weaken them; nothing was prepared to oppose them."[93] King William III warned Britain's would-be allies on the eve of the war that they must all "adopt such policies as may rescue and preserve the liberty of all Europe from the enormous power of the French aimed at establishing supreme domination."[94] And Queen Anne, William's successor after 1702, publicly declared that the aim of the settlement was preventing continental domination and "establishing a real balance of power in Europe" in order to combat French hegemony.[95]

"[T]he idea of 'universal monarchy' became essentially a propaganda slogan, a stick to beat France and Louis with, and ultimately yielded even in France to the guiding principle of 'balance of power,'" argues the historian Paul Schroeder.[96] In stigmatizing universal monarchy, British elites employed exclusion pathway #3, "severing social power." Building up "balance of power" as a more legitimate and natural state of affairs on the continent would help destroy Louis's pathway for amassing power and influence. To the extent that they were able to convince ordinary citizens—perhaps even those in France—of the desirability of a balance of power instead of a universal monarchy on the continent, they would have already gone far toward thwarting the Sun King's grandest ambitions.

The best available evidence with which to study British leaders' second fear—international dynastic connections being used to amass hegemonic power—is the written correspondence between the foreign ministers, Bolingbroke and Torcy, in 1711–1712, that produced the preliminary agreement and ultimately the final settlement. This correspondence reveals that British elites remained adamant throughout negotiations that the settlement had to satisfactorily put to rest the dynastic problems of European relations once and for all (rule #1). Bolingbroke from the beginning clearly wanted a peace based on joint moderation and general principle, as he feared that an imposed peace would both alienate France and prevent multilateral consensus for restraining destabilizing dynastic claims in the future.[97] Britain certainly sought (and largely achieved) a number of significant case-specific concessions in the negotiations. Yet much like Richelieu and Mazarin a generation earlier, British leaders prioritized a general and long-lasting settlement over specific territorial and commercial concessions. They ultimately achieved their goal in the 1711 London preliminary agreements.[98] By the start of the Utrecht conference in 1712, the powers had already agreed that the settlement must forever prevent the union of major power crowns in Europe for the sake of upholding a general equilibrium of power.[99]

What they still disagreed about, however, were the means to produce these ends. It was at this point in the negotiations—between the opening of the conference in early 1712 and the signing of the Utrecht accords the following year—that the Bolingbroke/Torcy correspondence became so crucial.[100] This correspondence ultimately produced the major order components of the Utrecht settlement signed in 1713. The predominant sticking point in the exchanges was the means for settling the Spanish succession crisis, and the arguments by Bolingbroke on this central issue in his correspondence with Torcy lend significant support to ordering-to-exclude theory.

Torcy's letters indicate that France wanted to end consideration of the succession issue with a *general* agreement that Spain and France would never be united, yet while leaving intact all *specific* rights of succession for members of the House of Bourbon. Tensions between these general and specific positions could then be addressed if or when they arose. The French minister at times tried to convince his British counterpart that "the union of the two monarchies would be a greater misfortune to France than to England" and thus would never be allowed to happen, while at other times arguing that formal and specific renunciations would "contravene the fundamental laws of this kingdom" since "we in France are persuaded that God alone can abolish it [divine rights]."[101]

Bolingbroke and Queen Anne strongly resisted these lines of reasoning, however, demonstrating that enacting general order principles was their top priority in the negotiations. On the point about divine right, Bolingbroke conceded God's ultimate role, but pointedly noted that in Britain, "a Prince can go from his right by a voluntary cession of it."[102] His letter to Torcy on March 23, 1712, was especially direct:

> In a word, Sir, the Queen orders me to signify to you, that this article [calling for blanket renunciations of succession rights] is of such vast consequence, as well to her as to the rest of Europe, as well to the present age as to posterity, that she will never agree to continue the negotiations for

peace, unless the expedient proposed by her be accepted, or some other equally substantial be adopted.[103]

Torcy tacitly conceded this point, but sought to introduce a new one: the timing of the renunciations. France again preferred to hold off until (and unless) future events warranted that specific renunciations be made by specific Bourbons, while Britain wanted them made immediately and proactively as a general rule at the heart of the settlement.[104] Again, Bolingbroke was resolute. As he put it, even if

> the Prince upon the Spanish Throne [made] his choice immediately [over whether to keep the Spanish crown or instead claim the French one], what additional security will that be to Europe, if the execution of that choice be deferred to a future period? . . . [M]ust we, on that account, after peace is signed, be perpetually armed, and live in constant expectation of a renewal of war? The Queen will never consent to this, and her Majesty believes, that not one of the allies will agree to such hard terms.[105]

Here Bolingbroke was activating pathway #2 for excluding a threatening force, "triggering tripwires." What British leaders wanted were specific, public, and preemptive renunciations by the Sun King's heirs to the thrones of multiple great power kingdoms at once. The point wasn't that renunciations alone would necessarily stop Bourbon leaders from backtracking later. But having the renunciations in writing would still create powerful symbolic and political barriers for these royals in the eyes of the European community, allowing elites across the continent to much more clearly identify what would constitute future Bourbon violations of Europe's political order.

On this point, Bolingbroke's demand again found success. Torcy relented in May, informing Britain that the Sun King had sent word to Madrid that Philip must immediately choose between the crowns of Spain and France. Torcy relayed Philip's decision to stay in Spain in early June.[106] Acknowledging receipt a few days later, Bolingbroke reiterated that although Queen Anne had indicated to Parliament that Britain would soon be at peace, there could be no backtracking on this central point: *"the expedient to prevent the reunion of the two monarchies of France and Spain, is the most important point of our negotiation, and her Majesty would give up all those that have been agreed upon, rather than leave it uncertain."*[107] Bolingbroke traveled to France shortly thereafter to negotiate directly with the French minister and his King, and a final agreement was ultimately reached precisely along the lines demanded by the British government. That these issues were of paramount importance to the most influential British elites is beyond dispute.

In fact, one of Bolingbroke's final acts as foreign minister came in writing Torcy a harsh letter warning that France must never "tamper with the 'great article', i.e. the renunciations" of the Bourbons that to Britain was the linchpin of the entire settlement.[108]

In sum, the content of the Bolingbroke/Torcy correspondence strongly supports the argument that British leaders used the settlement to address their greatest perceived threats—hegemonic domination of the continent and the linking of disparate kingdoms through dynastic claims—by imaginatively rewriting the rules of international order.

4.2.3 Alternatives

Binding

The binding thesis once again enjoys little support. As with the 1648 case, Ikenberry references the Utrecht settlement in *After Victory* but does not categorize it as an instance of hegemonic binding restraint.[109]

The way Britain treated its wartime allies in the postwar period also illustrates the weakness of the binding narrative in this case. Not only did British leaders go behind their allies' backs to sue for a separate peace with France, they also ceased hostilities before their Dutch and Austrian partners had agreed to do so and reneged on an agreement with the Dutch Republic to ensure that it received a security barrier from France.[110] In part because of Britain's opportunism in the war's endgame, the Dutch Republic was pushed to the side in European politics, never again to be considered a great power of the first rank.[111] These were not the actions, in sum, of an actor attempting to legitimate its leadership through binding restraint.

Exporting

In its strong form, the exporting thesis predicts that dominant actors will attempt to promote their ideological beliefs to the international system writ large. This strong form has no support in this case, where it is inapplicable in an age of ideological uniformity.[112]

The weaker version of exporting—emphasizing the influence of powerful domestic coalitions on order preferences—is potentially applicable, however. The early eighteenth century constituted an especially tumultuous period in Britain's domestic politics, particularly at the end of the War of the Spanish Succession. Under a Whig government throughout the war British leaders had been consistently unable to find compromise with France even when the conflict's outcome was no longer in doubt. It was only when the Tories, with the support of Queen Anne, took control of the government in the summer of 1710 that the decisive overtures for peace began.[113] Given their greater sympathy toward both absolute monarchy and Catholicism, a government controlled by the Tories naturally had reasons to find compromise with Louis in France while looking less favorably upon their own Dutch ally.[114] From this perspective, British domestic politics— and, specifically, the change from a Whig government to a Tory one—were crucial for explaining both the decision to end the war and British preferences in the peace negotiations.

Alas, this argument significantly overplays the independent influence of partisan differences on the timing and nature of the settlement. In actuality, the decisive events that led to Britain's fateful policy shifts at the end of the war were international, not domestic. Of particular importance was the death of Holy Roman Emperor Joseph I in 1711. The Imperial title now passed to his brother Charles, the same individual Britain had been planning to install as the King of Spain after overthrowing the Bourbon usurper, Philip V. Yet Joseph's death and Charles's ascension now made that possibility as dangerous and undesirable as the Bourbon domination they were fighting to prevent, since it would once again mean Habsburg expansion into Spain and a new "Universal Monarchy."[115] It was this event, more than partisan conflicts in Britain, that drove British leaders to sue for peace with France when they did.[116] The fact that this development may have forced Bolingbroke to refashion Britain's aims in the peace negotiations from the more particular (anti-French/Bourbon) to the more sweeping (anti-dynastic more generally) lends even greater support to ordering-to-exclude theory, as it demonstrates that Britain's evolving preferences were much more strategic than principled.[117]

Further casting doubt on a domestic politics explanation is the fact that upon taking power, the Tories actually pushed forward with Whig objectives that were seemingly at odds with their own ideological proclivities. These included securing French recognition of the Protestant line of succession in England (thus weakening Catholicism) and insisting upon the order principle devaluing dynastic ties (thus weakening absolute monarchism), both initiatives contrary to Tory ideological predilections. In short, while the Tories capturing power might have been a permissive cause for ending the war, it was not determinative. More importantly, there is little evidence that it played a role in determining the content of British order preferences in negotiating the Utrecht settlement.

Learning

The learning hypothesis again enjoys the most support among the alternatives. Because Britain's greatest perceived threat at the end of the war was the same as in the prewar period, learning and excluding once again predict similar order preferences. For this reason, observers like Kalevi Holsti argue that the framers of the Utrecht settlement "were mainly backward-looking. They concentrated on preventing a recurrence of French expansionism rather than examining the kinds of issues that were likely to spawn international conflicts in the future."[118] As discussed earlier, Louis XIV's power and bellicosity on the continent were clearly the greatest threats to Britain in the years prior to the war. Yet it was not until Louis's France proved to be both more nakedly bellicose and more successful in efforts than any power previously that Britain chose to directly target this threat in the settlement of Utrecht.[119]

Learning can thus account for both of Britain's order preferences, *for* a balance of power and *against* transnational dynastic claims. The core Utrecht agreement, as well as the Bourbon renunciations and Bolingbroke's correspondence, all clearly indicate that establishing and then permanently legitimating a balance of power was a direct reaction to the perceived causes of a war that had been ruinous for all parties involved. Learning also helps to explain the focus on international dynastic claims in general and the French-Spanish Bourbon succession issue in particular. The elements of the settlement involving dynastic claims were of paramount importance to British leaders and were not up for negotiation. At least in part, this is accounted for via the learning narrative: dynastic claims were the best vehicle for Louis to achieve the dominance across Europe he had been seeking for half a century, and Britain was determined to sever this pathway for the Sun King to achieve his ambitions once and for all. In that regard, they were attempting to put out the biggest fire of Europe's most recent past, a hallmark of the learning motive.

But like the post-Napoleonic settlement that would come a century later (chapter 5), the victors' aim after the War of the Spanish Succession was not solely to impose a backward-looking and punitive peace on the war's perceived instigator, France. If this had been the overriding goal, Britain would not have chosen to negotiate directly with France over the demands of its allies in war, all of whom wanted a much more punitive anti-*French* settlement (rather than a more general and anti-*dynastic* one). Indeed, there is near historical consensus that France escaped a war it lost with a surprisingly lenient peace settlement, one that ultimately left other actors far more discontented than the French regime. While the learning hypothesis correctly predicts the observed order preferences (congruence testing) and offers a plausible interpretation of the historical record for the origins of those preferences (process tracing), it thus does not tell the entire story. It cannot account for why British leaders chose to forego a more particularistic peace settlement focused on the immediate culprit of the most recent conflict, France, and opted instead for a more far-reaching agreement that would more fundamentally reshape the European international order. Ordering-to-exclude theory, which emphasizes the forward-looking threat perceptions of great powers, can better account for these decisions and developments.

In the long progression of international order, Utrecht is often treated as a quick stop along the road, one where much more could have been done to build consensus, erect foundational institutions, and deliver sturdier order principles.[120] This view is not entirely fair, however. While the settlement did not mandate lasting cooperation as a general principle, as later agreements would, and has not resonated in history as profoundly as Westphalia, it did advance two important rule changes that would remain consequential for at least the next two centuries of European politics.[121] As the historian Tim Blanning concludes,

> on the European continent, the best possible result was achieved: Louis XIV's bid for hegemony had been finally defeated; the Low Countries were buffered against French pressure; and a balance of power had been achieved. More generally, the peace treaties established the British objective of a continental "balance of power" as the goal of the European states-system.[122]

In this way, the settlement was as important and revolutionary for order as those more famous agreements that preceded and followed it.

4.3 *The Non-Reordering Moment of 1763*

Aside from the conclusion of the Great Northern War in 1721—a conflict that had coincided with the War of the Spanish Succession and marked the exit of Sweden from the ranks of great powers alongside Russia's corresponding entry— the European system remained stable in the decades after Utrecht.[123] Perhaps this was a consequence of the settlement itself, or instead the result of one of its other byproducts: Utrecht marked Great Britain's arrival as both a leader of the European system and a global great power of the first order.

While the settlement created an interlocking set of provisions for assuring equilibrium on the continent, it also made Britain the preponderant naval power and gave it a clear advantage in the overseas colonies.[124] With supremacy between them clear and their differences at least temporarily settled, Britain and France concluded an *entente* that would keep them at peace for the next twenty-five years.[125] They would not come to blows again until they found themselves on opposing sides of the War of the Austrian Succession, a conflict that marked the emergence of Prussia as a great power and was more about control of the Holy Roman Empire than it was about the larger system or order. By that point, however, another major Anglo–French conflict was probably inevitable. France's recovery by the 1730s from the setbacks of Louis XIV's late reign were impressive, and the growth of her overseas colonies was especially formidable (and to

Britain, especially threatening).[126] Even after the Treaty of Aix-la-Chapelle ended the Austrian succession conflict in 1748, many observers believed it was only a matter of time before the two foremost colonial powers engaged in another epic struggle for supremacy.[127]

This struggle, the Seven Years' War, is often referred to as the first truly global great-power conflict. Yet it was only global for two of the five powers, since for the Austrian Habsburgs, Russia, and Prussia the war was confined to Europe and almost exclusively to modern-day Germany. By contrast, the conflict that once again pitted Britain against France was waged across India, Africa, and most famously in North America, where it is better known as the French and Indian War. It was this Anglo–French conflict that was most important for international security and its corresponding resolution for international order. By 1763 Britain had emerged as the undisputed victor once again, achieving a position of dominance at war's end that no single European state—including Louis XIV's France—had ever before realized.

The endgame of the Seven Years' War has not received the scholarly attention of similar developments in 1648, 1713, 1815, 1919, or 1945, suggesting, perhaps, that there was less opportunity for order transformation here than in those other periods. Yet by virtue of the destruction and upheaval that it caused as well as the total involvement of all of the system's great powers, the Seven Years' War clearly constituted a shock to Europe commensurate to those of the Thirty Years' and Spanish Succession conflicts (see Table 2.2). It is studied far less than the other two cases of this chapter, I submit, not because it failed to present the dominant actor with a real opportunity to enact fundamental order changes, but because that actor—Great Britain—ultimately chose not to seize this opportunity.

Given its historically advantageous position at the end of the war, it might seem puzzling that British leaders did not pursue revolutionary order changes to cement their preponderance in the 1763 Peace of Paris. Britain's preferences for continuity are actually easy to understand from the perspective of ordering-to-exclude theory, however. Precisely because they had so thoroughly crushed and humiliated their chief rival and threat, France, *and* because the war had rendered the rest of Europe so depleted and exhausted, Britain found itself in an extremely benign security environment by 1763, with no major threats on the horizon. Their greatest danger, British leaders came to believe, came in the possibility of inciting revisionist backlash should they choose to impose too harsh a peace on the war's losing powers. With no new threats to exclude, it is little wonder that British statesmen chose implicit order continuity over pursuing order change in the aftermath of the Seven Years' War.

For a war notable for its disparate theaters, it should come as little surprise that it also had disparate origins. The Anglo–French antagonisms at its heart stemmed primarily from competition in their overseas colonies and especially in North America. Particularly in the Ohio Valley, where each power's territorial claims were vague, contested, and often contradictory, constant competition eventually bred deep antagonisms and mutual mistrust. Beginning in 1750, London received a steady stream of concerned messages from their governors in the colonies warning that France was preparing to seize the entirety of the Ohio Valley. What followed was a corresponding series of troop buildups across their respective holdings that would eventually spiral into armed conflict in the summer of 1754.[128]

Meanwhile, events in Europe gave each of these powers even more cause to fear one other. The impetus for conflict there revolved around the Austrian Habsburgs' strong desire to recapture the resource rich province of Silesia. That province had been taken by Prussia in 1740, a move that had ignited the Austrian Succession War. The Treaty of Aix-la-Chapelle had left the Austrian Habsburg Queen, Maria Theresa, dissatisfied and resentful that her longtime ally, Britain, had forced her to accept a peace that ceded Silesia to her now-lifelong enemy, Frederick II (the Great) of Prussia.[129] In the ensuing decade, Maria Theresa had plotted to steal it back by any means necessary.

It was in this context that the powder keg of Anglo–French conflict in North America took on a new and more dangerous meaning in Europe. When British leaders sent two regiments to Virginia in late 1754 to drive the French from the Ohio Valley, London feared that France would retaliate by attacking either Britain itself or Hanover, a close ally in Europe that also counted Britain's King George II as its sovereign. British leaders tried to enlist the help of their longtime allies, the Austrian Habsburgs, but received a cold response on account of Britain's unwillingness to help Austria reclaim Silesia. London's lack of reliable allies on the continent ultimately led British elites to seek a mutual security alliance with the Habsburgs' principal adversary, Prussia, culminating in the Convention of Westminster in early 1756.

This Anglo-Prussian pact shattered expectations and overturned the traditional alliance system in Europe. Free from the constraint of its traditional alliance with Britain, the Austrian Habsburgs immediately began readying for war against Prussia. In so doing, Maria Theresa also began cooperating with Empress Elizabeth of Russia, who had been similarly stung by the Anglo-Prussian alliance and aspired to make territorial gains of her own at Prussia's expense. Sensing encirclement, Frederick of Prussia launched a preventive strike against Saxony, a formidable Austrian ally, thereby triggering continental war. By the end of the year, Russia had joined a defensive Franco-Habsburg Versailles Treaty and in the following May the Austrian Habsburgs secured an offensive anti-Prussian alliance. By this time, the so-called Diplomatic Revolution precipitated by the shocking Anglo-Prussian alliance was complete. France supported the Habsburgs with troops but primarily through subsidies, while Britain backed Prussia exclusively through subsidies.[130]

The war went badly for Britain in its early years due in part to mismanagement in London. Yet this ship was soon righted by a political alliance that installed the Duke of Newcastle as Prime Minister and the irascible William Pitt (the elder) in charge of foreign affairs. For all of the controversy he inspired during his time in power, Pitt was a magnificently effective war manager. As early as 1759 it was clear that Britain was resoundingly winning the battle for colonial supremacy, an advantage it would make total by 1762. On the opposite side, France found itself spread too thin, having to commit too many resources to the anti-Prussian effort in Europe, facing the British on too many fronts across the colonies, and unable to raise enough revenue at home to effectively continue the war.[131]

Adding to the margin of Britain's victory was the fact that the European war ended much closer to stalemate than did the Atlantic and colonial fronts. Prussia was technically victorious on account of being Britain's ally and surviving a multi-front elimination campaign. Yet it was also ravaged and in significant debt by war's end, with dwindling financial and diplomatic support from British leaders who appeared to be washing their hands of further involvement in continental affairs. Russia, the Austrians, and France were all technically losers, though they suffered varied fates. Russia had performed well on the battlefield and benefited from exiting the war early, in 1762, after the death of Empress Elizabeth and the accession of the Prussophile Peter III, but was not yet considered a major player outside of its immediate sphere of influence. The Austrian Habsburgs were humbled and significantly weakened by the war, having suffered demoralizing defeats on the battlefield while failing to achieve their principal goal of reclaiming Silesia.

Still, the greatest setbacks were suffered by France. It had nothing to show for its new alliance with the Austrians in Europe, and, in spite of the fact that it had persuaded Spain to enter the war in the Americas against Britain in 1762, its colonial possessions were in an unprecedented state of disarray on the eve of the peace negotiations. As a result of all of these developments, Great Britain once again emerged as the undisputed victor of another major war by 1763.

4.3.1 Order Preferences

Notably, the British government that negotiated the peace was not the one responsible for waging and winning the war. The death of King George II in 1760 led to the accession of a ruler in George III who disliked both Pitt and Newcastle and favored his childhood mentor, the Earl of Bute (hereafter Bute), who was immediately installed on the Privy Council. Pitt resigned in protest in

1761 when the rest of the cabinet declined to preemptively declare war on Spain. Newcastle was pushed out the next year, and George III chose Bute to lead the government through the peace negotiations with France. Bute in turn selected his close ally the Duke of Bedford (hereafter Bedford) as his representative to the peace negotiations in Paris. The principal French negotiator at Paris was the Duke of Choiseul (hereafter Choiseul), Chief Minister of Louis XV and often simultaneously France's foreign minister.

The peace settlement of the Seven Years' War was comprised of two distinct treaties. A preliminary agreement was concluded at Fontainebleau in November 1762 by Britain, France, Spain, and Portugal. The resulting document, officially known as the Treaty of Paris, was signed by the same parties on February 10, 1763. At the same time, Frederick of Prussia made peace with the Austrian Habsburgs and the other German principalities in the Treaty of Hubertusburg on February 15. Because that agreement was negotiated between the lesser of the powers and largely restored the *status quo ante bellum* in Europe, I focus exclusively on the Paris treaty and negotiations here.[132]

For our purposes, the most notable facet of the Treaty of Paris was that it contained no new principles of international order or notable changes to old ones. Instead, it recognized the general principles consecrated at Westphalia and Utrecht "as a basis and foundation to the peace" moving forward.[133] The treaty went on to specify only the case-specific issues of returning and relinquishing of territories as had been agreed to in the preliminary negotiations in 1762.[134] France was virtually ousted from North America, allowed little more than fishing rights around Newfoundland and the St. Lawrence Seaway and the use of a number of small islands that it was nonetheless prohibited from militarizing.

And yet the peace was far less harsh than it could have been. Britain could have enacted order changes that would have consecrated its global hegemony in the colonized world—as it had "emerged from the Seven Years' War as the closest thing the eighteenth-century world had to a superpower"[135]—perhaps through a set of foundational new rules that would favor its existing imperial strengths and minimize its weaknesses. Britain's leaders also could have devised ways to exclude France and its allies from reaping any further gains in North America, not just in practice but also on principle, or destroyed French colonial power, or French continental power, or the Bourbon monarchy itself.[136]

Instead, Bute and Bedford not only sought no changes to the existing order but also showed remarkable leniency toward Britain's adversaries. Belleisle off of the Brittany coast, Goree near Senegal, and crucial colonies in the Caribbean— most notably Martinique, Guadeloupe, and St. Lucia—were returned to France, while Manilla and Havana were restored to Spain, France's ally in the later years of the war.[137] Understandably wanting to justify the settlement lest Britain decide to backtrack at the eleventh hour, the French negotiator Choiseul defended Britain's submissiveness, noting, "There is no modern example in which a peace has been made when the conquerors kept the whole of their conquests." "True as this dictum was," retorted an English historian later, "the contrast between what England retained at the peace in the New World, and what she restored [to her adversaries], was astonishing."[138]

4.3.2 Threats and Motives

The biggest threat to Britain's global interests in the prewar period had been a perceived "French attempt to subdivide the [North American] continent at the expense of further British westward expansion."[139] Yet in the wake of the global conflict, Britain no longer faced any such threat, either in North America or in Europe. That they ultimately decided against pursuing changes to order principles thus conforms to the expectations of ordering-to-exclude theory's hypothesis 1D: *"Dominant actors will not attempt major revisions to order principles when they perceive no major or new threat on the horizon, or where the immediacy of such a threat is perceived to be low."*

Plainly put, each of Britain's potential adversaries had glaring weaknesses by 1763. Austrian leaders found that they simply did not have the resources to raise a force large enough to take back Silesia. From 1761 on, they merely hoped for a peace that would restore the *status quo ante bellum*, a preference that was reinforced by Russia's exit from the war in 1762. Though Prussia had technically won the war, British leaders considered the Prussians neither permanent nor close allies. The only concrete bond linking the two during the war had been the annual British subsidy, a link that was promptly and abruptly terminated at war's end.[140]

Most importantly, Britain's principal threat before the war, France, was left utterly devastated and thoroughly humiliated by 1763. Figures 4.1, 4.2 and 4.3 display the severity of France's relative decline over the eighteenth century, particularly when compared to its earlier position. In retrospect, it is not difficult to see that French leaders had spread their resources far too thin to ever achieve victory in the Seven Years' War. While they may have had greater aggregate resources than Britain on the eve of war in 1756, that superiority alone should not have justified the dubious decisions to join a continental war against Prussia while at the same time fighting the mighty British Empire in various theaters across the world. When its leaders tried to extricate France from the European conflict as the global war bore on, Pitt made sure that this would be next to impossible by continuing Britain's generous wartime subsidy to Frederick in Prussia. As he would famously declare later, France in "America had been conquered in Germany."

French capabilities were decimated by the war. Her territorial losses "emphasized the low point her international prestige had reached by 1763. Her wretched performance in the war surprised contemporaries . . . and this decline was not speedily reversed."[141] Documents indicate that Choiseul hoped for a war of revenge to commence some years later and ordered a massive naval buildup in anticipation of this conflict. Yet French naval strength only increased from 60 ships of the line in 1763 to 62 in 1765, even after Choiseul had ordered an increase of 80 ships within five years.[142] French weakness also became manifest in numerous diplomatic failures, from her impotence in aiding the Ottoman Empire against Russia in 1766 to her helplessness in the first partition of Poland to her utter inability to deter Britain from taking the Falkland Islands from Spain in 1770.[143] The American colonies' successful war of independence may have shown France's continued ability to play kingmaker in contests outside of Europe. Yet as satisfying a poke in the eye against their British adversaries as that episode might have been, it "failed to revive France's overseas empire . . . and ultimately worsened France's naval position while restoring Britain's."[144]

British naval superiority was no less decisive in the latter years of the war and became magnified again at its conclusion. Its effective blockades of French Mediterranean and Atlantic ports had prevented France from getting needed supplies and reinforcements to North America, where she was thoroughly outmatched by 1758. After that year, Britain made extraordinary gains at France's expense in the colonial world, particularly in North America, the Caribbean, India, and West Africa.[145] Even the Franco-Spanish alliance that came to fruition in 1761 did little to reverse France's fortune. By 1763 Britain had captured Havana and Manila, two of the most crucial outposts for the already dilapidated Spanish Empire. In fact, Britain captured and kept numerous territories in the war and settlement that actually *enhanced* its preponderance and further ensured its security from future threats.[146]

Records also indicate that British leaders understood their preponderance at the war's conclusion. To that end, they recognized not only that they had little reason for imposing a harsh peace against France but also that it would actually be counterproductive to do so. Bedford, the British negotiator, recognized this as early as 1761, warning Newcastle in May of that year—when the cabinet was beginning to discuss the war's endgame—that such power "would be as dangerous for us to grasp as it was for Louis XIV when he aspired to be the arbiter of Europe, and might be likely to produce a grand alliance against us"[147]. In a crucial letter sent to Newcastle and Bute that July, Bedford argued that

> the endeavouring to drive France entirely out of any naval power is fighting against nature, and can tend to no one good in this country; but, on the

contrary, must excite all the naval powers in Europe to enter into a confederacy against us, as adopting a system viz. that of a monopoly of all naval power which would be at least as dangerous to the liberties of Europe as that of Louis XIV was, which drew almost all Europe upon his back.[148]

Bute replied that "I cannot help flattering myself that our ideas are nearly the same," while at the same time communicating his great fear that in demanding too sweeping a peace, Britain could "be deemed unreasonable, or thought to aim at *universal dominion*."[149] "We know the French are exhausted," he continued, and "that they in the most humiliating manner sued for peace: have they bettered their condition, or is ours become worse since their first offers?" Neither, he surmised: "All our foreign intelligence declares the impossibility of their continuing the war."[150]

This benign threat environment can help explain not only the decision for order continuity but also for much of Britain's leniency in the case-specific aspects of the settlement. Bute readily relinquished to France various important territorial acquisitions Britain had made in the war, reasonably stating his belief that attempting to hold them would drag out the negotiations, prolong the fighting, and potentially engender further ill will against Britain in the future.[151] As Fred Anderson summarizes the policy positions of Bute, Medford, and George III, they believed that

> an England that had thwarted Louis's attempts to impose a Catholic universal monarchy on Europe by the patient building and rebuilding of coalitions against him should never allow itself to be seduced by the temptations of dominion. The temptation was particularly acute, and thus most to be feared, now that hegemony over not just Europe but the Atlantic world itself seemed to lie within Britain's grasp.[152]

Prudently, British leaders concluded that they could live with this advantageous position without completely remaking the international order or more harshly punishing their competitors.

4.3.3 Alternatives

Binding

That Britain's advantageous threat environment in 1763 can best account for its order continuity preference is bolstered by the weaknesses of the alternative motives.

Since British leaders did not seek to enact a sweeping postwar settlement that would reorder the European system, the binding thesis is largely inapplicable in this case. It is true that they were worried about systemic backlash if they were to impose too harsh a peace, as was discussed in the previous section. Yet this hardly validates the hypothesis that they were motivated to enact an order that would make British hegemony more legitimate to others. Above all, the binding thesis is hampered here by the fact that Britain simply did not seek to impose any systematic restraints upon its own power in the war's settlement.

Exporting

Once again, there were no real ideological alternatives yet available to support the strong version of the exporting motive. As with the Utrecht settlement, however, the weaker version of exporting—focusing on the effects of British domestic politics on its order and postwar preferences—offers a more plausible interpretation. The twenty-two-year old George III had just become King in 1760 and relied tremendously on Bute, his mentor and tutor, for major policy advice.[153] The resulting leadership of a neophyte in Bute produced a settlement that was seen in some quarters as dangerously lenient on France. If Pitt had not resigned from Parliament in protest in 1761, he almost certainly would have pushed for harsher terms against France.[154] From this perspective, it was domestic political upheaval and the new government's belief that it needed to conclude a swift peace, rather than a benign threat environment, that informed British preferences and policy at the end of the war.

Upon closer inspection, however, this explanation does not stand up to scrutiny. Pitt certainly justified his preferences for a harsher settlement in a fear of French resurgence.[155] Yet his hardline demands appear to have been driven less by genuine fear of a resurgent French threat and more from a desire to permanently punish France by destroying her naval power as well as out of an "apparent lust for new conquests."[156] As one historian puts it most plainly, "no peace, other than one that humiliated France, would ever satisfy Pitt."[157] Furthermore, it is simply untrue that Pitt was powerless to pursue his policy preferences once he left the government. Still enormously popular with the general population, he remained a public figure throughout the peace negotiations. In a dramatic attempt to block the treaty's passage in Parliament, he came to the House of Commons and spoke against it for more than three hours. Bute, in turn, also defended the settlement in person, declaring that he "desired to have written on his tomb 'Here lies the Earl of Bute, who in concert with the King's ministers, made the Peace.'"[158] In spite of Pitt's efforts, the treaty was overwhelmingly approved. Its passage through the House of Commons demonstrated that if any elite's view of the settlement was an outlier, it was not Bute's but Pitt's.[159] Even without George II's death and the rise of Bute and Bedford to power, Pitt would have faced long odds for enacting a more punitive peace against France.

Learning

As with the exporting thesis, the learning motive would also predict Britain taking a harder line against France in a more sweeping postwar settlement. Surmises one historian, "those who imagined Bourbon intervention in the interior [of North America] were 'fighting the last war,' supposing that what happened in 1753-4 could easily happen again."[160] Indeed, if there was any consensus among the British people over how their leaders had treated France in the aftermath of the most recent prior wars—those of the Spanish and Austrian successions—it was that they had been too lenient rather than too harsh. The general unpopularity of the treaty among the British public is a testament to the fact that a simple review of the most formative recent events would have dictated a more sweeping and punitive peace. In short, no plausible interpretation of the learning motive for this case would predict Britain's actual preferences for the settlement they negotiated and achieved in 1763.

The 1763 case thus offers a striking instance of a dominant actor choosing order continuity over order change at a moment when it had the capacity to impose whatever sweeping order revisions it might have wanted. Yet Great Britain would find itself with more moments of opportunity to shape and change order over the next century and a half. For its principal adversary throughout the eighteenth century, however, even harder times were ahead. "By seeking to wage war simultaneously at sea, in the colonies and on the continent, France was defeated in all three theaters," writes Blanning. "Unwilling to recognize that their country was suffering from a decline that was both absolute and relative," the French public soon became bitterly disillusioned, further eroding support for their government and monarch.[161]

In fact, France's surprising loss in the Seven Years' War was the beginning of the end for the Bourbon monarchy. Less than thirty years later, Louis XV's grandson, Louis XVI, would lose his crown—and then his head—in one of the most significant developments for international order in all of history, the French Revolution. The reverberations of this transformative event are the focus of chapter 5.

5

Order in the European Concert Era

THE SETTLEMENTS IN the aftermath of the French Revolutionary and Napoleonic Wars are historically notable for creating the so-called "Concert of Europe," a pathbreaking cooperative endeavor among the continent's most powerful actors. The Concert "may not have fulfilled all the hopes of an idealistic generation, but it gave this generation something perhaps more precious," wrote a young Henry Kissinger in 1957: "a period of stability which permitted their hopes to be realized without a major war or a permanent revolution."[1] Kissinger hasn't been the only prominent American policymaker transfixed by the era: Woodrow Wilson referenced "the Vienna System" in constructing the Versailles peace settlement and League of Nations Covenant (chapter 6), while Franklin Roosevelt used the Concert as a guidepost for designing the great power consortium that would become the United Nations Security Council (chapter 7).[2] Indeed, the observation that policymakers today should adopt the grand strategic playbook of the European Concert's architects has practically become a truism.[3]

Yet what the Concert actually was, how it came to be, and how long it lasted are critical questions that continue to bedevil observers. In the first section of this chapter, I assess the scholarly debate over the Concert's substance and make the case that it represented a new rule-based order that decisively departed from the brand of realist balance-of-power politics that had dominated Europe since the War of the Spanish Succession.

And yet accepting such a conception of what the Concert was says little about how it came to be. Instead, I aim to show in the second section that an analysis of the motivations of its principal architects strongly supports the expectations of ordering-to-exclude theory, especially relative to the alternative explanations.

In the third section, I assess two more cases of order change opportunity where dominant actors elected not to recast the principles of the Concert order. The first—in the midst of the revolutionary wave of 1848—presents anomalies for ordering-to-exclude theory but also raises difficult questions for the alternatives.

The second—negotiations at the end of the Crimean War—fits more comfort-ably with the threat-driven logic at the heart of the book. This section concludes by assessing competing accounts for when and why the Concert order broke down. In the chapter's conclusion, I discuss the results across *all* the European cases detailed in this chapter and the last.

5.1 Bringing Order to the Concert
5.1.1 The Concert's Substance

Scholarly debate continues today over what the Concert of Europe actually was. This debate divides along the same battle lines as the larger IR debates over international order detailed in chapter 2. Realists are the Concert skeptics, arguing that all the talk about new principles was little more than high-minded rhetoric. These principles had negligible effects on actual great power behavior, realists argue, especially compared to the influence of the underlying balance of power that actually did the work of constraining behavior throughout this era.[4] Institutionalists treat the Concert as a primitive-but-successful version of a conflict-mediating organization that decreased the difficulties of negotiation among multiple actors (transaction costs) while increasing the reliable informa-tion each could learn about the others (transparency).[5] Constructivists focus less on these formal processes and instead treat the Concert as a successful instance of norm convergence among the great powers who together developed, depending on the particular account, a common conception of "European interests" or even a common transnational identity.[6]

A combination of aspects from each perspective is important for under-standing the Concert of Europe. Yet realists in particular have shortchanged the Concert in much the same way they have shortchanged the very concept of order (chapter 2). First, they fail to adequately address the considerable evidence that leaders spoke and states behaved much differently throughout the Concert era than realist theories would predict.[7] Second, the realist claim that the Concert rested on little more than post-Utrecht balance-of-power thinking is no longer regarded as tenable in historical scholarship. For all their disagreements over the Concert, diverse scholars actually agree that its architects viewed what they were doing as a repudiation of power politics as usual, not a reaffirmation of it.[8]

Though the institutionalist and constructivist views are more helpful, each also suffers from limitations. Characterizing the Concert as even a primitive intergovernmental organization comparable to the United Nations or NATO today seems problematic. The Concert had no formal or permanent bureaucracy and—outside of the initial treaties and whatever notes or declarations indi-vidual delegations decided to write down—codified virtually nothing about its proceedings. In fact, a number of scholars attribute the Concert's effectiveness not to robust collective security guarantees or institutionalized commitments, but to a distinct lack of these features. From this perspective, its very informality was what allowed it to remain flexible and adaptive to changing circumstances.[9]

Against the constructivist view, socialization in the Concert system was much weaker than in contemporary security communities. It was not nearly as socialized as the European Union, NATO, or even ASEAN are today—evidenced in part by states' frequent use of coercive threats against one another in Concert meetings (even as they hardly ever acted on them).[10] Furthermore, any normative consensus that did take place was almost entirely limited to a small group of elites, not their national publics. Notable constructivist accounts even admit that the lack of both broader and deeper socialization likely played a role in the Concert's eventual demise.[11]

Instead, I submit that the Concert of Europe was at its core simply an agreement among the elite statesmen of the great powers to adhere to a particular set of order principles. In this way, it fits comfortably within this book's conception of order established in chapter 2. Sometimes these principles appeared to be deeply felt and genuinely internalized by elites, resembling norms in the constructivist sense. At other times they were most useful for providing self-interested statesmen a forum and set of procedures to cooperate on common problems as institutionalists would expect. What mattered most, however, was that the Concert's principles were both recognized (in rhetoric) and practiced (in behavior) and had demonstrable effects on outcomes across the system. The Concert's rules established an unprecedented amount of elite-level contact through frequent meetings, resulted in a remarkably low incidence of interstate conflict, and led to an unparalleled degree of territorial stability on the continent.[12]

The Concert's set of order principles is sometimes called the "Vienna Settlement," a reference to the famous Congress of Vienna of 1813–1814. That months-long meeting produced only a small portion of that which came to define the broader postwar settlement. But the Congress fostered much of the *spirit* of the remarkable cooperation that would take place in the decades thereafter.[13] The major landmarks of the Vienna Settlement and their significance for the resulting Concert order are summarized in Table 5.1 and discussed in the next section.

5.1.2 The Concert's Principles

Much ink has been spilled attempting to capture the Concert's most important principles, such that one could easily cull a list of ten to twenty distinct rules from only a handful of historical sources on the Concert. I highlight four such rules that stand apart from the rest in importance and broad applicability, thus rising to

Table 5.1 The Vienna Settlement

Date	Agreement	Significance for Order
March 1814	Treaty of Chaumont	The great powers (GPs) pledge to negotiate with France to end the war only as a collective, not separately; agree to keep alliance together for an unprecedented length of at least 20 years
May 1814	First Treaty of Paris	The GPs grant themselves separate status and rights to dictate and enforce the terms of the peace on the continent in a separate, secret clause to the larger treaty that specifies the terms of the peace with France
June 1815	Vienna Final Act	This constituted a summary and collection of the massive territorial settlements produced through separate negotiations and treaties at the Congress of Vienna; significant for binding all of these settlements into one, implying they are part of a united whole
September 1815	Holy Alliance	Austria, Russia, and Prussia sign a short and vague agreement to come to each other's aid; today; while mostly meaningless at the time, it is only later repurposed by these eastern powers to justify anti-liberal interventions across the continent
November 1815	Second Treaty of Paris	This slightly more punitive settlement against France specifies the modified terms of the peace in the wake of Napoleon's escape and defeat at Waterloo; contains some of the most tangible language implying that anti-liberal/revolutionary sentiment is a significant component of the emerging order
November 1815	Treaty of Alliance (Quadruple Alliance)	This agreement renews the long-term and general alliance made in Chaumont, and establishes that there will be periodic GP meetings for the purpose of maintaining peace and tranquility throughout Europe
October 1818	Treaty of Aix-la-Chapelle	France is welcomed into the Quadruple (now Quintuple) Alliance, Concert system, and GP club; strongly reiterates the desire and intention for periodic GP meetings to deal with the geopolitical matters of Europe

the level of foundational order rules. Three were principles of behavior. The first involved the designation of a special status for the most powerful actors in the system. While today it is commonplace to differentiate "great powers" from all other states, this distinction would not have been recognized in Europe prior to the nineteenth century. But in the post-Napoleonic settlements, **the great power (GP) victors of the wars officially granted themselves new status as a separate, more important class of states uniquely fit to govern Europe (Concert rule #1).** Only *they* would be responsible for maintaining peace on the continent and determining what that peace would look like.[14] This differentiation was not a mere abstraction in the heads of statesmen. It also reflected a new material and social reality in which vast military power could be harnessed by the regimes with the largest populations, due in part to the advent of mass conscription.[15]

If this first rule accomplished a necessary preliminary task, a second articulated the single most important idea of the Concert: **an acknowledgement by the great powers that only *together* would they establish, defend, and redefine as necessary the political and territorial status quo on the continent (Concert rule #2).** Simply put, no unilateral territorial changes would be permissible without consent from (or at least consultation with) the great powers acting in concert. In the Treaty of Chaumont (March 1814), the four powers allied against France pledged to negotiate a final peace with Napoleon Bonaparte only as a collective, single unit. They also agreed to remain united against Revolutionary France's reemergence for at least twenty years after the war's conclusion, a commitment of unprecedented length for any state to make at the time, let alone the most powerful actors in the system.[16] Yet what started as a practical consideration in the war soon became a more general order principle of the settlement. The Congress of Vienna ultimately produced the Vienna Final Act (June 1815), an agreement notable for packaging all of the smaller territorial settlements negotiated at the Congress into a single treaty. As Jennifer Mitzen argues, "each individual agreement was given the additional endorsement of being part of the overall plan for continental peace and stability. Through the Final Act, European stability was made indivisible, and it was made the responsibility of all signatories."[17]

Yet the powers also recognized that simply acknowledging their responsibility to act in concert was not enough. They therefore built into this system **a loose mechanism for consultation and dispute resolution through periodic great power meetings (Concert rule #3).**[18] In the Quadruple Alliance (November 1815), they declared that "the High Contracting Parties have agreed to renew their Meetings at fixed periods" in order to continue with "the maintenance of the Peace of Europe."[19] If conflicts arose, the great powers would negotiate among themselves to reach some resolution, resorting to force only as agreed together and only for the purpose of containing larger disruptions to the status quo.[20] At the first of these meetings in 1818, held in Aix-la-Chappelle (Aachen, Prussia), the powers formally expanded their twenty-year Chaumont commitment to apply to *all* European security concerns more generally.[21]

It was at this same 1818 meeting that the powers formally ended the occupation of France mandated under the Second Treaty of Paris (November 1815) and welcomed their former adversary—now under a restored monarchy—into the Concert's great power consortium. The now-*five* powers then jointly declared that the "intimate union established between the Monarchs . . . offers to Europe the most sacred pledge of its future tranquility."[22] This declaration reiterated not only their commitment to the previously specified behavior principles but also articulated, for the first time in history, the addition of an order principle of membership: **in assessing polities across Europe that would seek the recognitions of sovereignty and protections built into the Vienna Settlement, the great powers would henceforth look favorably only upon those with legitimate (non-revolutionary) origins and conservative (non-liberal) institutions (Concert rule #4).**

In tracing the textual origins of this principle, Concert scholarship frequently highlights the so-called Holy Alliance (November 1815), a vague agreement formalized between Austria, Russia, and Prussia in Paris. While that agreement itself makes little reference to regime type, historians identify its significance in the way it was quickly repurposed by the masterful Austrian Foreign Minister Klemens von Metternich to justify interventions against liberal revolution across the continent.[23] Whatever its ultimate meaning, a much clearer articulation of this membership principle came in the form of the Troppau Protocol in 1820:

> States which have undergone a change of Government due to revolution, the results of which threaten other states, *ipso facto* cease to be members of the European Alliance, and *remain excluded from it until their situation gives guarantees for legal order and stability*. If, owing to such situations, immediate danger threatens other states, the Powers bind themselves, by peaceful means, or if be by arms, to bring back the guilty state into the bosom of the Great Alliance.[24]

The advent of this rule represented an important break from past practice in that it sanctioned great power interference in the *domestic* affairs of other polities as a general principle. As Andreas Osiander explains,

> it was the first attempt in the history of the states system of Europe to provide an abstract criterion for membership of that system. . . . [T]he concept did have a certain impact: the prominence given to it contributed, perhaps decisively, to the non-re-establishment of earlier non-dynastic actors (Genoa, Venice, Poland). At the same time, it helped to prevent the destruction of another (Saxony).[25]

The episodes Osiander refers to are illustrative: in the ensuing order, the great powers applied the rejection of unilateral conquest (Concert rule #2) selectively and only to protect the autonomy of "traditional" (conservative and non-revolutionary) regimes—Saxony, for example—while liberal and/or revolutionary regimes—Genoa, for instance—were either left to fend for themselves or allowed to be absorbed into legitimate polities.[26] When combined with great power supremacy (Concert rule #1), this membership principle provided a rationale for near-constant great power involvement in the domestic affairs of polities across Europe.[27]

Events would soon reveal that not all of the great powers shared the same level of enthusiasm for this new membership principle, however. In hindsight, the ambiguity with which it was codified in the agreements obscured a divide between the two more liberal powers, Great Britain and France, and the three conservative powers, Austria, Russia, and Prussia, over how far to push its implementation. The implications of this divide are explored in more depth later in the chapter.

5.2 The Transformative Reordering Moment of 1815

Great Britain, Russia, Austria, and Prussia were the great power victors of the French Revolutionary and Napoleonic Wars (1792–1815), while France was the sole great power loser. Britain was preponderant in terms of wealth and actualized resources, while Russia was destined to play a large role in the system as the polity with the most potential power (see Figure 5.1). Though Austria could not rival either of these states in material power, its centrality to the fate of the German states in the heart of Europe, combined with the diplomatic tact of its Foreign Minister, Prince Klemens von Metternich, assured it a first-tier position at the peacemaking table. Along with Metternich, the Concert's other principal architect was Britain's Foreign Secretary, Viscount Castlereagh. Russia's Tsar, the eccentric and unpredictable Alexander I, played a comparably lesser role in negotiating the final agreements, as did Prussia's Chief Minister Prince Karl August von Hardenberg and Prince Charles Maurice de Talleyrand, Foreign Minister to the newly restored Bourbon Monarchy in France. I focus predominantly on the motivations of Castlereagh and Metternich because they were the statesmen most responsible for crafting the foundational rules behind the Concert of Europe order.

5.2.1 Threats and Motives

In this section, I demonstrate that ordering-to-exclude theory offers a powerful explanation for the Concert of Europe's origins. This might seem odd in

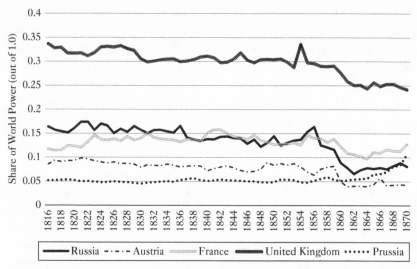

FIGURE 5.1 Relative power in the nineteenth century.

Source: Composite Indicator of National Capability (CINC) data set, version 5.0. See David J. Singer, "Reconstructing the Correlates of War Dataset on Material Capabilities of States, 1816–1985," *International Interactions* 14, No. 2 (1988).

an instance where the recent war's most threatening belligerent—France—was seemingly treated leniently and then quickly integrated back into the new order. Yet what the statesmen of Europe feared wasn't *France* per se, but destabilizing liberal revolutionary movements like those that had engulfed France and then many parts of the continent for so many years. Thus, much of what Castlereagh, Metternich, and their partners attempted to cultivate in Chaumont, Paris, Vienna, and Aix-la-Chappelle was an order that would delegitimate the sort of revolutionary regimes that had ravaged Europe throughout the French Wars. The order would do this by providing a rationale—through great power supremacy and consensus—and a mechanism—through face-to-face meetings—for multi-lateral action to suppress destabilizing movements and contain systemic distur-bances across the continent.

I unpack this larger narrative by developing five strands of argument and evidence. First, an examination of the perceived threat itself demonstrates its unprecedented nature for the elites across Europe. Second, the agreements that consecrated the Concert's order principles frequently reference this threat as the single most important reason for action. Third, a focus on the evolution of British strategic thinking shows how repeated failures to stop Revolutionary and then Napoleonic France gradually compelled elites to develop novel solutions focused on revolutionary rule-writing to combat this menace. Fourth, a major component of the French threat involved revolutionary subversion from below, a phenomenon that worried all of the relevant leaders but terrified Metternich in particular. Fifth, the differing levels of enthusiasm for enforcing the order's conservative membership principle track closely with the great powers' distinct perceptions of the threat itself: those who had the most to fear from revolutionary subversion advocated the toughest enforcement of the principle, while those who had less to fear were far more hesitant to treat this rule as a central component of the Concert order.

Unpacking the first point involves more precisely defining the threat posed by Revolutionary France at the turn of the century, a task not as easy as it may appear. To begin with, it would be inaccurate to claim that *every* European ruler feared *any* form of liberal government at this time. In fact, one form of liberalism called *monarchical constitutionalism*—which placed limits on a sovereign's powers while granting countervailing powers to members of the aristocracy—had previously achieved striking success on the continent, particularly after its adoption by Britain at the end of the seventeenth century. Instead, it was *republicanism*—casting aside monarchical authority altogether in favor of a government based entirely upon popular will—that represented the far greater ideological threat to Europe's elites. And yet even here, the great powers already had experience peacefully coexisting with a number of republics—tiny San Marino, the Dutch Republic, the Old Swiss Confederacy, and numerous quasi-states in Italy and Germany—and in some cases had done so for centuries. What had made *French* republicanism so threatening was the combination of Enlightenment principles with an era already characterized by civil unrest.[28] At the end of the eighteenth century, monarchs across Europe found themselves confronted by mass publics that were bigger (via population growth), angrier (via starvation and bread riots), and more armed than ever before with subversive ideas (via Enlightenment principles) that challenged the very legitimacy of absolutist rule.

Yet at first, even France's initial revolution was greeted with ambivalence across much of Europe. Contrary to their radicalized counterparts later on, the revolution's early leaders favored only the establishment of a British-style constitutional monarchy in 1789 and 1790. Furthermore, the sentiment for reigning in the French crown's excesses was one that was shared—or at least understood—by many elites across Europe.

The major polarizing event of the revolutionary era came not from the initial revolution, but with Louis XVI's failed flight from Paris to Varennes, a small town on the border of Austria from which the French King intended to instigate a counterrevolution. Instead, his capture and imprisonment in June of 1791 demonstrated to Europe's royals that the revolution had now become alarmingly anti-monarchical in nature. Most immediately, it led to an anti-French alliance between Austria and Prussia via the Declaration of Pillnitz, a decree which more generally called for Europe's dynasts to restore France's monarchy. These powers were at war with France by April of 1792. For those European elites still sitting on the sidelines, an alarming series of events soon conclusively demonstrated the novelty and potency of this French Revolutionary threat. Beginning in August of 1792, France's revolutionary leaders: suspended and then abolished the monarchy in favor of a republic; surprisingly halted the Austrian/Prussian offensive and repelled their armies from France's borders; vastly expanded their war aims by issuing anti-monarchical decrees across Europe in November; executed Louis XVI and Marie Antoinette in January of 1793; declared war against Britain and the Dutch Republic in February; and, perhaps most consequentially, essentially invented the concept of mass conscription out of thin air, and with smashing success. With the announcement of the *levée en masse* in mid-1793, the revolutionaries were able to raise an army of over six hundred thousand patriotic Frenchmen by the end of the year. The military and ideological menace created in the French Revolution would completely consume European domestic and international politics for over twenty years thereafter.[29]

After more than two decades of brutal warfare, elites of the victorious states thus sought to use the postwar settlement to forestall two interrelated concerns for the future: subsequent bids for continental hegemony as destructive as France's had been; and revolutionary movements that could inspire likeminded revolts in far-off countries as France's had.[30] The first was merely the latest manifestation of the old and reoccurring fear of a single power dominating all of Europe, addressed previously in the settlements of Westphalia and Utrecht (chapter 4). Yet this older threat had been given new life by a revolutionary nationalism that had transformed France into an entirely different beast. Under the command of Napoleon Bonaparte, the brilliant military leader who had been coronated Emperor of the new French Empire in the Revolution's final phase, France came closer in 1811 than any power in history to achieving total hegemony over all of Europe.

The second point of evidence in support of ordering-to-exclude theory is the most straightforward, and follows directly from the first: the treaties themselves frequently highlight the Revolutionary French threat as the principal reason for taking extraordinary action. The GPs agreed to an unprecedented alliance commitment in the Chaumont Treaty because they would need to protect Europe "against every attempt which France might make to infringe the order of things resulting from such Pacification."[31] Similar threats were cited in the agreements made at Aix-la-Chapelle in 1818, at which time British elites reiterated how the "Treaty of Chaumont gave to this Alliance that character of permanence which the deep-rooted nature of the danger against which it was intended to provide appeared to require."[32] They rationalized the Quadruple Alliance in 1815 by citing the possibility that "the same Revolutionary Principles which upheld the last criminal usurpation, might again, under other forms, convulse France, and thereby endanger the repose of other States."[33] At the same time, they aimed with the Second Peace of Paris at "restoring between France and her Neighbours those relations of reciprocal confidence and goodwill which the fatal effects of the Revolution and of the system of conquest had for so long a time disturbed."[34] In short, the agreements themselves name the revolutionary threat as the principal impetus for action.

The evolution of British threat perceptions and corresponding proposals for action is the third point of evidence for ordering-to-exclude theory, as the increasing ambition of these proposals tracks closely with heightening realization of the French menace's novelty. Foreign Secretary Castlereagh is rightly portrayed as the Concert's principal British architect. Yet he was not actually Britain's first high official to advocate for something like it. After the collapse of the First Coalition against Napoleon (1793–1797), the Foreign Secretary at that time, Lord Grenville, proposed an early prototype of the Concert (rules #1 and 3) to elites in Russia, Prussia, and Austria. He argued in 1798 that the continent could be "saved only by a union of the Great Powers which would have for its purpose the establishment of a general peace" that would guarantee the territorial possessions of each GP.[35] Following the disintegration of the Second Coalition (1798–1802) and the gradual realization that Napoleon would never be satiated, Russia and Britain entered into negotiations for a security alliance in late 1804. After hearing Tsar Alexander offer an expansive-but-vague vision of what their partnership might look like, Britain's William Pitt (the younger) went further. In a now-famous January 1805 memorandum, the Prime Minister called for "a general agreement and Guarantee for the mutual protection and security of different Powers, and for re-establishing a general system of public law in Europe," thus advocating an approximation of Concert rules #1, 2, and 3.[36] The point here is that in both instances elites at least momentarily recognized the necessity of unprecedented cooperation in order to meet the novelty of the French threat. Yet at the same time, they succumbed to routine mistrust and petty rivalries that ultimately kept these proposals on the drawing table.[37]

Through observing the failure of each previous coalition to stop France, Castlereagh became convinced that only entirely new mechanisms of statecraft would stand a chance at vanquishing the threat, an experience he was not reticent about noting in his writings.[38] He freely admitted that in drafting his important "Project of Alliance" memo in 1813, he had been inspired by his mentor Pitt's 1805 memorandum to Alexander.[39] The "Project" document also reveals that by late 1813 Castlereagh understood that the novel threat Europe was facing required an equally novel response. "How many years since would war have been terminated if the expectation of dividing her opponents ... had not tempted France to persevere?" he asked rhetorically on the eve of traveling across the Channel to personally oversee the war's endgame.[40]

Castlereagh arrived on the continent at a momentous time in 1813: the Sixth Coalition (1812–1814) had finally scored a decisive *military* victory against Napoleon at Leipzig, but appeared ready to surrender *political* victory by succumbing to the same intra-alliance grievances that had scuttled earlier coalitions. Fearing that individual powers would again attempt to negotiate separately with Napoleon, Castlereagh came to the continent to urge Britain's allies to keep their eye on their larger common adversary.[41] "It is this common danger which ought always to be kept in view as the true basis of the alliance, and which ought to preclude defection from the common cause," he argued. He saw "their only rational policy then is inseparable union," and urged that "a peace concluded in concert, though less advantageous in its terms" to any single GP, "would be preferable to the largest concessions received from the enemy as the price of disunion."[42]

It was Castlereagh more than any other who recognized, in preeminent Concert historian Paul Schroeder's words, that "a united Europe would be secure even against Napoleon; a divided one would soon fall into new conflicts, regardless of the kind of victory it won or the terms of peace it imposed."[43] It was at this critical moment that his "Project" memorandum—which called for "a perpetual defensive Alliance" to continue even past the defeat of France—would make all the difference.[44] It soon became the foundation upon which the fateful Chaumont Treaty would rest. Chaumont was the agreement that kick-started the entire Vienna Settlement. Castlereagh built into it the unprecedented commitments he did because he believed they had to be made "upon a scale which must envelope and overwhelm the enemy," convinced as he was that neither Napoleon nor the French people would ever sue for long-lasting peace unless they were confronted by a coalition demonstrating unprecedented unity.[45]

If Castlereagh was responsible for forging that momentous demonstration of unity, it was Metternich who took the lead in combatting the subversive and ideological component of the threat. This is the fourth major point of evidence supporting ordering-to-exclude theory: elites came to realize that the threat wasn't just invasion from above, but now, and for the first time in history, also revolution from below. Metternich in particular was obsessed with the subversive effects of liberal revolution. This obsession would continue from the war through his subsequent decades overseeing the survival of the Austrian Empire. In his own words, he focused throughout the Concert era on "the urgent necessity to put a stop to ... the principles subversive of the social order, on which Bonaparte has founded his usurpation."[46] He understood that the patchwork, multinational nature of the Austrian Empire and the repressive regime needed to keep its disparate parts together meant that Austria had the most to fear from revolutionary contagion seeping out of France.[47] Of particular concern was the Austrian Empire's uneasy relationship with the semi-autonomous Kingdom of Hungary, which was a constant source of agitation for imperial reform or outright Hungarian independence. In complaining about one such Hungarian campaign, Metternich revealed his belief that such movements were uniform and monolithic: while its leaders always professed limited aims, their ultimate goal was "a subversive one which exploits moderate constitutionalism in order to overthrow the government and the constitution. . . . It cannot be accommodated to democratic institutions. Such institutions are in contradiction with the existing order."[48]

Tangible action followed from ideological antipathy. It was Metternich who insisted that only a "legitimate" French regime be left in place at war's end lest the coalition be seen as legitimizing democratic governance more generally across the continent. Whether that "legitimate" regime should be the restored Bourbon monarchy or even Napoleon himself, Metternich surprisingly cared little.[49] He was the main proponent of transforming the Holy Alliance from a vague spiritual doctrine to a tangible conservative one, and was also the principal author of the Troppau Protocol justifying anti-liberal interventions across the continent (Concert rule #4). He continued to regularly articulate his belief that revolutionary liberal movements constituted the paramount security threat to Europe, and he sometimes referred to himself as "the Chief Minister of Police in Europe" for his role in combatting it. As he wrote to a colleague in 1833,

> for many years all those who pointed to the existence of a *Comité directeur* working secretly for universal revolution were met everywhere only by incredulity; today, it has been shown that this infernal propaganda exists, that it has its centre in Paris and that it is divided into as many sections as there are nations to regenerate. . . . Every thing that refers to this great and dangerous plot cannot, therefore, be observed and surveyed with too much attention.[50]

Though he was the most forceful anti-liberal advocate, Metternich was never alone in harboring such fears. Russia was often an enthusiastic proponent of anti-democratic interventionism, while Prussia also played a passive but supportive role. Talleyrand, the conservative French representative in Vienna, circulated a popular note at that conference advocating a principle in the settlement "that everywhere and forever the spirit of revolt be quenched, that every legitimate right be made sacred."[51] And even Castlereagh observed, in giving voice to British thinking in 1813, that "the whole military history of the Revolution has taught us to dread that the monster once engendered on French ground may break loose to seek its sustenance elsewhere. This is the true danger against which the Continent . . . has to provide. . . . And she may thereby lay the foundation for a long peace."[52]

That Castlereagh understood the threat of revolutionary subversion does not mean he felt it as strongly as his eastern counterparts, however, thus connecting point four to the final point of evidence for ordering to exclude: the theory's logic can best make sense of Britain's halfhearted enthusiasm for the conservative membership rule (Concert rule #4). Britain's startling decision in 1820 to break with elements of the Concert system less than a decade after its formation—and soon followed by France—is sometimes treated as the most glaring anomaly of the Concert project. Yet the divide between Western and Eastern powers over how to interpret the order's anti-liberal membership principle is one that likely existed from the start. Only a lack of clarity about how this principle would be enforced led both Castlereagh and Metternich to believe that their respective interpretations had carried the day in those initial negotiations.[53]

Their differences became alarmingly clear, however, with the outbreak of multiple revolutions across the continent in 1820.[54] Alexander demanded an immediate meeting to suppress the revolts. Metternich soon relented, leading to the Troppau and Laibach (Ljubljana) Congresses that produced the controversial Troppau Protocol. Yet Britain and France strongly resisted and essentially boycotted these meetings, arguing that only revolutions that endangered the more general tranquility of Europe could be subject to the Concert's purview.[55] In his rebuttal to the Troppau Protocol, Castlereagh emphasized that the British people could not

> admit that this right can receive a general and indiscriminate application to all Revolutionary Movements, without reference to their immediate bearing upon some particular State or States, or be made prospectively the basis of an Alliance. —They regard its exercise as an exception to general principles of the greatest value and importance, and as one that only properly grows out of the circumstances of the special case.[56]

In exploring the reasons for this difference, British and French elites believed they had less to fear from the very notion of liberal revolution than did their eastern counterparts. This variance in threat perceptions came through differences not in elite personalities but in domestic institutions, an explanation that fits well within the security-driven logic of exclusion. Britain's unique brand of constitutional monarchy had in important ways already solved the dilemma of incorporating liberal ideas into a stable monarchical system.[57] As a result, its leaders were less inherently threatened by liberal ideas and instead singled out only those particular movements they deemed the most dangerous to international harmony in Europe. Castlereagh even couched Britain's rationale in threat-related language in a famous 1820 state paper: "It was the Revolutionary power more particularly in its Military Character actual and existent within France against which it [the Concert order] intended to take Precautions, rather than against the Democratic Principles" more generally.[58] The more conservative eastern great powers, by contrast, constantly viewed *any* liberal movements as existential challenges to the legitimacy upon which their regimes depended.[59] "The so-called 'British school' has been the cause of the French Revolution," complained Metternich, "and the consequences of this revolution, so anti-British in tendency, devastate Europe today."[60]

Some scholars use this early divide over liberal revolutions to argue that the Concert order actually broke down soon after it began in the 1820s.[61] Advocates of this interpretation have a point in that the particular issue of how to respond to revolutions was never resolved, weakening but not eliminating rule #4 of the Concert order. Additionally, after 1822 the most important elites of each country almost entirely dispensed with the practice of regularly meeting with one another directly (congresses), opting instead to let their intermediaries represent them (conferences), thus weakening but not eliminating Concert rule #3.[62]

Yet it goes too far to suggest that this was simply the Concert's end. For one thing, there is considerable evidence that the break was less a fissure through the *entire* order and more a tacit agreement to occasionally disagree over one particular principle without letting this disagreement disturb their consensus over the other three. Richard Elrod has argued that in spite of this ideological rift,

> concert diplomacy continued to function. It did so because a great-power consensus persisted that transcended political ideology. . . . Despite ideological divergences, the European powers still agreed upon the necessity of peace among themselves and accepted concert diplomacy as the means to manage crises that might jeopardize that peace.[63]

Concert rules #1, 2, and at least a weakened variant of 3 thus remained intact. Moreover, Castlereagh's stand on the revolutions issue was predicated not on abstract principle but on the belief that these developments did not threaten Britain like they did the conservative powers. In instances where elites believed British interests were imperiled by revolution, however, their principles quickly shifted. In the Greek revolts against Ottoman rule throughout the 1820s, for example, British leaders stood shoulder to shoulder with Austria in opposing the destabilizing effects a full-fledged Greek revolution could have for Europe if it was allowed to succeed. Here, Kissinger's analysis of British policy is especially illuminating:

> The policy of Castlereagh in the Greek crisis revealed that the doctrine of non-interference did not reflect a superior morality, nor even entirely a difference in domestic structures, but primarily the consciousness of safety conferred by an insular position. For in Greece, where Austrian and British interests were about equally involved—where, in other words, Britain felt as vulnerable as Austria—it suddenly appeared that the insular power, too, could appeal to the Alliance, and, by implication, even to the Holy Alliance. Here, surprisingly, even Castlereagh emerged with a doctrine of the wickedness of revolution and of the danger of an international [ideological] conspiracy, no less eloquent, if more ponderous, than that of Metternich.[64]

Castlereagh was, after all, preparing to travel to the Congress of Verona to assist Metternich's diplomatic efforts on this very issue when he shocked both country and continent by committing suicide in 1822.

5.1.3   Alternatives

Binding

Of all the European cases of order change examined in this book, the 1815 settlement is the single instance where the binding motive stands a chance. The Concert order did, after all, represent an attempt by the victorious powers to enact something radically different from all that had been tried before. Furthermore, this new order appeared to be characterized by remarkable pronouncements of great power restraint. It is thus not surprising that John Ikenberry has devoted significant attention to the Concert in *After Victory*. "Great Britain pursued an institutional strategy aimed at establishing formal processes of consultation and accommodation among the postwar great powers," he writes. "These institutional proposals—in particular, the alliance and the congress system—were novel in the way they attempted to bind potentially rival states together."[65] In support of this interpretation, Pitt's 1805 memorandum even called for the European powers to collectively "*bind* themselves mutually to protect and support each other," a sentiment echoed by Castlereagh's call for them to "solemnly *bind* themselves to each other . . . for the purpose of procuring for themselves and for Europe a general peace, under the protection of which their rights and liberties may be secured" in his fateful "Project" blueprint in 1813.[66]

That a full system of institutional binding was never implemented isn't nec-essarily evidence against the binding motive here. Ikenberry openly admits that such a system was not realized, after all. Furthermore, he effectively explains its failure by pointing to structural factors clearly identified in his theory that pre-vented binding *preferences* from becoming binding *outcomes*: Britain was not yet powerful enough relative to the other powers to enact such a system on its own, while its partners were not yet democratic enough to fully desire such an order or credibly commit to implementing it even if they had wanted to.[67] Binding might still serve as a powerful explanation for what British elites *attempted* to enact at this time, which is a principal focus of Ikenberry's study and the singular focus of this book.

Alas, the binding thesis suffers from a dearth of evidence even when it comes to accounting for Britain's preferences. First, it has no expectation nor offers any explanation for the preference for an anti-liberal membership principle as an important part of the Vienna Settlement. While Britain wasn't the most enthu-siastic proponent of this principle, I have already shown that it was still generally supportive of the spirit of this rule in particular circumstances.

Second, the hypothesized motives behind binding do not align with the his-torical record regarding *why* British leaders acted as they did. Ikenberry admits as much, noting how his theory "is less helpful in identifying the specific intellectual breakthrough that led Britain to seize on institutional mechanisms as a tool of order building."[68] In fact, much of his evidence regarding British motives points less to a desire to increase the longevity of British preponderance (as his theory hypothesizes) than it does to a perceived need to do something unprecedented in the face of a revolutionary new threat (as ordering-to-exclude theory predicts).[69]

Finally, there is little indication that Britain ever actually made the kind of hegemonic bargain—systemic stability in exchange for leading actor restraint—that is at the heart of the binding model. Once again, Ikenberry is surprisingly forthcoming in this regard: "There is no clear evidence that Britain actually gave up substantial short-term gains in exchange for institutional agreement on the continent," he admits.[70] In spite of some surface-level evidence for the broad applicably of binding as a motivation in this period, its logic breaks down upon closer inspection.

Exporting

That the most conservative regimes—Austria and Russia—were often the most eager to suppress liberal revolutions seemingly supports the exporting motive for at least the membership principle (Concert rule #4).[71] And indeed, supporting like-minded regimes across Europe was clearly a priority for decision-makers at Vienna, Paris, and beyond. I have already indicated how the powers' different

domestic institutions played a significant role in their divergent threat perceptions, differences that only grew wider as the Western powers liberalized even
further in the 1830s and 1840s.

Yet this interpretation also does not fully stand up to scrutiny. Simply put,
no great power consistently sought to export its own domestic institutions as an
overriding strategy throughout the Concert era in the first half of the nineteenth
century. Britain's hybrid regime certainly affected its leaders' threat perceptions.
Yet there is little evidence that these same leaders attempted to proactively export
their system as a part of the Concert order. Castlereagh was clear in his 1820
state paper that Britain had little interest in doing so unless European stability
required it, as "to generalize such a principle and to think of reducing it to a
System, or to impose it as an obligation, is a Scheme utterly impracticable and
objectionable."[72] Russia's Alexander was never a reliable proponent of any one set
of ideological principles. While the Tsar sometimes sought to proactively spread
autocratic principles, at other times he focused more upon exporting Christian
principles or even liberal ideals. Most surprising is that even Austria never consistently sought to install its own institutions across Europe. The ultimate foe of
liberalism though he was, Metternich was actually most concerned with preserving the status quo across Europe—even at times propping up regimes that he personally loathed—rather than proactively crusading on behalf of monarchism.[73]
He even characterized himself in such a way after his tenure was over: "For thirty-
nine years I played the role of rock, from which the waves recoil . . . until finally
they succeed in engulfing it."[74]

A telling example of Metternich's surprising passivity here came in the early
1820s. This was a period when Alexander, at the urging of his cunning foreign
minister Ioannis Kapodistrias, sought to transform the Concert into an order
that would proactively install conservative regimes across the continent. Yet
Metternich resisted, demonstrating that he bore no desire to be an ideological
crusader when security did not necessitate it. Instead, he was successful in enacting a *negative* doctrine at the Troppau Congress—against destructive, liberal
revolutions—rather than the *positive* one in favor of monarchism that Alexander
and Kapodistrias had hoped for.[75] In sum, the reluctance of any of the powers
to embrace an order premised on proactively externalizing their own domestic
ideals suggests that the exporting motive lacks explanatory power for the order
vision of this era.

Learning

As it was throughout chapter 4, learning is again the most formidable of the alternatives. Once again, the prior trauma and the perceived future threat were one
and the same to the statesmen of Europe after 1815: it had been Revolutionary

France's internal crises and resulting outward aggression that had so badly disrupted Europe in the first place, and both of the elites' greatest fears for the future—hegemonic bids for supremacy and waves of radical revolution—were inspired by what had just happened with France. Unsurprisingly, then, learning provides a plausible rationale for each of the implemented order changes after 1815.

Yet like in the Westphalian case (chapter 4), there is some evidence to suggest that the architects of the Concert were more interested in creating a forward-looking settlement than a backward-looking one. For one thing, the series of peacetime congresses and conferences that followed from the settlements (Concert rule #3) had no precedent in prior history.[76] For another, Schroeder has effectively demonstrated that the Vienna Settlement represented the first decisive victory for "systemic" thinking wherein states thought proactively about the larger European system when making decisions. Moreover, he points to the necessity of the revolutionary threat in bringing about this sea change: "Europe's leaders ... did not actively look for new and better ways of thinking about international politics," he argues. Instead, "they were forced into systemic thinking by repeated failures, the exhaustion of alternatives, their inability to make any form of the old and the new politics work—and finally, by the ruthless imperialism of one of the most insatiable conquerors Europe has ever seen."[77] Finally, the forward-looking nature of the 1815 settlement was recognized even by its most reactionary architect, Metternich. "It does not require any great political insight to see that this Congress could not model itself on any predecessor," he acknowledged. Instead, "the Congress is brought into being of itself, without having received any formal authority, there being no source which could have given any."[78]

That the Concert's architects were responding more to future challenges than past ones is also evident in their dealings with France. In retrospect, it is remarkable how leniently she was treated after Napoleon's defeats and then welcomed into the Concert system only a few short years later. Earlier in the wars, elites had at first planned to impose a more punitive settlement. "As it became clear in practice, however, that [Napoleon's] power rested less upon the power of France and more upon the international disruption caused by the revolution," argues one historian, "the doctrines and fact of revolution became a kind of common enemy."[79] By 1814, it was the emerging and *prospective* ideological movement that had possessed France, not the *retrospective* of France itself, that elites saw as the real threat to the future of Europe.[80] Perhaps this is why the diplomats at Vienna, upon hearing of Napoleon's escape from Elba and return to power in Paris, effectively declared war not against the country but against the man, an act without precedent in history.[81] "Revolutionary France is more likely to distress the world than France, however strong in her frontier, under a regular [monar-chical] government," argued Lord Wellington, Castlereagh's successor at the Congress of Vienna, "and that is the situation in which we ought to endeavor to place her."[82] Had they been motivated more by a desire to simply extinguish that which had previously tormented them, they would have chosen to treat France far less hospitably.

In sum, the great power victors of the Napoleonic Wars had certainly greatly feared the reemergence of France, that perennial European troublemaker throughout this era, much as their predecessors had a century earlier at Utrecht. Yet unlike their forebears, they also feared a menacing ideological threat that had made *this* iteration of the French menace so uniquely formidable. The most nota-ble departure from past practice in the settlement of 1815 was the incorporation of a membership principle into the resulting order. I have argued that we can best account for this deepening of order preferences by focusing on the emergence of threats of an ideological nature, manifested most dangerously in the potent combination of revolutionary liberalism and revolutionary nationalism that had captured Revolutionary France. Conversely, elements of this order slowly began decaying in subsequent decades in large part because of the diverging internal characteristics of the great power order builders. These domestic changes then engendered ever-widening external disagreements, particularly over which enti-ties and movements were most threatening for the continued tranquility of the European system.

5.2 Reordering Dogs that Didn't Bark and the Concert's Unraveling

Until at least the 1880s, the same threats confronted by the architects of the Vienna Settlement remained at the forefront of European politics. Just as these statesmen had predicted, national liberation movements and liberal unrest became much more frequent causes of conflict in the decades ahead.[83] New nation-states gradually but persistently emerged as nationalism grew more potent, while demonstration effects from the American and French Revolutions continued to reverberate. The Greek Wars of Independence in the 1820s tested the unity of the Concert over preventing or at least containing revolution. In the late 1820s, France's new king, the reactionary Charles X, attempted to regain many of the absolutist powers enjoyed by his predecessors. Instead, he found himself forced to abdicate in the midst of another liberal revolution in the sum-mer of 1830. The Duke of Orleans was installed as King Louis-Philippe under the new "July Monarchy" (1830–1848) that was even more limited than that of the Restoration (1815–1830). The resurgence of French liberalism in 1830 empowered likeminded activists to push for change in Switzerland, Poland, and in the German and Italian states. Most importantly, they also did so in the Belgian province of the United Kingdom of the Netherlands (1815–1839), a neutral polity that had been created by the great powers in 1815. The GPs flirted with going to war over this Belgian revolution—France to support it and champion liberalism, the three eastern powers to combat it while backing the Dutch King's conservative legitimacy. Yet they were ultimately able to avert conflict by working together to negotiate a controlled Belgian independence from Holland in 1831.[84]

In spite of this victory for Concert unity, the fact remained that France's 1830 revolution, coupled with Britain's 1832 Reform Act, installed considerably more liberal governments in Paris and London. In Britain this government included Lord Palmerston, the bombastic and powerful foreign minister and, later, prime minister who would almost singlehandedly control British foreign policy for the next thirty-five years. As an unapologetic liberal, he not only continued Castlereagh's tradition of opposing concerted anti-liberal interventions but also began lending rhetorical and even material support to *pro*-liberal causes abroad. These actions, usually undertaken with the support of France, unsurprisingly often provoked some or all of the eastern powers (depending on the particular episode) to double down on their anti-revolutionary interventionist practices, each time eroding at least some of the powers' trust in the Concert order and each other.[85] The rest of the 1830s saw periodic GP interventions, with the conservative powers taking action in Poland, Germany, and Italy and the liberal powers intervening in Spain and Portugal. Yet aside from these defections, none of the powers radically overstepped the boundaries imposed by the order principles of the Vienna Settlement.[86]

In short, the Concert order remained intact. Through these challenges, it helped to prevent the spread of revolution beyond manageable boundaries and kept peace between the great powers in the first half of the nineteenth century, thus succeeding at its most fundamental objectives. Alas, the most fateful disturbance for the Concert would come not from war between the great powers but again from revolution from below, this time in a newly potent wave that nevertheless began in that traditional epicenter of liberal unrest, France.

5.2.1 The Revolutions of 1848

The 1848 revolutions seemed almost predesigned to fulfill Metternich's worst fears about liberalism and revolutionary contagion. When France had previously succumbed to a revolution in 1830, at least a version of the monarchy had been restored. This was not to be in 1848, as that country now declared itself a republic for the first time since Napoleon's wars, and in fact installed that leader's nephew—the erratic populist, Louis-Napoleon—as its first president. Soon thereafter, its leaders announced that "the treaties of 1815 have no legal existence in the eyes of the French republic."[87] And, unlike in 1830, much of Europe outside of France was now also agitating for reform. Across the continent, this revolutionary wave marked the culmination of a tacit alliance between radicals—those who prioritized universal male suffrage above all other issues—and liberals, who sought more general reforms such as written constitutions, more representative institutions, and greater civil liberties.[88]

The shockwaves across Europe were swift and severe.[89] When uprisings reached Vienna in March, the royal family declared it could no longer guarantee Metternich's safety, resulting in his resignation and flight from the country. French demonstration effects had led to Metternich's fall, but this momentous event itself only further galvanized revolutionaries in places like Italy and Hungary. Just days after Metternich's fall, for instance, King Frederick William of Prussia pledged to adopt a much more liberal constitution as multitudes of protestors in Berlin demanded.

In sum, a new revolutionary wave brought revolutionary regime changes across many of Europe's most significant polities in 1848. And yet, perhaps surprisingly, there was no major reordering reaction from Great Britain, the sole power unscathed by this wave and Europe's most dominant actor at this time. Britain at midcentury was in fact at the height of its global reach and influence (to an extent that Figure 5.2 can only partially capture), and she remained free from the domestic disturbances afflicting the other powers. "So absolute was this British supremacy that it hardly needed political control to operate," observes E. J. Hobsbawm. "There were no other colonial powers left, except by grace of the British, and consequently no rivals."[90] Palmerston, at this time foreign minister, was known as a fierce interventionist who championed liberal movements abroad. And yet aside from offering rhetorical support to liberals in select areas and episodes, he and others chose to keep Britain out of the revolutionary turmoil on the continent. More importantly, Britain sought no revisions to the rules of the Concert order in spite of possessing a clear opportunity for pursuing such changes. Why? And does the answer to this important question challenge or bolster ordering-to-exclude theory?

In brief, I argue that it does a bit of both. On the one hand, the lack of preferences or plans on the part of British leaders to reorder the system against this revolutionary wave defies the core expectation of ordering-to-exclude theory. Clearly, there *was* a formidable new threat tearing apart the continent in 1848. Furthermore, this revolutionary wave had been made even *more* potent through a

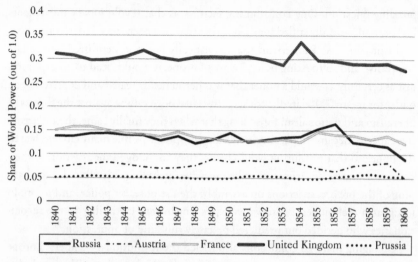

FIGURE 5.2 Relative power at midcentury.

Source: Composite Indicator of National Capability (CINC) data set, version 5.0. See David J. Singer, "Reconstructing the Correlates of War Dataset on Material Capabilities of States, 1816–1985" *International Interactions* 14, No. 2 (1988).

combination of technological advancements, economic disturbances, and social discontent that together created a perfect storm for revolutionary upheaval.[91] On the other hand, this wave was also in other ways *less* potent to British elites than what they had seen in the original French Revolution decades earlier. This was due not to international developments but domestic ones: the political reforms that Britain had made at home in the years since the Napoleonic Wars made her more liberal and thus less vulnerable to the dangers of another transnational wave. Furthermore, at almost precisely the time that Palmerston and others in Britain began to more seriously worry about the radicalization of the 1848 movements, many of these movements imploded.

The Threat: Formidable or Fatigued?

On its surface, the buildup to the 1848 revolutions looked similar to the upheaval surrounding the original French Revolution. And once again, conservative elites were determined to respond in kind. "Sovereigns should not yield to [any] demands, not even in an effort to make timely concessions to avoid revolution," implored Metternich, giving voice to a longstanding hallmark of his diplomacy.[92]

Yet in spite of Metternich's decades-long efforts, by the 1830s a truly transnational network of underground liberalism had been established across Europe. Why this threat became particularly pronounced by 1848, however, remains a puzzling question. One contributing factor was that revolutionary movements had been successfully stifled for so long that they had been forced to become more sophisticated.[93] As Palmerston characteristically put it in deriding Metternich's "repressive and suffocating policy," across Europe, it would "lead to an explosion just as certainly as would a boiler that was hermetically sealed and deprived of an outlet for steam."[94] Relatedly, conservatives had been railing against the threats of liberalism and nationalism for so long that when they finally came, their destructive capacity became in part a self-fulfilling prophecy. While many citizens feared the upheaval that revolution would bring, they also judged the reaction of their own conservative governments to be excessive, including as it often did the banning of the press, restrictions on assembly, the use of secret police, and so on. In using such techniques, conservative elites lent instant credibility to the revolutionaries who derided but predicted precisely this kind of oppression.[95]

Changing material conditions also fueled the revolutionary embers. Europe was rife with significant economic downturn by the late 1840s. The much discussed "social question" of the times referred to "the problem of poverty and the dislocation caused by the painful economic transformation that was under way," as the benefits of industrialization and capitalism for classes other than those at the very top would not become apparent until the 1850s.[96] The lack of strong social welfare programs only exacerbated miserable conditions for much of Europe's working poor, breeding anxiety and resentment. These forces coincided with the rise of a vibrant civil society across Europe that was both more educated and more detached from the existing political system than prior generations.[97] This emerging middle class was also now more conscious of international events in a way they hadn't been previously, in part because of the tremendous growth of newspaper presses and universities across the continent. "I deplore that the censorship cannot be instated for all writings without exception," complained Metternich, predictably.[98]

On the other hand, the ways in which these disturbances threatened Britain in particular were not obvious. Like other radical movements across Europe, the "Chartist" movement in Britain sought to institute full (male) suffrage along with other reforms considered radical at time. Drawing support from the February revolution in France, the Chartists staged protests throughout the spring of 1848 that were at least temporarily disruptive in London. Yet in spite of the inspiration they took from Paris, these protesters never posed a viable threat to Britain's leaders or institutions.[99] This was due in no small part to the fact that British elites had already previously satisfied the goals of many moderate liberals in their country. Shortly after capturing power from the long-ruling Tories, the Whigs had in 1832 passed the momentous Reform Act. It significantly extended the franchise across the country and made the House of Commons far more representative of constituent populations than ever before.[100] Partly as a consequence, by 1848 "most Chartists did not see themselves, like French workers at the barricades, as potential revolutionaries," writes one historian of the movement. "Those who did made only a spotty appearance in Chartist ranks and were disparaged vehemently by the overwhelming majority in the movement as well as by the English middle classes."[101] If Britain's leaders were already comparatively less threatened by liberal revolutions in the 1820s—a theme of the previous section on the Concert's founding—this was only more true after 1832.

Apart from long-term developments in Britain, the revolutionary movement on the continent was also starting to splinter and in some places implode by the time it might have begun to threaten English shores. Following their smashing successes across the continent in February and March of 1848, differences between revolutionary factions soon became apparent. As in the original French Revolution, the radicals in that country again overreached by pushing for too much—promises of universal suffrage, full employment, and absolute freedom of assembly and press—all at once.[102] The socialists and liberals soon split apart and the factions came to blows, resulting in the French military stepping in to restore order by June. The new constitution, revealed in November, was certainly more liberal than the July Monarchy and yet still established a strong central state with a powerful executive.[103] By the end of the year France had ejected the revolution's original leaders from power and instead elected Louis-Napoleon Bonaparte as President of the new French Republic. When he soon after installed a conservative government populated by members of the old guard, it became clear that the results of *this* revolution would not be what the radicals who started it had hoped for.[104]

Across other countries touched by this revolutionary wave, the pattern was similar. Radicals seized power early on, but then just as quickly lost much of their influence as their demands for immediate and universal voting rights quickly abandoned liberals (who sought more moderate reforms) and disillusioned socialists (who at best saw suffrage as a means to an end).[105] The revolutionaries thus lacked "agreement over the form that the new political order would take: republic or monarchy, democratic or liberal, unitary or federal." Liberals and radicals "did not see eye to eye over the extent to which the revolutions should overhaul social relations—how far the state should intervene to alleviate poverty, to mediate in labour disputes, and to regulate economic activity."[106] Recognition of these differences started the process of redrawing the ideological fissures along which the next generation of elites and revolutionaries would do battle.

As in France, counterrevolutionary reverberations across the continent were swift and sharp. By summer's end, revolutionary gains had been rolled back across Germany and Italy. In the Austrian Empire, Hungarian freedom fighters had escalated conflict to the point where Vienna could no longer peacefully grant

Hungary the autonomy it had long sought. Austrian elites soon secured Russia's intervention to beat back the Hungarians' bid for independence. By early 1849, the Austrian and Prussian kings had rescinded many of their earlier concessions and dissolved newly created parliaments.

Thus, as dangerous as the revolutionary wave of 1848 at first appeared to conservative elites, its very radicalism also paradoxically helped many of these same elites once again secure their hold on power (albeit often in a less absolutist form). After 1848, those "transnational liberal networks continued to exist, but were decimated" by counterrevolutionary responses.[107] The 1848 wave also represented the last ideologically pure battle between absolutism and radicalism. By the 1860s, these extremes would give way to more moderate and pragmatic reformers who succeeded in forming constitutional governments in united Italy, Austria, Prussia (later Germany), and France. This happened at least in part because prudent conservatives saw the reformist writing on the wall and began to recognize—particularly after Metternich's fall and flight—that resistance to *all* forms of liberalization would likely bring a fate far worse than the modest curtailment of their powers.

This conservative-liberal reconciliation also received a push from the emergence of a new ideological menace on the horizon after 1848: the tactical marriage of anarchists and socialists, united by their common disillusionment with moderate, limited liberalism. "In Paris, Vienna, Berlin, and other places," observes John Owen, "conservative and liberal alike caught glimpses of something" that would become even more threatening to each than one another: "power in the hands of those who did not respect private property or the ways it had always been acquired and transferred."[108] The great ideological threat to the Western world in the twentieth century—revolutionary socialism—had already begun stoking fears of upheaval by the middle of the nineteenth.

British Threat Perceptions and Order Preferences

In sum, the revolutionary threat in 1848 contained both new and old elements. British elites therefore rightly feared it in some ways while at the same time recognizing that their country was perhaps uniquely equipped to combat it in others. As Palmerston put it at the time, "the revolutionary movements could be lowered to their real importance if foreign powers would not attach to them exaggerated significance and would rather redress their peoples' grievances" in the ways Britain's leaders had.[109] Far from viewing the revolutions with dread, Palmerston actually saw some positives in the anticipated changes that would come. "Happy would it have been for the Continent if this had happened some years ago," he wrote to a confidant upon hearing of Metternich's fall from power.[110] Britain simply had less to fear from the revolutionary wave than others. As a result, ordering-to-exclude theory generates indeterminate predictions as to whether or not British leaders should have pursued significant order changes in response.

Even so, process tracing indicates that the excluding motive did not play a primary role in Britain's response to continental events in 1848. Instead, elites seemed motivated more by a desire to preserve the territorial status quo on the continent. This corresponded with more traditional geopolitical concerns—French or Prussian expansionism in the west and Russian expansionism in the east—and less with the ideological threat posed by the new revolutionary liberal wave.

British policy toward numerous revolutionary causes throughout the year exemplified this focus. Officials evinced ideological fears only when upheavals appeared to increase the territorial ambitions of continental powers, such as when the revolutionary poet Lamartine declared that France now "reserve[d] the right to question the legality of the 1815 treaties."[111] Palmerston's reaction to the liberalization movement in Prussia is indicative of Britain's larger policy tendencies throughout these months. He was generally predisposed to favor the reformers' proposals for limited liberalization there. He was even initially unconcerned when Prussia soon after went to war against Denmark for control of the long-disputed duchies of Schleswig and Holstein. But when it was revealed that the Prussians were attempting to cooperate with France in Schleswig in exchange for help in liberating Poland from Russia, British officials quickly came to fear that the revolutions might be used as a guise to unleash revisionist ambitions across the continent.[112] In fact, evidence indicates that British elites were actually relieved rather than dismayed when counterrevolutionary forces returned a more oppressive regime to Prussia later in the year, believing it indicated a return to a status quo–oriented foreign policy.[113]

The British government's position on the Austro-Hungarian conflict also followed this now-familiar trajectory. Palmerston publicly offered rhetorical support for the Hungarian independence movement. Yet even his public displays of sympathy came only at times when the Hungarians appeared to be damaging *Russia*—who had intervened on the side of Austria—rather than weakening *Austria*. In direct conflict with the Hungarians' ultimate goal, Palmerston continued to view Hungary as a vital part of the Austrian Empire, in large part because a strong Austria had to remain a bulwark against both Russian *and* French expansionism on the continent. Accordingly, he communicated to Austrian elites that "the British government had no knowledge of Hungary, except as a component part of the Austrian Empire."[114] He also rejected numerous personal appeals from the Hungarian leader, Lajos Kossuth, for British aid against Austria and Russia.[115] Public opinion in Britain began to turn against these conservative powers by the end of the year as accounts of the atrocities committed against the Hungarians became widely reported in the English press.[116] Nevertheless, Palmerston never wavered. He rejected Kossuth's final plea for aid in mid-1849 and made clear that he would support nothing less than Austro-Hungarian political reconciliation as an acceptable outcome.[117] Hungary's revolution was defeated by the end of that summer, and British leaders cheered the restoration of a modified version of the status quo in Austria.

Alternatives

If ordering-to-exclude theory cannot definitively predict or adequately account for British order preferences in the wake of the 1848 revolutions, two of the three alternatives do not fair substantially better. Binding is at best inapplicable, as there is no indication of the Concert order imposing constraints on Britain after the revolutions.

Like excluding, learning provides indeterminate predictions. On the one hand, perhaps British leaders learned between 1815 and 1848 that revolutions on the continent posed less danger to their country than they had believed decades earlier. On the other hand, the lessons of the last formative foreign policy event—when the original French Revolution had ignited the most destructive wars Europe had ever seen—might have left British leaders fearing that 1848 could soon become another 1789.

Ultimately, exporting provides the strongest explanation among the motives examined in this book for Britain's order preferences in response to the 1848 revolutions. First, it offers a logical correlation for British threat perceptions in congruence testing: moderation/toleration of liberalism at home translated into a more pragmatic and less ideological perspective on liberal revolution abroad. Exporting also provides the best explanation in process tracing for why Britain's leaders felt less threatened in 1848 compared to (a) the other more conservative great powers, but also (b) the prior generation of British elites back when Britain was less liberal. Ultimately, their lack of existential alarm was vindicated when the Chartist movement remained generally peaceful, non-revolutionary, and only minimally disruptive in 1848.

What exporting cannot totally account for, however, is the *variation* in British reactions to various revolutionary and counterrevolutionary gains in 1848–1849. Exporting fails to explain in particular why Palmerston did so little to aid moderate liberals in places like Prussia, Italy, Hungary, and France, even when evidence indicates he recognized that their leaders held likeminded views to his own. If anything, British elites appeared on average to slightly prefer counterrevolutionary advances on the continent over even moderate liberal ones. Where exporting would expect stronger preferences for and defense of liberal movements, British policies instead seemed to follow the predictions of basic balance-of-power realism.[118] In places where Palmerston declined material support to revolutionaries and reformers, he frequently cited a longstanding British desire to uphold the continental status quo. "Austria stands in the centre of Europe, a barrier against encroachment on the one side, and against invasion on the other," he told Parliament in defense of his government's unwillingness to aid Hungary in 1849. "The political independence and liberties of Europe are bound up, in my opinion, with the maintenance and integrity of Austria as a great European power."[119]

To the extent that British elites equated the Concert order with territorial stability, this interpretation remains consistent with one of ordering-to-exclude theory's most basic predictions: in the absence of a pressing threat, dominant actors should explicitly or implicitly favor order continuity. That said, it simply does not appear that British leaders had the larger European order on their minds in 1848, focused as they were on power calculations instead. If this was indeed the case, perhaps balance-of-power realism offers the most complete explanation for Britain's inaction in and after the revolutionary wave of 1848.

5.3.2 Crisis and Crimean War

At first glance, the lack of order changes following the Crimean War (1854–1856) appear to offer another anomalous case for ordering-to-exclude theory. After all, this conflict constituted nineteenth-century Europe's most destructive shock as the only new war involving more than two great powers. It also pitted the system's two most dominant actors—Britain and Russia—directly against one another. In spite of its significance, however, neither its causes nor its outcome introduced any new threats to the actors most able to steer the course of order at war's end, Britain and France.

I explicate these dynamics in this section by briefly chronicling the war's origins and endgame, detailing the precise nature of the 1856 Treaty of Paris, and then exploring how and why the great power victors of the Crimean War came to moderate earlier demands for a more order transformative and punitive settlement. In brief, I posit that the absence of a major new threat had a dampening effect on these actors' preferences, leaving them more ambivalent about pursuing their more expansive aims and less politically able to act on them even if they had wanted to.

The Convoluted Causes of Crimea

The Crimean War's immediate causes in 1853–1854 at first appear to be religious—feuding Christian factions in the Holy Lands ensnaring their great power benefactors into a larger conflict over prestige and resolve—and this popular interpretation holds some truth.[120] Yet its origins were also rooted in deeper structural factors: the steady decline of the Ottoman Empire's power in Europe, Russia's desire to solidify access to a permanent warm-water port that could not be easily cut off by the Western powers, these Western states' fears of an expansionist Russia upsetting the balance of power in Europe, and the desire of Louis Napoleon (or, after 1851, Napoleon III) to ignite a crisis that would help France break out its perceived Concert constraints.[121]

The greatest fear of the Western powers, and Britain in particular, was Russia achieving disproportionate gains at the expense of the Ottomans. For decades, the great powers had together been able to successfully stave off conflict over this "Eastern Question," a shorthand term for the uncertainty produced by the Ottoman Empire's decline.[122] Yet prudent statesmen on all sides remained consistently wary that the next crisis over this issue would prove to be the breaking point. Turkey (the Ottoman Empire)[123] and Russia had fought numerous wars over a series of buffer zones throughout these years, and the Danubian principalities of Moldavia and Wallachia (modern Romania) in particular had changed hands multiple times. These zones were in Ottoman control in the early 1850s, and Russia wanted them back. Moreover, the most recent Russo–Turkish conflict had also ended with religious implications: its settlement had given Russia permission to build an Orthodox Christian church in the Ottoman capital of Constantinople. Like his predecessor Alexander, Tsar Nicholas I was a deeply religious leader who enthusiastically embraced this claim. He was so enthusiastic, in fact, that he interpreted this provision as a more general right to speak for and protect *all* Orthodox Christians living in the Ottoman Empire.[124] It was this interpretation, coupled with new developments on the ground, that set the stage for crisis.

The spark that eventually lit the powder keg had an especially obscure starting point: conflict in the spring of 1853 between the Latin (Catholic) and Orthodox Christians over each group's access to some of Christianity's most sacred locations in Jerusalem. Hoping to shore up both nationalist and Catholic support in France by playing the part of the Catholic protector against an Orthodox/Russian menace, Napoleon III sensed an opportunity. He persuaded the Turkish Sultan to grant him the title of "Protector of the Christians in the Ottoman Empire" as well as to give the keys to the holy places most under dispute to the Latin (Catholic) Christians in Jerusalem. Outraged, Nicholas demanded the keys' return to the Orthodox Christians. More significantly, he also demanded the return of his "Christian Protector" title and along with it an open-ended guarantee of Russia's right to intervene in Turkey on behalf of Orthodox Christians. The Tsar threatened to occupy the Danubian principalities if Turkey refused, and followed through on this threat in June of 1853.

The great powers met in Austria later that summer in the hopes of staving off a larger crisis. The result of these negotiations was a proposal (informally referred to as the "Vienna Note") that appeared likely to peacefully resolve the dispute. It did not, and for two reasons. First, the Ottomans were never fully sold on the need for such a compromise and had reason to believe the Western powers—Britain and France—would back them in any war with Russia. Second, Russia immediately asserted a "violent" interpretation of the agreement under which it would seemingly still gain all that the Tsar had previously demanded. With the diplomatic backing of Britain and France, the Turkish sultan repeatedly refused to submit to this interpretation and decisively abandoned *any* compromise based on the Vienna Note in September. When Russia again refused to withdraw from the principalities, Turkey declared war. After just a month of fighting, however, the Russian fleet completely obliterated the Turkish squadron in the Sinope harbor on the Black Sea. Fearing a decisive Russian victory at the Ottomans' expense, Britain and France sent their navies into the Black Sea in early 1854, agreed to a formal alliance with Turkey, and declared war on Russia in late March.[125]

After two years of miserable fighting and shockingly high body counts on all sides (many of which came from disease), Britain and France emerged as the clear victors of the Crimean War. Britain was led throughout the crisis by Palmerston. Whether as Home Secretary (during the escalation and fighting) or as Prime Minister (as he became again in early 1855), he remained the indisputable architect of British foreign policy before, during, and after the conflict. By virtue of her alignment with Britain as well as Russia's surprisingly poor showing in war, France also emerged empowered from the conflict. Victory was technically shared by Austria and the Ottoman Empire, the latter of which was even invited into the great power consortium as a part of the peace settlement. Yet neither actor had much say in the settlement, and I therefore focus here upon the preferences of France and, especially, Britain.

Allied Threat Perceptions and Order Preferences

What did these powers want from the Crimean War? This remains a difficult query to answer, and was even less clear to observers at the time. As the historian Orlando Figes has argued, "it was far from clear what the allies would be fighting for. . . . The reasons for the war would take months for the Western powers to work out through long drawn-out negotiations between themselves and the Austrians during 1854."[126] Even as the war continued, Austrian elites convened the Vienna Peace Conference in 1855 in an attempt to find common ground between the belligerents. Though all parties seemed to come to agreement on the terms for a settlement—centered around what they referred to as the most critical "Four Points" of the dispute—these negotiations were ultimately unsuccessful. This was due in large part to secret war aims on both sides incompatible with those of the other: Russia and Austria were determined to avoid a settlement humiliating to Russia, while Britain and France were committed to decimating Russian naval strength.[127]

Though fighting would continue into 1856, it became clear with Russia's loss of Sebastopol in the fall of 1855 that she would eventually lose the war. A more definitive peace conference was convened in Paris where the great powers successfully negotiated a settlement in the spring of 1856.[128] The settlement was similar to the aborted Vienna agreement from the prior year in that it included three of the "Four Points" Russia had already accepted: the transfer of the "Protector of the Ottoman Christians" title from Russia to a collectivity of the great powers (point 4), the opening of the Danube river to all great powers (point 2), and the stripping from Russia of the Danubian principalities in favor of a joint power protectorate (point 1).[129]

Debate over the final issue—the status of Russian war ships in the Black Sea (point 3)—generated the most controversy in the negotiations. The Straits Convention of 1841 had closed the Bosporus and Dardanelles to all foreign warships whenever Turkey was at peace, an agreement all sides believed they could live with at the time. Seeking to implement something reminiscent of this status quo, the Austrians' original point 3 proposal in 1855 would have allowed Russia the same number of ships she had there prior to the outbreak of hostilities.[130] Instead, and at the insistence of Britain and France, the final agreement neutralized the entire Black Sea and thus prohibited the presence of *any* warships in times of peace.[131] Though this might sound evenhanded, it was in fact devastating for Russia. She was deprived of the crucial warm-water port she had long sought, and having to back down in such a way was seen by Russian elites as both a humiliating concession and an egregious violation of Russian sovereignty.[132]

Upon closer inspection, however, what was most remarkable about the settlement wasn't its sweeping and punitive nature but the fact that it actually wasn't very sweeping or punitive at all. First, by dealing only with case-specific issues rather than general order principles, the treaty was forged within the boundaries of the Concert order instead of fundamentally challenging it.[133] This was contrary to the stated preferences of Napoleon III, who had justified the war at home by appealing to the public's desire for overturning the Concert order. Second, both the war's endgame as well as the peace negotiations themselves were concluded far short of the brutal punishments British and French leaders had promised to inflict upon Russia throughout the war. In spite of such promises and threats, the final settlement was very close to the original Four Points agreement that Palmerston had declared totally unacceptable only a short time earlier. As one historian observes, "the terms of the final treaty were remarkably lenient, especially when compared with the extravagant war aims formulated by Palmerston."[134] What had happened?

I argue that the absence of a novel and unifying existential threat at war's end moderated the demands of both great power victors. At the onset of fighting,

Britain and France thought they were united in their ultimate goals of fundamentally rolling back Russian strength and ambition. And yet in the wake of the Crimean War, there was no new balance of power, technological revolution, or transnational ideological threat to capture the attention of these allies. Most importantly, Russia had been strategically stunned and both materially and psychologically humbled by war's end. As Grand Duke Nikolayevich lamented after the war, "we are both weaker and poorer than the first-class powers, and furthermore poorer not only in material but also in mental resources, especially in matters of administration."[135] As this became more apparent to all actors involved, it ruined the allies' appetites for forging a transformative settlement designed to forever decimate Russian power.

That Britain originally had such revisionist aims is beyond dispute. Even as it was clear to all participants in late 1855 that Russia would lose the war, Palmerston threatened to open a new offensive in the Baltic and continue to fight until the Crimean and Caucuses regions were definitively separated from Russia. After the fall of Sebastopol, he privately complained about how "Austria will try to draw us again into negotiations for an insufficient peace, and we shall not yet have obtained those decisive successes which would entitle us to insist on such terms as will effectively curb the ambition of Russia for the future."[136] The goal was to deprive Russia of so many territories that she would be unable to threaten British imperial interests for at least a generation.[137] Palmerston envisioned the Crimean campaign as but the first step in a larger war that would annihilate Russia. The British press and public were often behind him, in part due to years of the country's elites across the political spectrum stoking rampant Russophobia. "We went to war not so much to keep the Sultan and his Musselmens in Turkey as to keep the Russians out of Turkey," Palmerston wrote to his Foreign Minister Clarendon that fall, "but we have a strong interest also in keeping the Russians out of Norway and Sweden and *if we can do so by ink shed instead of by bloodshed* surely it is wise to take the opportunity to do so."[138] Interesting here is Palmerston's recognition that if Russia couldn't be crippled through military might (bloodshed) she could still be punished by Britain's strategic use of an order-transformative settlement (ink shed).

In spite of Palmerston's determination to punish Russia, however, the lack of a unifying threat soon spelled trouble for allied unity. Particularly after the fall of Sebastopol, British elites were surprised to find that they could no longer count on French support for a punitive settlement. Napoleon III had certainly supported such an endeavor earlier. Yet it soon became clear that for France this was only a means to an end for accomplishing their ultimate objective—breaking out of the perceived shackles of the 1815 settlement—rather than a genuinely held conviction. Instead, French elites most desired a revision of the Concert order that would link territory more closely with nationality. Napoleon wanted these things in part because of his own tenuous political base at home, yet also because nationality had been the unifying principle behind the various liberal revolutions of the prior century that had so often empowered France in Europe.[139] To the extent that France at times directed its ire against Russia in this period, it was only as a means to achieving this larger goal.[140]

Consistent with the expectations of ordering-to-exclude hypothesis 1D, it remained difficult to maintain allied unity over postwar order in the absence of a unifying existential threat. Palmerston was thus surprised to find little support from France for his proposals to indefinitely continue the war. "When you talk of 'we' and of 'our' going on with the war if the Russians are intractable," Clarendon warned him in the midst of the peace conference, "you are probably thinking of the France of two years ago." By this point in time, however, "we have nobody here who is not prepared to make *any* peace."[141] Napoleon III was by this time searching for a formidable partner to endorse his vision of a Europe organized more by nationality and less by commitment to the territorial status quo. In the absence of a pressing postwar threat, however, London saw no reason to go along with such ambitious changes to an order that had served its interests well. The Prime Minister thus reacted coolly to more specific French proposals to insert into the Crimean settlement clauses that would help liberalize Poland, unite the Danubian principalities under a liberal government, and provide aid for liberal Italian revolutionaries to fight against Austria.[142] Undeterred, Napoleon soon did an about-face and sought a revisionist pact with the power he had just helped to defeat. Far from seeing her as a threat, French elites were now convinced that Russia, under its new Tsar, Alexander II, was "the only power who will ratify in advance any aggrandizement of France" and overturn what remained of the 1815 order.[143]

Even more critical than the loss of French support, however, is evidence that Britain itself was wavering on Palmerston's hardline preferences. According to hypothesis 1D, even the most hawkish elites will find themselves stepping back from the brink when their greatest perceived threat appears to dissipate. Palmerston's hawkish views on Russia were increasingly seen as extreme to other elites in the British government as the war went on. Over time, Queen Victoria, Foreign Minister Clarendon, and much of the cabinet began finding ways to work around his continued bellicosity.[144]

More telling is evidence that even Palmerston himself was not as wedded to a punitive peace as his public statements suggested. In the absence of an existential threat, his hardline views were apparently not intensely held preferences and were thus subject to alteration. "Palmerston's demands were in a state of flux," writes one historian.[145] He accordingly gave up much of his defiant stance in the negotiations in late 1855. He wrote to Clarendon in November that while France doubted the seriousness of the ongoing Austro-Russian negotiations, he was surprisingly optimistic: "I may be mistaken, but I am much inclined to think its character much more real and serious; I think it highly probable that Austria has privately ascertained that Russia will accept the terms specified, and that we are therefore on the eve of a 'practical negotiation.'"[146] Most importantly, Palmerston both publicly and privately claimed to be satisfied with the peace agreement resulting from the Paris negotiations—giving Clarendon "the credit for having obtained very good terms"—even as the settlement was much less encompassing and punitive than what he had only recently and very publicly demanded.[147]

Alternatives

The binding motive once again enjoys little support. Britain's stated preferences for a sweeping and anti-Russian peace during the war show that she was not motivated by strategic restraint, while France sought to break out of the constraints of the Concert rather than tie them any tighter. These are not only inconsistent with the binding motive but closer to its opposite.

The learning motive is similarly limited, as there was not a single salient event in recent history for leaders to draw upon or attempt to rectify. It is true that France fought the Crimean War in part to overturn what it perceived as injustices previously imposed against it. Yet by the conflict's end, Napoleon III declined to push very hard for such changes as the war had become deeply unpopular in France. British deliberations similarly reveal little about past events influencing present policy. Russophobia was certainly potent among the British public, but there is little evidence to show that it came out of any specific injustice or formative event.[148]

The strong version of the exporting thesis would expect to find the victorious powers motivated to externalize their liberal ideals, perhaps for the purpose of rolling back the influence of the reactionary regimes in the east. As in 1848, Britain "dabbled in promoting liberalism on the Continent [and] played at substituting a new liberal system [of the kind favored by France] for the old conservative Concert," according to Schroeder. Yet she "never worked at it, never finished what she started."[149] Even more than in that earlier period, foreign regime promotion simply never appeared to be an important British goal.

The weak version of the exporting thesis, on the other hand, can account at least for French preferences at the end of the war. The Paris regime was almost certainly forced to moderate its war aims due to public opinion turning sharply against the war at home. "Palmerston was driven by one popular movement to continue the war; Napoleon, by another, to make peace at once," observes the historian Harold Temperley.[150]

Yet domestic politics cannot alone account for the preferences of the stronger power, Britain, to sue for a lenient and non-transformative settlement. After all, while British *elites* were reasonably satisfied with the settlement they had made, the British press and public most decidedly were not.[151] Fevered Russophobia certainly helps explain Britain's role in escalating the crisis to war in 1853–1854.[152] Yet precisely because it had not yet abated by late 1855, that same Russophobia cannot then also explain why British leaders did an about-face to accept a much more moderate settlement than their domestic audience had been primed to expect.

Ultimately, the negative logic of ordering-to-exclude theory provides a better explanation for this shift than does exporting: in spite of their rhetoric, British and French elites were simply unwilling to pay the major material and political costs for achieving a more transformative and anti-Russian settlement in the absence of a pressing menace on the horizon. From this perspective, it is not surprising that these powers ultimately decided against major changes to the Concert order in the peace forged at Paris after the Crimean War.

5.3.3 The Concert's Demise

Observers continue to disagree about the timing of the European Concert's demise, and scholarship has generally divided into three camps. One argues that the Concert ended soon after it began, disintegrating with the rupture between Britain and the eastern powers over how to deal with liberal revolutions in the 1820s. I responded to this line of reasoning earlier by highlighting how this disagreement over the order's membership principle (Concert rule #4) did not prevent the powers from continuing to work with each other to uphold the order's three behavioral principles (Concert rules #1–3). Indeed, some of the Concert's greatest successes—fostering Russian restraint in the Greek and Turkish Wars, deterring unilateral opportunism against the crumbling Ottoman Empire, and successfully limiting the systemwide effects of various liberal revolutions on the continent—came in the years *after* the Troppau and Laibach congresses where this fateful early rupture supposedly occurred.

A second camp argues that the Concert order continued functioning all the way until the outbreak of the First World War.[153] Support for this perspective comes from the near-continuous series of ambassadorial conferences (a la Concert rule #3) that persisted right up until 1914, many of which proved reasonably successful in resolving particular territorial or colonial issues while also allowing the GPs to continue acting in concert. Alas, this camp's position is undermined by the failure of even these continuous meetings to stop the kinds of transgressions that had been far less frequent in prior decades. These failures included: a new scramble for colonies outside of Europe that nevertheless began infecting continental politics;[154] an inability to control or shape developments regarding the Polish, Italian, and especially German nationalist movements; and, most importantly, a failure to prevent the outbreak of the significant Crimean, Austro-Prussian, and Franco-Prussian conflicts.[155] After the peaceful interlude of the Concert era, major power antagonisms had clearly returned to Europe by midway through the nineteenth century.

I submit that it is a third camp that offers the strongest perspective on the Concert's demise by splitting the difference between the first two and highlighting the two critical midcentury shocks I have focused upon here.[156] The revolutionary wave of 1848 might not have produced a significant reordering response, but it nevertheless mortally wounded the Concert in a number of ways. It completed the cycle of pushing the last of its architects, Metternich, out of power, thus entrusting its maintenance to a set of elites who had little prior experience operating within its rules or placing faith in one another.[157] Such a setback might have been surmountable except for the fact that this new generation of leaders was the first to be significantly more accountable to—and thus often preoccupied with—their national publics. When the Concert was no longer shielded from domestic politics in this way, it became difficult for elites to justify their continued cooperation with what were often seen at home as odious foreign regimes. Instances of great powers defecting on the order principle of concerted action multiplied, thus slowly undermining Concert rule #2. And each time one power pursued unilateral gain at the expense of this most fundamental of Concert rules, it became a little easier for others to break out of the Vienna Settlement's virtuous cycle and give in to their most immediate temptations.

The Concert order's demise wouldn't become as clear to the participants themselves, however, until the outbreak of the Crimean War. On balance, it seems fair to say that the Crimean War was more a symptom of the Concert's demise than a cause of it. After all, this was precisely the kind of conflict that an *effective* Concert order had done so well to avert in the decades prior.[158] Yet this time, an obscure series of disagreements was allowed to spiral into a full-blown great power conflict. Russia was left utterly defeated, demoralized, and profoundly dissatisfied with the settlement imposed upon her. The bellicose and arrogant Tsar Nicholas I rightfully bears much of the responsibility for his country's plight here. Yet in their dealings with that eastern power with whom they had so often worked in concert before, Britain and France were also culpable. For in their treatment of her—especially their unprecedented demand for Russia's forced disarmament on the Black Sea—the Western powers ultimately "broke the first law of the Concert, 'Thou shalt not challenge or seek to humiliate another great power,' and thereby helped ensure" the ultimate destruction of the European Concert order.[159]

Concert-like conferences continued in the decades after the 1856 settlement, sometimes even helping to resolve smaller disputes. Yet the order left in place was no longer capable of forging consensus on those issues that were most controversial and important to the great powers. A shell of the Concert order—agreement over great power supremacy and a weakened version of the rule encouraging multilateral meetings (Concert rules #1 and 3)—remained in place up until the First World War. But transnational liberalization had by this time rid the system of any solidarity between the Concert's elites, thus destroying one important rule (#4).[160] Most importantly, the principle most central to the order's effectiveness—that of settling European political and territorial questions in great power concert (#2)—had clearly withered away by 1856.[161]

5.4 Conclusion: Order Construction in the European Cases

The last two chapters have offered substantial support for ordering-to-exclude theory across a broad tapestry of Europe's diplomatic history. In so doing, they have highlighted continuities across two eras that are often compared more for their differences than similarities. Yes, the Concert era of the nineteenth century saw the development of more general order principles than had the seventeenth and eighteenth centuries, and it was an order distinct from those in the past in its inclusion of a novel membership rule. And yet across both eras, major advances in order came about only when the most powerful actors had both the opportunity to reshape these rules and the motivation to do so in the face of some significantly threatening force or entity.

As Table 5.2 indicates, ordering-to-exclude theory performed very well in accounting for most of these actors' order preferences. In all but two instances, its expectations matched the actual observed preferences (congruence testing). Furthermore, there was also an abundance of evidence for excluding as the primary motivation of the relevant policymakers (process tracing). Of the two instances where the theory at least partially failed, one came in a case where the order rule in question—regular great-power meetings—was not directly predicted by ordering-to-exclude theory but is nevertheless reconcilable with it in combination with the other principles of the European Concert. In the other anomaly—the aftermath of the liberal revolutions of 1848—two of the three alternatives were equally unsuccessful in accounting for Britain's order preferences.

On the whole, none of the alternative motives fared nearly as well. Though learning performed the best, it was perhaps falsely boosted by the fact that the enemy of the most recent conflict and the perceived future threat were either related or one in the same across a number of cases. Exporting performed poorly

Table 5.2 Results: European Cases

Era	Order Preferences	Exclude	Bind	Export	Learn
1648	1: Enhanced autonomy for territorially bounded polities	Y/Y	N/N	Y/N	Y/N
1713	1: Delegitimating transnational dynastic claims	Y/Y	N/N	N/N	Y/Y
	2: Legitimating "balance of power" as a desirable end / state objective	Y/Y	N/N	N/N	Y/Y
1763	(Preferences for continuity)	Y/Y	N/N	N/N	N/N
1815	1: Great powers designated special status/ rights	Y/Y	A/N	A/N	A/N
	2: Defend territorial-political status quo through multilateral consensus	Y/Y	Y/N	A/N	Y/Y
	3: System management through regular congresses and conferences	A/Y	Y/N	A/N	Y/N
	4: To anti-liberal, monarchic regimes	Y/Y	N/N	Y/Y	Y/Y
1848	(Preferences for continuity)	A/N	N/N	Y/Y	A/N
1856	(Preferences for continuity)	Y/Y	N/N	N/N	N/N

Pass congruence test? / Pass process tracing test? Y = Yes; N = No; A = Ambiguous
Shading = passed both tests.

in the absolutist era (chapter 4) and only slightly better in the Concert cases (chapter 5). This is to be expected, since it was the French Revolution that first unleashed the kind of ideological competition that made exporting an important component of statecraft.

Across both European eras, the binding thesis found virtually no support. This is not necessarily as damning as it may seem, however. While it is technically a general theory of order preferences, binding's logic is also predicated on the empirical observation that the American order project of the twentieth and twenty-first centuries has been fundamentally different from those that came before it. It is to those cases—binding's strongest historical instances, we have been led to believe—that we now turn.

6

The Wilsonian Order Project

IN THIS CHAPTER and the next, I seek to show that American leaders in the twentieth century came to prefer, advocate, and enact order principles out of the same kinds of exclusionary impulses that motivated European statesmen of prior centuries (chapters 4 and 5). Yet unlike in those earlier eras—when the perceived threats of the great powers were transitory—in the twentieth century there loomed a single overarching threat to American leaders: the ideological appeal fostered by the Bolshevik Revolution and the ideological *and* military might of that revolution's creation, the Union of Soviet Socialist Republics (USSR). In the pages ahead, I argue that the pattern of American order building in its century can best be explained as an attempt to exclude and delegitimize the looming ideological power of revolutionary socialism along with, later, the massive traditional state power of the USSR itself.

More specifically, I seek to account for the distinct visions of order advanced by US leaders following the two world wars and the superpower Cold War, events that dominated great power politics in the twentieth century. Accordingly, the next three chapters are dedicated to explaining American preferences for international order in three key moments: 1918–1919, 1945–1950, and 1989–1990. Overall, I posit that to understand continuities and changes in the evolving American vision of order in the twentieth century, we must study continuities and changes in its perception of the Soviet threat over the same era.

This chapter focuses on the first of those moments, the aftermath of the First World War and the construction of a new order centered around a revolutionary new international institution, the League of Nations. The Paris Peace Conference of 1919 was, in a sense, both the last and the first of its kind. It was the last time that virtually all of the world's most important leaders came together in a single forum for such an extended period of deliberation, as they had previously at momentous occasions like Westphalia (chapter 4) and Vienna (chapter 5). But the conference also marked the first time that leaders attempted to enact such far-reaching changes to the international system using complex institutional mechanisms designed to permanently lock a settlement in place. Rather than tweaking the existing order by simply adding or eliminating an order principle here or there, the statesmen at Paris grappled with proposals that would fundamentally transform the way polities had interacted since the advent of the Westphalian states system (chapter 4). And driving the terms of this settlement was an American president who consciously put himself at the center of these negotiations for a new world order.

Perhaps more than any other statesman or historical figure, Woodrow Wilson is the archetype of the inclusive liberal in international relations. He is, after all, the president who called for a "peace without victory" in the midst of the First World War, a settlement where victors would forego the typical spoils of conflict. He argued in his famous Fourteen Points address that a revolutionary new institution was necessary for making that conflict the last of its kind, and a few short months later set sail for Paris to personally negotiate the details of that organization himself. These events transformed Wilson into the great hope of oppressed peoples across the world. Events at the time suggested that the masses were not foolish to place their faith in him. Wilson's agenda dominated the Paris Peace Conference in the first half of 1919, pushing the leaders of America's wartime allies into accepting a much more liberal vision of international order than they ever would have entertained in the US president's absence.

How do we account for the Wilsonian vision of order, manifested most concretely in the Covenant (or charter) of the League of Nations? The dominant inclusive narrative of order construction in 1919 emphasizes America's own liberal institutions at home coupled with its president's progressive ideals and sense of ideological mission in international politics. What this narrative overlooks, however, are the ways in which American perceptions of threat shaped aspects of both the general Wilsonian vision of order and the mechanics for translating that vision into a workable international institution. In particular, I contend that after the Bolshevik Revolution of 1917 in Russia, the new ideological threat posed by radical socialism actually played a critical role in shaping the order preferences of Wilson and his principal foreign policy advisers. While this threat cannot explain all of the proposed order changes before and at the Paris Peace Conference, it can account for a surprising amount of the League Covenant's specific and most important content, particularly those parts that originated in the mind of the American president.

This is not to argue for a conspiratorial account of Wilsonian peacemaking where some revisionist agenda was crafted in smoke-filled rooms by elites secretly consumed above all, and much more than they admitted in public, with strangling the Bolshevik menace in its infancy. What I seek to show instead is that for a number of Allied elites—Wilson foremost among them—the Bolshevik Revolution opened a window into the kind of radicalism they feared might soon consume the world if the rules of international order were not substantially recast. The degree to which broad and inclusive "Wilsonian" ideals thereafter gave way to a more tangible and specific set of order rules designed not to accommodate but to forestall this contrary movement, I will argue, has not often enough been highlighted in the conventional narratives of Wilson, the Paris negotiations, and the birth of the League of Nations.

Because of the prominence and supposed power of the inclusive narratives of Wilsonian order building, this episode constitutes a "least likely" case for ordering-to-exclude theory.[1] For this reason, I depart in this chapter from the structure of the case studies for the rest of the book in two significant ways. First, after elucidating the order preferences of the Allies in the first section, I examine the liberal alternative motives for order building—binding, exporting, and learning—*before* assessing the excluding motive. I proceed in this fashion because of the sheer weight of these arguments in the prevailing wisdom about and major historiography on Wilson and the birth of the League of Nations. Second, I go into greater depth here than for the other cases in the book, utilizing the vast amount of published primary source material available on the Wilson administration and international order construction at the end of the First World War. If ordering-to-exclude theory can explain order preferences in this period—the strongest case for some of the liberal alternative narratives and a hard case for my argument—it will strengthen the case for the theory's explanatory power across time and circumstance.

6.1 Allied Order Preferences after World War I

As the clear victors of the First World War, the Allied great powers—Great Britain, France, and the United States—possessed both the coercive power and the recognized right to dictate the terms of the peace. Yet of these actors, the United States was, for the first time in its history, clearly the foremost preponderant power on the world stage. Aside from its sheer material strength and status as the primary creditor of the Allied war effort, America's role in the peace process was also notable because of Wilson's immense popularity. Due to the acclaim of a number of his speeches in 1917 and 1918—especially the Fourteen Points address—Wilson became a global political celebrity the likes of which had never before been seen. At a time when leaders in Europe, none more so than Georges Clemenceau of France, were calling for a more conventional and far less transformative postwar settlement—one including traditional alliance guarantees, reparation payments by the war's losers, and colonial spoils for the victors—the American president articulated a need for more fundamental changes to world politics and sought what was considered at the time to be a radical liberalization of the international system.

Consideration of Wilson's seemingly radical agenda consumed the Paris Peace Conference. The president and his foreign policy views similarly dominated politics at home and framed the domestic debate in the United States over the shape of the postwar order as well. As the historian Thomas Knock has argued, perhaps no US president has exercised as much personal control over major foreign policy decisions in the history of the American republic. "Wilson the diplomatist made all final decisions himself, routinely composed important diplomatic notes on his own typewriter, and, in many instances, conducted diplomacy without informing the State Department of his actions."[2] Because of the unusually significant role that Wilson personally played in the deliberations over the postwar international order, I focus more on his agenda, motives, and beliefs in this chapter than I do on any other single leader examined in the book.

Yet while the United States was certainly the global leader by the end of the First World War, it was not nearly as omnipotent as it would become two and a half decades later. Unlike in the aftermath of the Second World War, writes historian Margaret Macmillan in her magisterial account of the Paris Peace Conference, America's European allies in 1919 "were not exhausted and desperate, prepared to take American aid, even at the price of accepting American suggestions" on all aspects of the postwar settlement. "In 1919, they still saw themselves as, and indeed they were, independent actors in world affairs" rather than merely junior partners of the American colossus.[3] Great Britain and France in particular were not nearly as decimated in 1919 as they would be in 1945, a point that the CINC power data depicted in Figure 6.1 helps to illustrate. Like Britain after the Napoleonic Wars, American statesmen in Paris had to contend with and accommodate the preferences of their great-power wartime allies. In that earlier period, however, Britain had found herself in the fortunate position of sharing nearly identical threat perceptions with her allies, at least in the initial years after the wars (chapter 5). As we will soon see, the United States enjoyed no such luxury in 1919.[4]

6.1.1 The Order Principles of the League of Nations Covenant

The main questions at stake throughout the Paris Peace Conference were how harsh a peace to impose on the primary defeated belligerent, Germany; what if anything to do about Germany's colonies and the great power colonial system more generally; and whether (and how) to create institutional commitments to

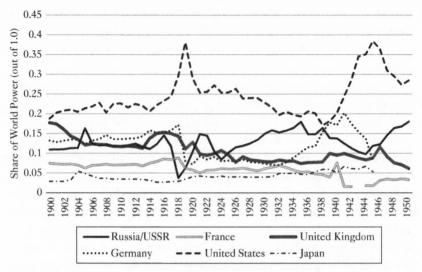

FIGURE 6.1 Relative power, 1900–1950.

Source: Composite Indicator of National Capability (CINC) data set, version 5.0. See David J. Singer, "Reconstructing the Correlates of War Dataset on Material Capabilities of States, 1816–1985," *International Interactions* 14, No. 2 (1988).

guard against another brutal and destructive systemic war. But the most important *order* questions at the conference focused on what the acclaimed but still only vaguely outlined "League of Nations" would actually look like in practice. Using the text of the principal ordering document of the time—the League of Nations Covenant—I submit that we can identify preferences for four major changes to international order in 1919.[5]

Three were behavior rules, and of these two were deeply interconnected. **First, the Covenant essentially outlawed the initiation of interstate wars of aggression (League rule #1). Second, it established in the place of war institutionalized mechanisms for non-violent dispute resolution that member states pledged to utilize as an alternative to war (League rule #2).** In practice, this second rule was to be realized by the establishment of a permanent supranational organization focused on international security, the first of its kind in the modern system. Together, these two rules went further than any of those of the European Concert, since that earlier arrangement had established only that no territorial changes in Europe could be made without multilateral great-power consent (chapter 5). The heart of the League Covenant, by contrast, essentially outlawed the unprovoked use of force in virtually any circumstance (League rule #1).[6]

The new order would realize this rule in practice through a variety of institutional mechanisms that constituted the core of the League of Nations organization itself (League rule #2), each of which would curtail member states' sovereignty in specific ways. Three of these mechanisms bear mentioning. First, League members committed to negotiations in the future aimed at significantly reducing national armaments and limiting munitions production past whatever was necessary for basic self-defense.[7] Second, members agreed to submit their disputes to the League itself for open deliberation or arbitration of some sort instead of—or at least prior to—resorting to armed conflict.[8] Third, members pledged to both punish breakers of the rule against aggressive force (League rule #1) with economic and political sanctions (Article 16 of the Covenant)[9] and come to the aid of any League member whose territorial sovereignty was violated in this way (Article 10).[10] Regardless of whether or not Article 10 constituted a true collective security pact—an issue I return to later in the chapter—the Covenant clearly called upon members to punish aggressive defectors and assist states that were the victims of aggressive acts.

The Covenant's third behavioral principle stood almost entirely apart from the first two, yet was no less consequential: **in determining the governance of dependent people and nations, the "self-determination" of those people and nations must be given significantly greater consideration in the future than it had in the past (League rule #3).**[11] Codified in Article 22, this rule established the League's colonial mandate system. In theory, this provision acknowledged that any nation in the world was entitled to eventual self-government, a process that would presumably culminate in full sovereignty for any and all who wanted it. In the meantime, nations not yet deemed ready for self-government would be placed under the trusteeship of a great power state that, in consultation with the League, would ease the transition to independence through tutelage and the gradual devolution of power.

In practice, the mandate system allowed the Allied victors of the First World War to (mostly) preserve control over their existing colonies in the postwar period. Yet in spite of its dearth of immediate far-reaching consequences, it still constituted a major rule change to international order for at least three reasons. First, it imposed stricter rules over the mandatory power's methods of control and coercion in dealing with its colonies (now mandates). Second, it required that mandatory powers allow full economic and cultural exchange between their mandates and all other League members. Finally, it for the first time explicitly codified a promise by the mandatory powers for at least the gradual transfer of power to the people of each designated mandate.[12]

The fourth and final order change seemingly came in the form of a new membership principle. The Covenant's preamble declared representative political institutions the single most important condition for membership into the League. This appeared to establish that the League of Nations would be a league of democracies. Under Article 1, eligibility for membership was open only to "any fully self-governing State, Dominion or Colony," a requirement that could be scrutinized in the future by existing League members since subsequent admission required the support of two-thirds of them. Non-democracies could not become members,[13] and non-members lost out on the benefits of the multilateral arbitration and dispute-resolution mechanisms, the freer exchange of goods and services through the expected lowering of tariff barriers, and the Article 10 guarantee of assistance against unprovoked aggression.

Yet it is more accurate to say that **the Covenant required *orderly* democratic institutions as a condition for entry into the League (rule #4).** I emphasize *orderliness* here because the focus was less on enforcing strict adherence to some tightly defined set of domestic criteria than about promoting orderly or lawful behavior both domestically and internationally. In the meeting where this principle was ultimately codified into the Covenant, Woodrow Wilson himself defined the parameters of what he had in mind by "orderly democracy":

> I have spent twenty years of my life lecturing on self-governing states, and trying all the time to define one. Now whereas I haven't been able to arrive at a definition, I have come to the point where I recognize one when I see it. For example, regardless of how it appeared on paper, no one would have looked at the German government before the war, and said that nation was self-governing.... On the other hand, some governments are in terms less liberal than Germany was, and yet we would agree in calling them self-governing.... I should be sorry not to see some recognition of the principles of self-government in the Covenant.[14]

"Orderly democracy" was thus something of a moving target, referring to the domestic makeup of a polity, but also with reference to how it behaved on the international stage. Aside from the "self-governing" provision, the Covenant also called for and codified respect for the rule of law, adherence to existing contracts and obligations, and domestic moderation on particular issues (those viewed as important by the members of the League Commission). For instance, Article 1 explicitly required members to "give effective guarantees of [their] sincere intention to observe [their] international obligations," as well as to "accept such regulations as may be prescribed by the League in regard to [their] military, naval and air forces and armaments." Article 23 made additional demands for orderliness by mandating "fair and humane" domestic working conditions, "just treatment of the native inhabitants of territories," and "freedom of communications and of transit and equitable treatment for the commerce of all Members of the League." It is thus more accurate to say that this fourth order principle of the League

Covenant fell somewhere between membership and behavior, since it prescribed and proscribed both domestic and international patterns of behavior. I nevertheless classify it as a membership rule because it was the principle subsequently used more than any other to actually exclude particular states from joining the League of Nations.

Overall, then, these proposed order changes indicate that the Covenant's authors had strong preferences for a stable, predictable, and orderly international system characterized both within and across polities by formidable respect for the existing rule of law.

6.2   *Alternatives*

How can we account for these new foundational rules, order principles that at the time looked like a radical departure from those that had governed world politics for centuries? In this section I address how the binding, exporting, and learning narratives have sought to answer this question. All appear highly plausible from the start. I aim to show, however, that after peeling away some initial surface-level support for each of them, one quickly encounters serious deficiencies in their ability to explain the most important elements of the American-driven order project in 1919.

6.2.1   Binding

With a true international institution in the League of Nations that was premised on codified rules and sophisticated mechanisms of conflict resolution, the binding thesis instantly has greater plausibility in this case than it did for any of those examined in chapters 4 and 5. Perhaps the United States attempted to create this revolutionary institution to bind its power to a liberal order that would achieve buy-in from allies and subordinates while helping the world's first truly liberal hegemon foster security and stability "on the cheap."

We do not have to blindly extrapolate on binding's expectations for 1919, as John Ikenberry devotes significant attention to the Wilsonian order-building project in *After Victory*. The United States tried "to use its momentary power advantages during and after the war to secure a postwar settlement that locked in a favorable order," he argues, "and it attempted to use offers of restraint on and commitment of its own power to gain an institutional agreement with European states."[15] More concretely, Ikenberry posits that Wilson's postwar vision was premised on (a) a desire to construct a binding security institution among the world's leading democracies that would forestall the return to the kind of balance-of-power politics predominant before the war; and (b) the belief that a democratic revolution about to sweep across Europe would make possible this consortium based upon shared ideological principles.[16] The American president thus sought to protect America's foreign interests by "transform[ing] European politics without getting too involved in actually working with or protecting Europe" via traditional alliance commitments.[17] America ultimately rejected Wilson's optimistic vision, Ikenberry argues, because Europe demanded too *great* a binding commitment from the United States while the American public and US Senate, concerned above all with preserving their country's freedom of action, demanded too *small* a commitment.[18]

Ikenberry's narrative of the "Wilsonian moment" has its merits. To be sure, the United States under Wilson did seek to cement in place the favorable asymmetries of power in 1919, and sought to do so through a revolutionary security institution in the League of Nations. In Wilson's vision, this institution would at least partially obscure any threatening shadow of America's overwhelming power, while at the same time serving as a vehicle for that power in Europe after the war. Wilson himself appeared to believe that "the League will act as a permanent clearinghouse where every nation can come," making it the indispensable forum through which problems of international security would be handled.[19] There is also some evidence to support the claim that American leaders sought to use institutional burden-sharing in the League to exercise maximum dominance at minimum cost.[20] "There must now be not a balance of power, not one group of nations to set off against another," the president argued, "but a single overwhelming, powerful group of nations who shall be the trustee of the peace of the world," in part by acting in concert to divide up the costs of and responsibilities for preserving international stability.[21] Binding thus offers a plausible account for at least the first two out of four proposed order changes, those stigmatizing war and promoting institutional mechanisms for conflict resolution (League rules #1 and 2).

Nevertheless, any account highlighting binding as the *principal* motive for order building in 1919 must contend with at least two important discrepancies. First, there is a dearth of evidence indicating that Wilson or his advisors were driven with any real conviction by a desire to rapidly democratize the world. This at first might seem surprising, since Wilson had, after all, declared in 1917 that America was entering the war to combat German autocracy and make the world safe for democracy. Yet a closer look suggests that Wilson himself had actually been privately resistant for some time to using the democracy/autocracy cleavage as the principal justification for American entry into the war in 1917. While he eventually agreed to publicly use this narrative as justification, it was in fact just that—a *justification*—rather than a genuinely held underlying belief that motivated major decisions.[22] Up until Germany's resumption of unrestricted submarine warfare a few months prior, Wilson had been convinced that, in spite of its autocratic institutions, Germany could still be fully reintegrated into his emerging vision of a liberal order. The impossibility (or at least undesirability) of doing this only became clearer to him later and largely in reaction to changes in Germany's *international* behavior rather than to its domestic politics.[23]

Relatedly, it is difficult to find any evidence that Wilson or those around him harbored any real illusions about orderly democratic governments soon spontaneously emerging in Europe, at least throughout the time of their deliberations at the Paris Peace Conference.[24] I contend instead that the American negotiators actually saw greater evidence that Bolshevism, not orderly democracy, was the ascendant ideology on the continent after the war, an argument I develop in the pages ahead. In short, both the necessity of democratization for Wilson's order vision and his optimism for it soon spontaneously occurring seem at best to be overstated in this interpretation of 1919.

The second and strongest indictment against the binding thesis comes, however, when we contrast the expectations of this motive for order building with the actual stated motives of the American negotiators in Paris. To put it plainly, there is little evidence that demonstrating hegemonic restraint motivated any of the relevant US statesmen during this period. Ikenberry is correct to note that the Europeans—and the French in particular—were insistent on receiving an American security commitment to Europe. But what they wanted here—security *commitment*—is not the same as security *restraint*, and is in fact closer to its opposite. A core component of the binding explanation for order building is that "the leading state gives up some freedom on the use [of] its power in exchange for agreed-upon principles and institutional processes that ensure a durable and predictable postwar order."[25] In 1919, however, the Americans were not offering any explicit promises of restraint, nor were European leaders asking for any such commitments. Ikenberry even admits as much, noting that "specific sacrifices are difficult to identify" on the part of American leaders, while Wilson himself "did not offer specific concessions on short-term gains in seeking agreement with European leaders."[26]

The best case one can make for a self-imposed binding restraint on American power centers around the Covenant's famous Article 10. As its text reads, "the Members of the League undertake to respect and preserve as against external aggression the territorial integrity and existing political independence of all Members of the League."[27] Many of Wilson's supporters and opponents alike saw Article 10 as the linchpin of the entire settlement, as have a number of contemporary scholars.[28] If it was truly the collective security promise that his supporters hoped for and his opponents feared, it might represent the kind of binding commitment at the heart of this explanation.

The problem with this interpretation of Article 10 as an ironclad and binding security commitment, however, is that its very architect, Woodrow Wilson himself, did not view it in this way. While he believed it to be "a very grave and solemn moral obligation," above all he argued that it was "a moral, not a legal obligation, and leaves our Congress absolutely free to put its own interpretation upon it in all cases that call for action. It is binding in conscience only, not in law."[29] It would be through not legally binding commitments, but instead the "moral force of men throughout the world" shining the "searching light of conscience" upon aggressors through which the League would "settle most questions," Wilson posited.[30] In fact, he actually argued *against* an automatic and institutionalized military response to aggression of the sort that France wanted built in to the Covenant. "We are ready to fly to the assistance of those who are attacked," he argued in a heated meeting of the League Commission, "but we cannot offer more than the condition of the world enables us to give."[31] Robert Cecil, British representative to the League Commission, concurred. While he and Wilson "desired to enforce on the parties a delay of some months before any war took place . . . they did not think that it would be accepted by the nations if there was an attempt to compel them to agree to a solution dictated" by the League. It was Cecil's opinion that "all that the Covenant proposed was that the members of the League, before going to war, should try all pacific means of settling the quarrel," not that they could be coerced into any form of positive action to which they objected.[32]

In short, the best case one can make for Article 10 as a binding mechanism is that its architects were not exactly sure what it would do in practice. More likely, however, was that they saw it as a general deterrent to or a temporary pause on aggression, not a literal and truly binding obligation that each member was legally compelled to follow at the critical time. Moreover, recent scholarship on Wilson in particular has emphasized how he repeatedly eschewed an excessively legalized League, preferring instead an open-ended forum for deliberation between principled members of the international community (a point developed in more detail in the next section).[33] Simply put, this is not the kind of heavily institutionalized and power-restraining organization that we would expect to find if the binding motive had been truly paramount.

6.2.2   Exporting

The narrative that the Versailles peace settlement was heavily influenced by an American desire to export its domestic ideals and/or institutions is a prominent one. A popular variant of this argument posits that President Wilson, as a preeminent scholar of America's political institutions and liberal traditions, sought to impose the architecture of the American federal union onto the international system via the League of Nations. For instance, Kalevi Holsti has argued that Wilson was influenced more "from his analysis of American domestic politics than from any deep familiarity with the practices or history of European international relations."[34] Andreas Osiander similarly posits that "Wilson believed that the international system could be pacified by introducing into it the peacekeeping mechanisms of domestic society."[35] And in a variant of the exporting thesis, Colin Dueck argues that American ideational traditions help explain both the loftiness of Wilson's transformative plans for order and the domestic fears of foreign entanglements that ultimately led to his country's rejection of his plans.[36]

General aspects of this perspective find support in the evidentiary record. Wilson's pre-presidential writings confirm that he informed some of his early ideas about reforming the international system at least in part on novel elements of the American federal union.[37] Trygve Throntveit has similarly posited that Wilson and his confidant "Colonel" Edward House came to the conclusion in their earliest drafts of the League Covenant in 1918 that "just as the states of the Union had ceded powers to the federal government in return for long-term security and growth, the states of the world must formally abandon their claims to absolute national sovereignty, authorizing and equipping a deliberative organization to resolve their conflicts."[38]

Exporting thus generally fits as a motive for American order preferences in and around the settlement. Upon taking a closer look at this narrative, however, significant problems emerge. What becomes most evident is that it was not Wilson's version of the League that was the most beholden to America's domestic political traditions, but an alternative vision of postwar order (and the League) propagated at the same time by some of Wilson's fiercest domestic critics. This coalition was led by the most prominent Republican foreign policy minds in the country and included former Presidents Theodore Roosevelt and William Howard Taft and former Secretary of State Elihu Root. Though these three men at different times offered separate blueprints for an American-led world order, their plans were united in envisioning a version of the League much more in line with the legalist—or "legalist-sanctionist"—tradition of American jurisprudence than was Wilson's.[39]

Whereas Wilson wanted a broad but loosely organized League that could evolve over time, the legalist-sanctionists advocated something closer to the polar opposite of this vision: a narrowly defined League that nonetheless had the power to execute and enforce its clearly codified legal principles. In 1915–1916, Root sketched perhaps the most sophisticated variant of this vision, one that would look much more like an international court than the political debating society Wilson would come to champion. In advocating for such a vision, he "was simply applying the theory behind criminal municipal law to international relations" under which "criminal offenses in international relations were treated like domestic civil disputes."[40] It wasn't Wilson's vision, but instead this kind of legalism—defined as externalizing the laws of advanced societies like the United States to the international system[41] —that would most closely constitute an attempt to export American institutions and ideals onto world politics after the First World War. As Root prominently complained in 1919 after the president's alternative vision had become clear, Wilson's League would place "the whole subject of arbitration back where it was twenty-five years ago. Instead of perfecting and putting teeth into the system of arbitration provided for by the Hague Conventions, it throws those conventions upon the scrap heap."[42] To Root and his sympathizers, Wilson's vision was a radical departure from the American political tradition, not an attempt to extend that tradition to the international sphere. The main problem with Wilson's League, Root would later argue, was that it "rests the hope of the whole world for future peace in a government of men, and not of laws."[43]

Wilson's implicit reply to such criticism was dismissive and perhaps even disdainful. "I should say of this document that it is not a straitjacket, but a vehicle of life," he said of the completed Covenant in Paris. "A living thing is born, and we must see to it that the clothes we put upon it do not hamper it" with burdensome legal provisions, he argued in what was a clear jab at the legalist-sanctionists.[44] In point of fact, the president believed that in "matters that relate to the good faith of nations . . . the only sanction" that would be effective wasn't a legal one but "that of public opinion." The "moral judgment of peoples is more accurate than proceedings before a tribunal," he argued.[45] What Wilson had in mind was an ever-evolving organization that would begin with only a few codified principles, rather than the more formal and detailed organization his domestic legalist critics desired.[46] Only an open-ended and political institution, the president believed, could provide both the elasticity and the security that would be needed in a dangerous world.[47]

The point here isn't to adjudicate between the League visions of Wilson and the legalist-sanctionists. Instead, it is to demonstrate that there are good reasons for treating Wilson's particular ordering vision as an *aberration* from American traditions more than a faithful extension of them. Upon closer inspection, the exporting narrative isn't nearly as helpful for understanding the president's ordering motives as it first appears.

6.2.3   Learning

Adopting the learning motive as narrative for this case, one would expect to find the victorious powers focused on opposing the recent war's perceived belligerents—or preventing the reemergence of the war's perceived causes—when constructing the postwar order. In either case, the focus in 1919 should have been on addressing German militarism. This was, after all, the force that most occupied Allied leaders during the war, and it remained the focus of much of their enmity in the negotiations in Paris.

There is some support for this narrative. Evidence indicates that at least some of the important actors in the peace negotiations were preoccupied with this pre-existing menace—German militarism—more than any other threat or issue. To a number of European elites—particularly Vittorio Orlando of Italy and especially France's Clemenceau—the biggest foreseeable threat at war's end remained the prospect of a militarily resurgent, expansionist, and imperialistic Germany.[48] Clemenceau was adamant that the settlement had to impose severe limits on traditional German power and provide guarantees against subsequent future German aggression. Moreover, France and Italy were not alone in these views, as important British and even American policymakers shared these fears. In particular, prominent Republican Party leaders like Roosevelt and Senator Henry Cabot Lodge, the Chairman of the Senate Foreign Relations Committee—both fierce political adversaries of Wilson—viewed the peace negotiations as an opportunity to permanently curtail Germany's power base. Doing so, they believed, would sap Germany of both its international ambition and its geopolitical greed, which these Republican elites saw as the principal causes of the Great War.[49]

There can be little doubt that the settlement imposed harsh and perhaps untenable terms upon Germany, seemingly supporting this variant of the learning thesis. It must also be remembered that Wilson himself famously took the United States into the war in April 1917 by condemning Germany's autocratic institutions and militaristic leaders. For the president's Republican critics at home, this remained the prime objective of the war and the peace negotiations. As Chairman Lodge publicly declared in reference to the settlement, "no peace that satisfies Germany in any degree can ever satisfy us.... [We] must go to Berlin and there dictate peace."[50] So much did Republicans agree with Allied leaders like Clemenceau and disagree with their own president on the goals of the peace settlement that Lodge and Roosevelt went so far as to set up backchannel communications to work around Wilson, encouraging European elites to stand firm against their own government's efforts to promote leniency for Germany.[51]

On the subject of that leniency, what of the Wilson administration's motivations vis-à-vis Germany? There is certainly evidence to suggest that administration officials were at least in part responding to the perceived causes of the war when negotiating the peace: balance-of-power politics, imperialistic expansion, and the destructive actions taken by a less-than-democratic Germany. The learning motive thus has some explanatory power for this case. Yet three important caveats also merit attention here. First is the fact that any evidence of Allied statesmen focused on combatting Germany while crafting a new order can be used to bolster the excluding motive as much as the learning one. After all, just because a perceived future threat remains the same as a past threat doesn't necessarily mean that the resulting order is more backward- than forward-looking (a point highlighted in the 1648 and 1713 cases in chapter 4). To the extent that Allied leaders thought that Germany would remain a significant threat into the future, constructing an order to combat that threat would still fit comfortably within the logic of excluding even if it would also remain consistent with learning.

Second, while a narrative focused on targeting Germany can account for some of the order principles at the heart of the League Covenant, it cannot account for all of them. Logic and evidence suggest that proposed League rules #1 and 2—those stigmatizing aggression and promoting institutionalized conflict resolution—could have been designed in part to prevent the resurgence of a threatening Germany. There is less evidence, however, that the future threat of Germany can account for the self-determination or orderly democracy principles, proposed League rules #3 and 4. The administration's lack of concern over regime type in private was discussed earlier (#4). And while it was understood that great power rivalries and nationalist movements stemming from imperialism might have helped exacerbate the conflict, there isn't much evidence that notable administration officials saw those things as a *primary* cause of the war. At best, then, learning might be able to partially explain only half of the relevant order preferences in this case.

The third and final caveat is the most consequential, and one that sets the stage for the rest of the chapter: while there is *some* evidence that the Wilson administration did in part respond to the threat of a resurgent Germany while forging the postwar order in Paris, there is *overwhelming* evidence that they were concerned far more with a new menace than with this old one. This is the focus of the next section.

6.3   *Threats*

Across the rest of the chapter, I contend that officials in the Wilson administration were preoccupied with resurgent German power only in the context of two broader fears. "There are two great evils at work in the world today," wrote Secretary of State Robert Lansing to Elihu Root, the man who had formerly held his job, in 1918: "Absolutism, the power of which is waning, and Bolshevism, the power of which is increasing."[52] Lansing's first evil captured the administration's fear that the world would soon return to the imperialistic and balance-of-power system of shifting alliances that had brought about the Great War in the first place, a point that Wilson himself often reiterated in public and in private. And since this was precisely the type of system that many European elites hoped to reaffirm rather than repudiate, calling for its fundamental overhaul and reform often put Wilson at odds with other Allied elites.

Yet by the end of 1917, I contend that Wilson and his principal advisers were often even more concerned about Lansing's second stated evil: revolutionary socialism, a radical and violent offshoot of liberalism that many observers now feared would spread like a poison across Europe. The principal catalyst for this fear, of course, was the Bolshevik Revolution in November 1917 that brought Vladimir Lenin to power in Russia. "Over the longer term," writes Stephen Walt, capturing the significance of this critical development for Wilson and other Western elites, it "created a new state that was fundamentally hostile to the prevailing international order and openly committed to spreading its principles to other countries."[53]

In the next section, I connect advocacy for the main order principles of the League of Nations Covenant to an ordering strategy focused on countering and containing the revolutionary threat of Bolshevism. In *this* section, I examine the Wilson administration's threat perceptions from the end of the war through the peace negotiations. In so doing, I make three interrelated arguments: First, the Bolshevik threat represented a more existential challenge to the Wilsonian worldview than did a reversion back to the old prewar system. Second, the Bolshevik Revolution's possible demonstration effects were the primary vehicle through which elites feared developments in both Russia and Germany during the critical stages of the peace negotiations. Third, some of these same elites recognized that this was a threat of ideology rather than traditional state power, thus necessitating a response that did not rely foremost upon military force.

First, evidence suggests that members of the Wilson administration feared the possibility of a new world order based on Bolshevik principles much more than a reversion to the previous order epitomized by the belligerent practices of Imperial Germany. The reason for this was simple. As an older generation of revisionist scholarship has highlighted, Wilson's ordering vision, though portrayed as revolutionary at the time, actually shared much more in common with the status quo of European balance-of-power and imperialist politics than it did with the kinds of practices advocated by revolutionary socialists.[54] After all, American elites recognized that their country's recent global ascendance had much to do with their continuing ability to export large amounts of industrial output.[55] Part of their dislike of the old order came from the existing practices of frequent war (a product of balance-of-power thinking) and imperial preferences in trade (a product of colonialist thinking) that oftentimes left much of the world impenetrable to US commerce.[56] A substantial opening of those parts of the world currently closed off to American economic penetration was needed, they believed.

Yet Lenin's calls for the immediate self-determination of *all* dependent peoples, coupled with his repudiation of *all* elements of the global status quo, quickly and naturally became much more troubling to many of these same elites than did the prospect of reversion back to the prior order. For all their talk of a new world order, the American political class disagreed more with the form than the substance of the old system. The radical new ordering vision propagated by the Bolsheviks, in contrast, seemed completely antithetical and alien to both American interests and American values, and thus represented the far greater threat.

What exactly was the Bolshevik vision for international order? Lenin actually agreed with Wilson that the status quo of imperialistic and power politics was untenable. Yet he radically disagreed with the American president's stated belief that such a system could be peacefully and gradually liberalized. Instead, he judged the traditional order to be wholly irredeemable, dominated as it was by the most exploitative of the capitalist great powers. He therefore advocated not only the violent overthrow of national governments across the world but a radical restructuring of the very foundations of international relations under which class-identification would replace national allegiance as the basic building block of international society. "Very few of Lenin's followers saw a sharp distinction in terms of political activity between what had been the Russian empire and countries outside it," writes the historian Arne Westad. In fact, "to Lenin, the main purpose of his revolution had been to prepare the ground for other revolutions to come; first, in the developed capitalist countries of Europe and then, as their social conditions allowed for it, in the colonial territories."[57]

Well before the revolution in Russia Western leaders had been aware of Lenin, who even prior to the war had become associated with slogans calling for "complete equality of rights for all nations; the right of nations to self-determination, [and] the unity of the workers of all nations."[58] But fears exploded out into the open once his radical Bolsheviks captured control of Moscow in November 1917. He immediately publicized the Allies' secret treaties for the division of Germany and its spoils after the war,[59] and his government routinely began speaking past Allied leaders to instead call upon "'the class-conscious workers of England, France, and Germany' to 'bring to a successful end the cause of peace . . . and the liberation of all who labor.'"[60] When the Wilson administration officially (though coldly) congratulated Lenin on forming a government in Russia, the Bolsheviks answered not with likeminded restraint but instead with further calls for revolutionary upheaval in countries across the world including the United States itself.[61] Wilson himself was deeply unsettled in March of 1918 by the dissolution of the Russian Constituent Assembly, which in its brief tenure had been the most democratic institution that country had ever seen.[62] "If the Bolsheviks intend to suggest that every community . . . can determine its allegiance to this or that political state or to become independent," wrote Lansing to Wilson in early 1918, "the present political organization of the world would be shattered and the same disorder would generally prevail as now exists in Russia. It would be international anarchy."[63]

Events throughout 1918 and 1919 demonstrated the terrible possibility of Lenin's transnational vision of European revolution, or even global anarchy, coming to fruition. The Bolsheviks quickly negotiated a separate peace with Germany in December 1917—culminating in the Treaty of Brest-Litovsk—in which they ceded vast territories to the German Empire while allowing German leaders to rededicate their efforts to fighting the Allies along the Western front. Socialists led by Béla Kun seized power in Hungary in early 1919, demonstrating that the simple fact of the Bolshevik regime's continuing survival in Russia could produce disturbing and tangible demonstration effects across national borders.[64] Fears of ideological subversion were heightened by the proliferation of workers' movements and protests across the world, many of them demonstrating their strength at precisely the time that leaders gathered in Paris to negotiate the peace.[65] Herbert Hoover, then head of the American relief effort in Europe, captured the sense of dread engulfing Eastern Europe during the first half of 1919:

> Bolshevik ideas were impregnating the working classes throughout the area. Unless some means could be devised of abating the infection, the economic regeneration of Central and South-Eastern Europe would be difficult. Béla Kun's government was spending a great deal of money on sending Bolshevik missionaries to industrial centers outside Hungary."[66]

Hoover clearly associated the provision of aid to Eastern Europe with holding back a dangerous Bolshevik ideological wave. "It is my view that the critical moment is right now," he wrote to Wilson late in 1918. "It is not necessary for me to mention how fundamental it appears to me that this is, if we are to preserve these countries from Bolshevism and rank anarchy."[67]

At the same time, Lenin's challenge also immediately created dangers for Allied leaders within their own borders. This was true not only in Europe but also in America itself. Public consciousness was seized with fear of Bolshevik subversion in the First Red Scare in 1919 and 1920.[68] "Most Americans were more concerned with Bolshevism at home than with Bolshevism abroad," writes the historian Melvyn Leffler. These concerns led to red-baiting rhetoric from US elites including Wilson himself, not to mention Justice Department raids against supposed leftwing radicals. At the same time, thirty-five of the forty-eight states of the union passed new sedition laws and took unprecedented additional steps such as banning the public display of red flags.[69] "No man is fatuous enough to suppose that if the rest of the world is disturbed and disordered," Wilson argued about Bolshevism in the fall of 1919, "the disturbance and disorder are not going to extend to the United States."[70] In short, the transnational threat that the Bolshevik Revolution posed outside of Russia had quickly become apparent to Wilson and other Allied elites.

None of these observations is meant to imply that the peacemakers in Paris were preoccupied *only* with the revolutionary regime in Russia. They were not, and there were certainly important meetings where Russia was not directly discussed. Naturally, much of elites' attention in Paris was devoted to their principal adversary in the war, Germany. Yet significant evidence also suggests that American leaders in particular seemed to fear postwar Germany not because it was likely to return to its prewar composition or behavior but because of the potential for a socialist, Bolshevik-style revolution there. This is my second major argument in this section.

Many of the discussions over the fate of Germany in Paris—both in intra-American and intra-Allied deliberations—were focused more on the possibility of Bolshevik subversion in that country than on the resurgence of traditional German power. Influential officials such as Lansing, Assistant Secretary of State Breckinridge Long, and State Department Russia expert (and, later, Wilson's emissary to the Bolsheviks) William Bullitt reported to the president in the midst of Germany's November Revolution that it was being influenced by Bolshevik ideals if not also by actual Bolshevik agents.[71] Wilson himself was preoccupied with this possibility throughout the end of 1918 and the first half of 1919. "The spirit of the Bolsheviki is lurking everywhere, and there is no more fertile soil than war-weariness" of the type that was taking hold in Germany, he remarked in private in 1918.[72] In a crucial March 1919 meeting of the Council of Four—those deliberations between Wilson, British Prime Minister Lloyd George, Clemenceau, and Orlando in Paris—the American president argued that the most urgent danger was not the present German regime but the frightening possibility that "it will be replaced by a government with which we cannot negotiate. . . . We owe it to the peace of the world not to tempt Germany to plunge into Bolshevism; we know only too well the relations of the Bolshevik leaders with Germany."[73] This was far from an irrational fear: records indicate that the Bolsheviks themselves considered Germany among the ripest targets for revolution, actively targeting its unstable regime in the months after their own ascendance to power in Moscow.[74]

These myriad developments help cast light upon a third major point: Allied and especially American fears of socialism derived *not* from Russian military might but from the ideological draw of the Bolshevik Revolution and regime, a force that was novel, unconventional, and unpredictable. Accordingly, key elites correctly perceived that because this threat didn't come in the form of traditional state power (military force), it could not be combatted in a conventional way (countervailing military force). Wilson in particular "recognized that since communism could not be defeated with 'barbed wire' alone it was imperative to oppose it with a rival ideal,"[75] noting at one point that trying "to stop a revolutionary movement with ordinary armies is like using a broom to sweep back a spring tide."[76] In his speeches throughout 1919, the president consistently highlighted that the "ugly, poisonous thing called Bolshevism" was an ideological disease that would soon produce very material symptoms.[77] He publicly worried, for instance, that it would become increasingly difficult to "prevent the Germans from forming a powerful industrial and commercial union with Russia" once revolutionary socialist ideas united them into a single super-state. [78]

The belated and halfhearted nature of American intervention in the Russian Civil War is sometimes used to combat the narrative that the Wilson administration worried much about Bolshevism.[79] Indeed, Wilson was far from enthusiastic about intervention, especially compared to hardline European officials like British War Secretary Winston Churchill and Marshal Ferdinand Foch in France.[80] Though he eventually agreed to send a limited number of troops to Russia to fight alongside those of the Allies, Wilson did so with great reluctance and in the belief that they would ultimately fail.[81] Yet this is less a sign that the president did not care about or fear Bolshevism than it is an indication that he did not believe Bolshevism could be stopped through military force. By opposing the Bolsheviki by armies," he argued at the peace conference, "the cause of the Bolsheviki was being served by the Allies. . . . It was therefore desirable that the Allies show that they are ready to hear the representatives of any organized group in Russia," he noted in defense of a plan to invite all of Russia's competing political factions to a concurrent peace conference. If the Allies followed through on this course of action instead of continuing to use overt force, he argued, it "would bring about more reaction against the cause of the Bolsheviki than anything else the Allies could do" militarily.[82] Though this plan soon failed, it was not Wilson's last attempt to combat Bolshevism with weapons far removed from military might.

6.4 Motives

Instead of inadvertently stoking the fires of Bolshevism through foreign intervention, the Wilson administration worked to undercut its momentum through a fundamental reorganization of international order. The influence of this threat upon the Wilsonian vision of order is thus a crucial but often neglected factor in the narrative of the League of Nations' origins.

My goal in this section is to link advocacy for and implementation of the order principles articulated in the League Covenant to a concerted effort to

combat the emerging Bolshevik threat. To do so, I highlight four elements of
Wilsonian foreign policy in this period that are puzzling for more conventional
and inclusive narratives of the peace deliberations but that make more sense
through the lens ordering-to-exclude theory. They are: (a) the curious timing
as well as the content of Wilson's most famous speech about and blueprint for
world order, the Fourteen Points address; (b) Wilson's tortured relationship with
the concept of "self-determination" and that concept's circuitous path into the
Covenant via the League of Nations mandate system; (c) the strange demand of
Wilson and others for making the idea of "orderliness" a foundational component of the Covenant; and, finally, (d) the shocking failure of the United States to
join the very League—and the vision of order it represented—that had been the
brainchild of its own sitting president. We can best make sense of each of these
apparent puzzles, I argue, by employing the logic of ordering-to-exclude theory.

The first of these puzzles is the easiest to illuminate. Primary source evidence
suggests that both the timing and the content of Wilson's famous Fourteen Points
speech in January 1918 were clearly spurred by the Bolshevik Revolution. The
speech's specific content detailing for the first time Wilson's vision for postwar
order, as well as the perceived need for the president to give such a speech at that
particular time in the first place, reflected decisions made privately by Wilson
and his confidant Colonel House in a series of meetings at the end of 1917. These
meetings came as a direct result of the Bolsheviks seizing power in November
and then quickly reaching an armistice with Germany in December.[83] Wilson
reportedly framed the speech with three purposes in mind: answering and countering the Bolshevik messages to the world, appealing to the German Socialists to
prevent them from joining with the Bolsheviks, and serving notice to European
elites that the forthcoming peace settlement must be a liberal one.[84] The immense
appeal of Bolshevism to the war-weary and desperate peoples of central Europe
clearly troubled Wilson. As he noted in private on January 3, "it was evident that
if the appeal of the Bolsheviki was allowed to remain unanswered, if nothing were
done to counteract it, the effect would be great and would increase."[85]

In crafting the speech itself, Wilson and his advisers were careful not to *directly*
challenge Lenin for fear of legitimating the Bolshevik narrative of world events.[86]
This was advice they had received from a representative of the very Provisional
Government that the Bolsheviks had overthrown in Russia, who argued that not
answering the Bolsheviks at all or answering with overt hostility would only serve
their radical cause.[87] Yet Wilson's message to the world about these revolutionaries was nonetheless clear: "Whether their present leaders believe it or not, it is
our heartfelt desire and hope that some way may be opened whereby we may be
privileged to assist the people of Russia to attain their utmost hope of *liberty and
ordered peace*."[88]

It is too simple to frame the entire speech solely as a counter to Lenin. Yet what is clear is that it took the Bolshevik Revolution to finally convince Wilson to share with the world his blueprint for an alternative vision of order, a blueprint for which elites both at home and abroad had been clamoring in vain for months.[89] As we will see, Wilson's vision of order soon came to be seen as antithetical to the Bolshevik vision being concurrently developed by his rival in Russia.

6.4.1 Selling a Slippery Self-Determination

A second puzzling aspect of Wilsonian diplomacy from a conventional perspective was the American president's tortured relationship with the idea of "self-determination." The traditional narrative has been that Wilson consciously championed the elimination of imperialism around the world after the war. As a wealth of more recent historical work has shown, however, this was simply never the case.[90] Wilson did not in fact coin the term "self-determination," nor did he even use it in his Fourteen Points address. Instead, Lloyd George had been the first Allied leader to invoke the term in his notable Trades Union Speech days before Wilson's famous address. The American president, by contrast, was immediately skeptical of the concept upon first hearing it, confessing privately that "pushed to its extreme . . . the principle would mean the disruption of existing governments to an undefinable extent."[91]

This was consistent with Wilson's earlier thinking and writing. "Freedom is not giving the same government to all people, but wisely discriminating and dispensing laws according to the advancements of a people," he had argued years earlier.[92] In a 1919 press conference, he similarly posited that countries like Mexico and Costa Rica would not be admitted as full members to the League because "they've got to find themselves to qualify as respectable nations."[93] Simply put, Wilson had never envisioned immediate success for all national liberation campaigns, nor full equality for all the world's polities. He favored only a general spirit of self-government taking hold in select areas of the world through which groups of like-minded people might develop a sense of civic responsibility. At some point in the distant future, he reasoned, such developments would perhaps allow them to play a more direct part in their own governance.[94]

Ironically, it had been Lenin and the Bolsheviks, not Western elites, who had first brought the concept of self-determination into the global public consciousness. They had done so by advocating for the *immediate* emancipation of oppressed (that is, colonized) peoples *everywhere* around the world. At least as early as 1916, self-determination was a major facet of Lenin's publicly articulated worldview. He hardly could have been clearer on the topic than in a publication entitled *Theses on the Socialist Revolution and the Right of Nations to Self-Determination*:

Socialists must not only demand the unconditional and immediate liberation of the colonies without compensation—and this demand in its
political expression signifies nothing more nor less than the recognition of
the right of self-determination—but must render determined support to
the more revolutionary elements in the bourgeois-democratic movements
for national liberation in these countries and assist their rebellion—and
if need be, their revolutionary war—*against* the imperialist powers that
oppress them.[95]

"All nations have the right to self-determination," Lenin declared at the Eighth
Party Conference in 1919. "The vast majority, most likely nine-tenths of the population of the earth . . . come under this description" and must be liberated, he
argued.[96] Furthermore, the Bolsheviks believed that using violence in support of
this cause could be justified, or even glorified, so long as it served proper revolutionary ends. Lenin's foreign minister and ideological right hand, Leon Trotsky,
defended such action if it was "the violence that is supported by millions of workers and peasants and that is directed against a minority [the Western imperialist
powers] which seeks to keep the people in servitude; this violence is a holy and
historically progressive force."[97] Finally, it was the Bolsheviks who first brought
ideas of self-determination into actual diplomatic negotiations, demanding their
inclusion in the Brest-Litovsk negotiations with Germany in 1917.[98] This was
weeks before Lloyd George would give even a vague tip of his hat to the idea of
self-determination as a *possible* ordering principle in his Trade Unions Speech.

So, given that it was originally a Bolshevik proposition, and in combination
with Wilson's private trepidation over the core of the idea behind it, why did
the American president subsequently seem to embrace "self-determination" as
a necessary bedrock of the League of Nations? Evidence points to two motivations here, both of which are consistent with a logic of excluding. First,
when Wilson and other Allied leaders first began using the term, they were
most often doing so in reference to a very specific part of the world. It was not
in the colonies of the Global South—in Africa or Asia, for instance—but in
Central and Eastern Europe where these leaders actually meant to encourage
orderly emancipation from imperial rule, particularly with the founding of new
states like Poland, Czechoslovakia, and Yugoslavia. Furthermore, these leaders
advocated independence not out of altruistic or principled motives but from
strategic ones. Specifically, they believed that encouraging self-determination
for the peoples of the disintegrating Austro-Hungarian Empire (the tenth of
Wilson's Fourteen Points) would ensure that neither Imperial Germany nor the
Bolsheviks in Russia would gain further influence at the expense of crumbling
Austrian authority.

Wilson's "Inquiry"—the group of academics he had House assemble to help formulate the administration's peace plans—stressed to the president the need to square a delicate circle on this front. On the eve of the Fourteen Points address, for instance, the Inquiry recommended a policy in Eastern Europe characterized by the "stirring up of nationalist discontent, and then . . . refusing to accept the extreme logic of this discontent" that would otherwise entail allowing the region to fall into Bolshevist-like extremism and anarchy.[99] Poland was particularly important to Wilson, evidenced by the fact that the Poles were the only "self-determining" people to receive special attention in his Fourteen Points address.[100] By stoking the fires of nationalism and creating new nation-states in Central and Eastern Europe, administration officials aimed to create both ideological barriers (against Bolshevism) and political and geostrategic barriers (against Germany in the west and Russia in the east).[101] This is consistent with pathway #2 of ordering-to-exclude theory, "triggering tripwires" beyond which threatening forces cannot continue expanding their influence.

Wilson's second motive for co-opting the language of self-determination centered around both controlling a trend he was coming to see as inevitable—nationalist independence movements—and simultaneously working to discredit its more radical variant, Bolshevism. In practice, the American president himself did this through constantly emphasizing the virtues of *gradual* progress and the dangers of rapid and especially *violent* change. In the words of the historian Erez Manela, Wilson hoped that his evocation of the self-determination concept "would serve precisely in the opposite role, as a bulwark against radical, revolutionary challenges to existing orders, such as those he saw in the Russian and Mexican revolutions," while also helping to "remove the revolutionary impulse and promote change through rational, gradual reforms."[102] Soon after his Fourteen Points address, Wilson argued in front of Congress that "all well-defined national aspiration shall be accorded the utmost satisfaction that can be accorded them without introducing new or perpetuating old elements of discord and antagonism that would be likely in time to break the peace of Europe and consequently of the world."[103] Giving this theme more urgency in an address in Paris the next year, Wilson noted how

one of the things that has disturbed me in recent months is the unqualified hope that men have entertained everywhere of immediate emancipation from the things that have hampered and oppressed them. You cannot in human experience rush into the light. . . . You cannot throw off the habits of society immediately. . . . They must be slowly got rid of, or, rather, they must be slowly altered. . . . That is the process of law, if law is intelligently conceived.[104]

Aside from the newly designated states in Central and Eastern Europe stipu-lated in the treaties, the most concrete manifestation of the self-determination principle enacted in the settlement was the League of Nations mandate system. Before traveling to Paris, Wilson had only vaguely sketched the outlines of a trusteeship program for former colonies.[105] Yet upon arriving at the conference, he came to be greatly influenced by a pamphlet written by Jan Smuts, a prominent South African statesman and advocate for the British Commonwealth.[106] Smuts identified the postwar problem of many peoples "either incapable of or deficient in power of self-government." These people now nevertheless had to be helped lest they be driven "to that despair of the state which is the motive power behind Russian Bolshevism."[107] He used this predicament to establish a rationale for the League mandate system, and the conference subsequently relied on Smuts' vision more than any other in bringing this system into being.

In establishing the mandate system for the colonial world, the peacemakers at Paris performed another delicate balancing act. On the one hand, designing mechanisms to reform deeply unpopular colonial practices allowed Allied elites to demonstrate to the restless masses of the subjugated world—especially those who seemed most susceptible to Bolshevik appeals—that their imperial overlords were committed to ending the excesses of imperialism through gradual liberalization.[108]

On the other hand, doing so also helped these elites work to simultaneously counter the threat of revolutionary socialism. The decision in January of 1919 to classify and differentiate mandates into three categories of current "advancement" essentially legitimated the European powers' existing colonial holdings as well as their larger spheres of influence. Having the League give these empires at least a temporary stamp of legitimacy reaffirmed and even expanded the areas in which radical revolutionaries would not be tolerated by allowing the traditional powers to keep control over their imperial possessions (pathway #2, "triggering tripwires").[109]

More importantly, however, the mandate system undercut one of the greatest appeals of Lenin's message and model—speedy emancipation—by delegitimizing abrupt demands for immediate and violent self-determination (via pathway #3, "severing the social power" of the Bolsheviks' appeal). Coupled with the prohibi-tion on the use of interstate force (League rule #1)—a principle further bolstered in the League Covenant through Wilson's own forceful language regarding future disarmament—the Allies were able to speak to some demands for the liberaliza-tion of international relations while excluding others.[110]

6.4.2 Making Democracy Safe for the World

A third puzzling aspect of Allied diplomacy throughout this period was elite insistence—most notably from Wilson himself—on the "orderly" nature of the peace settlement. This included calls for League membership to be limited to *orderly* democracies (League rule #4) and advocacy for *orderly* transitions as the only legitimate form of international change (aspects of League rules #1 and 3). I contend that in both instances, the Allies and Wilson in particular intentionally emphasized orderliness to stigmatize alternative models of political representation, as well as alternative means of bringing about international change, that were both closely associated with the Bolsheviks specifically and radical socialist movements more generally.

First, it was Wilson who led the way in insisting that League membership be limited to *orderly* democratic states. While the president had publicly crusaded for a League made up of democracies, a wealth of evidence indicates that it was only the Western flavor of democratic institutions that truly fit his mold. Ray Stannard Baker, Wilson's confidant in Paris and later his biographer, captured some of the president's tortured thinking on this point: "With political revolution, up to the point of introducing democratic institutions of the type he knew and believed in, he was thoroughly in sympathy. With anything beyond and more radical—especially with social and economic revolution—he was just as thoroughly out of sympathy."[111] This description fits with the more conservative and orderly flavor of domestic liberalism Wilson had championed for years. Like his intellectual hero Edmund Burke, he consistently highlighted the peaceful and orderly nature of the American Revolution prior to his presidency, contrasting America's process of independence favorably with the types of violent and radical social revolutions he abhorred.[112] "Wilson's 'good society' was that of the nineteenth century liberal," adds historian John Thompson: "a self-disciplined, ordered society adhering to moral principles and based on the consent of the governed," one where "social change was a gradual and continual process, which could not be forced."[113]

Speaking to Thompson's last point—social change—the second facet of Wilson's interest in orderliness came in his consistent championing of gradual and peaceful progress against rapid and violent change. As highlighted earlier, the president repeatedly made the case that violence of any sort remained a dangerous and illegitimate means to achieve one's objectives, no matter how lofty and legitimate the end goals might be. "The danger of conflagrations and revolutions menaces all organized states if the necessary precautions are not taken in time to assure the maintenance of order and the triumph of law," he confided to the French ambassador in September 1918.[114] And as he imaginatively argued in his Armistice Address two months later,

> excesses accomplish nothing. Unhappy Russia has furnished abundant recent proof of that. Disorder immediately defeats itself. . . . The peoples who have but just come out from under the yoke of arbitrary government

and who are now coming at last into their freedom will never find the trea-
sures of liberty they are in search of if they look for them by the light of
the torch. They will find that every pathway that is stained with blood of
their own brothers leads to the wilderness, not to the seat of their hope.[115]

In legitimating a particular conception of both democracy and change, Wilson
led the Allies in using the idea of orderliness to stigmatize their greatest perceived
threats: the Bolshevik ideological model along with Bolshevik promises of speedy
emancipation through violent worldwide revolution. On the latter—stigmatizing
rapid and radical change—the president seemed almost obsessed with promoting
the idea of orderly transition. The best way to "cure" radicalism, he argued at the
peace conference, was through a process of "constant discussion and a slow process
of reform."[116] He began the preamble to his first draft of the League Covenant with
the stated goal of securing "peace, security, and orderly government by the prescrip-
tion of open and honorable relations between nations."[117] "Disordered society is
dissolved society," he later declared. "There is no society when there is not settled
and calculable order. . . . The conditions of civilized life must be purified and per-
fected, and if we do not have peace, that is impossible."[118] Domestic order was a
prerequisite for peace and prosperity, he argued, reiterating his belief "that the most
disastrous thing that can happen to the underman, to the man who is suffering, to
the man who has not had his rights, is to destroy public order."[119]

This narrative intensified throughout the president's US speaking tour in the
summer and fall of 1919, where the contrast he drew between his idea of orderly
change and Bolshevik methods became even clearer. At one point, Wilson referred
to Bolshevik ideas as "the poison of disorder, the poison of revolt, the poison
of chaos," something that "is the negation of everything that is American."[120] At
another, he posited that "Minorities have often been right and majorities wrong,
but minorities cease to be right when they use the wrong means to make their
opinions prevail. We must have peaceful means."[121] By institutionalizing an end
to violent conflict, he sought to outlaw the means through which the adversary could most effectively expand. "Liberty is a thing of slow construction," he
argued in St. Paul, Minnesota. The "lesson is that nobody can be free where there
is not public order and authority."[122] This vision not only contained no room for
Lenin's revolutionary model for speedy emancipation through violent class war,
but it was in large part explicitly designed to exclude it.

In regard to the other target of the Allies' "orderliness" emphasis—
stigmatizing radical regimes as a principle of order membership—the Covenant's
hazy definition of democratic institutions afforded Western leaders the freedom
to include or exclude whichever polities they desired in the League of Nations. In
practice, this meant that they were easily able to legitimize the total exclusion of

Germany and Russia from both the peace conference and the League itself. This was not simply the work of the more recalcitrant Allies like France but a preference of Wilson himself. In public and private, he consistently articulated his view that Germany would be prohibited from joining the League until it had made meaningful changes.[123] "The membership is open only to self-governing nations," Wilson declared on his speaking tour. "Germany is for the present excluded, because she must prove that she has changed the processes of her constitution and the purposes of her policy."[124] His indictment of Germany here also harkens back to an important point made earlier about the Covenant's orderly democracy membership requirement: for Wilson, membership standards were predicated not just on domestic structures but also on international-level behavior.

The promotion of orderly democratic regimes in the Covenant allowed the Allies to stigmatize not just the German and Russian *states* but also the Imperial and Bolshevik *models* of statehood and behavior. This was done most concretely via Covenant Article XI, that which declared it "the friendly right of each [member state] to draw the attention" of the League "to any circumstances affecting international intercourse which threaten to disturb international peace or the good understanding between nations upon which peace depends."[125] This provision came to be seen by supporters and opponents alike as the League's version of the Holy Alliance (chapter 5), as it would allow members to make all revolutions the League's business while picking and choosing which ones would be allowed to proceed or be stamped out.[126] Wilson occasionally referred to Article XI as his favorite of the Covenant, and on his speaking tour he played up its ability to be used as a bulwark against Bolshevism.[127]

Even while the precise contours of the orderly democracy "in group" were vague, it wouldn't have been difficult for observers to comprehend that following the path of "out-group" pariahs like the Bolsheviks would earn them the wrath of the Western powers. Allied advocacy for this orderly democracy principle thus demonstrated to other nations, especially those that were newly "self-determining," that following Russia's recent trajectory would lead to a path of isolation from the community of nations and away from the protections this community afforded to weak states through the League's rules of behavior (pathway #1, "commonalities for contrast"). "We are at present helpless to assist Russia, because there are no responsible channels through which we can assist her," Wilson noted on his speaking tour, as if in warning to other polities contemplating the Bolshevik path to modernity. "Our heart goes out to her, but the world is disordered."[128] The meaning behind these sentiments was clear: The League would not welcome regimes that were considered radical or recalcitrant, even if the precise contours of those things had been left, perhaps intentionally, unclear in the League Covenant.

It would be misleading to claim that the perceived Bolshevik threat motivated *all* the ideas behind Allied or even just American order preferences. Records indicate, after all, that Wilson and others on both sides of the Atlantic had been thinking about a momentous institutionalization of world politics (League rules #1 and 2) for years prior to the Bolshevik Revolution in Russia.[129] Yet before the emergence of a Bolshevik threat, the specific ideas for institutionalization later codified in the Covenant were far from fully formed in any of its authors' minds, least of all Wilson's.[130] His first Covenant draft, for instance, contained no mention of colonial mandates, democratic membership requirements, or the promise of humane labor conditions. All of these important elements were only added later, once Wilson was in Paris, and at a time when the transnational threat of Bolshevism was at its apex.[131]

In sum, there is compelling evidence that the Wilsonian vision of order, so often thought to be the embodiment of international liberalism, was actuality designed to a surprising degree to liberalize the principles of order just enough to, first, ensure the system's survival against radical challenges, and second, better serve America's increasingly global interests. Through encouraging *limited* self-determination and *orderly* democratization (League rules #3 and 4), this new order would correct for some of the excesses of balance-of-power imperialism. But more important to the new order's proponents was demonstrating that a liberalized version of the status quo could persevere even in revolutionary times, a message they hoped would forestall the appeal of Lenin's calls for radical upheaval. "Although many misconceived his purpose, fundamentally Wilson was a conservative, hoping to preserve the status quo by improving it," writes Thompson.[132] Consistent with hypothesis 1B of ordering-to-exclude theory, their hope was that elements of this revised order would neutralize the most ominous elements of the Bolshevik threat.

If the system worked well enough in this regard, perhaps a neutered Russia could even be invited back into this order somewhere down the road. "If the Bolsheviks really accepted the conditions and stopped their aggression upon their neighbors" in exchange for League membership, argued one of Lloyd George's chief advisers, "they would in fact [begin] to cease being Bolsheviks."[133] Until that time, however, they were to be completely excluded from all elements of the new order embodied in the League of Nations.

6.4.3 Explaining Wilson's Failure

A final surprising development of the Wilsonian order-building saga remains perhaps the most puzzling of all: why, after getting so much of what American statesmen supposedly pushed for in Paris, would the United States then turn around and reject that very settlement? None of the liberal alternative arguments discussed earlier are able to adequately account for the ultimate failure of the United States to embrace and ratify the Wilsonian vision of order. Ikenberry admits as much for the binding perspective, conceding that his "model cannot account fully for the failure of the American government to ratify some version of the peace agreement." Instead, he lays the blame primarily on "Wilson's own highly personal and stubborn convictions" for not accepting modifications made to the Covenant and the larger treaty by the US Senate.[134] Ikenberry is not alone here, as numerous scholars of the era invoke Wilson's personal unwillingness to budge or bargain to explain the otherwise inexplicable decision of the United States Senate to reject the League Covenant.[135] Because this thesis—that Wilson's personal failures derailed American entry into the League—is one that is so powerful and prevalent in the historiography of the era, I conclude the chapter by inspecting it more closely.

Two specific arguments are often made about President Wilson's failings in the negotiations following the First World War: (a) He was naïve to or ignorant of the backlash he would receive back home for conceding so much to the Allies in Paris regarding the punitive terms imposed against Germany;[136] and/or (b) once he had negotiated the League Covenant in Paris, he stubbornly refused to compromise with his Senate critics at home, many of whom had legitimate concerns over US obligations but likely could have still supported some version of American participation. Both arguments perform surprisingly poorly when assessed against the evidence, however.

Contrary to the first argument—the president giving away too much in Paris—Wilson himself often demonstrated his understanding of the dangers of imposing too harsh of terms against Germany in the Versailles Treaty. But he also recognized that keeping France—whose leaders he knew were ambivalent on the need for a League of Nations—onboard for his vision of postwar stability was critical to its overall success. As Leffler summarizes, "there was considerable tension between Wilson's sympathy for France and his desire to reintegrate Germany into a prosperous world order, between his concern for French security and his antipathy toward balance of power politics, and between his desire to preserve Allied unity and his aversion to alliances." Not unrealistically, perhaps, Wilson hoped that "these apparent inconsistencies and contradictions could be reconciled through the creation of the League of Nations," an organization that would remain fluid and flexible enough to deal with formidable future challenges.[137]

On the other hand, he was only willing to go as far as he believed the US Senate would allow him in accommodating France on the structure of the League. "We must make a distinction between what is possible and what is not," he argued in opposing a French proposal to give the League a permanent standing army comprised of compulsory member-state contributions. "To propose to realize unity of command in time of peace, would be to put forward a proposal that no nation would accept."[138] One can fault Wilson's precise calculation on the details here, but his focus on achieving maximum Allied buy-in yet balancing it with a realistic vision of the League that his own Senate could accept was certainly a defensible endeavor.

Regarding the second argument—Wilson's stubbornness in the face of legitimate League criticism at home—it is true that the president often seemed at his most obstinate on the issue of his Senate opponents' "reservations" to the Covenant. Yet contrary to the larger narrative that Wilson would never negotiate, the president actually worked hard to address some of their most serious critiques before the treaty officially came to a vote on the Senate floor. Upon his return to Paris in the summer of 1919, he succeeded in modifying the Covenant to address critics' concerns regarding: member freedom to exit the League (made easier with a clause inserted into Article 1); the League's effects on the Monroe Doctrine (a special exemption was inserted into Article 21); and the League's ability to exercise judgment on members' domestic issues (a clarification on its limits was inserted into Article 15).[139]

Debate continues over whether the treaty could have cleared the Senate had Wilson accepted passage with *additional* reservations presented by recalcitrant senators on top of the ones he had just succeeded in addressing in Paris.[140] Yet proponents of this view fail to note that further amendments would have necessitated sending the entire Versailles Treaty back to its other signatories, further complicating the process of reaching a final agreement. And because states like France had already expressed concerns about the sincerity of America's security commitment to Europe under its existing terms, Wilson giving in to yet another round of Senate reservations might have irreparably harmed the Allied unity the president saw as so crucial to the League's success. Once again, one can fault particular aspects of Wilson's negotiating skill here, yet do so without succumbing to the faulty view that a more reasonable individual in his place could have fundamentally changed the course of history.

By contrast, and without falling back on Wilson's personal failings, ordering-to-exclude theory can account for the seeming anomaly of America's failure to join the League of Nations. The principal problem throughout Wilson's negotiations both abroad and at home remained that *there were two vastly different views about the most dangerous forces on the horizon in world politics.* While Wilson and many of his advisers were most concerned with the radical and revolutionary socialist threat manifested by the Bolshevik regime, it was the more traditional state power threat of German dominance over Europe that occupied the attention of states like France (perhaps understandably)[141] and Wilson's Republican opponents at home (perhaps less understandably).[142]

As excluding hypothesis 1C would predict, those elites that were focused more on traditional state power threats remained less convinced of the need for such deep changes to the fabric of international order compared with those who believed they were witnessing the birth of a revolutionary ideological menace in Russia.[143] "The Conservatives do not realize what forces are loose in the world at the present time," Wilson privately lamented while sailing to Paris. "Liberalism is the only thing that can save civilization from chaos—from a flood of ultra-radicalism that will swamp the world."[144] As we would expect from hypothesis 1A, lack of consensus on the nature and urgency of the threat will drastically decrease the likelihood of strong and unified preferences for deep changes to international order.[145] In sum, the failures of important Allied and American elites to agree on the most threatening forces in world politics likely would have caused as many difficulties for *any* adept leader as they did for Woodrow Wilson after the First World War. Wilson's plight thus remains tragic, even as he was decidedly *not* the inclusive order-building hero that liberal internationalists have made him out to be.

For all that has been written about Wilsonian diplomacy in the hundred years hence, it was not a Western liberal who captured the essence of Woodrow Wilson's diplomacy in Paris in 1919 but, ironically, a contemporary of his who observed the president from a distant and perhaps surprising vantage point. "Comparing the Versailles conference to the congresses of Vienna, Paris and Berlin in the nineteenth century," Soviet Commissar for Foreign Affairs Georgy Chicherin argued in a 1919 article that "the current meeting was simply a continuation of the European concert of reaction, directed now against the world proletarian revolution," casting Clemenceau as Metternich and Wilson as Tsar Alexander.[146] Perhaps surprisingly, Chicherin got the hard part—the plot—right, but the easier task—the casting call—wrong. For by playing the role of the postwar order's most important architect in 1919, Wilson was every bit as cunning, farsighted, and strategic—though perhaps only less adept at navigating the treacherous waters of domestic politics—as Klemens von Metternich had been a century before him.

7

Birthing the Liberal International Order

FOR MANY OBSERVERS of history, the liberal order forged after the Second World War appears to be fundamentally distinct from international orders of the past. Policymakers and scholars often attribute this break to a simple, single development: the United States of America becoming the first truly liberal hegemonic actor in history. A "distinctive type of international order was constructed after World War II," argues John Ikenberry. At this moment of opportunity, "the United States engaged in the most ambitious and far-reaching liberal order building the world had yet seen" to create "a hierarchical system that was built on both American power dominance and liberal principles of governance." While America would hold some privileges as its natural leader, "its power advantages were muted and mediated by an array of postwar rules, institutions, and reciprocal political processes" where, for the first time, "weaker and secondary states were given institutionalized access to the exercise of [the hegemon's] power."[1] Many prominent American politicians and foreign policy practitioners—as well as a good number of IR scholars[2]—agree with this sentiment, which has practically been embraced as conventional wisdom. When it comes to international order building, this consensus suggests, the United States of America simply "does it differently."

One of the many elements that make this case unique is the fact that there were actually multiple layers of order built after World War II. More specifically, there was a universalist *global* order vision—manifested in the United Nations system—and a smaller *Western* order vision—comprised of the Bretton Woods economic and NATO security systems. Observers often posit that these layers were complementary, representing an evolving but not contradictory strategy by the United States to build a multilayered institutional order that would preserve world peace and enhance global prosperity. For instance, Ikenberry conceives of the Western vision as an inner layer, a "Western core of the order ... built among democratic societies and organized around layers of institutions" that would gradually allow the thicker principles of that core to diffuse outward to other regions of the world.[3]

On both of these points reflecting the conventional wisdom, I beg to differ. Against the first point, I argue that the order changes advocated by American leaders after the Second World War—while they were certainly the most far-reaching and complex the world has ever known—can nonetheless still be best explained by the logic of excluding threats. That makes American motives for order construction unexceptional compared to those of prior order builders. Against the second point, I argue that the Western order was never intended to fit within the global one. Instead, Western order emerged as an *alternative* to global order only when that system unexpectedly failed to deliver on what its founders had envisioned. The story of order building after World War II, I posit, is the extraordinary transition away from a vision of global order to a more circumscribed and exclusive Western vision of order.

Bringing both of these points together, I argue in this chapter that this transition can be best explained by American leaders' shifting threat perceptions during this extraordinary period of order construction. While they began with a global plan for order that served their interests so long as they were most focused on the Nazi/fascist threat, US elites soon shifted to a more exclusive and adversarial Western order idea as they became increasingly wary of the threat posed by their former wartime ally, the Soviet Union.[4] In short, I argue that American apprehension over the daunting material and ideological gains made by the USSR in the late 1940s—coupled with increasing fears about Soviet intentions—is the single most important element in explaining the United States' founding blueprint for a liberal international order that remains with us to this day.

Whereas the last chapter assessed a hard case study for ordering-to-exclude theory, this chapter analyzes what is actually a "most likely" and therefore "crucial" case for the theory.[5] Baldly stated, it is not difficult to link America's construction of the liberal international order to the looming threat of Soviet power and communist ideology, both significantly more potent in the 1940s than they had been in the 1910s (chapter 6). It has only been a more recent trend to decouple the origins of the liberal order from the origins of the Cold War, as a number of scholars have sought to argue that this order's origins have their own separate history and logic.[6] In this chapter, I seek to recouple them.[7]

The construction of the liberal international order was complex and multifaceted, stretching over numerous years, locations, leaders, and negotiations. There was no single equivalent to the 1919 Paris Peace Conference. Instead, aspects of the new order were proposed, debated, and negotiated at numerous formal conferences and informal meetings across time and space. More specifically, the principles of the emerging *global* order were consecrated at conferences in Washington (Dumbarton Oaks, 1944) and San Francisco (1945), while those of the more circumscribed *Western* order came predominately in the negotiations over finance in Bretton Woods, New Hampshire, in 1944, over US aid to Europe in Paris and Washington in 1947, and over Western security cooperation in Washington in 1948 and 1949. Various aspects of both order visions were also debated at the wartime summits between the "Big Three" actors in Tehran (1943), Yalta and Potsdam (1945), and in numerous meetings of the Council of Foreign Ministers (CFM) between 1945 and 1948.

The sheer scale and complexity of this period warrants another chapter-long investigation of a single case. Yet in this instance, my priority returns once again to breadth of explanation over depth. Between the origins of the Cold War and the birth of the United Nations, Bretton Woods institutions, Marshall Plan and NATO, the postwar era of the 1940s is perhaps the most studied in modern history. The relevant events worthy of analysis are ubiquitous. The way these events fit together is complex and at times contradictory. And the documentary and secondary historical evidence on each of them is vast. For these reasons, my principal objective is to provide a broad overview of the changing logic of American order building in the 1940s rather than a comprehensive analysis of all these developments. Above all, I aim to demonstrate how the US movement away from a global order vision and toward a Western-oriented one can best be seen as a logical and even effective response to the most threatening aspects of the perceived and emerging Soviet menace. Accordingly, I divide this postwar period in two, focusing first on American order building *before* the Soviet threat became fully manifest—up until 1946—and then on American order building *after* elite focus and fear had fully shifted to the USSR—in and after 1946. Before getting there, however, I begin with a broad overview of the American order-building project in and after the Second World War.

7.1 *American Order Preferences after World War II*

Much more than in 1919, the United States was truly hegemonic by 1944. The extent of its preponderance in virtually every measure of national power—exports, gold reserves, standard of living, per capita productivity, military spending, and military technology—was unprecedented in modern history.[8] The traditional European powerhouses were left utterly defeated (Germany) or greatly weakened (France and Great Britain). France had been invaded and occupied, its true government in exile in London, while Britain was considerably crippled by the war.[9] That said, Prime Minister Winston Churchill was a veteran statesman and master tactician. Though he and American President Franklin Delano Roosevelt (FDR) had held mixed feelings about one another before formally meeting as their countries' respective leaders, they formed a close partnership in 1941 that lasted until Roosevelt's death, a relationship that gave Britain an important role in aspects of the postwar planning.

Aside from the United States, the only other country that could be considered a great power at war's end was the Soviet Union, whose massive army was spread over half of Europe by war's end. Yet while its resource base and population served as natural strengths, the economic and especially the human costs of the war—27 million Soviets dead—had been staggering. Adding to this was the fact that achieving their vast military might at the orders of a brutal and paranoid despot—Generalissimo Joseph Stalin—had come at a high cost paid by millions of starving and enslaved Russians in the years before the war. "In essence," writes the historian Paul Kennedy, "the Russia of 1945 was a military giant, and, at the same time, economically poor, deprived, and unbalanced."[10] In short, the United States had an enormous opportunity to set the agenda for international order after the Second World War, perhaps the greatest such opportunity in modern history.

Though no single meeting or resolution captured every significant aspect of the new vision for order, one came close. In the Atlantic Charter of 1941, Roosevelt and Churchill explicitly enumerated "certain common principles in the national policies of their respective countries on which they base[d] their hopes for a better future for the world." Their declaration was based in part on Roosevelt's address earlier in the year in which he articulated "four freedoms": of speech, of religion, from (economic) want, and from fear (of war).[11] The Atlantic Charter was only an aspirational statement of principles, and as such was hardly binding. Yet FDR saw its maxims as universal and accordingly declared that it "didn't refer only to the Atlantic. It referred to the whole world." It only "happened to be made on the Atlantic Ocean."[12] Overall, the Charter "articulated a community of Anglo-American values to complement the new Atlanticist framework for U.S. security," argues the historian David Reynolds. "The global impact of the declaration was profound."[13]

It was through the Atlantic Charter that Roosevelt and Churchill first consecrated their postwar goals and revealed them to the world. In particular, they articulated three general principles that would serve as the foundation for more concrete order changes in subsequent years: greater economic openness, stability, and standardization in the international system; greater collective security guarantees through a modified great power concert; and greater domestic expectations that regimes would provide for their citizens' welfare. While the first two principles were important, it was the third—domestic welfare—that represented the Charter's most striking departure from the past.[14] "It posited the individual as being in a relationship with a wider international order," writes the historian Elizabeth Borgwardt, "and, by extension, implied that the individual" and no longer only the state "was a legitimate object of international concern."[15]

7.1.1 Envisioning a Global Order

The United Nations organization (UN) was envisioned to be the primary vehicle for achieving the Atlantic Charter's aims. It was negotiated at the Dumbarton Oaks estate in Georgetown in the summer of 1944 and then in more formal proceedings the following summer in San Francisco.[16] Much like the League of Nations, its primary purpose was to avert destructive and destabilizing wars. Unlike the League Covenant, however, the UN Charter aspired to form a collective security system based less on moral or legal obligation than on ensuring both the material capacity and the political will necessary for deterring major threats to international security.

Specifically, the UN Charter aimed to facilitate true collective security through reasserting an important order principle of behavior: **the reaffirmation of the special status and privileges of the great powers.** Not since the Concert of Europe had an international agreement so formally differentiated great powers from "normal" states.[17] This special status was codified in the United Nations Security Council (UNSC), an entity that was to enjoy precedence over all other organs of the United Nations.

The League of Nations had also contained a Council dominated by great powers. But in a number of ways, the UNSC's great powers were privileged far beyond those of the League's Executive Council. First, League decisions had to have unanimous support, thereby giving significant influence to the Council's non-great powers. In the UNSC, by contrast, only a supermajority would be needed to pass resolutions. Second, the great power permanent members of the UNSC were granted the enormous institutional advantage of an unconditional veto, a controversial benefit never afforded to the leading states of the League's Council.[18] Third, and most importantly, on issues where the Council and Assembly might have both claimed jurisdiction in the League, the UN Charter gave the UNSC clear authority over the most consequential issues.[19] In the League Covenant there was both greater balance between the Assembly and Council and greater ambiguity about their powers relative to one another.[20] In the UN Charter, by contrast, the UNSC was given both the tremendous authority to "determine the *existence* of any threat to the peace, breach of the peace, or act of aggression" as well as the power to decide how to deal with those threats.[21]

The reaffirmation and extension of great power privileges was important. Yet it was also the only major rule of this *global* vision of order to be successfully enacted and subsequently observed after World War II. Unsuccessful efforts were made to enact others. First, the UN Charter contained more progressive language on self-determination than had the League Covenant, suggesting to some that colonial independence had become, by rule, an inevitability. In its actual details, however, the subsequent United Nations Trusteeship Council did not significantly differ from the League's mandate system.[22] Second, the great powers attempted to establish an effective collective security mechanism for the UNSC. In one sense this was begun via the structure of the UNSC itself. But the next logical and planned step—an integrated, multinational fighting force ready for rapid deployment by the Security Council—never materialized, and the idea of truly global collective security slowly withered away.[23] Third, the United States and its wartime allies had also sought more tangible membership principles for the UN. In its final form, the Charter called for membership predicated on democratic institutions and open economic exchange. Yet from the beginning these principles were treated as merely aspirational, and any hope of enforcing them quickly faded with the emergence of Cold War tensions. In fact, *all* of these global order aspirations failed to materialize in large part because of emerging fault lines between West and East, rifts I contend led to fundamental changes in American leaders' order preferences.

7.1.2 Enacting a Western Order

For the first time in history, and for reasons explored throughout this chapter, the dominant actors succeeded in building multiple orders, or at least multiple layers of order, after World War II. Alongside the global order described in the prior section, some leaders also sought to build what became a less-than-global *Western* variant of order.

Originally meant to complement the UN's focus on security, the Bretton Woods system became a key component of this more circumscribed order vision instead. The United Nations Monetary and Financial Conference in Bretton Woods, New Hampshire, produced two formal organizations, the International Bank for Reconstruction and Development (IBRD, or World Bank) and the International Monetary Fund (IMF).[24] Through these organizations—particularly the IMF—Western leaders enacted two important rule changes that became foundational principles of the Western order. First, **they pledged to work multilaterally on economic issues in the interest of advancing economic openness, economic standardization, and international economic stability (liberal order rule #1).** Its founding Articles of Agreement identified as the IMF's principal objectives to (a) "promote international monetary cooperation through a permanent institution"; (b) "promote exchange stability, to maintain orderly exchange arrangements among members, and to avoid competitive exchange depreciation"; and (c) set up "a multilateral system of payments" between members that would all serve to "shorten the duration and lessen the degree of disequilibrium in the international balances of payments of members."[25]

Second, Bretton Woods also advanced a new standard of membership: **governments would now be held more directly responsible for the general welfare of their citizens (liberal order rule #2)**. The focus here was on basic human and, above all, economic rights. The Bretton Woods framers agreed that the permanently open global economy they were creating (via liberal order rule #1) necessitated a second principle to ensure that governments would protect their citizens from the ebb and flow of the free market.[26] Regimes were now expected to take greater responsibility for national employment as well as to ensure their citizens access to an assortment of basic social services.

To be sure, this principle was not as formally negotiated and prominently celebrated as behavior rule #1; yet it was nevertheless still codified in the IMF Articles of Agreement, which pledged "to facilitate the expansion and *balanced* growth of international trade" in a way that would "contribute thereby to the promotion and maintenance of high levels of employment and real income and to the development of the productive resources of all members as primary objectives of economic policy."[27] Together, argues Borgwardt, the two foundational order principles of Bretton Woods served "two interlocking goals—global economic stability and local individual security" for the citizens of member countries, a combination that has come to be known as "embedded liberalism."[28]

The other new principles of this Western order vision either focused more on security or transcended the economic/security divide altogether. Perhaps the principle most central to this entire vision was a behavior rule that proved to be truly novel: **the establishment of a liberal security community and society among the Atlantic democracies that, above all, promoted porous boundaries between members (liberal order rule #3)**. This principle was first consecrated in the American decisions in 1947 to send extraordinary amounts of aid to Europe through the European Recovery Program (ERP), more commonly known as the Marshall Plan. US officials both publicly and privately advocated for the ERP by stressing America's cultural and ideological ties with Western Europe, a point discussed in more detail later in the chapter.[29] This principle was later strengthened in the declarations of common cultural and civilizational heritage that were at the heart of NATO.[30] Signatories to the North Atlantic Treaty (NAT) in 1949 pledged to "safeguard the freedom, common heritage and civilization of their peoples, founded on the principles of democracy, individual liberty and the rule of law."[31] As Dean Acheson would later describe it, the security arrangement was "far more than a defensive arrangement. It is an affirmation of the moral and spiritual values which we hold in common."[32]

Importantly, NATO was *not* simply a smaller version of the United Nations. Where the UN failed to achieve a reliable collectively security mechanism, NATO resoundingly succeeded in achieving **a new behavior rule for true collective security (liberal order rule #4)**. Article 5 of the NAT, the treaty's core provision, stated that an attack against one NATO member was to be considered an attack against all members.[33] While the organization went through notable changes in its early years and the US eventually achieved a special role and privileged status within it, NATO nonetheless succeeded in building a true multilateral burden-sharing security apparatus the likes of which the UN did not and would never even approximate.

Yet NATO did more than simply correct for the UN's institutional defects. It also consecrated an explicit **membership requirement for its signatories to maintain free and representative political institutions (liberal order rule #5)**. Where membership principles quickly proved to be empty rhetoric in the UN, they became a tangible reality in NATO. New membership was contingent upon the unanimous consent of existing members and open only to "any other European State in a position to further the principles of this Treaty and to contribute to the security of the North Atlantic area."[34] NATO was thus not only a true collective security organization but also an organization among democracies.[35]

Figure 7.1 depicts the organization and logic of American order-building efforts after World War II. The Atlantic Charter was the linchpin, a declaration

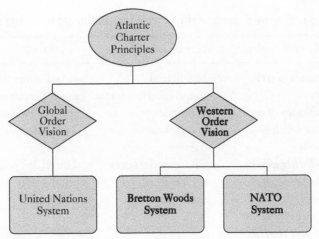

FIGURE 7.1 The logic of American order building after World War II.

of general objectives that would remain the foundation of both visions of order. Roosevelt intended to implement its principles alongside Churchill and Stalin via the United Nations. As we will see, however, events intervened in ways that soon led Western leaders to doubt the UN's ability to deliver on its objectives. When this happened, the United States pivoted instead to fortifying a smaller and more exclusive Western order vision. Through the Bretton Woods and NATO systems, they implemented sweeping changes to order, some of which they had previously attempted through the UN.

The totality of these order changes is summarized in Table 7.1. This table highlights that as important as the UN seemingly was, in the context of international order it really only reiterated and strengthened a prior order principle—the supremacy of the great powers—rather than advancing any new ones. Instead, the major changes to order that we most associate with the postwar era came via the new institutions of the *Western* order—Bretton Woods and NATO—rather than the United Nations.

As noted in the chapter introduction, John Ikenberry has also highlighted a distinction between global and Western orders after World War II. The difference, however, is that he depicts the relationship between these order visions as complementary. I advance an alternative interpretation. In my view, the Western order does not neatly fit within the larger global order vision, in large part because it was never intended to do so. Instead, the Western vision of order emerged as an alternative only *after* the global vision unexpectedly failed to deliver on its initial promise.[36] In the two major sections of the chapter that follow, I seek to further explicate this interpretation by examining American motivations for order

Table 7.1 Proposed Rules of the Liberal International Order, 1944–1949

United Nations	Bretton Woods	NATO
Reaffirmation of great power supremacy	Multilateral cooperation to advance economic openness, standardization, and stability	Establishment of security community with porous boundaries
Liberalization of colonial mandates/trusteeship system (FAILED)		*True collective security*
True collective security with tangible guarantees (FAILED)	Greater social safety net membership requirement	*Liberal democracy membership requirement*
Democracy member requirement (FAILED)		

building throughout the 1940s, both before and after the perceived threat emanating from the USSR became manifest.

7.2 Postwar Order, Take One

Even without the emergence of the Soviet threat, the United States would have
advocated for a United Nations system encompassed within a broader vision of
global order. This does not mean that ordering-to-exclude theory is unhelpful
for explaining American order preferences prior to the emergence of Cold War
tensions, however. To the contrary, I argue in this section that the origins of the
UN and especially the order principles behind the Bretton Woods institutions
still broadly fit with the theory's core expectations. That the Soviets were not initially excluded from either of these systems is not a violation of the theory but an
affirmation of it, since US threat perceptions were not focused on the USSR in
1944–1945. Moreover, once we have a clearer understanding of what entities *did*
worry US elites in this period, it becomes clear that ordering-to-exclude theory
actually performs quite well in explaining American order preferences prior to
the emergence of the Cold War.

7.2.1 Threats to 1946

Not surprisingly, in the midst of World War II American elites' initial attention
was on the threat posed by Nazi Germany and the fascist ideological model, not
the USSR and communism. Three aspects of this threat seemed to have most
concerned FDR.

First was the threat of fascism as an ideological model. The president identified it as "the ideological challenge to 'our American civilization'" in a critical
fireside chat in late 1940, agreeing with Adolf Hitler's recent pronouncement
that "there are two worlds that stand opposed to each other" with no chance of
coexistence. "They may talk of a 'new order' in the world," warned Roosevelt,
"but what they have in mind is only a revival of the oldest and the worst tyranny.
In that there is no liberty, no religion, no hope."[37] Like many Americans, FDR
particularly abhorred fascism's militant nationalism and, in the case of Nazism,
its focus on racial cleavages.[38] This likely contributed to his belief that there
would be an international "race war" in the near future unless drastic measures
were taken to reverse the subjugation of dependent peoples across the world.[39] In
this sense, the Nazi threat only strengthened the president's anti-colonial feelings
and made eliminating colonial empires a cornerstone of his postwar vision.

Second, and aside from ideology, Roosevelt believed that fascism promoted
extremely dangerous economic policies of the type that had so decimated the

global economy in the 1930s, perhaps even causing the Second World War. John Ruggie effectively describes the nature of the fascist economic order:

> Nazi Germany had negotiated with and/or imposed on its trading partners a series of trade and monetary clearing arrangements. Each was specific to a particular trading partner, who often became locked into dependence on Germany. This was achieved by, for example, Germany importing more from its trading partners than it exported to them, but requiring them to liquidate their claims on Germany through reinvestment there or by purchasing deliberately overpriced German goods.[40]

The connections between fascism, mercantilist economic policies, and autarkic spheres of influence were identified early and often by American policymakers. As was repeatedly stressed by Cordell Hull's State Department, "the connection between politics and economics was central to the very way Nazism was interpreted as a regime. American commentators viewed Nazism as an abusive political economy: a cartel of monopolists who subordinated the public sphere to private forces."[41] Giving voice to this fear as early as 1938, Roosevelt argued that the "liberty of a democracy is not safe if the people tolerate the growth of private power to the point where it becomes stronger than their democratic state itself. That, in its essence, is Fascism."[42] This aspect of Nazism convinced elites that an open economic order free from autarkic spheres of influence would be critical for achieving postwar peace.

Third, as the tide gradually turned against Hitler, American elites also feared for the revitalization of German power even once Nazism was vanquished. Roosevelt therefore maintained that Germany would have to be partitioned and most likely disarmed after the war, and even surprised Churchill at the Casablanca Conference by announcing that the Allies would insist upon nothing less than the unconditional surrender of the Axis powers.[43] In administration debates between those that would revitalize Germany and those that would more harshly punish and partition her, FDR declared, "Most decidedly I belong to the latter school."[44]

Perhaps surprisingly, this apprehension over Germany did *not* come with a corresponding fear of Russia. Far from fearing the Soviets, in fact, Roosevelt believed that continued cooperation with Russia would be a crucial component of the global order's success. He had engaged in a public information campaign—starting after his confidant Harry Hopkins's trip to Moscow in 1941—to make the USSR appear more tolerable, tolerant, and democratic than Nazi Germany and its fascist allies.[45] By 1942, and through to his death in 1945, he worked to bring Stalin into "the family circle," enlisting the Soviets as a permanent partner for securing postwar stability.[46] He considered the USSR the most important power for his "Four Policemen" consortium that would be responsible for managing a largely disarmed world of regions after the war.[47]

That Roosevelt so valued cooperation with the Russians demonstrated not only his belief that the Soviets would possess extraordinary power after the war but also a conviction that they were actually in agreement with the United States on many important issues. Ideologically, they were aligned with the American aversion to imperialism and desire to rid the world of colonial empires. Similarly, no one was more adamant than Stalin on the necessity of dismembering German power. The possibility of the Soviets pursuing a closed sphere of influence after the war was a potential sticking point. Yet Roosevelt was confident that Russian participation in the Bretton Woods system—coupled with Stalin's numerous public observations that states in the Soviet sphere "should maintain friendly relations not only with the Soviet Union but with the other Allies"—meant that the USSR did not necessarily hold antithetical positions even in this regard.[48]

Surprisingly, it was actually the other member of the Big Three, the United Kingdom, that more consistently expressed opposition to Roosevelt's postwar objectives. Churchill's adamancy for preserving the British Empire clashed with the first two of these objectives, freeing the colonies and breaking down closed economic blocs. As we will see, the American negotiators at Bretton Woods viewed Britain's imperial preference system as a critical threat to postwar stability. Churchill also envisioned a much less punitive settlement for Germany than did Roosevelt and Stalin.[49] This stemmed in part from his profound mistrust of the Soviet Union and Stalin, another point that divided him from Roosevelt. Whereas Churchill consistently pleaded with the United States to take a harder line on the necessity of establishing independent governments in Eastern Europe, Roosevelt strongly rejected both the inclination to make the issue a sticking point that would divide the powers and the suggestion that the United States should meddle in the intricacies of continental affairs after the war.[50] None of this is to suggest that the United States feared Britain more than it did the USSR. Yet if forced to choose between his two greatest wartime allies, the historical record reveals far more ambivalence on the part of Roosevelt than conventional wisdom would suggest.[51]

Furthermore, while FDR's views were not universally shared across the US government, they also were decidedly not his alone. Up until the beginning of 1946, major portions of the government and military did not view the USSR as an implacable threat. To the contrary, a dominant belief in official circles was that cooperation with the Soviets was *the* critical ingredient to postwar security. "Soviet Russia is a power whose good intentions must be assumed until there is incontrovertible evidence to the contrary," argued a group of preeminent IR academics in a report so influential with military officials that it became a Joint Chiefs of Staff

(JCS) paper.[52] "This is the age of the Big Two," they made clear, and the "Soviet-American relationship is the key to American and to general security." Maintaining good relations was so critical, in fact, that the United States should consider publicly breaking with Britain on issues where the British position appeared to antagonize the USSR. This fit with an earlier and influential JCS paper that had reflected the military's skepticism about British intentions, particularly its desires to maintain its empire and confront the Soviets in Eastern Europe. Even though it identified the USSR's monumental rise as "a development which seems certain to prove epochal," it nonetheless encouraged cooperation with Russia.[53] In the most comprehensive report yet prepared on Soviet postwar capabilities and intentions, moreover, US Soviet experts argued in early 1945 that while Russian power might be cause for concern in the distant future, Soviet objectives were likely to remain defensive and non-ideological for the time being.[54]

To be sure, threatening elements of the USSR were apparent to American policymakers well before 1946. Yet even after Roosevelt's death and the new administration's early clashes with Russia over its actions in Eastern Europe, most of the key American players appeared to believe throughout 1945 that fundamental cooperation with the USSR was both possible and desirable.[55]

7.2.2 Building Bretton Woods

Given these threat perceptions, even ordering-to-exclude theory would predict that the order principles successfully advanced at Bretton Woods were not designed to target the Soviet Union, at least at first. After all, the principal negotiations took place in the summer of 1944, well before the emergence of Cold War tensions. The USSR was invited into the Bretton Woods system and, initially at least, had been expected to play a significant role in its management. The primary author of the accords and chief US negotiator at the conference, Harry Dexter White, was even a Soviet sympathizer.[56]

Instead, the threats targeted at Bretton Woods were fascism and, to a lesser extent, imperialism. The targeting of fascism was most manifest in the membership rule charging regimes with greater responsibility for citizens' economic and social livelihoods (liberal order rule #2). The narrative behind the push for this principle emerged as greater respect for "human rights," a new concept at the time. Elites hoped that this focus on individual rights would provide a favorable contrast with fascism's total subordination of the individual to the nation or race.

Though Roosevelt had clearly done some thinking on this front prior to fascism's rise, evidence suggests that it was only the full emergence of the fascist threat that provided him with both the rationale and the political will to pursue such changes. FDR himself crafted the "four freedoms" theme and content for his famous 1941 address. He was motivated to do so out of a desire to demonstrate, in the words of one speechwriter, "that what we were fighting for was economic as well as political democracy." In preparing the speech, Roosevelt relied in part on a letter from his adviser Harold Ickes championing "the need for an 'economic bill of rights,' to defeat Hitlerism in the world forever by establishing 'minimum standards of housing, food, education, and medical care,' along with free speech, free press, and free worship."[57] Coming less than a year after that notable speech, the Atlantic Charter leaned heavily on the four freedoms. Roosevelt used the pact with Churchill to construct a postwar agenda that would make clear "our alternative to Hitler's new order" in part by focusing on social welfare.[58]

He finally brought all these strands together in his 1944 State of the Union address. "We have come to a clear realization of the fact that true individual freedom cannot exist without economic security and independence," he declared. Unless the United States and its allies around the world adopted something akin to an "economic bill of rights" after the war, then "even though we shall have conquered our enemies on the battlefields abroad, we shall have yielded to the spirit of Fascism here at home."[59] This gave voice to the ideological threat of fascism that he and others feared was seeping into politics at home, temptations to emulate those states that "removed those four freedoms in the interest of a greater efficiency" in particular.[60] By advocating for an expansive conception of human rights, however, Roosevelt sought to highlight a new commitment to "fundamental freedoms that differentiated the Allies from their totalitarian rivals."[61]

The other Bretton Woods rule change, behavioral guarantees of economic openness, standardization, and stability (liberal order rule #1), was initially designed to target another major component of the fascist threat: autarkic and mercantilist policies that led to closed economic blocs.[62] That fascism was the target here was made clear in Harry White's first draft of what would become the IMF's Articles of Agreement. It declared that pursuing a visionary open economic system in the present would "be a factor in winning the war" for the future. Defeating the Axis powers would be far easier, he argued,

> if the victims of aggression, actual and potential, could have more assurance that a victory by the United Nations will not mean in the economic sphere, a mere return to the pre-war pattern of every-country-for-itself, of inevitable depression, of possible wide-spread economic chaos with the weaker nations succumbing first under the law-of-the-jungle that characterized international economic practices of the pre-war decade.[63]

Yet while the policies of Germany and Japan had been the most egregious on this front, these states were not the sole offenders. Instead, it was the United

Kingdom's resistance both to ending its discriminatory preference system and to allowing sterling to once again become a true international currency that emerged as considerable sources of tension in the Bretton Woods negotiations.[64] In particular, US officials hated the so-called Ottawa System established in 1932 whereby the UK had abandoned the gold standard and ostensibly set up its own closed trading and monetary bloc among the polities of its empire. Though American elites knew the British were *internally* liberal, they nonetheless saw Britain's *external* relations as belonging "to the abnormal world of the 1930s, characterized by such aberrations as German autarchy in Central Europe, Japan's so-called 'Co-Prosperity Sphere' in Asia, Italian fascism in the Mediterranean, and the Soviet Union's state trading system."[65]

In sum, while Bretton Woods' new membership principle targeted fascism in particular, its new behavioral principle was aimed at behaviors that US policymakers associated with fascist and non-fascist states alike. A closer look at the Bretton Woods negotiations reveals the degree to which the United States successfully achieved these objectives, and often at the expense of their allies in Britain. Because this analysis undermines a key claim of the binding thesis, I review that argument in the next section before more closely examining the Anglo-American negotiations at Bretton Woods.

7.2.3   Alternatives

Binding

Bretton Woods is a crucial case for the binding motive, perhaps even serving as the case that generated the theory.[66] Ikenberry argues that the "embedded liberal" that resulted from the negotiations order represented a true compromise between the dominant United States and subordinate United Kingdom. This was primarily the result of an Anglo-American expert consensus that essentially created a third way in their previously intractable negotiations and gave both actors parts of what they had initially wanted. While the United States got what it wanted in the new behavioral rule—economic stability and openness—it was the British who succeeded in getting the domestic welfare membership rule inserted into the agreements.[67] The resulting order thus represented multiple compromises: between "the conservative free traders and the new profits of economic planning," between "a nineteenth century style free trade system and regional or national capitalist arrangements," and, above all, between the United States and United Kingdom.[68]

Binding makes logical sense in accounting for the order principles advanced at Bretton Woods, thus passing both congruence tests. Analysis of the negotiations themselves, however, reveals much more American dominance than compromise. Three points support this thesis while undermining the binding narrative.

First, the most important battle for determining the shape of the Bretton Woods system wasn't between the US and Britain but between different factions of the American government itself. Specifically, a large divide over postwar foreign economic policy had emerged between the State and Treasury Departments. Led by Cordell Hull, the State Department was preoccupied above all with ending discriminatory commercial practices and ushering in an era of unprecedented free trade, yet without much regard for the revolutionary domestic safeguards that would come to be associated with embedded liberalism. Even early on they treated Germany as less of a threat in the postwar period than Soviet Russia, whom State Department experts immensely mistrusted.

The Treasury Department, by contrast, was filled with committed New Dealers—none more so than Secretary Henry Morgenthau—who wholeheartedly bought into FDR's four freedoms and second Bill of Rights mantras. More closely aligned with FDR on geopolitical imperatives, they hoped to integrate Russia into the postwar economic system while burying Germany and fascism.[69] More important for our purposes, the Treasury Department repudiated the simplistic classical economic vision of the State Department.[70] And when Roosevelt chose his friend Morgenthau to take the lead on postwar financial matters by 1943 (while handing commercial issues to State), he had effectively already guaranteed an "embedded liberal" outcome before the international component of the negotiations with Britain even began.[71]

Second, when divides between British and American negotiators did emerge, they had less to do with abstract and principled ideals and more to do with their countries' respective international positions. One can really only claim that Bretton Woods was a true compromise if we equate general "Keynesian" economic ideas directly with John Maynard Keynes himself as Britain's chief negotiator at Bretton Woods. Yet in this capacity, Keynes was clearly acting more as an advocate for Britain's national interests. In fact, both the White and Keynes proposals had already embraced "Keynesianism" prior to the negotiations. Contra Ikenberry, the biggest differences between their proposals wasn't Britain favoring domestic protections and America opposing them, but instead between the British favoring a system that would benefit debtor countries at the expense of creditor states and the Americans favoring the precise opposite. "In short," summarizes Benn Steil in his magisterial account of the negotiations, "where White and Keynes stood on the question of the postwar global monetary structure was determined by where they sat—Washington and London, respectively," rather than by any larger theoretical or philosophical differences.[72]

Third and most importantly, the final agreement was less a compromise than it was an outright victory for the American blueprint with only slight modifications. As the Council on Foreign Relations' Stewart Patrick summarizes, the two coun- tries "differed about the burden of adjustment to be placed on deficit versus sur- plus countries, the magnitude of liquidity any new international monetary regime should provide, the role of the dollar as the world's key currency, and the pace at which countries should move toward full currency convertibility."[73] The United States won on nearly all these issues. The dollar would become the anchor of a Bretton Woods system that would be physically headquartered in Washington. And the IMF would be a limited stabilization fund with an "active" role in the loan-making process, not a liquidity-rich but "passive" bank allowing debtors to almost automatically borrow deeply, frequently, and without conditionality.[74]

The Americans got what they wanted not only because of their dominant bar- gaining position but also from clever negotiating. They used a Joint Statement of Principles to which the British had serious reservations as the basis of negotia- tions with other countries prior to the conference, falsely implying that Britain was fully committed to that agreement. Harry White in particular organized the pre-conference meeting in Atlantic City as well as the Bretton Woods conference itself in such a way as to avoid actual substantive changes to his ideal draft of the accords, a document he kept hidden from observers throughout the proceed- ings.[75] During the conference he quietly slipped a provision into the Fund's char- ter that would essentially make the US dollar the reserve currency of the world, an important detail that Keynes would not notice until after the negotiations had ended. And White and Morgenthau succeeded in using private bilateral meet- ings with country delegations to buy votes to base the institutions in the United States over British objections.[76]

By contrast, the issues over which Britain negotiated some leniency were ones tangential to the lasting structure of the institutions and the larger economic order established at Bretton Woods. US officials agreed (a) to the temporary con- tinuance of monetary controls during a transition period of 3 to 5 years; (b) to the retention of capital controls that would nonetheless fall out of fashion in subsequent decades; and (c) to soon supply Britain with a substantial infusion of postwar credits to help its struggling economy.[77] This last concession resulted in a $3.75 billion loan in early 1946. Ironically, American elites in the State Department—now back in charge of economic policy after FDR's death and the subsequent shift back to trade—used negotiations over the loan to extract *further* concessions from the United Kingdom, finally achieving promises for a return of sterling to full convertibility and, especially, for an end to the impe- rial preference system. Though it eventually passed the House of Commons, the loan and accompanying Bretton Woods ratification package was lamented there as "an economic Munich" amid accusations that the new Labour government had "[sold] the British Empire for a pack of cigarettes" to the free trade vision of the United States.[78] In sum, Bretton Woods is far better characterized as an outright American victory than an Anglo-American compromise. Binding thus fails both process tracing tests for this critical case.

Exporting

Numerous historians have argued that the postwar order's origins reflected a revolutionary internationalization of the American system, a "New Deal for the World" to use Borgwardt's memorable phrase. Exporting passes both congruence tests, as both the behavior and membership principles advanced at Bretton Woods were consistent with domestic economic ideals of and practices in the United States. Many New Deal policymakers had taken important foreign policy positions by the war's end, and some even gave voice to the belief that it was their mission to apply New Deal principles to the international system.[79] In Jeffry Frieden's words, with the final Bretton Woods agreements the "organized capitalism of the new social democracy, which had swept the domestic political economies of the Western capitalist nations, was applied at the international level."[80]

Surprisingly, however, there isn't much process tracing evidence to support an exporting narrative here. As we have seen, Roosevelt was only motivated to advance his expansive new membership principle (liberal order rule #2) once he came to believe that the Allies needed to forge a favorable contrast with the fascist model. Similarly, saying that exporting can explain the behavior preference for economic openness would mean having to ignore striking American hypocrisy when it came to its own closed economic sphere in the Western hemisphere. As Herbert Feis put it, "the American trading system in Latin America was fully as monolithic as any communist state-trading organization" at this time.[81] In conversations with Stalin, Roosevelt even attempted to use American regional hegemony in Latin America as a model for the "spheres of responsibility" order he hoped to create for the postwar system.[82] Finally, the exporting motive appears convincing only if one ignores America's weaponization of the Bretton Woods system in subsequent years once Cold War tensions became manifest. This is a development I return to in more detail later.

Learning

Learning certainly played an important part in shaping order preferences after the Second World War, and it is practically undeniable that the calamities of the interwar period weighed heavily on American order builders during critical negotiations. According to a number of accounts, learning was particularly influential for these economic aspects, and especially in FDR's State Department. "Above all," argues Stewart Patrick, "postwar American commercial multilateralism derived from the disastrous experiences of the 1930s and new ideas about the institutional requirements for economic growth and political stability."[83] As the historian Melvyn Leffler puts it, "For U.S. officials, the most decisive and lasting legacy of the wartime experience was that potential adversaries must never again be allowed to gain control of the resources of Eurasia through autarkical economic practices, political subversion, and/or military aggression."[84] These lessons clearly played a part in the Bretton Woods behavior rule change. And on the membership principle, learning was also evident in the notions "that stabilization of capitalism begins at home" and that it was necessary to "reframe international economic stability as a national security issue."[85] Learning thus passes both congruence and process tracing tests for both the economic principles of the Western order.

To be sure, changing American preferences toward free trade and greater economic and monetary coordination all reflected significant learning from the past. That said, the effects of such "lessons" should not be overstated. First, we have already seen how the US and Britain had come to significantly different conclusions about the economic lessons of the 1930s. As one account summarizes, "Keynes argued that the lesson of the 1930s was that international obligations to sustain a fixed exchange rate . . . were politically unsupportable; White argued that the lesson of the 1930s was that exchange rate instability was politically disastrous."[86] In other words, the lessons to be learned were not as obvious as they might appear in retrospect.

Second, it is important to remember that these changes also came as a consequence of America's changing position in the world economy. By the time the most consequential decisions were being made, it was clear that America's enormous economic power advantage would give it *the* central place in any postwar arrangement. Accordingly, US statesmen realized that American exports would be highly competitive in virtually every category, a factor that goes a long way toward accounting for their push for greater openness.[87] This alternative explanation is supported by the fact that in those categories where Americans still feared the perils of open markets and international competition—most notably, in agriculture—policymakers insisted on exemptions and continued protections for important domestic constituencies.[88]

7.3 Postwar Order, Take Two

It was not this global vision that proved to be the most consequential and enduring, however. Instead, a Western vision of order superseded the global one for the United States and much of Europe. This section details this conversion, chronicling the origins of the more exclusive Western order in the later 1940s.

More specifically, it performs four tasks: First, I track significant changes in American perceptions of the Soviet Union between the end of 1945 and the beginning of 1948, demonstrating that the USSR became the United States' principal perceived threat during this time. Second, I highlight an increasing American disillusionment with the United Nations in this same period that corresponds with the perceived emergence of the Soviet threat. Third, I return to the Bretton Woods institutions to show how they were turned against the Soviets in the years after their founding. Fourth and most importantly, I closely examine the American origins of the Marshall Plan and North Atlantic Treaty Organization ideas. Above all, I argue that both the timing behind the birth of these institutions and the shape each ultimately took are clearly accounted for by an overriding desire to exclude the perceived Soviet menace from participation in the emerging liberal international order.

7.3.1 Threats from 1946

As I argued earlier, American leaders had not particularly targeted the Soviet Union at the end of the Second World War for the simple reason that they had not seen the USSR as a primary threat. This began to change late in 1945 and especially in 1946, however. Narratives of the Cold War's origins are ubiquitous, and the complete story need not be recounted here. Instead, I aim to synthesize the best of these accounts in making four points: first, American leaders were profoundly affected by what they perceived to be increasingly aggressive Soviet behaviors; second, these developments took place at the same time that elites were fully comprehending the destruction caused by the Second World War; third, extraordinary Soviet gains in material power led to two more specific fears related to Germany and American society at home; and fourth, the ascendance of the Stalinist-communist ideological model at this time made the Soviet threat appear even more potent to Western observers.

First, and beginning in late 1945, US elites believed that they were witnessing increasingly uncooperative and ambitious Russian behaviors that could not be as easily justified by legitimate claims of insecurity as FDR had been wont to do. Officials had been frustrated by Soviet heavy-handedness in Eastern Europe in 1944 and 1945, yet also recognized that the Russians had a legitimate interest in seeing friendly regimes installed there. They would grumble but ultimately accept Soviet domination of the region so long as Stalin repaid this flexibility by demonstrating restraint elsewhere.[89] Yet it was in this context that subsequent actions in other areas began alarming American officials. Three bear mentioning.

First, the Russians were late in moving their military forces out of Iran in early 1946 as all members of the Big Three had agreed to do, while at the same time demanding oil concessions in and political autonomy for northern Iran as a condition of their withdrawal. The crisis was resolved when the Soviets belatedly removed their troops in May, yet only did so with an agreement on oil concessions and in response to strong condemnation at the newly formed United Nations.[90] Second, Stalin's infamous "election address" in February 1946 surprised US officials for its ideological bellicosity. His declaration that the recently concluded war had been "the inevitable result of the development of world economic and political forces on the basis of monopoly capitalism" signaled that ideological zealotry was apparently now returning to Soviet foreign policy after a welcomed interlude, a development that shocked even the most knowledgeable Russian experts in the State Department.[91] Third and perhaps most ominous were Stalin's attempts beginning in 1945 to coerce Turkey into granting the Soviets special naval rights as well as a base on the strategically vital Turkish Straits. American concerns over Soviet troop movements near Turkey in the summer of 1946 provoked the first major power war scare of the postwar era, even as the Soviets rescinded their demands and the crisis abated without incident by the end of the year.[92]

Together, these developments led to a marked shift in officials' beliefs both about long-term Soviet intentions (downward) and about the short-term probability of American–Russian military conflict (upward).[93] New interpretations of Soviet conduct coinciding with these events—none more influential than Russian expert George Kennan's "Long Telegram" in February 1946 and the "Clifford-Elsey Report" later in the year—convincingly articulated the view that Soviet behavior was based on a hostile ideology and offensive ambitions, not weakness and fears of insecurity.[94]

Second, structural conditions coinciding with this perceived behavioral shift magnified American fears. Advances in military technology made rapid attack— even against the American homeland—much more feasible than it had been just a few years earlier.[95] As President Harry Truman warned the Congress in the fall of 1945, "never again can we count on the luxury of time with which to arm ourselves. In any future war, the heart of the United States would be the enemy's first target."[96] And the USSR was in a much better position to capitalize on others' weaknesses after 1945 compared to 1919 thanks to Stalin's forced industrialization programs of the interwar years and the positioning of Soviet troops at the end of the war. Strategic assessments by the Joint Chiefs recognized as early as 1943 that "Russia's postwar position in Europe will be a dominant one. With Germany crushed, there will be no power in Europe to oppose her tremendous military forces," a position that was reinforced in study after study in the years following.[97]

In addition to those concerns, the wartime damage to America's European allies was much greater than in 1919. As Leffler has summarized, "during 1946 and

1947, defense officials witnessed a dramatic unraveling of the geopolitical foundations and socioeconomic structure of international affairs."[98] It wasn't until these years that elites realized the extent of the upheaval not only in Europe but across the world, and at precisely the time that they were witnessing the retreat of British hegemony that had served as a stabilizing influence. "The commercial and financial situation of the world is worse than any of us thought a year ago it would be," testified Under Secretary of State Dean Acheson in 1946. "Destruction is more complete, hunger more acute, exhaustion more widespread than anyone then realized."[99]

Third, the Soviets' newfound material power manifested two more specific fears in the minds of American strategic thinkers. Most immediate were fears over the fusion of Soviet and German power. Initially, American statesmen had agreed to work with the Soviets for a negotiated settlement over Germany, one where disarmament, deindustrialization, and permanent partition were all on the table. This settlement would include reparations for the USSR, not only out of the eastern zone the Russians occupied but from the Allies' more resource-rich western zones as well. Yet as elites began to doubt Soviet intentions, they also came to fear for Russian plans in Germany and the capabilities they could potentially amass from German resources.[100] "The only really dangerous thing in my mind," worried Kennan, "is the possibility that the technical skills of the Germans might be combined with the physical resources of Russia."[101] Early indications of the Soviets ransacking their zone and suppressing noncommunist political movements there weren't promising. Yet Western officials became truly alarmed in the first half 1946, first by Russian pressure on the popular social democrats (SPD) to fuse with the unpopular communists (KPD) in their zone, second by the Soviets' rejection of a US-initiated treaty for the occupying powers to demilitarize Germany for twenty-five years.[102] To American officials, both moves indicated that Stalin aimed to install a communist regime across *all* of Germany and appeal to a reunified German state to join the emerging Soviet sphere of influence. "Unless western Germany during the coming year is effectively associated with the Western European nations, first through economic arrangements, and ultimately perhaps in some political way," warned Truman's third State Secretary George Marshall by 1948, "there is a real danger that whole of Germany will be drawn into eastern orbit, with obvious dire consequences for all of us."[103]

The second specific concern in the face of Soviet material gains was what hypothetical Russian domination of Europe would mean for life at home in the United States. Policymakers became preoccupied with the possible necessity of excessive state intervention in or militarization of American society.[104] If Soviet autarkic practices became more influential in world affairs, the United States would have "to find itself in the business of allocating foreign goods among importers and foreign markets among exporters and telling every trader what he could buy or sell, and how much, and when, and where," Truman argued in a notable address at Baylor University in 1947. "It is not the American way. It is not the way to peace."[105] Secretary of Commerce Averell Harriman's influential committee on the European Recovery Program came to a similar conclusion later in the year. "The domestic consequences are such as no American could easily tolerate," the committee concluded, arguing that it would lead to "the swift and complete conversion to a military footing which national security would require," as well as "the immediate and sweeping limitation of our economic and political life, perhaps extending even to our very form of government."[106] Marshall agreed. "We must not permit the free community of Europe to be extinguished," he testified. "It would impose incalculable burdens upon this country and force serious readjustments in our traditional way of life."[107]

Fourth, the perceived ascendance of the Soviet ideological model at a time when liberal democracy and, especially, capitalism appeared to be on the defensive only heightened all of the rest of these fears. As chapter 6 demonstrated, American fears of socialist ideological contagion were nothing new. In the years after the First World War, however, that threat had seemingly abated. Socialism's ideological momentum had stalled, and, after an initial wave of optimism, Bolshevik Russia had proven incapable of marshaling either the material resources or the ideological appeal to project influence very far outside its borders.[108]

Yet the gaping vacuum opened by destruction across Europe by 1945 was not only material but also ideological. The traditional political landscape had been decimated, leaving politicians and political parties in an unprecedented environment of ideological uncertainty. And peering into this vacuum, it often appeared to be the Stalinist-communist ideological model that had the greatest momentum throughout Europe. The Soviets had "a strong drawing card in the proletarian philosophy of Communism," lamented Truman's director of the Office of Strategic Studies (OSS), the precursor to the CIA. The United States and the West, by contrast, had "no political or social philosophy equally dynamic or alluring."[109] Prominent American officials recognized this reality, even as they worked to forestall it. The Europeans "have suffered so much, and they believe so deeply that governments can take some action which will alleviate their sufferings," predicted Acheson, "that they will demand that the whole business of state control and state interference shall be pushed further and further."[110]

For impoverished peoples throughout Europe—as well as those across the developing world—the Soviet model held tremendous appeal for a number of reasons. First, Stalin's speedy industrialization seemingly offered a blueprint to others looking to rapidly build or rebuild their societies in a way that ideological alternatives did not. "We could point to the economic benefits of Capitalism," noted a US War Department study in 1946, "but these benefits are concentrated rather than widespread, and, at present, are genuinely suspect throughout Europe and in many parts of the world."[111] Second, Stalinist-communist ideology could easily be fused with the national independence narratives that were taking hold across many parts of the world, narratives that could not as easily be coopted by Western states tarred either by their own imperial legacies or by their close relationships with other powers that had them.[112]

Given this charged ideological atmosphere, it shouldn't be surprising that contestations over the domestic makeup of regimes quickly pitted the United States and USSR against each other. Even when they were still wartime allies, tensions arose in Italy in 1943 when the Americans insisted, and over Soviet protestations, that the post-fascist Italian government adopt a liberal constitution. Less than a year later, and citing Italy as precedent, the USSR forcibly imposed a communist government in Bulgaria. Both sides recognized a need to reach some consensus on regime imposition, and probably thought they had done the best that they could do with the Yalta agreements in early 1945. Yet though the Truman administration had expected the imposition of Soviet-backed communist regimes in Poland and Romania, the manner in which this was done nonetheless disturbed them. While US officials had previously pleaded for Soviet help in the Pacific War, they worked in the summer of 1945 to bring that conflict to as quick an end as possible in part to forestall Russian entry—and communist subversion— into East Asia.[113] At America's urging, France forcibly punted the communists out of its government by 1947. This coincided with Truman's public pledge of aid to Greece and Turkey and any other democratic country fighting communist influence, as well as secret authorization of covert action against the communists competing in Italy's upcoming elections.[114] The creation of the Cominform later in the year—a heavily ideological wing of the Soviet state designed to coordinate communist party messaging across the world—again raised suspicions that Stalin was now returning the USSR to an ideological footing in global affairs. Shortly thereafter, both US elites and the American public were shocked when a Soviet-backed coup toppled the democratic government of Czechoslovakia in early 1948 and installed a communist dictatorship.[115] These last two events— Cominform and Czechoslovakia—appear to have shattered any doubts about the disparate nature of various local communist movements, as it signaled in the estimation of the CIA "the clear identification of Communist parties as agents of the Kremlin."[116] The belief thus took hold in 1946 and 1947 that the Soviets were building a potent and united communist bloc.[117] Well before the more well-known and infamous crises in Berlin and Korea, then, ideological polarization had been locked in place, triggering a corresponding pattern of forcible foreign regime promotions on both sides.[118]

Subsequent events only hardened these views. Germany became more permanently divided, with the east firmly under Soviet control and the west sometimes drifting dangerously close to neutralism. China's unexpected fall to communism in 1949 demonstrated the viability of the Soviet model in vital power centers outside of Europe, while the unexpected revelation of Russia's nuclear capacities that same year eliminated the one advantage American statesmen believed could limit Stalin's ambitions. Between 1945 and 1949, then, the Soviet Union had gone from wartime ally to implacable adversary and existential threat in the eyes of America's foreign policy elites.

7.3.2 Giving Up on Global Order

The UN system's founding clearly preceded the perceived emergence of the Soviet threat. Moreover, without the emergence of this threat that system likely would have looked similar to what it actually came to be: a modified great power concert, circumscribed by a lower assembly with near-universal membership and universalistic aspirations.[119] This reflected Roosevelt's views about the necessity of a great power consortium (via the UNSC) while also speaking to his belief in the need to appeal to universalist values to satisfy American public opinion (via the United Nations General Assembly [UNGA], for example.) Simply put, the perceived Soviet threat is not necessary for explaining American advocacy of the UN system.

Yet the United States did not prioritize its *global* order vision for very long. Over the course of a few short years, it became clear to elites that the UN would fail to deliver on its objectives in the face of increasing disagreements between the two superpowers. The biggest impediment, these officials believed, was the fact that Stalin's USSR shared equal authority with the United States on the UNSC, especially when it became apparent that the Soviets would not be shy about using their veto power to stymie perceived threats to their own interests.

The shift in American elites' attitudes toward the UN between 1945 and 1947 is striking. When Soviet actions in Iran became one of the first diplomatic standoffs of the UN era in late 1945, US officials worked hard to shield the new organization from fatal blows to its legitimacy. American elites also defended the veto from numerous early complaints against it, and more generally attempted to help the organization project an image of fairness and impartiality.[120] By the second half of 1947, however, these same elites had shifted to using the UN as yet another forum to voice to the world that America's cooperative endeavors had "been consistently frustrated by the obstructionist policies and tactics of the U.S.S.R."[121] Most egregiously, they used George Marshall's UNGA speech in November of that year to launch an initiative to bypass the UNSC (and the Soviet veto) altogether. Instead, their proposed "Interim Committee" of the UNGA would take over the most important responsibilities related to peace and security from the Security Council.[122]

Though the Interim Committee proposal would amount to little, it predictably agitated the Soviets and demonstrated that American elites no longer believed in the UN's founding vision. President Harry Truman had once been an enthusiastic supporter of the UN's promise, vowing in the midst of a troubling episode in 1945 that "the United Nations must be made to work and we [will] *make* it work." Within a few short years, however, he joined others around him in lamenting the organization as little more than a "mirror in which the state of world affairs is reflected" rather than a vehicle for effectively addressing the international community's greatest challenges.[123] Perhaps no one better captured what the UN system had become by this time than Britain's first UN representative: "It seems to me plainer than ever that the Council is being used solely as a sounding board for mischievous propaganda," Alexander Cadogan complained. "It is not used for reaching useful agreement on policy, . . . remedying unsatisfactory situations or averting the danger of threats to peace."[124] By 1947, in sum, it was clear that Western elites had largely given up on the United Nations as the primary ordering vehicle for accomplishing their objectives.

7.3.3 Weaponizing Bretton Woods

The subsequent targeting of the Soviets with a Bretton Woods system they had originally been invited into may seem contradictory. In fact, America's adoption of "economic containment" against the Soviets in 1946 and 1947 was not as much of an about-face as it first appears. Enthusiasm for bringing the Soviets into Bretton Woods in the first place had not been universal. Consistent with ordering-to-exclude theory, including was supported most strongly by those who were most focused on the threat of Germany/fascism, primarily Roosevelt and his allies in the Treasury Department. Those that were already skeptical of Soviet Russia even by 1944—the British government and hardliners in the State Department, for instance—were not enthusiastic about Russian participation but had acceded to the wishes of Roosevelt, Morgenthau, and White.[125]

Yet even among those supportive of Soviet inclusion, it remains unclear how serious their efforts had really been. While bringing the Soviets into Bretton Woods was a political priority for those like White who admired the Soviet system and those like Roosevelt who believed Big Three cooperation was critical, there isn't much evidence of intricate plans for or thoughtful understandings about how it would actually work.[126] For their part, the Soviet delegation showed remarkably little interest in the nature of the proposed institutions during the negotiations and only spoke up on issues that would directly affect their country. Moreover, their efforts were directed less at changing the broader rules of the new organizations than carving out special exemptions for the USSR and its satellites.[127] As one American official observed, the Soviets "counted not on logic and persuasion for winning their point but upon sheer doggedness and the fact that they knew that the United States delegations would make every effort to satisfy them" for political purposes.[128] A British representative was less kind, observing that there was "something morally impressive about such monumental selfishness" on the part of the Russian negotiators.[129] More to the point, an American economist serving as a technical adviser at the conference concluded that the Soviets really couldn't have become meaningful participants in the resulting system even if they had shown more interest in doing so. This was the case, he argued, *not* because of the Soviets' domestic system but because of their international practices. As he put it,

> it is difficult to see how Russian membership in the Bretton Woods institutions could have contributed to their success without a substantial change in the whole economic and political philosophy of the Soviet Union. . . not based on the fact that the USSR has a socialist economic system and maintains a state monopoly of all foreign trading. . . . The difficulty lies in the fact that the USSR is not willing to organize its trade on a purely commercial basis and conduct its buying and selling in world markets in a non-discriminatory manner and in accordance with the principles of maximum advantage from international specialization and trade. Russian trading practices violate these principles in several ways. . . . [Most importantly,] the USSR uses its trade as a means of gaining political objectives. Economic cooperation for the development of a multilateral trade and payments system is of course impossible to achieve with a country whose foreign trade is an instrument of power politics.[130]

It would also be misleading to characterize the economic order created at Bretton Woods as "inclusive" to the Soviets simply because they had been formally invited into it. As the last quote indicates, American leaders would only permit Soviet participation on Western terms. This meant that the USSR would have to open its economy to supranational scrutiny and market forces.[131] For a non-democracy to do all of this just to join an organization openly premised on promoting *private* enterprise would be a tall order.[132] As if these domestic intrusions weren't enough, however, joining could also have dire implications for Moscow's *international* relationships with its satellites and subordinates. "American support of an open sphere was designed, at least in part," observes Leffler, "to circumscribe the very predominance [in the Soviets' designated sphere of influence] that

Americans sometimes said they were willing to accept."[133] In Eastern Europe in particular, US policymakers understood that they were in effect demanding that the Soviets take actions that would drastically undercut their ability to maintain a sphere of influence, a sphere these same officials had previously acknowledged as legitimate given the Soviet experience in the war.[134]

Whether or not to join the Bretton Woods institutions likely posed a genuine dilemma for Soviet elites. On the one hand, they must have known that *not* joining would give Western and particularly American elites free reign to shape an economic order explicitly on Western terms that could revitalize capitalism and, in the future, encircle and isolate the USSR (thus setting off pathway #2, "triggering tripwires"). On the other hand, joining would mean abandoning policies Stalin believed were necessary for Russian security, thereby potentially triggering pathway #3, "severing the social power" of Soviet control over its vital sphere of influence. The limited documentary evidence available shows that Stalin indeed feared for how Bretton Woods might embolden Western efforts to pry Eastern Europe out of its special relationship with Moscow.[135] Soviet elites worried that American elites "were trying to draw us into their company, but in the subordinate role," recalled Stalin's longtime confidant and foreign minister, Vyacheslav Molotov. "We would have got into the position of dependence, and still would not have obtained anything from them" that might have made this capitulation worthwhile.[136]

When the Soviets declined to ratify the Bretton Woods Agreement by the end of 1945 (and again failed to meet an extended deadline for ratification in 1946), it was the former pathway that came to pass. Yes, the Bretton Woods system hadn't been initially designed to target the Soviets. Yet revisionist historians have a point in that its institutions were soon redirected in an anti-Soviet direction. Even though aid decisions were supposed to be devoid of political considerations, for instance, the World Bank denied loans to Poland and Czechoslovakia at America's urging, even though both states were Bank members, and it only extended aid to Yugoslavia once its leader, Josip Broz Tito, had publicly and dramatically broken with and embarrassed Stalin on the world stage.[137]

These developments aligned with other American efforts to economically isolate the Soviets. Officials at first believed that economic inducements could be used to buy Soviet cooperation on American postwar priorities. Yet by the end of 1945, this approach was abandoned in favor of economic containment.[138] In an important directive that fall, James Byrnes (Truman's second State Secretary) advocated for a shift away from administering postwar aid according to need alone:

> The situation has so hardened that the time has now come, I am convinced, in the light of the attitude of the Soviet Govt and the neighboring

states which it dominates in varying degrees, when the implementation of our general policies requires the closest coordination. In a word we must help our friends in every way and refrain from assisting those who either through helplessness or for other reasons are opposing the principles for which we stand.[139]

Accordingly, American officials abruptly cut off Soviet Lend-Lease aid before curtailing it for other allies, and continuously put off negotiations for a large loan to the USSR that never materialized. They became increasingly opposed to UN Relief and Rehabilitation (UNRRA) aid to countries in the Soviet bloc and were responsible for the sidelining and eventual dismantling of that institution as the premier vehicle for postwar relief.[140] Though Stalin was in many ways heavy-handed in his treatment of Eastern Europe, even he did not favor a policy of abso-lute autarky from Western commerce in this early period. It wasn't the USSR but instead "the United States that adopted a policy" by 1946, Eduard Mark reminds us, "of halting all trade with the Eastern Bloc that might aid either its economic development or its ability to wage war."[141] This effort remained ad hoc until 1949, when American leaders led the way in forging a secret but coordinated export control regime with their European allies—the Coordinating Committee, or CoCom—through which they would engage in outright economic warfare against the Soviet sphere for years to come.[142]

Finally, these developments behoove us to examine an important question about the role that timing played in the shape and character of the Bretton Woods institutions: what might they have looked like if they had been negotiated later than 1944, once Cold War tensions had become manifest? To speculate, we need only look to the fate of what was intended to be the third leg of the Bretton Woods tripod, the International Trade Organization (ITO).

Though its charter had been negotiated in Havana in 1948, the ITO never materialized in large part because the United States showed little enthusiasm for joining. This is sometimes explained by American anger over a lack of pro-tection for its agricultural sector, as well as too many anti-free trade exceptions for other countries in its charter.[143] Yet the influence of those factors pales in comparison to that of emerging US–Soviet tensions. The ITO was ultimately undone by "the ideological struggle of the Cold War," argues historian Thomas Zeiler in his account of the trade regime's origins. "By imposing regulations on open competition, the charter contradicted the precepts of market capitalism, now under attack by the Soviet Union. That was unpalatable in the Cold War, a contest between capitalist and communist ways of life." The Truman administra-tion was unwilling to spend political capital on ratifying the ITO charter in large part because "the Cold War atmosphere undercut universalist projects," while

Congress and the business community disliked that it "represented a huge planning mechanism, a global bureaucracy" that was "flawed by statist provisions" of the sort that characterized the Soviet sphere. Both sets of actors concurred that "free trade was a weapon [to be used] against the Soviets," but also came to agree that it was not the ITO that would best serve this goal but the smaller and less ambitious General Agreement on Tariffs and Trade (GATT) that had already quietly been put in place in 1947.[144]

As a result, the GATT—initially intended to serve only as a precursor to the ITO—became the Western order's premier free trade regime.[145] The GATT was appealing to many American constituencies precisely because of its limitations: it had fewer members, most of whom were already Western allies, lacked a formal architecture or sizable bureaucracy, had no real international legal standing, and only loosely obligated signatories to act in ways that would encourage freer trade.[146] In sum, had the other Bretton Woods institutions similarly been put off until the later 1940s, they likely would have endured a fate similar to that of the ITO.

7.3.4 From Noncommittal to North Atlantic Alliance

The path to the other Western order principles—liberal security community, democratic membership, and true multilateral collective security (liberal order rules #3, 4, and 5)—offers a number of more straightforward instances of ordering to exclude. Here I focus first upon the impetus for and evolution of the Marshall Plan before exploring the development of the NATO alliance.

Uniting Europe

Evidence is clear that the perceived emergence of the Soviet/communist threat supplied the impetus for a liberal security community with porous borders (liberal order rule #3). The principal objective behind that community's earliest manifestation, the Marshall Plan, was to provide Europe with the capacity to halt the westward movement of Soviet influence.[147] Secretary of State Marshall later admitted that he first gave serious thought to a major recovery program as "an outgrowth of [his] disillusionment over the Moscow Conference" in the spring of 1947, where frustrating meetings with Molotov and Stalin convinced him that the Soviets were negotiating in bad faith on a number of issues.[148] The urgency for the program at this point demonstrated an understanding that with the growing appeal of communist ideology the Soviet threat was not limited in type (to coercion alone) or in scope (to Eastern Europe alone). By the spring of 1947, even the US military had come around to the belief that "the next war will be ideological," leading them to enthusiastically support the use of order building via economic aid as a component of national security.[149]

Accordingly, aspects of the ERP were designed to forestall the ideological power of communism from spreading across Europe. Two of these aspects in particular are worth noting. First, American leaders sought to use aid to stop democratic communist movements in their tracks. Implicitly, they did so by using the promise of inducements to drive a wedge between radical communists and less radical labor movements still willing to pursue their objectives through the regular democratic process.[150] Explicitly, they pursued this objective by overtly declaring to European regimes that kicking or keeping communists out of their governments was a quid pro quo for the closer cooperation implied by the ERP.[151]

Second, the launching of the Marshall Plan was to be used not only for defensive purposes in Western Europe but also for offensive ones in the areas of Eastern Europe seemingly already under Soviet control. Like with Bretton Woods, American officials invited the Soviet Union and its satellites to participate in the ERP. This time, however, their motives were quite clearly exclusionary from the start.[152] The plan would be offered "in such a form that the Russian satellite countries would either exclude themselves by unwillingness to accept the proposed conditions or agree to abandon the exclusive orientation of their economies" toward Moscow, argued George Kennan, now the head of the State Department's newly created think tank, the Policy Planning Staff.[153] Either outcome would serve American purposes. The Marshall Plan would thus "put Russia over the barrel," Kennan declared. "Either it must decline or else enter into an arrangement that would mean an ending of the Iron Curtain."[154]

In the less likely event that states in the Soviet orbit chose to participate, the very nature of the ERP's intrusive economic and pan-European cooperation requirements would force these states out of the USSR's exclusive sphere. This would drastically weaken if not outright decimate the Kremlin's grip over its subordinates, thereby undermining Soviet strength (pathway #3, "severing social power").[155] Yet the more likely outcome, State Department officials believed, was that Stalin would reject the ERP offer and forbid his satellites from participating.[156] If this happened, it would demonstrate to the rest of Europe both that Soviet control over Eastern Europe was hierarchical rather than consensual and that the Soviets were the ones most responsible for the emerging division of Europe (pathway #1, finding "commonalities for contrast" to unite would-be allies against the threatening entity). But key American officials still believed it was crucial to *offer* the Soviets the opportunity to participate.[157] Consistent with pathway #1, they believed this was critical because it would maximize the chances of Western Europe fully participating in an arrangement that at least on its surface was not divisively anti-Soviet. It would thus begin the process of recruiting states reluctant to join an overt standoff against Russia into what would nevertheless become an anti-Soviet bloc. "Many people in Europe were very timid about opposing the Soviet Union," Marshall would later explain. He feared that "if we started our plan by throwing the Soviets out it would scare these [European] people and perhaps keep some of the European countries out of the program."[158] This had been the mistake of the recent and more provocative Truman Doctrine announcement, he and others believed, and the ERP afforded them an opportunity to more adeptly court allies for the larger struggle ahead.[159]

As it turned out, American officials were right on both counts, about the USSR's inclination to reject the ERP and the anticipated result of this rejection. Stalin sent Molotov to Paris to gather information about the program in a preliminary meeting with Britain and France in June of 1947. From these tense meetings—tense in part because France and Britain actually wanted the Soviets to reject the ERP[160]—Molotov concluded that Soviet participation would be unacceptable precisely for the reasoning discussed already.[161] Shortly after the Soviet delegation stormed out of the Paris negotiations, the Kremlin instructed its satellites that still hoped to participate—Poland and Czechoslovakia—to decline the invitation. When the Czechoslovak government demurred, Stalin dramatically called its leaders to Moscow to force their compliance, thereby demonstrating to any remaining skeptics the coercive relationship between the USSR and its subordinates. The American gamble had succeeded, and even the typically understated Kennan could barely contain his pleasure at the result:

> Strain placed on communist movement by effort to draw up plan for European rehabilitation. Communist Parties in West forced to show their hand. Russians smoked out in their relations with satellite countries. Maximum strain placed on those relations. Events of past weeks the greatest blow to European Communism since termination of hostilities. If same line can be continued on our part we can weaken movement still further.[162]

To address the *material* aspect of the Soviet threat—Russia's preponderant military power in Europe—the American architects of the ERP used the program to advance another novel diplomatic weapon: unprecedented European cooperation that could eventually lead to integration. US officials pursued this objective by ultimately requiring ERP countries to create a multilateral structure—the Committee for European Economic Co-operation (CEEC)—and then a new supranational institution—the Organization for European Economic Co-operation (OEEC)—through which they would collectively determine their aid needs, make aid requests, and distribute aid amongst themselves. From the very genesis of the ERP idea in 1947, American officials made clear that they would only support an aid package that demonstrated "substantial evidence of a

developing overall plan for economic cooperation by the Europeans themselves"
that could culminate in an "economic federation."[163]

This was an extraordinary development that, in the words of one scholar,
"marked the first time in history that a preponderant power had pursued a policy
promoting unity rather than division in an area under its influence."[164] It was
also clearly designed to build Europe into a third force that could better resist
a Soviet invasion. While ideas for European integration had been floated in US
policy circles prior to this point, it was only after the rupture with the Soviets
at the Moscow CFM meeting that such ideas gained influential supporters in
the State Department.[165] By May and June of 1947, American officials had come
to believe that their best chance to effectively balance Soviet power was to foster unprecedented cooperation in Western Europe.[166] "By insisting on a joint
approach, we hoped to force the Europeans to begin to think like Europeans,
and not like nationalists, in their approach" to dire continental issues, recalled
Kennan on the impetus for the ERP. "If the people of Western Europe were to
reject American aid on those terms, then that in itself would be equivalent to a
final vote for Russian domination."[167]

In numerous subsequent policy battles over the Marshall Plan, the officials
most responsible for launching it fought to maximize its ability to meet the goal
of unprecedented cooperation above all others. They decided early on to keep
ERP aid away from UN agencies like the Commission for Europe where states
in the Soviet sphere had representation.[168] When it became clear that the CEEC
was falling short on its integrative aspirations in the deliberations in Paris, State
Department officials sacrificed their hands-off approach to more directly dictate
what its final report needed to look like (i.e., much greater European cooperation).[169] They fought with Congress to keep State Department control of the
ERP and then, later, to ensure that the newly created European Cooperation
Administration (ECA) remained attuned to the strategic rather than just the
economic objectives of the Marshall Plan.[170] They tussled with the British over
whether the OEEC would have supranational powers to *compel* European states
to integrate rather than just consulting powers as the British wanted.[171] And they
battled the French over the necessity of West German revitalization as a key component of the ERP.[172] They did not win all of these battles, and sometimes had
to compromise in order to ensure that the program continued moving forward.
Yet the fact that they fought them demonstrates that the main objective of the
ERP remained the promotion of European cooperation for the sake of forestalling Soviet advances.

Finally, the Truman administration was only able to build the necessary public and congressional support for the ERP in late 1947 and early 1948 by invoking a narrative of existential conflict between the free world and the communist

one.[173] "Our deepest concern with European recovery," Truman argued in a special address to Congress, "is that it is essential to the maintenance of the civilization in which the American way of life is rooted. . . . If Europe fails to recover, the people of these countries might be driven to . . . the surrender of their basic rights to totalitarian control."[174] Marshall emphatically stated that European "unification is a necessity to the plan" in congressional testimony.[175] Consistent with ordering-to-exclude theory, it was only when the public relations campaign to sell the Marshall Plan turned to a full-blown anti-communist message that both Congress and the public bought in.[176] As the *New York Times* put it: "The Marshall Plan appears to draw its greatest strength not from any special feeling that other peoples should be helped for their own sake, but only as a demonstration against the spread of communism."[177] Dean Acheson concurred, recalling that "what citizens and the representatives in Congress alike always wanted to learn in the last analysis was how Marshall aid operated to block the extension of Soviet power and the acceptance of Communist economic and political organization and alignment."[178]

Arming Europe

Though NATO would come to be the most resonant institution of the Western security order, its origins were really only a continuation of the processes launched for the Marshall Plan.[179] While the ERP was first conceived as an alternative to an American military commitment to Europe, it soon became clear that economic aid could only supplement military cooperation rather than replace it. "I have done and will continue to do all I can to bring the Marshall Plan to fruition," cabled UK Foreign Minister Bevin to Marshall in early 1948. "But essential though it is, progress in the economic field will not in itself suffice to call a halt to the Russian threat."[180]

The North Atlantic Treaty was finalized and formalized in 1949, yet the most critical period for its negotiation came in the first half of 1948. Documentary evidence indicates that a number of specific events triggered American leaders to relent on giving Europe—particularly France—the permanent peacetime military commitment they had long sought. Especially important here were (a) the utter deadlock at the London CFM meeting at the end of 1947; (b) the shocking Soviet-led coup in Czechoslovakia in February 1948; (c) evidence that March that the Soviets were pressuring the Nordic countries into signing Eastern Europe–like "mutual assistance" pacts; (d) French resistance throughout the spring to Anglo-American plans to more rapidly revitalize Western Germany absent a concrete American security commitment; and, finally (e) the total blockade of Berlin by the Soviets in late June.

Throughout these developments, it was in those moments when the Soviet threat appeared most imminent that American elites took the most significant steps toward committing to the ordering ideas behind NATO.[181] The London CFM meeting convinced Marshall that cooperation with the Soviets—doubtful as it was after the earlier CFM meeting in Moscow—was now out of the question. From this point on, he believed the Americans, British, and French should proceed with their own plans, particularly in regards to Germany, on the assumption that the USSR was now more adversary than ally.[182] Before Marshall departed from London, he met with Bevin for a series of important conversations about the possibility of an unprecedented security arrangement between their countries.[183]

Bevin soon put his ideas into writing and sent them to the State Department.[184] US officials offered general but noncommittal support and, as with the ERP, encouraged the Europeans to first take action among themselves.[185] This led to the Treaty of Brussels declaring a Western European defense pact in March of 1948, a pact that Marshall and Truman quickly and publicly supported.[186] It was only in response to the Soviet-backed coup in Czechoslovakia, the Soviet "request" for a treaty with Finland, and rumors of a similar initiative being forced upon Norway that Marshall finally offered to begin negotiations for an Atlantic security pact.[187] The next push forward came in the midst of French resistance to revitalization plans for Western Germany, resistance that became increasingly problematic for the United States as talks progressed in London that spring. In the end, France only reluctantly approved the "London Declarations" on West Germany because of increasingly tangible American promises of a security guarantee to Europe.[188] Finally, it was the Soviets' most provocative response to the London Declarations—the blockade of Berlin—that seemed to ultimately convince reluctant American officials to commence official negotiations for a more formal security commitment.[189]

The Vandenberg Resolution passed the US Senate on June 11, and on the 23rd Marshall cabled Ambassador Jefferson Caffery in Paris to say that the United States was now prepared to participate in "top secret exploratory talks" in line with that resolution, a position the National Security Council (NSC) and Truman himself officially endorsed in early July.[190] The first meeting of the "Washington Exploratory Talks on Security" commenced on July 6, and ultimately produced a joint policy paper by early September that would serve as the blueprint for the NAT.[191] Though the final negotiations would have to wait until after the contentious American elections later in the year, the Rubicon had essentially been crossed by the end of summer in 1948.[192]

The Soviet threat can thus precisely account for the timing, demand for, and supply of the order principle changes behind the North Atlantic alliance. Yet can that threat also account for NATO's shape and character? A number of observers posit that it cannot. In particular, they argue that Western leaders often chose to subordinate military effectiveness to other intra-alliance considerations, suggesting that NATO was *not* simply a defensive alliance but reflected a deeper logic built on Western commonalities that predated and transcended the Soviet threat. "Despite its obvious importance," argues David Lake, "the Soviet threat is insufficient as an explanation of American security relations" after the Second World War.[193] Steve Weber posits that "the principles on which an alliance is constructed and its institutional form are blind spots for neorealism."[194] Similarly, Mary Hampton argues that "the political goal of Allied cohesion would over time often take precedence over narrowly conceived military considerations. . . . "[195] Hampton's point in particular is certainly true: other considerations like Allied cohesion often *did* take precedence, leaving the alliance less militarily potent than it could have been. With relative ease, the United States could have formed a rigid and hierarchical alliance that maximized its freedom from and coercive capacity over its European subordinates.[196]

What this criticism ignores, however, was recognition by American elites that the Soviet Union was not only threatening for its military capacity. Accordingly, and in the words of Under Secretary of State Robert Lovett, "efforts to meet it should be directed to the ideological as well as the military threat. The respective countries should be strengthened to resist internal as well as external threats."[197] Throughout the Washington talks that ultimately produced the NAT, American officials were emphatic that the proposed agreement be a consensual and positive one—a genuinely multilateral pact directed toward a common vision of shared values in defense of a singular civilization (liberal order rules # 4 and 5)—rather than hierarchical (clearly dominated by America) and negative (purely reactive to the Soviet threat).[198] "It should be more than an arrangement for defense alone; it should serve both to preserve the common civilization and to promote its development by increasing the collaboration between the signatories," collaboration where US aid "must supplement rather than take the place of the maximum efforts" of all parties, they jointly declared in a policy paper that served as a basis for the treaty.[199] On the surface, this emphasis might look like an indictment of the excluding motive. Yet what becomes clear from assessing the 1948 Washington and State Department talks is that key officials favored this particular vision of NATO precisely *because* they believed it would be superior to a traditional military alliance for countering the Soviet menace.

Specifically, a truly consensual pact stressing a positive message would serve at least four strategic purposes related to targeting the Soviet/communist threat. First, downplaying the exclusively military nature of the pact would allow the United States to emphasize the continuing necessity of European nations practicing further integration among themselves. [200] Rearmament that "proceeds at any appreciable cost to European recovery," Kennan warned, "can do more harm than good."[201] Averell Harriman, now serving as ERA administrator in Europe, posited that the ultimate "objective should continue to be the progressively closer integration" of Western Europe.[202] "We are not thinking in terms of 'lend-lease' but of 'mutual aid,'" argued Dean Acheson shortly after becoming Truman's fourth Secretary of State in 1949, emphasizing that "it is our policy that economic recovery must not be sacrificed to rearmament and must continue to be given a clear priority."[203] As with the Marshall Plan, multilateralism was to be at the fore-front of this emerging vision to emphasize the necessity of Europeans continuing to act for themselves.

Second, this particular version of NATO would help the requisite states fight the most immediate threat—internal communist subversion—better than a sim-ple military alliance ever could.[204] "The problem at present is less one of defense against overt foreign aggression than against internal fifth-column aggression supported by the threat of external force, on the Czech model," argued John Hickerson, the State Department's Director for European Affairs and a key NATO architect. The response therefore had to go beyond simply rearming Western European states in isolation: "No security arrangement for Europe can be effective unless the free European governments and peoples are prepared to pool their resources and to resist by every means at their disposal," he emphasized, arguing that this was much more likely to happen through a positive unifying message than a negative one.[205] The participants in the Washington talks came around to a similar view, that emphasizing "the common Western approach" and "the Western attachment to the worth of the individual would be the best cement" for standing together against the threat of communist subversion.[206]

Third, emphasizing both a positive message and the multilateral nature of the pact would help attract skittish would-be allies into the arrangement (pathway #1, "commonalities for contrast"). The former attribute, the pact's positive message, was particularly important to the Scandinavian countries that had been enthusi-astic participants in the less overtly anti-Soviet ERP but were fearful about sign-ing onto a military pact.[207] As it was, Sweden ultimately declined to take part out of fear of provoking the Soviets, while Denmark and Norway only agreed to join very late in the process after receiving these kinds of assurances.[208]

The latter element, the pact's truly collaborative and multilateral nature, would soon prove crucial to courting West Germany. The United States was constantly fearful of the West Germans drifting toward neutralism (or worse) if they were courted by the Soviets or became disillusioned with the West.[209] As a result, American officials put a premium on bringing West Germany into the Western order, and did so in part by emphasizing the consensual and equality-based nature of the North Atlantic pact.[210] That West Germany's first Chancellor, Konrad Adenauer, leveraged these features to win his country greater concessions than the West had anticipated giving can be seen as the United States simply making good on the attractive promises of the NATO system.[211] A more assertive Germany was a price they were willing to pay for forever anchoring a crucial ally to the Western order.

Finally, Western officials recognized that a consensual and positively purposed alliance would offer a favorable contrast to the coercive and hierarchical Eastern Bloc in the eyes of the international community. The Western order would be more principled than the Soviet bloc, pronounced Bevin during his dramatic call for a North Atlantic alliance before the House of Commons in 1948. "It [hierarchy and coercion] is not in keeping with the spirit of Western civilization, and if we are to have an organism in the West it must be a spiritual union. . . . It must be on terms of equality and it must contain all the elements of freedom for which we all stand."[212] This is why American negotiators were so adamant that NATO have a normative component agreed to by all members. The pact "would lose a great deal of its moral strength," argued Lovett, "if it appeared merely to be aimed at the Soviet Union."[213] Its positive and genuinely multilateral nature was thus designed at least in part to highlight and delegitimate Soviet practices in their own sphere (pathway #3, "severing social power").[214]

In sum, there were very good strategic reasons for NATO taking the shape and character it did that were intimately connected to the threat it was designed to combat. Furthermore, the preceding analysis demonstrates that US officials fully recognized the benefits of constructing the pact in this way, and often insisted on doing so to maximize its effect in combatting the USSR. Both the shape and character ultimately taken by NATO, in short, can be fully accounted for by ordering-to-exclude theory.

7.3.5 Alternatives

Binding

Binding performs strongly in congruence testing for all three of the remaining rule changes in what is seemingly its strongest case. Advocacy for democratic membership (liberal order rule #5) fits well with the theory's contention that democratic regimes are the most able to commit to institutional settlements. A liberal security community with porous borders (liberal order rule #3) fulfills binding's expectation that members should seek to become increasingly enmeshed in one another's decisions. And the manifestation of true collective security through NATO (liberal order rule #4) appears to be a textbook example of the binding motive in action: the dominant state foregoes coercion in favor of constraints on its own power that give smaller members more decision-making authority. In short, it appears highly plausible that American leaders were cognizant of the need to make their empire one of invitation, not domination, in the aftermath of the Second World War.[215]

Important to note, however, is that demonstrating that the United States reaped the benefits of an institutionalized order after World War II is an altogether different task from demonstrating that elites were *motivated* to create that order for reasons consistent with the binding logic. Ikenberry has done well on the former—outcomes—effectively showing how the benefits of that system have accrued to the United States both during and after the Cold War.[216]

Yet he has been less convincing on the latter—motives—as evidence is scant that American elites actually acted as they did in the 1940s *because* they had binding foremost on their minds.[217] Evidence for this case once again does not support binding's logic of incentives for dominant and subordinate states. As with the post–World War I era, Ikenberry concedes that "European leaders were more concerned with American *abandonment* than with *domination*, and they consistently pressed for a formal and permanent American security commitment" that eventually came through NATO.[218] Yet as was discussed in chapter 6, the dominant actor will have different motives—and more leverage—when its principal veto power is abandonment rather than domination. Because American leaders knew that Europeans knew that they needed US engagement, the United States had negotiating leverage that a dominant actor most fearful of being labeled a bully would not. While it is certainly true that elites were concerned with how they would be portrayed in Europe, they were not nearly as open to compromise over the character and shape of the order as the binding logic anticipates.

This fact gets masked in congruence testing because the resulting alliance seemingly put restraints on American power. As I argued in the last section, however, *it was the United States, not Europe, that insisted on a truly multilateral alliance built around a positive message*. Whereas European elites would have been happy with a hierarchical anti-Soviet arrangement in which America provided all the security, US leaders insisted that the pact must be something more. As I have argued, their goal here was a continuation of their objective with the ERP: to get Europe to shoulder greater responsibility for defending itself by banding together in unprecedented ways.

Finally, it is worth noting that from his first major exploration of the post–World War II period in *After Victory* to his second in *Liberal Leviathan*, Ikenberry has substantially amended his interpretation of the settlement in ways that move away from a narrative of pure binding and closer to one of excluding. As he puts it in *Liberal Leviathan*, the "weakness of Europe, the looming Soviet threat, and the practical requirements of establishing institutions and making them work" transformed the trajectory of order building in ways American leaders had not previously envisioned.[219] On the consecration of stronger bonds within a liberal security community, he admits that "the Cold War alliance system and security commitments provided a wider and deeper foundation for cooperation among the 'free world' countries" than what had been imagined earlier.[220] In other words, the need for a deeper logic of cooperation among the liberal core of the order—my focus throughout this chapter—was not anticipated from the start. The original order vision had to be substantially amended most immediately due to the emergence of the Soviet/communist threat. That threat is thus *the* critical causal force in explaining this important shift in America's ordering strategy, and the story of the liberal international order's origins simply cannot be told without it.

Exporting

On the surface, exporting can seemingly account for most if not all elements of the Western security order. A liberal democratic membership principle clearly mirrors the American domestic system, a truly multilateral collective security system fits with US traditions of opposing excessive hierarchy, and a liberal security community is at least not inconsistent with the porous and open nature of the American polity.

Yet as in the 1919 case, the question is not about general influence but instead about what specific aspects the exporting motive can actually account for. Let us take each of the three order principles in turn. Unprecedented cooperation among a liberal security community? The historian Charles Maier has advanced a variant of this perspective by arguing that American leaders used their country's "politics of productivity"—the ways they overcame political and labor strife at home through redefining the debate as one over production, efficiency, and growth—as a model for how to help Europe overcome its own disagreements.[221] This is a thesis that nicely aligns with the exporting perspective advanced by Michael Hogan in his pathbreaking study of the Marshall Plan. Yet for all of their considerable merits, these accounts highlight the importance of the threat environment at least as much as they do exporting impulses. Maier admits that policymakers were also strongly influenced by their desire to undercut the appeal of communist parties across Europe.[222] And while Hogan's account convincingly demonstrates that the Marshall Plan's *implementation* fits well with American corporatist traditions at home, the early chapters of his study analyzing the *origins* of the ERP actually lend stronger support to an excluding narrative than an exporting one.[223]

The true multilateralism inherent in NATO? "America's historical experience, political culture—and national biases," argues one scholar evincing this perspective, "drove its multilateral approach to the military element of containment."[224] Yet while this might initially make some sense, upon further reflection it isn't clear why US domestic traditions would dictate that it *had* to support this type of international arrangement over all other options available at the time. As John

Ruggie rightly asks, "why would a system of bilateral alliances have been incompatible" with American values, particularly since NATO as a permanent alliance was seen at the time as such a *deviation* from prior US traditions?[225] It must also be remembered that at the same time as policymakers chose multilateralism and institutionalization in the Atlantic community, they chose bilateralism and ad hoc relations with their East Asian allies.[226] If exporting domestic traditions was truly a major impetus behind the postwar order, this vision should have been consistently implemented across the world.

Democratic membership principles? True, American statesmen strongly articulated in public the importance of liberal values for their postwar decision-making. Yet as the Cold War progressed beyond the time period and region analyzed in this section (1945–1949 in Europe), it became clear that US officials were less committed to the positive principle of liberal democracy than they were to the negative one of forestalling communism. As Leffler concludes, policymakers often treated ideological principles like their commitment to liberalism "as tools and levers to be used to constrain potential foes, influence prospective allies," and generally serve strategic interests. "Rarely does a sense of real compassion and/or moral fervor emerge from the documents and diaries of high officials."[227] These officials would continue to espouse the virtues of democracy in public when it served their interests, but they ultimately appeared less interested in advancing ideology for its own sake than they were in halting the advance of a contrary set of ideas. As George Kennan himself plainly put it in 1950, "it is better to have a strong regime in power than a liberal government if it is indulged and relaxed and penetrated by Communists."[228]

Overall, evidence simply does not square with an interpretation that attributes *primary* importance to America's liberal values for generating its postwar order preferences. Exporting arguments appear better equipped instead to explain order paths *not* chosen. More specifically, exporting provides perhaps the most convincing explanation for why a "spheres of responsibility" (SOR) global order vision was effectively taken off the table by American policymakers at numerous critical junctures.

Two variants of an SOR order seemed viable at the time and merit consideration. The first was encapsulated in Roosevelt's "four policemen" vision whereby America, the USSR, the UK, and China would assume responsibility for their respective geographical region. Roosevelt had long favored such a vision of global order. Yet he came to realize as the war drew to a close that the American public would likely only support an order vision that centered around a universal organization that carried worldwide appeal. Accordingly, he moved away from his bare-bones policemen idea and toward a universalist vision focused on the United Nations.[229]

The second SOR vision was encapsulated in the "percentages" agreement reached by Stalin and Churchill in late 1944, in the "spirit" of the Yalta understandings between the Big Three over Eastern Europe in early 1945, and then, more explicitly, in the agreement at the Potsdam conference that had been the brainchild of Secretary of State Byrnes. I focus here on the last of these agreements, that seemingly forged by Byrnes at Potsdam: while the superpowers would disband their wartime alliance and essentially go their separate ways in postwar reconstruction, each would also recognize the other's legitimate control of the region it occupied at war's end. This included a tacit acknowledgment of a division of Germany specifically and of Europe more generally.[230]

Once again, however, this deal was scuttled by public resistance (both real and anticipated) in the United States. For different reasons, both the political right and left objected to any deal that would consign millions of Europeans to oppressive and autocratic rule while consecrating the permanent division of Germany.[231] As a result of outcry at home, FDR and then especially Truman adopted a harder line on Soviet behavior in its sphere, particularly in Poland and then in Germany, even after the Soviets believed they had received permission for a live-and-let-live SOR order at Yalta and Potsdam.[232] Exporting impulses thus appear to have played an important role in limiting the ordering choice-set of American elites, even as these impulses were not powerful enough to dictate what the alternative to an SOR order would look like.

Learning

Learning cannot account for the liberal security community order preference, and it is ambiguous as to whether or not the promotion of democratic regimes as a membership principle fits as a "lesson" of the Second World War. Yet the learning motive has a strong claim on the American preference for a true collective security system (liberal order rule #4). In particular, scholars have argued that the United States learned an important lesson after the Second World War that it had refused to properly internalize after the First: America's fate, as well as the fate of the world, would forever be tied to the stability of Europe.[233] Jeffrey Legro offers a powerful variant of this argument, showing how "the notion developed that trouble on the Continent—even if it were not an imminent military threat—could have profound implications for U.S. security."[234] The strength of Legro's account is its ability to document and track changes in the collective ideas of the American public, beginning with skepticism for international organizations and global activism but dramatically moving in the early 1940s to much greater openness to both.[235]

The difficulty for this variant of the learning motive is substantial evidence of a strong desire on the part of American officials at the end of the Second

World War to once again get out of Europe as quickly as possible. Forsaking the reconstruction of an independent and unified Germany remained a viable policy option in the United States and was not truly taken off the table until the emergence of significant problems with the USSR and corresponding fears of the Soviets harnessing German power.[236]

More broadly, the "automatic" nature of the American commitment to Europe has often been drastically overstated in historical accounts. As a number of scholars have more recently demonstrated, it remained an American priority in the late 1940s—and even throughout much of the 1950s—to get Europe to shoulder the burden for its own defense so that the United States could withdraw from the continent.[237] American officials ultimately failed on this front, becoming more permanently entrenched in Europe than they had envisioned or wanted. Yet the fact that US elites actively resisted this commitment for so long is a blow to the learning argument. This resistance was evident at each step along the way to greater commitment, from the advent of the ERP to the NAT negotiations to the restructuring of NATO after the Korean War to the (failed) American attempts to hand off security responsibilities to Europe in the 1950s, first in conventional forces with the European Defense Community (EDC) and later with nuclear weapons through the Multilateral Force (MLF).[238] Given the effort US leaders put into these struggles and the depth of their resistance to making a long-term commitment to Europe, the full-throated embrace of internationalism and sharp break from the past do not look nearly as striking or as clear-cut as Legro and others have characterized them.

7.4 Conclusion: Order Construction in the American Century

The two most far-reaching cases of order building in the twentieth century provide strong support for ordering-to-exclude theory relative to the alternatives (see Table 7.2), stronger even than the European cases of chapters 4 and 5. In the "least likely" case of 1919, the theory can fully account for two out of four order preferences and partially account for one of the others. In the post–World War II case that has been the focus of this chapter, it can fully account for all five American preferences for major order changes in the 1940s.

The alternatives do not perform nearly as well. In what are supposed to be the strongest cases for the binding motive, its logic can often correctly predict the United States' expected preferences (congruence testing). Yet the case for the binding logic falls apart due to a dearth of evidence for its influence upon key decision-makers (process tracing). Exporting successfully predicts some of the observed order preferences—predominantly and predictably those

Table 7.2 Results: American Cases

Era	Order Preferences	Exclude	Bind	Export	Learn
1919	1: Institutionalized dispute resolution mechanisms	A/N	Y/N	A/N	Y/Y
	2: Abolition of inter-unit war initiation	A/Y	Y/N	A/N	Y/Y
	3: Gradual transition from imperial system to colonial mandates system	Y/Y	Y/N	A/N	A/N
	4: To orderly and nominally democratic regimes	Y/Y	A/N	Y/N	A/N
1945	1: Cooperation on economic openness, standardization, and stability	Y/Y	Y/N	Y/N	Y/Y
	2: To social welfare–enhancing regimes	Y/Y	Y/N	Y/N	Y/Y
	3: Establishment of a liberal security community with porous borders	Y/Y	Y/N	A/N	N/N
	4: True collective security through mutual guarantees	Y/Y	Y/N	A/N	Y/N
	5: To liberal democratic regimes	Y/Y	Y/N	Y/N	Y/N

Note: Pass congruence test? / Pass process tracing test? Y = Yes; N = No; A = Ambiguous; Shading = passed both tests.

involving membership rules—but finds surprisingly little support in process tracing. Strongest among the alternatives is learning, which can once again explain some aspects of American decision-making after each of the World Wars. As in the previous cases, however, this could be due to the interconnectedness of the prewar and postwar threats decision-makers faced in both cases, rather than the inherent strength of the learning logic itself.

Overall, then, ordering-to-exclude theory significantly outperforms the alternatives for the major American instances of order building. Seen from this perspective, and particularly when compared to the motives of European leaders in previous centuries, the American order-building projects of the twentieth century look far less exceptional than they have conventionally been portrayed.

8

Consolidating the Liberal International Order

WHILE LUNCHING WITH a foreign leader on November 9, 1989, Secretary of State James Baker received an unusual note from his aide: "The East German Government has just announced that it is fully opening its borders to the West. The implication from the announcement is full freedom of travel via current East German/West German links between borders." Excusing himself as soon as he could, Baker rushed to discuss the shocking news with his boss, President George H. W. Bush.[1] The utterly unanticipated fall of the Berlin Wall was a momentous event that capped a year full of them. Most notable was the unexpected end of the Brezhnev Doctrine, the policy of the Soviet Union to keep the states of its informal empire in line through the threat or use of force. Yet when Soviet General Secretary Mikhail Gorbachev signaled that he would no longer do so, the world witnessed unprecedented displays of autonomy and defiance throughout Eastern Europe that culminated in the rapid disintegration of the communist regimes there.[2] Observers believed they were seeing the beginning of a new world order, and the American president would soon employ that very phase to describe the unanticipated but rapid transition taking place from the Cold War to a post–Cold War era.

And yet for all the talk about revolutionary transformation, American leaders ultimately came to prefer, in the words of one historian, "to retool and refurbish old institutions rather than construct new ones."[3] In contrast to the extraordinary transformations after World War II, the pivotal changes in international power and influence that took place between the end of 1989 and 1991 did not correspond with matching changes in American order preferences or, more importantly, in order outcomes. Instead, US leaders ultimately chose to stick with existing order principles, maintaining continuity of the Western order in the transition from the Cold War to a post–Cold War international system. We can account for this continuity in American order preferences, I argue, by examining American perceptions of the lack of new threats in this critical period.

In this chapter, I focus on the principal security component of Western order at the end of the Cold War, NATO. This is not to say that the economic components of that order are unimportant, or even that their continuity cannot also be explained by ordering-to-exclude theory.[4] Instead, I focus on security because it was the element of the Western order that was most controversial at the end of the Cold War and seemingly had the greatest chance for fundamental transformation. More than the economic parts, the security elements of the American-led order seemed especially "up for grabs" in the pivotal years of 1989 and 1990. This was an extraordinary moment rife with enormous potential for transformation. That US preferences over the security aspects of order remained constant even in the face of powerful calls for change is a puzzling development that requires explanation.

8.1 Order Preferences

Order continuity wasn't simply a shortsighted or default policy position unthinkingly implemented across the United States government. It was consciously chosen by statesmen who were thoughtfully considering the larger Cold War endgame. Key members of the George H. W. Bush administration were distinctly aware of the critical juncture they were navigating. National Security Adviser Brent Scowcroft supervised a comprehensive review of US–Soviet relations across the government's major foreign policy agencies when the Bush administration first came into office.[5] In meetings of the principals, Scowcroft would consistently ask, "'Where do[es the United States] want to be twenty years from now?'"[6] And for all of the popular attention to President Bush's discomfort with the "vision thing" of the office, his was not an administration that lacked historical perspective or understanding of the monumental legacies their decisions would have. "I don't want people to look back 20 or 40 years from now and say, 'That's where everything went off track. That's where progress stopped,'" Bush privately confided to his advisers early in his term.[7] "Bush and Scowcroft mused about this remarkable opportunity to pick up where Roosevelt had left off in 1945" while fishing in Maine in the summer of 1990, the same occasion where Scowcroft began referring to the "new world order" that would soon make its way into the president's speeches.[8] "Historians are likely to view 1989 as a year, like 1848, which transformed a continent," Scowcroft wrote privately to Bush.[9] This was not a team, in short, that made major policy decisions without considering the larger ramifications.

The order contest at the end of the Cold War came to the forefront of international politics via the rapid and revolutionary process of German reunification.

Grappling with the fate of Germany involved answering difficult questions at both the intra-German level (addressing questions over how to reunify) and the international level (addressing questions over which order/orders reunified Germany should join).[10] The positions of the Soviet Union, as well as American allies Britain and France, evolved throughout the period. Even the West German government would shift its stance on reunified Germany's international status in response to developments. Yet from the beginning of the process to its end, American preferences remained remarkably fixed and firm: they would accept nothing less than a fully reunified Germany fully integrated into a NATO alliance that would remain the premier security institution of Europe.[11] As Bush and Scowcroft have freely admitted in the time since, they recognized that this was an issue area where they "could exercise real, perhaps decisive, influence" over the future of Europe and the wider world. Yet they had to remain unyielding to achieve success, as the "outcome was not at all foreordained."[12]

Throughout this critical period, key members of Bush's administration made both implicit and explicit decisions to advocate continuity in the Western order established after the Second World War. What continuity meant above all was the preservation and then the expansion of the existing NATO system. Bush officials not only chose to fiercely protect NATO's right to continue on after the Cold War but also supported efforts to actually increase its power and influence. While NATO would endure, the institutions of the Soviet-led eastern order—especially the Warsaw Pact—would not. Furthermore, newer institutional competitors to NATO that would more comfortably fit the vision of a united Europe supported by a growing number of leaders around the world—most notably, the Conference on Security and Cooperation in Europe, or CSCE—would be kept subordinate to the existing Western order. On all of these things, the Bush administration explicitly chose and forcefully pursued preserving the Western order and then expanding it eastward rather than working with allies and former adversaries to start anew.[13]

While the Bush administration decided soon after the Berlin Wall's fall to fight for continuity, other foreign leaders were more intent on transforming order. Had the Soviet leader Mikhail Gorbachev had his way, both NATO and the Warsaw Pact would have been either disbanded or integrated into what he envisioned as a new pan-European order.[14] "What I dislike is when some U.S. politicians say unity of Europe should be on the basis of Western values," Gorbachev told Bush at their first summit meeting, in Malta, at the end of 1989.[15] If either of the Cold War alliances remained in place and invited a united Germany to join, the other should do so as well. "You are a sailor," he said to Bush at their second summit meeting. "You will understand that if one anchor is good, two anchors are better."[16]

Parity between the Cold War orders and dual German membership was one option. Yet Gorbachev's clear preference was for getting rid of these old institutions altogether in favor of something new and more inclusive. "I too believed that we needed a 'safety net' which would protect us and the rest of Europe from any 'surprises' from the Germans," recalled the last leader of the USSR. "However, unlike the Americans, I thought that these security mechanisms should be provided not by NATO but by new structures created within a pan-European framework."[17] Gorbachev referred to this new framework as "a Common European Home," and argued that reunified Germany should remain detached from the existing alliances until this new institutional web could be constructed.[18] "I was thinking about the common roots of this multiform and yet fundamentally indivisible European civilization," he later recorded in his memoirs, "and perceived with growing awareness the artificiality of the political blocs and the archaic nature of the 'iron curtain.'"[19]

Other prominent elites shared the Soviet leader's inclusive vision or at least something akin to it. French President François Mitterrand spoke of creating a European confederation that, like in Gorbachev's plan, would become the premier pan-European forum for security issues.[20] Hans Dietrich Genscher, West Germany's Foreign Minister, aimed to make the CSCE the focal point of German reunification negotiations while attempting to sideline the Cold War alliances and superpowers.[21] Even the West German Chancellor Helmut Kohl—who would soon become closely associated with the American position—at first supported the "embedding of the future structure of Germany within the pan-European process."[22]

In spite of America's immense power advantages, Gorbachev and his perestroika platform were immensely popular across Europe and around the world, and the outcome of this order contest was by no means certain. At the beginning of the fateful year of 1990, it became clear that the United States would have a fight on its hands over the order's future shape. "Our nightmare was that Gorbachev would announce in March 1990 that he would accept German unity but not NATO membership," recalled a prominent Bush adviser.[23]

Yet through the combination of America's preponderant power and the tactful negotiating of Bush, Baker, and the German leader Helmut Kohl, the West achieved total victory in translating these preferences for continuity into outcomes. Somehow, Bush and Baker were able to convince Gorbachev and his influential Foreign Minister Eduard Shevardnadze to allow NATO to become the linchpin of post–Cold War Europe and the institutional home of reunified Germany. Nearly all observers of the negotiating process—policymakers and academics, Americans, Europeans, and Russians alike—agree that this outcome was a remarkable victory for America. "For the United States, and

ultimately for Europe," recalled Bush, "reunification was an astonishingly successful achievement." And for Scowcroft, quite simply, "the Cold War ended
when the Soviets accepted a united Germany in NATO."[24] Overall, American
leaders grasped the monumental importance of the moment and vociferously
pursued the goal "to bribe the Soviets out of Germany, not to set up long-term
cooperation or structures in which Gorbachev and his successors would be full
partners."[25]

8.2 Threats and Motives

In this section, I make the case that America's diminishing threat perceptions can
convincingly account for its preferences for order continuity in the fateful year of
1990. I do so by making five points. First, while the Soviet Union was no longer
an ideological threat, it remained for the United States a formidable material one.
Second, the Bush administration not only passively resisted order transformations but also actively worked against other actors that were pursuing such transformations. Third, American elites adopted assumptions about the need for order
continuity in Europe that only make sense if we take the motives highlighted by
ordering-to-exclude theory into account. Fourth, US elites used their advantages
in the existing order to shut out or hold down the Soviets wherever they could,
and in novel ways consistent with the theory. Fifth, though US elites targeted the
Soviet Union throughout this period, they chose to emphasize only the aspects
of the Western security order that corresponded with the parts of the USSR they
still found threatening. .

First, and after decades of relative stability, the United States entered 1990
in a drastically altered and significantly less threatening security environment.
The late 1980s were characterized by the United States making remarkable gains
in both material and especially ideological power at the Soviet Union's expense.
The collective threat perceptions of the Bush administration thus appropriately
vacillated between *continuity*—the Soviet Union (and later, post-Soviet Russia)
was still the foremost threat—and *ambiguity*, an acknowledgment that the
Cold War as an ideological and global geopolitical struggle was likely ending,
but with fundamental uncertainty as to what would come next. On the latter,
ambiguity, one of Bush's diary entries from early 1990 is particularly instructive: "Who's the enemy? I keep getting asked that. It's apathy; it's the inability
to predict accurately; it's dramatic change that can't be foreseen. . . . There's all
kinds of events that we can't foresee that require a strong NATO, and there's all
kinds of potential instability that requires a strong U.S. presence."[26] This was a
sentiment Bush would repeat over and over again throughout the year, in public

press conferences and in private conversations with foreign leaders: uncertainty was no excuse for complacence, and no reason for fundamental change in Europe.[27]

As for the continuity of the Soviet/Russian threat, it was clear by the critical juncture of 1989–1990 that ideological momentum was no longer on the Soviets' side. The USSR was obviously in rapid economic decline, while Gorbachev's policy of easing its control of Eastern Europe had led those polities to cast off communist ideology much more quickly than Moscow had anticipated. Aside from a handful of isolated regimes in far corners of the world, the only other stable communist state, China, was succeeding precisely because of capitalist market-based reforms rather than socialist ones. While the Cold War as a European diplomatic and military standoff may not have been over by 1990, it was thus clear by this time that the Soviet Union had decisively lost the global ideological contest.[28]

What nearly all of the principals of the Bush administration agreed upon, however, was that Russia would remain an important security challenge moving forward. Consensus existed that a sizable American military presence must continue in Europe. Bush himself agreed wholeheartedly with Mitterrand's assessment during a friendly meeting with the French leader in 1990: "The risk of war has decreased.... Nevertheless, a threat remains. Gorbachev may have to make certain dangerous postures if he is forced by necessity, so we must retain our security arrangements.... The Soviet Union is not reassuring: a great power in a weakened condition is dangerous."[29] Yet overall, the concern now was not for ideological and traditional power together, but instead for the latter—military power—alone.

It was precisely this military component that still deeply concerned American elites. "The administration held this view," recall two prominent Bush foreign policy officials, "because the political situation seemed so turbulent and unsettled, because U.S. forces in Europe had become vital to projections of American power in other areas such as the Middle East, and because Soviet military power would inevitably remain large enough to overawe Western Europe if the Americans departed."[30] The changes of the past year had been significant, Bush told British Prime Minister Thatcher in early 1990, but "the jury is still out on the changes we may see" going forward, particularly in the military sphere.[31] He wrote the next month to Kohl, the West German Chancellor at the time, that "Even if, as we hope, the Soviet Union withdraws all its troops from Eastern Europe, it will still remain far and away the most powerful single military power in Europe."[32] Even if it was now less of an existential menace than it had seemed at the height of the Cold War, the traditional threat of the Soviets using their massive military superiority to overwhelm Eastern *and* Western Europe still haunted American observers. We "believe caution is in order," said Bush's incoming Defense Secretary,

Richard Cheney, summing up the administration's view of the Soviets. "We must guard against gambling our nation's security on what may be a temporary aberration in the behavior of our foremost adversary."[33]

Second, evidence suggests that this altered threat environment is critical for explaining American order preferences—as well as its general foreign policy behavior—during this critical juncture. In particular, it lends support to hypothesis 1D's expectation that continuity of threat engenders continuity of order preferences. Like in 1763, 1848, and 1856, the dominant power pursued order continuity in the absence of new perceptions of threat (chapters 4 and 5). Yet unlike in those previous cases, an investigation of US actions at the end of the Cold War shows not simply a passive preference for order continuity but instead a rigorous campaign to defeat the transformative order plans of other actors.

US leaders insisted on a post–Cold War vision of a "Europe, Whole and Free"—Bush's rhetorical alternative to Gorbachev's "Common European Home"[34]—that would see the eastern order dismantled and pan-European solutions subordinated while NATO would not only endure but expand to include a reunified Germany. Bush's team was adamant throughout 1990 that they could not allow the fate of Germany to be subsumed within some kind of new pan-European security order in which the United States might be sidelined. The most likely venue for this new order was the CSCE, the preferred institutional forum of the Soviets (and sometimes the British, the French, and factions within both Germanys as well). American elites therefore imagined themselves in a race against time to get the two halves of Germany reunited with an agreement on NATO membership *before* a crucial fall meeting of the CSCE. Bush personally took it upon himself to secure Kohl's pledge prior to his May summit with Gorbachev that the West German government would "be unshakable on the question of Germany's membership in NATO and the need to maintain the American military presence, including both nuclear and conventional forces" no matter what Gorbachev or others attempted to persuade him of otherwise.[35] Through the entirety of the diplomatic battle, the American position remained that while they were willing to help Gorbachev save face in the negotiations for the sake of his domestic political position, they would not budge on their underlying order preferences.

Third, behind the American preference for continuity were two assumptions that largely seemed to go unquestioned by US elites. Specifically, they couched their preferences on their stated beliefs (a) that the United States would only be able to maintain a major military commitment to Europe if it did so via NATO; and (b) that NATO would provide the most effective institutional environment to bind a united Germany to Europe (as well as preserve European stability more generally).[36] Both of these positions merit additional scrutiny.

On the first assumption—the necessity of NATO for continued American engagement in Europe—it is difficult to derive where this position came from, who genuinely rather than just strategically supported it, why why. Key administration officials certainly stated it as fact in important venues. Bush wrote to foreign leaders that "NATO is the only plausible justification in my country for the American military presence in Europe," yet without specifying why he believed this to be the case.[37] He agreed with the NATO Secretary General's assessment that "If Germany is out of the integrated NATO structure, the United States will be out of Europe. This will lead to great destabilization in Europe."[38] Scowcroft believed that on the subject of America's long-term commitment to Europe, "the vehicle for that role must be NATO. The alliance was the only way the US could keep forces in Europe as a visible commitment to its security and stability. In addition, a united Germany as a full member of the alliance was key to our presence. . . . If it left the alliance, it would be difficult if not impossible to retain American troops in Europe."[39] NATO was "the raison d'être for keeping US forces in Europe," echoed Baker, and "we couldn't have US forces in Europe on the soil of a non-full member of NATO."[40]

On the second issue—NATO as the superior apparatus for German and European security—American officials again held firm to a position they regarded as self-evident, yet without providing consistent justification. "I hope that you agree that the North Atlantic Alliance is an essential component of Europe's future," Bush conveyed to Mitterrand in early 1990. "Indeed it is difficult to visualize how a European collective security arrangement including Eastern Europe, and perhaps even the Soviet Union, would have the capability to deter threats to Western Europe."[41] "The most dangerous course of all," Scowcroft warned Bush, "may be to allow others to set the shape and character of a united Germany and of all future structure of European security."[42] In reaction to a proposal by the West German Minister Genscher to allow the CSCE to take the reins of the reunification negotiations, Scowcroft was adamant that "there was no way we could accept [the CSCE] absorbing NATO and its functions."[43] The president also complained to Kohl at Camp David about the Soviets attempting to keep Germany out of NATO, but without justifying why he believed that institution was the best (or only) option for containing German power.[44]

Sometimes officials explained that these positions came from a fear that Gorbachev's pan-European vision would bring too many players to the table for effective diplomacy to succeed. Robert Zoellick, a Counselor to the Department of State and trusted advisor to Baker, warned his boss that "we must avoid any 'Congress of Vienna' effort to draw up rigid guidelines for a new European order."[45] Baker evidently shared his aide's views, writing that "a CSCE conference on German unification [what Gorbachev wanted] was a non-starter. It was

difficult to understand how such delicate diplomatic negotiations could be managed with thirty-five participants, and CSCE's rule of consensus would give the
smaller states of Europe veto power over issues far beyond their standing."[46] In
nearly identical reasoning, Scowcroft argued that "CSCE, with its consensus
procedures, allowed any country uneasy with the prospect of a large Germany
much greater potential to stall or delay."[47] Rejecting Thatcher's suggestion to
take Gorbachev's vision more seriously, he indicated that it "was an unacceptable
notion, both because of the centrality of NATO to US strategy and because, to
me, collective security, as typified by the League of Nations and United Nations,
was, in the end, no security at all."[48] In the end, he successfully counseled Bush on
the need to avoid the dangers of "an open-ended negotiation about the future of
Europe in about the worst multilateral settling one can imagine."[49]

Yet from the standpoint of the overall stability of Europe, the American
position did not make much sense.[50] In the short term, it is no doubt true that
American elites saw the CSCE route as detrimental to achieving rapid German
reunification, a goal they understandably wanted to achieve before disingenuous
objectors found ways to delay or derail the project. Yet it remains unclear why US
officials could not have embraced the pan-European vision as a *long-term* solution
to European security, especially after Gorbachev proposed a transition period
whereby Germany would become a member of both Cold War alliances before
eventually joining a "Common European Home" sometime in the future. As the
Soviet leader angrily indicated to Baker, the American positions on Germany and
Europe were contradictory:

> You've said to us that both Germanys want peace, they both want democ-
> racy, and, therefore they pose no danger. . . . So when you are talking
> about a united Germany and you say that if Germany is not in NATO, it
> would create problems, what you are really saying is that you don't believe
> Germany can be trusted. . . . [I]f you *are* saying that, then there's a prob-
> lem. Because you are saying you continue to need a bloc even when the
> other alliance is disappearing.[51]

Aside from the simple fact that NATO was *their* alliance, Bush administration
officials did not and perhaps could not articulate why that order would make a
more appropriate home for Germany than either a reorganized eastern order or a
new pan-European one.

I submit that this obstinate insistence on continuity makes sense only when we
take ordering-to-exclude logic into account. American elites were naturally more
inclined to support an order vision that would best protect the power and security of the United States, not necessarily one that would include other European

actors. While a transformational pan-European order might have been better for the Russians—not to mention other marginalized actors across Europe—American leaders had little incentive to pursue such significant changes. "I don't want to see us fettered by a lot of multi-lateral decisions," Bush recorded in his diary in late February, arguing that "we've got to lead, so we should not be just kind of watered down, picking up the bill, and acquiescing in a lot of decisions that might hurt us."[52] For one thing, they already possessed what they believed was the ideal institution for reconciling their level of involvement and freedom of action in Europe security affairs on American terms. More importantly, while US leaders did not yet perceive a major new threat horizon, they remained significantly wary of the old one. Simply put, suspicions remained high even in 1990 that the Soviets would succeed in "tricking" the West into relaxing Cold War suspicions just enough to gain a decisive advantage.[53] Scowcroft's study group in the administration's first year expressed the fear that they were being lulled into a false sense of security whereby the Soviets would achieve their goal of "disband[ing] the Western coalition by smothering us with kindness."[54]

American elites appeared especially apprehensive about the Soviets cutting a separate deal with European states. After claiming concerns over too many voices at the negotiating table as his principal objection to elevating the CSCE, Baker revealed that his greatest fear was *actually* the possibility of "the Germans and the Soviets going off alone and cutting a private deal disadvantageous to Western interests."[55] Zoellick recalls that a major objective throughout the period was "to counter initiatives such as Gorbachev's 'Common European Home'" that he and others believed would have intentionally "marginalized the United States in Europe."[56] "What worries me is talk that Germany must not stay in NATO," Bush confided to Kohl at Camp David, laying the reasoning behind his preferences bare. "To hell with that! We prevailed, they [the Russians] didn't. We can't let the Soviets clutch victory from the jaws of defeat."[57] Overall, American officials indicated that they were not about to willingly surrender an order that had served their interests for over forty years for one that would invite their adversary into the fray and give it a privileged place at the table. Consistent with hypothesis 1D the lack of a new threat on the horizon, coupled with fears over a diminished but still dangerous Soviet adversary, gave US statesmen little reason to embrace proposed order changes.

Fourth, and most importantly, American leaders used their advantages in the existing order to shut out, disadvantage, and generally weaken the Soviets throughout the negotiations over Germany and NATO. In so doing, they employed each powerful pathway of an ordering-to-exclude strategy. First, they utilized pathway #1 ("commonalities for contrast") by coopting other European actors, particularly the newly autonomous and non-communist regimes in

Eastern Europe, to embrace America's vision of order continuity. They did so by offering them membership into the Western economic order, most notably dangling the inducements of bilateral aid and GATT membership. The effect of this leverage can be seen by examining the public pronouncements of Václav Havel, Czechoslovakia's new president at the time. Initially a vocal opponent of *any* role for Cold War institutions in the future of Europe, he was soon turned from NATO skeptic to one of the alliance's most prominent champions after promises of Western inducements.[58]

Next, the Bush administration employed pathway #3 ("severing social power") by structuring the very negotiations over the fate of Germany in a way that would privilege the American position and sideline the Soviet one. Though their position was sometimes difficult to pin down, the Soviets seemed to prefer a pan-European forum—likely the CSCE—to negotiate about Germany. Instead, the United States succeeded in instituting a "2 + 4" format whereby the two—West and East Germany—would play the foremost role while supported by the four former occupying powers of postwar Germany, the US, USSR, Britain, and France. This transformed the negotiation forum from one that would have involved numerous disparate actors on equal footing into one dominated by NATO advocates while the Soviets would be outnumbered and sidelined.[59] Administration officials couldn't have been much clearer about their aims here in private correspondence and recollection. "Frankly, it's in our interest," posited Baker, "as it prevents separate German-Soviet deals that could be prejudicial to our interests."[60] "I prefer to call two plus four the 'two-by-four,'" argued another diplomat, "because it represents in fact a lever to insert a united Germany in NATO whether the Soviets like it or not." CIA Director Robert Gates referred to 2 + 4 as an ideal way "to give the Russians a feeling that they're a participant in this and it's not done over their heads," even as the ultimate plan was to "roll them."[61] "Such a forum also would ensure that reunification was not the result of a deal between the Soviets and Bonn in which [West Germany's] tie to NATO would be jettisoned as the price for Soviet agreement," he added, getting to the heart of the policy disagreement.[62] "The real purpose of Two-Plus-Four," argued Scowcroft, pulling all of these points together, "was to bring the Soviets along while preventing separate German-Soviet deals."[63]

Yet as advantageous as 2 + 4 seemingly was for the United States, the Bush administration still left nothing to chance. "In no event will we allow the Soviet Union to use the Four Power mechanism as an instrument to try to force you to create the kind of Germany Moscow might want, at the pace Moscow might prefer," Bush wrote to Kohl shortly their fateful Camp David meeting in February.[64] Instead, he made sure to work out a unified position with Kohl—and then to get approval on it from Thatcher in Britain and Mitterrand in France—before presenting a unified front (and a fait accompli) to the Soviets.[65] "We need to be low-key about our activities at One Plus Three," Bush said privately, appropriately updating the math on the negotiation forum to more accurately reflect reality. "We don't want to give the Soviets the impression that they are being dealt out."[66] Yet by design, that is exactly what was happening.

This was no small feat. Between the trips of Kohl and Baker to Moscow in early February and the conclusion of the Bush-Kohl Camp David summit at the end of the month, American officials were able to pull off a remarkable sleight of hand. At the beginning of the month, all of the principals had seemingly backed a plan announced by Genscher—the West German Foreign Minister who supported Gorbachev's pan-European vision—that would have seen a reunified Germany with an extremely limited and special status in NATO. Specifically, NATO troops would agree to never enter the territory of the former East Germany, and the alliance itself would pledge that "whatever happens to the Warsaw Pact, an expansion of NATO territory to the East, in other words, closer to the borders of the Soviet Union, will not happen."[67]

Yet by the conclusion of the Camp David meeting between Bush and Kohl only two weeks later, the Americans had succeeded in getting the German leader to back a remarkably different arrangement much more in line with US preferences. "We share a common belief that a unified Germany should remain a *full* member of the North Atlantic Treaty Organization, *including participation in its military structure*," Bush pointedly declared to the press at the conclusion of Kohl's visit.[68] This rhetorical shift was intentional, as documents reveal Bush stressing before the meeting the urgency of getting "Kohl to agree that a unified Germany would be a full member of NATO and a participant in its integrated military structure, and to state that *publicly*."[69] By transforming 2 + 4 to 1 + 3, the Bush administration was able to achieve a united Western front on order continuity in Europe where none had previous existed, and in a matter of mere days.[70]

Most striking on this front, however, was their subsequent utilization of pathway #2 ("triggering tripwires") to turn Gorbachev's own rhetoric against him at a decisive moment in the negotiations, thus toppling the last remaining hurdle to reunified Germany in NATO, Soviet opposition. This moment came on the first day of the Washington summit late May of 1990. Administration officials were not anticipating a breakthrough on Germany at the summit. Indeed, throughout the spring Gorbachev had conveyed time and time again the impossibility of the American position on Germany and NATO for the Soviet Union.[71] Yet US officials had also previously noted how Gorbachev's affinity for new thinking "makes it difficult for him to appear unresponsive to bold, new ideas" and sought to use this observation to their advantage.[72]

The trap was set by Bush using the carrot of the CSCE to engage Gorbachev in a discussion of the principles behind the Helsinki Accords' Final Act, the agreement that had established the CSCE in the first place. "CSCE had long been the Kremlin's preferred security institution," remembers Baker about this critical meeting, "and when the President relied on CSCE principles to explain a united Germany's choice of NATO as its alliance, Gorbachev was in the difficult position of having to refute an argument that depended on CSCE principles."[73] The Helsinki principle that Bush invoked to trap Gorbachev was that any state, large or small, should be afforded the self-determination to choose its own fate, including its own alliances. "Gorbachev had often adopted the rhetoric of free choice and national self-determination," surmise Zelikow and Rice. "So when Bush struck the wall of resistance from this new angle, it suddenly cracked," forcing the Russian leader to give in.[74] The Helsinki Final Act said that "all countries had the right to choose their alliances," Bush noted. To him, "that meant Germany should be able to decide for itself what it wanted."[75] Shouldn't the Germans have the right to choose their own foreign policies? he asked. Wasn't this the only position truly consistent with Helsinki? "To my astonishment," Bush later recalled, "Gorbachev shrugged his shoulders and said yes, that was correct."[76]

This was a remarkable concession, one that delighted American officials while horrifying those on the Soviet side. Still, Bush pushed even further. Gorbachev wanted their joint statement on the matter to read, "The U.S. and the USSR are in favor of Germany deciding herself in which alliance she would like to participate." Bush insisted upon something different: "The United States is unequivocally advocating Germany's membership in NATO. However, should Germany prefer to make a different choice, we will respect it."[77] Once again, Gorbachev gave in.[78] He would backtrack in the comings days, only to relent once again later in the summer upon Kohl's next visit to the Soviet Union.[79] Yet the principals knew he had ultimately given the game away in Washington, allowing himself to be rhetorically trapped into a position that would assure America's victory on the crucial matter of Germany in NATO. Yes, his country's dire economic position and America's vast influence both contributed to the outcome.[80] But as the historian Jeffrey Engel has argued, what decisively tipped the scales wasn't coercion, but logic:

> Gorbachev conceded Germany's right to choose its own alliances because it made sense. He'd lived his life driven by the pursuit of philosophical truths, and he ultimately could not sustain an illogical argument past its breaking point. He believed in self-determination. He'd staked his entire political philosophy on it. How could he publicly state that the fundamental principle he upheld as a universal truth applied only when convenient?[81]

As Gorbachev himself confirmed years later, if Germany was to be fully "sovereign, its people should decide for themselves. As someone devoted to democracy, how could I object? To have done so would have been unworthy."[82] Bush and his advisers masterfully used Gorbachev's own stated positions against him in a way that assured the victory of the American position. In combination with their expert use of other advantages in the Western order, they achieved total victory in the diplomatic battle to define the shape of post–Cold War Europe.

Fifth and finally, it is also important to note what American officials did *not* advocate in this diplomatic battle. While frequently invoking NATO's behavioral characteristics centered on collective defense and democratic security community (chapter 7), they chose not to emphasize its founding membership principle of free and representative political institutions. In fact, the Bush administration chose not to prioritize democracy promotion more generally throughout this period. Instead, they emphasized only the inter-unit behavioral principles of multilateralism through coalition building, respect for state sovereignty, and the value of upholding international stability.[83] This change of emphasis is consistent with hypothesis 1C of ordering-to-exclude theory. Because the United States no longer feared the USSR for its ideological power, American elites did not feel the need to strategically emphasize the Western order's ideological aspects.

Examples of this abound.[84] Even as they continued to compete with the Soviets on other fronts, administration officials sought to avoid gloating over the ideological defeat of communism. Bush himself drew fire from his conservative base at home for his reticence to support, first, the Eastern European independence movements and, later, the independence movements of the socialist republics of the Soviet Union itself. When the president warned of the dangers of "suicide nationalism" while in Ukraine, for instance, the conservative columnist William Safire lambasted Bush's "Chicken Kiev" speech that made the "American President appear to be anti-liberty."[85] In Operation Desert Storm, Bush successfully led a massive diplomatic and military coalition to roll back Iraqi dictator Saddam Hussein's invasion of Kuwait, a coalition that the Soviet Union had joined. But his administration was careful to justify the coalition's authority to intervene with inter-unit behavioral principles—respecting sovereignty, upholding the rule of law, opposing unilateral aggression—and not with reference to undesirable domestic attributes of the Iraqi regime itself. "We are not going to Baghdad," Defense Secretary Cheney stated flatly at the time. "Our military objectives [do] not include changing the Iraqi government."[86] Ironically, the administration's tendency to forgo ideological posturing was striking enough to catch the attention of Democrats eager to weaken Bush for the 1992 presidential election. As Democratic nominee Bill Clinton told a Milwaukee audience only weeks before the election, "Mr. Bush's ambivalence about supporting democracy and his eagerness to befriend potentates and dictators has shown itself time and again. . . . [President Bush] simply does not seem at home in the mainstream prodemocracy tradition in American foreign policy."[87]

In sum, there was both a constraining factor *and* a propelling factor pointing American leaders toward order continuity as a diplomatic battle raged over Germany, NATO, and the future of Europe in 1990. On the constraining side, American leaders perceived no new threats that would warrant the effort and resources necessary to build a transformative order from scratch, especially when they still had one that continued to serve American interests so well. On the propelling side, a continuing fear of Soviet capabilities and mistrust of Soviet intentions made these officials wary of any order revisions that might allow their Cold War adversary greater future influence in Europe. Even if they were not eager to see the chaos that would soon engulf the Soviet Union itself, they advocated what they did in 1990 knowing full well that it would, to use Scowcroft's words, "rip the heart out of the Soviet security system" that had dominated Eastern Europe for a generation.[88]

8.3   *Alternatives*

In general, the alternative arguments do not provide convincing explanations for strong American preferences for continuity at the end of the Cold War (see Table 8.1).

8.3.1   Binding

Binding is the most viable of the alternative motives, as John Ikenberry provides a logically sound account of order continuity at and after the Cold War's end in *After Victory*. He argues that the open and multilateral character of the Western security order gave the United States "the ability to reassure Soviet leaders that they would not exploit Soviet troubles, and that German integration within Western security and economic institutions would provide an effective guard

Table 8.1 Results: Order Continuity at the End of the Cold War

Era	Order Preferences	Exclude	Bind	Export	Learn
1989	(Preferences for continuity)	Y/Y	Y/N	A/N	N/N

Note: Pass congruence test? / Pass process tracing test? Y = Yes; N = No; A = Ambiguous; Shading = passed both tests.

against the resurgence of German power." Ikenberry concludes that the "willingness of the Soviet leaders to accept a unified Germany within NATO was partly linked to the way the alliance bound the United States to Europe."[89] He points in particular to the fact that, led by the Americans, Western leaders announced changes to the NATO alliance at a summer 1990 meeting that were designed to reassure the Soviet Union.[90] Overall, binding weaves a logically powerful narrative of the end of the Cold War: the inclusive and restraining characteristics of the Western order had finally succeeded in co-opting even its greatest adversary into accepting its universal benefits.[91]

The weaknesses of the binding account come not from logic (and congruence testing), but from history (and process tracing). It *is* true that NATO's publicized changes in the summer of 1990 succeeded in winning the Soviets' final acquiescence to united Germany's membership in the Western alliance. Yet a closer look at those changes reveals that they were more cosmetic than actual. American elites carefully crafted them to make the Western alliance *appear* less threatening to the USSR—designed to "sweeten the pill" for the Soviets in one NATO official's words—yet succeeded in doing so without altering NATO's fundamentally anti-Russian mission or offering the Soviet Union membership, both conditions that Gorbachev had at one point or another demanded as the price of his acquiescence.[92] The biggest tangible effect of these announced changes wasn't in actually transforming NATO but in providing Gorbachev political cover at home for capitulating on the German membership issue.[93] Gorbachev had, after all, conceded Germany's membership in NATO more than a month before these announced changes, back at the summit meeting with Bush in Washington.

More broadly, there is certainly evidence of the United States seeking to reassure the Soviets as to the benign nature of the Western order, much as the binding motive would expect.[94] There is virtually *no* evidence, however, of Soviet elites coming to believe what American officials were telling them, particularly about the order's restraining effects on Germany. In a meeting with Baker, for instance, Gorbachev agreed with the Secretary of State that "we needed a safety net which would protect us and the rest of Europe from any 'surprises' from the Germans," but strongly *disagreed* on the guarantor of that safety net, stressing that it "should be provided not by NATO but by new structures created within a pan-European framework."[95] "Having Germany in NATO might be good for West Germany and the United States, but don't expect me to say that it would be good for the Soviet Union," complained one Soviet official on the eve of Gorbachev's capitulation at the Washington summit. "Don't treat us like kids," added another.[96] Instead, it appears that by the summer of 1990 Gorbachev and Shevardnadze simply came to realize that the Bush administration's position was unyielding and that they had little leverage to change the terms of the settlement. When Gorbachev was rhetorically trapped into admitting that Germany had the right to choose its own military alliances, their lack of leverage became even starker.

One final point on the binding thesis and the end of the Cold War bears mentioning. If binding American power and reassuring would-be allies had really been a foremost concern of American elites, then they should have been more receptive to the Soviet leader's inclusive vision of a pan-European order in the first place. At times, this is indeed what Bush administration officials seemed to promise the Soviets, holding out vague suggestions of a more inclusive and CSCE-focused Europe in the future. As Baker explained to his NATO colleagues in Brussels in May of 1990, for example, "adaptation of NATO, the EC, and the CSCE to new European realities" avoided "a loss to Moscow" and helped prevent "creating the image of winners and losers." He was even clearer on the possibility of institutionally fortifying the CSCE, telling Shevardnadze in Moscow soon thereafter that "it can create a sense of inclusion not exclusion in Europe. . . . I see it as being a cornerstone over time in the development of a new Europe."[97]

The problem, of course, was that American leaders never followed through on these promises and often seemed to actively work against the realization of this more inclusive order vision. Analyzing the nature of American promises to the Soviets regarding the future of NATO, Joshua Shifrinson has captured the nature of US duplicity here:

> The available evidence suggests a sharp disjuncture between what the United States told the Soviet Union and what U.S. policymakers privately intended. For Soviet and other external audiences, U.S. policymakers depicted a world in which the United States would forgo NATO expansion and craft a mutually acceptable European order. Privately, however, U.S. policymakers sought to expand the United States' presence in Central-Eastern Europe; they discounted the importance of the cooperative and pan-European security structures presented to the Soviet Union; and they opposed arrangements that would foreclose future U.S. options in Europe. As part of this effort, the United States was also actively considering expanding NATO despite assurances to the contrary.[98]

As late as the summer of 1992—after the Soviet Union had already collapsed—Bush administration officials were still pushing to keep the CSCE from becoming a more prominent forum for European security issues at NATO's expense.[99] These were not the actions, in sum, of elites who had binding American power and forging a more inclusive order foremost on their minds.

8.3.2   Exporting

Exporting yields ambivalent congruence test predictions for this case. A preference for continuity in the liberal security order is of course consistent with the view that the United States seeks to export its ideals and institutions to the international system. Then again, numerous paths *not* chosen at the end of the Cold War could also have been consistent with this narrative and motive. A more soft-line position of disbanding *all* Cold War institutions and starting anew would have appealed to Americans' representative history at home, as well as to the liberal desire to afford the peoples of Europe the most say in their own affairs, for example. Conversely, a more hardline position of opportunistically and forcefully promoting democratic revolutions across Eastern Europe at Moscow's expense *also* would have been consistent with American traditions and values.

While congruence testing yields ambivalent results for exporting, process tracing is more damning: while Bush's speeches were sometimes filled with idealistic rhetoric about American values, private negotiations among the principals over the fate of Europe were remarkably devoid of the kind of ideological language commensurate with the exporting motive. Behind the scenes, Bush took pride in the fact that he did not give in to triumphalist and overtly ideological posturing in the midst of events that would make doing so easy and politically expedient for him, a point he repeatedly emphasized to Gorbachev.[100] In the end, the exporting narrative is not helpful for differentiating between the plausible policy options on the table, or for explaining the motivations of key US elites at the most decisive moments in this period.

8.3.3   Learning

Similarly, if learning had been a motivating factor in American foreign policy at the end of the Cold War, we should have seen greater inclusive tendencies on the part of US officials toward their weakened Soviet competitors. After all, the lessons of the last great transformative events—the World Wars—had been that integration of a fallen adversary, Germany, into the Western system after World War II produced far more desirable results than had its oppression and exclusion after the First World War. Bush, Scowcroft, and Baker have all paid lip service to these lessons in their memoirs, noting the importance of not leaving the Soviets feeling isolated or disillusioned at the end of the Cold War.

In the end, however, these sensitivities apparently did not matter enough to significantly alter their order preferences. There was no new Marshall Plan for the Soviets or Eastern Europeans, and the architecture of European security institutions would not be overhauled to accommodate and include them. As we have seen, in fact, American elites explicitly blocked attempts to supplant the existing Western security order with fora that would be more representative of all European actors. Overall, the fact that American leaders' tactics and objectives at the end of the Cold War were more exclusionary than inclusionary is underscored by Russians' continued bitterness about the persistence and, later, the expansion of NATO, as well as by their resentment toward Gorbachev for seemingly giving so much away for so little in return. These resentments became evident soon after the events of 1990 and endure to this day.[101]

In sum, and at a time when themes of "transformation" and "inclusion" dominated the major diplomatic addresses of US officials, America's order strategy was ironically anything but. As Mary Sarotte aptly summarizes, evidence does not support the contentions either that "U.S. foreign policy at the end of the Cold War was generous and inclusionary" or that "integration of the Soviets into new or existing institutions was dominant" in the thinking of the principal American officials in 1990. Instead, "shielding that status quo in an era of dramatic change became the United States' highest priority."[102] In that endeavor, they succeeded beyond what their wildest expectations must have been when that wall in Berlin had come crashing down only a year earlier. "Mikhail Gorbachev's new world order had been a slogan," writes one historian of the era. But "George Bush's new world order was becoming a reality."[103]

8.4   Conclusion: From Cold War to New World Order

The choices for order continuity made by the Bush administration in the critical juncture of 1989–1990 had profound legacies that long outlasted George H. W. Bush's time in office. Continuities in order would continue into the 1990s, as the Clinton administration struggled to identify what new threat might next challenge American security and supremacy. The decade after the Cold War was similar to the interwar years of the 1920s in that American leaders could not agree on what, if any, international force vitally threatened American interests. "The problem during those years," as two scholars of the era have put it, "was that with no common threat to unite them, Americans couldn't come together to define the national interest."[104] The ambiguity and uncertainty that defined this new interwar period—the era between the fall of the Berlin Wall and the terrorist attacks of September 11, 2001—were as prevalent in American foreign relations as they had been during the first interwar saga.

This isn't to say that there was an entire absence of perceived threats. But when particular elites did perceive menacing forces in this period, they often profoundly disagreed on their nature as well as the urgency with which they needed to be addressed. In congressional testimony about the future of American foreign policy, for example, Cheney acknowledged that threats were now so "remote" that "they are difficult to discern," while Chairman of the Joint Chiefs of Staff Colin Powell admitted that he would not be able to tell "where the next . . . Saddam Hussein will appear to threaten stability in the world. . . . The key to preparedness," he argued, was in "building forces flexible enough to react to the unknown."[105] In spite of such warnings, US elites struggled to agree upon the nature of the next great threat to American interests. Continuity in order preferences thus persisted throughout the 1990s and into the 2000s.

If history has indeed "returned" for the United States in recent years, as some commentators have argued[106]—with a renewed focus on rising great power competitors such as China—what does it mean for US attitudes about the liberal international order, not to mention the future of order more generally? I take up these issues in the concluding chapter.

9

The Future of Order

OBSERVERS OFTEN ARGUE that the key to overcoming emerging fault lines in global governance will be Western (particularly American) accommodation in fundamentally reforming the institutions at the heart of the liberal international order. So the argument goes, if governance arrangements could just be restructured to reflect new realities of power, breakthroughs in cooperation—namely, concessions from rising and emerging powers on important issues—will soon follow. The United States must "lead by inducing greater cooperation among a greater number of actors," argued former Secretary of State and 2016 presidential candidate Hillary Clinton, who has advocated for putting "special emphasis on encouraging major and emerging global powers to be full partners in tackling the global agenda."[1] The lesson is clear, posits a prominent former official of George W. Bush's State Department: "the international system cannot function unless it incorporates the largest and fastest-growing countries. If it fails to adequately include China, India, and other emerging economies, they will simply turn elsewhere."[2] Only assimilation will break the emerging global impasse, this consensus suggests.

By contrast, I contend that this impasse is not a temporary phenomenon or one amenable to these kinds of quick fixes. Instead, it reflects the coming clash between two visions for international order that will increasingly butt heads as time progresses. If the past is any guide, the disagreements of today are a direct manifestation of the brewing competition over who will shape the order of tomorrow. After reviewing the principal arguments I have made in this book and discussing its most important findings, I turn to its greatest theoretical and practical implications for the future.

9.1 Arguments and Evidence
9.1.1 Orders of Exclusion

When and how do powerful actors attempt to fundamentally change the rules of international order? I have argued that dominant-actor preferences for order are conditioned above all by their perceptions of threat in the international system. The propelling motivation for order building is the fear of long-term threats on the horizon, threats to dominant actors' security, threats to their enduring primacy, or both. In short, actors use the principles that constitute order less to include as many allies as possible than to exclude those actors or entities they find most threatening.

As I have sought to show, the implications of ordering-to-exclude theory have varied over international history. Prior to the French Revolution, the theory's expectations largely mirrored those of IR realist balance-of-power arguments: the victors of the major European wars after 1648 and 1713 advocated new rules of behavior designed to target and weaken their principal geopolitical foes. And when they perceived no major foe on the horizon, as after the Seven Years' War, they advanced no new principles to condition states' future interactions (chapter 4). The dynamics of order building became forever more complex after the French Revolutionary and Napoleonic Wars, however (chapter 5). That series of events introduced an ideological component to competition that has come to characterize all of world politics ever since. The advent of this new kind of threat complicated the logic of order building and took my theory's predictions far beyond balance-of-power realism: when dominant actors confront threats with an ideological component, they will advocate not only new principles of behavior but also rules that reach into the very core of states' traditional prerogatives, their domestic politics.

It thus isn't a coincidence that the advent of ideological competition in the nineteenth century and its prevalence ever since has correlated with the advent of deeper, more textured international orders. The nineteenth century pitted great powers supporting absolutism against those supporting liberalism (chapter 5), just as great power politics in the twentieth century took place against a backdrop of ideological struggle between capitalist liberal democracy and communist authoritarianism (chapters 6–8). The latter contest ultimately ended with the collapse of the USSR. Yet as I discuss later in this chapter, there are good reasons to believe that a new fusion of geopolitical and ideological competition between the United States and China could make order building in the twenty-first century at least as complex and contentious as it was in the nineteenth and twentieth centuries.

9.1.2 The Results

In chapter 3, I also detailed three alternative motivations for dominant-actor order preferences. The first, *binding*, predicts that dominant actors will advance new order principles to make their leadership appear more benevolent and less coercive to many of the other less powerful actors with which they interact.

The second, *exporting*, predicts that dominant actors will seek to export their domestic ideas and institutions to the international system writ large. I also introduced a weaker version of this motive predicting that domestic political battles could shape dominant actors' order preferences at the international level. The final alternative, *learning*, predicts that dominant actors will advocate order changes to avoid or prevent the recurrence of recent and negative events in their history.

Chapters 4 through 8 evaluated the utility of these arguments relative to ordering-to-exclude theory, and Table 9.1 summarizes the results. Ordering-to-exclude theory significantly outperformed the alternatives, plausibly passing both congruence and process tracing tests in 80 percent of the case instances examined. Of the few outliers, only one case—order-building inaction in 1848—presented a true anomaly for the theory and was ultimately better explained by a mix of exporting and another explanation outside of those examined in this study. The other anomalous results came in the post–World War I US order-building episode, one that I have argued is a "least likely" case for ordering to exclude but where the theory nevertheless performed as well as or better than the alternatives. Aside from these anomalies, ordering-to-exclude theory performs remarkably well across time and space in both predictions for and explanations of dominant-actor order preferences.

By comparison, learning, exporting, and binding fared considerably worse. Of the three, learning achieved the most success, fully passing both evaluative tests in 40 percent of the cases. Curiously, it fared slightly better in the European cases than in the later US-centric periods. Aside from the straightforward interpretation—that learning offers a powerful explanation in more than a third of these cases regardless of time period—two additional possibilities bear mentioning.

One possibility stems from the fact that in the older cases, dominant actors' perceived threats and their most recent past adversaries were more often one and the same than in the later cases. For example, elites' perceived threat after the War of the Spanish Succession and French Revolutionary Wars were closely connected to the same French menace they had previously just gone to war to vanquish. Support for the learning hypothesis in these cases might therefore be less a sign of its true explanatory power and more an indication of the difficulties in adjudicating between the excluding and learning motives when both predict similar outcomes. A second possibility is that, for whatever reason, learning is a less powerful motivation for order building in more recent times than it was in the past. Perhaps dominant actors have evolved over time from thinking about order more *re*actively to approaching it in a more *pro*active manner. That powerful states think much more about order today than ever before is a truism in

Table 9.1 Final Results

Era	Order Preferences	Exclude	Bind	Export	Learn
1648	1: Enhanced autonomy for territorially bounded polities	Y/Y	N/N	Y/N	Y/N
1713	1: Delegitimating transnational dynastic claims	Y/Y	N/N	N/N	Y/Y
	2: Legitimating "balance of power" as a desirable end / state objective	Y/Y	N/N	N/N	Y/Y
1763	(Preferences for continuity)	Y/Y	N/N	N/N	N/N
1815	1: Great powers designated special status/ rights	Y/Y	A/N	A/N	A/N
	2: Defend territorial-political status quo through multilateral consensus	Y/Y	Y/N	A/N	Y/Y
	3: System management through regular congresses and conferences	A/Y	Y/N	A/N	Y/N
	4: To anti-liberal, monarchic regimes	Y/Y	N/N	Y/Y	Y/Y
1848	(Preferences for continuity)	A/N	N/N	Y/Y	A/N
1856	(Preferences for continuity)	Y/Y	N/N	N/N	N/N
1919	1: Institutionalized dispute resolution mechanisms	A/N	Y/N	A/N	Y/Y
	2: Abolition of inter-unit war initiation	A/Y	Y/N	A/N	Y/Y
	3: Gradual transition from imperial system to colonial mandates system	Y/Y	Y/N	A/N	A/N
	4: To orderly and nominally democratic regimes	Y/Y	A/N	Y/N	A/N
1945	1: Cooperation on economic openness, standardization, and stability	Y/Y	Y/N	Y/N	Y/Y
	2: To social welfare–enhancing regimes	Y/Y	Y/N	Y/N	Y/Y
	3: Establishment of a liberal security community with porous borders	Y/Y	Y/N	A/N	N/N
	4: True collective security through mutual guarantees	Y/Y	Y/N	A/N	Y/N
	5: To liberal democratic regimes	Y/Y	Y/N	Y/N	Y/N
1989	(Preferences for continuity)	Y/Y	Y/N	A/N	N/N

Note: Pass congruence test? / Pass process tracing test? Y = Yes; N = No; A = Ambiguous; Shading = passed both tests.

contemporary commentaries, but one that may very well be right. Regardless, this is a topic that merits further scholarly attention.

The exporting motive found some validation in congruence testing (35%) but only rarely passed process tracing tests (10%). Not surprisingly, it was most applicable in instances where actors advocated for new membership rules, as it is relatively unsurprising that often advocate for their own domestic arrangements when advancing a blueprint for the internal makeup of other polities. More surprising was that this surface-level support in congruence testing was rarely validated in the process-tracing search for underlying motives. This finding suggests that while actors often advocate for their own domestic characteristics, they do not typically do so for the simplistic reasoning advanced by the exporting hypothesis. Also surprising was the dearth of support for *either* variant of the exporting motive in accounting for behavioral rule preferences. Though this is a motive that historians and political scientists often ascribe to statesmen in foreign policy decision-making, it found virtually no support in my analysis.

It was with the binding thesis where I observed the greatest discrepancy between congruence and process tracing, however. Overall, binding performed reasonably well in congruence testing (55%). It did even better, moreover, if we limit analysis to the cases where at least one of the dominant actors was a democracy (close to 69%). The binding motive thus established itself as a plausible motivation for order preferences in many cases—particularly those involving the United States—because it could often correctly predict the observed preferences in congruence testing. This, I believe, is one of its principal strengths, *plausibility*. It provides a plausible and at times compelling logic for what farsighted dominant actors could do to perpetuate their position in the system. Aside from plausibility, binding's other strength is *desirability*. In an age where democratic ideals are among the easiest to defend around the world, binding provides a logic for what many no doubt believe dominant actors *should* spend their time building: democratic, institutionalized, and above all legitimate international orders that limit the exercise of brute force in favor of the rule of law. Putting these points together, binding provides a coherent and appealing narrative of American exceptionalism: in constructing the liberal order still with us to this day, the United States has done something different with its dominance—and something better—than any other dominant actor in history.

The binding theory's difficulties came not from correlation, but in the search for causation via process tracing. Quite surprisingly, I found no instances where binding could adequately account for the motives behind dominant-actor order preferences. This is most damning in the American cases where the theory is supposed to be most powerful. Yes, there were isolated instances—and, occasionally, powerful quotes—showing American officials recognizing the benefits of ruling by consent rather than by coercion. Yet such instances are hardly definitive support for the binding motive alone, and in fact could support any of the motives examined in this study in the right context.

Moreover, such instances should not be taken to imply that the more specific and controversial claims of binding theory are also supported by the historical record. Binding predicts that a dominant actor will seek to legitimize its dominance over smaller actors by (a) limiting its own exercise of power and (b) giving those smaller actors more voice opportunities in global governance, all for the purpose of (c) locking in place an order that continues to benefit that dominant actor far into the future. Yet in my estimation, evidence is scant for American leaders *ever* being motivated by this reasoning in the most defining and consequential historical moments. The binding logic does not appear in American deliberations behind the League of Nations, the Bretton Woods institutions, the Marshall Plan and NATO alliance, nor even in the diplomacy that brought about the peaceful end to the Cold War. For those who believe in American exceptionalism in world politics, this will be a particularly troubling yet important negative finding.

One additional point is worth mentioning in regard to John Ikenberry's pathbreaking scholarship on international order closely associated with the binding motive. Though the present study has cast doubt on the motivations he champions for dominant-actor order preferences, the binding thesis is only one of several important arguments Ikenberry raises in *After Victory* and *Liberal Leviathan*. My analysis does not directly speak to what is perhaps his most powerful thesis in those works, that the liberal international order *itself* is imbued with exceptional qualities that have rendered it far more durable than all orders before it. In other words, one could embrace the arguments of this book and yet still subscribe to the view that the contemporary order is uniquely capable of enduring beyond the current distribution of power. I happen to be skeptical that such a fortuitous arrangement could have emerged by accident, and without careful American planning. Yet evaluating this powerful claim is a matter of international outcomes, whereas I have limited my analysis to explaining foreign policy preferences and decision making.[3] In short, this is far from the last word on the nature of the liberal international order, and much important work remains to be done.

9.2 Theoretical Implications

The theory I have advanced in this book bridges the gap between two types of arguments that have typically remained separate in IR scholarship: those demonstrating that actors are strategic and keep their security and relative position in the international system foremost in their considerations, and those arguing that there exists something akin to "order" in world politics that is weighty and consequential. I have sought to show that these two strains of thought do not have to be mutually exclusive and can in fact fit together quite easily and logically.

Keeping this in mind, ordering-to-exclude theory both supports and challenges aspects of the liberal paradigm in international relations. It supports the liberal contention that even the most powerful states understand that rules and institutions often significantly matter in world politics. At moments in history when they have the opportunity to do so, great powers have often devoted significant resources to shaping the rules behind order to advance their interests. Realist and rationalist scholars who dismiss the importance of order thus do so to the detriment of their theories' empirical accuracy and policy applicability.

Yet my theory also challenges popular and prominent liberal explanations for why powerful states act as they do. Just as realists should not accept the false premise that states do not care about order, liberal scholars should not mistake the fact that powerful actors are concerned with order for those actors forgoing a pursuit of their self-interests and primacy above all. If ordering-to-exclude theory has merit, it suggests that dominant actors do not typically advocate major order changes out of altruism, to demonstrate their benevolence, or to promote national values as various liberal theories suggest, but instead for more strategic and sometimes even nefarious purposes.

Likewise, ordering-to-exclude theory supports and challenges aspects of realist IR theory. Broadly speaking, realists get the "why?" question correct: powerful states most often act as they do out of a fear of long-term threats. I have added some nuance to that general proposition by detailing how states work to exclude threatening forces, as well as how threats with or without an ideological component can affect dominant actors' ordering strategies and perceptions. But overall, my theory's basic proposition about dominant actors' motives is fundamentally realist at its core.

Yet if the realists get the "why?" right, my analysis also shows that realism falls short on answering the "how?" question. Outside of building up military force, forming alliances, or going to war, realists have had little to say on how powerful states deal with long-term threats and existential challenges. This failing comes, I suspect, from the overly sparse worldview of neorealism, one that affords no significant place to the ideational and institutional phenomena that are often at the core of international order. Yet without first acknowledging that order exists and is often consequential for both foreign policy decisionmaking and international outcomes, realists are unlikely to recognize that strategic order building has been an important and often even essential component of great-power grand strategies for centuries. The attention being paid to international order is growing and will likely only continue to do so as the twenty-first century progresses.

If realists want to remain relevant and indeed "realistic" in their predictions and prescriptions for international relations, it is time for them to relax some of their more rigid and outdated theoretical assumptions and join the order party. John Mearsheimer's recent admission that "because states in the modern world are deeply connected in a variety of ways, orders are essential for facilitating efficient and timely interactions" is a good start, but much more progress needs to be made to drag realism into the twenty-first century.[4]

Finally, ordering-to-exclude theory also speaks to aspects of the constructivist IR paradigm. More specifically, I have highlighted three pathways through which dominant actors have attempted to use the ideas behind order to target, weaken, and above all exclude actors and entities that they perceive as threatening. In one sense, this component of my analysis supports constructivism by showing that intersubjective understandings are weighty and have significant effects on material outcomes. After all, the idea of territorial sovereignty might have only begun as an abstract conception of authority in someone's head, but its advocacy had very real (and detrimental) consequences for universalist actors like the Holy Roman Emperor and Empire.

On the other hand, the fact that my analysis has highlighted the *strategic* origins of foundational rules also challenges aspects of constructivism. The more convincing ordering-to-exclude theory is, the less it means that dominant actors actually truly value the order principles they have advocated throughout history. The emergence stories for ideas about sovereignty, balancing power, great power responsibility and self-determination are recast not as genuine arguments between principled actors but as instances of cunning agents finding new weapons with which to beat down their competitors. What we are left with is an uneasy and uncertain balance between some actors that truly believe and internalize normative values and others who merely observe and advance them for strategic and non-principled reasons. Future constructivist scholarship must attempt to sort out these ambiguities.

9.3 Practical and Political Implications

Ordering-to-exclude theory also offers predictions for the future of world politics. And two questions about the future of international order loom above all others. In the near term, what changes to the existing liberal international order will the United States advocate as it declines in relative power yet remains preponderant in relative influence? And in the long term, what if anything is the United States' projected hegemonic successor, China, likely to do with the liberal international order when it finds itself in a position to fundamentally recast its underlying principles?

I consider each of these questions by way of concluding. Before proceeding, however, it is worth at least briefly considering whether either of these states will even have an opportunity to revise or replace the liberal order in the first place. This book has, after all, focused on cases that were preceded by large exogenous shocks, shocks that at least momentarily gave actors both the enhanced capacity and special legitimacy to pursue foundational rule changes. It may well be the case that neither the United States nor China will be able to change international order in the coming years and decades, even if they develop strong preferences for doing so.[5] Yet while I have focused only on cases of order change opportunity in this book, in chapter 2 I also acknowledged that it is likely that orders can change outside of these types of moments as well. With this acknowledgment in mind, I set aside the question of whether either of these actors will have such opportunities in the following analysis and focus instead on using ordering-to-exclude theory to predict their underlying order preferences.

9.3.1 American Order Preferences in the Near Term

An influential component of the American policymaking and academic communities has been optimistic about the prospects of the liberal order remaining intact even after the United States declines. If American leaders were smart, according to this optimistic view, their future policies should entail simply more of the same, doubling down on America's commitment to the existing order. Assuming this logic is true, Ikenberry has charted a prudent course for American elites going forward:

> The idea is to make the liberal order so expansive and institutionalized that China will have no choice but to join and operate within it. . . . America's goal should be to see that Chinese power is exercised as much as possible within rules and institutions that we have crafted with other liberal states over the last century, and in which we ourselves want to operate, given the more crowded world of the future.[6]

While this may indeed be a prudent course of action, the argument and findings of this book suggest that it is not the path that the United States is likely to take. It belies a historical pattern of exclusionary order building that has taken hold time after time in decisive moments of power transition. And if American leaders are motivated by the same impulses that ordering-to-exclude theory has highlighted throughout history, when it comes to thinking about order in the future their focus will be on combatting perceived threats rather than assimilating them. And for the United States, no threat looms larger today than the geopolitical challenge—if not also the ideological one—posed by a rising China.[7]

Assuming that projections about China's rising power hold, ordering-to-exclude theory offers two predictions about US leaders' corresponding order preferences. First, if China continues to gain on the United States in aggregate power, American leaders will increasingly attempt to redirect the principles of order against China. Their focus in particular will be on using order to target the types of international behaviors that most benefit Chinese power and influence. Second, if China continues to rise without the Chinese Communist Party (CCP) having to make significant political concessions at home, we should expect to see American leaders redirecting the principles of order to counter not only Chinese behavior but also the Chinese ideological model, oftentimes referred to as "authoritarian capitalism."[8] An ideology-fueled ordering battle against authoritarian capitalism seems especially likely if this domestic model makes notable gains in and with states in the developing world looking to emulate China's successful rise. I believe it is this kind of scenario that poses the most immediate danger for a tense and potentially conflict-laden power transition in the coming decades.

Taking these considerations into account, President Donald Trump's "America First" foreign policy begins to look less like a bug and more like a feature of America's post–Cold War ordering strategy. Ikenberry has recently lamented that "Across ancient and modern eras, orders built by great powers have come and gone—but they have usually ended in murder, not suicide."[9] As I have argued throughout this book, however, great powers have consistently tweaked, manipulated, or entirely replaced order rules for the purpose of targeting threatening forces. When old threats change or dissipate and new ones arise, we should expect dominant actors to pursue appropriate changes to order, even if they are the same dominant actors who engaged in the most recent prior round of order building to begin with.

Trump's critical statements about the United Nations, NATO, free trade, and multilateralism more generally have struck many observers as signs of his administration's irrational contempt for the liberal international order. Yet this belies the fact that the United States had already been subtly tweaking the order's principles for years even before the unexpected rise of Trump. Since the end of the Cold War, American leaders across different political parties and administrations have actively moved to enforce and expand the liberal order's membership requirements—social safety and especially liberal democracy—not just within its traditional Western orbit but across the entire world. They have done so not only through persuasion—using the perks of membership in NATO and free trade institutions to expand the size and scope of both—but also through coercion.

Accompanying a more forcible approach to membership principles has been American advocacy for a new behavioral principle whereby problems previously identified as domestic—most notably, civil wars and human rights abuses—are now treated as threats to the international community, legitimating increasingly frequent interventions in those polities' internal affairs in ways that never would have been tolerated before.[10]

While Trump's forceful rhetoric against China has been jarring, it too is not inconsistent with a broader trend in American behavior. China has, after all, reaped enormous benefits from the contemporary order, rising from a third-rate country to the brink of superpower status in less than forty years. This wasn't a problem for the United States so long as its principal perceived threat remained the Soviet Union or, more recently, Islamic terrorism. But in the years since the Cold War's end—and especially as perceptions of a radical and transnational Islamic threat have faded since the 9/11 attacks and the rise and decline of ISIS—China has become a—if not *the*—top security challenge for the United States.[11]

Though it is too early to say for certain, we are perhaps witnessing the beginnings of an American attempt to revise the behavioral principle of unfettered economic openness, stability, and standardization that has been at the core of the liberal order since the 1940s. This rule was an asset so long as it was viewed as a net benefit for the United States against its perceived competitors. But if it comes to be seen instead as disproportionately benefiting rather than hindering America's emerging adversaries, its days as the order principle most forcefully defended by American elites are likely numbered.[12]

None of the preceding discussion is meant to imply that Trump's surprising victory in 2016 and inartful (some would say appalling) language about the pillars of the postwar order were inevitable developments. Yet if history is any guide, the emergence of an American ordering strategy premised on the sentiment *behind* Trump's bluster was likely only a matter of time. If anything, and regardless of the ultimate fate of Trumpism, we should expect to hear more of this kind of sentiment, not less, from American elites in the months and years ahead.

9.3.2 Chinese Order Preferences in the Long Term

Recent commentary on China's preferences for order can largely be sorted into two camps.[13] A more pessimistic camp that we can associate with the exporting perspective argues that China will advocate a significantly different conception of order for the purpose of bringing the international system more in line with particular characteristics and traditions of Chinese society and history.[14] A more optimistic camp that we can generally associate with IR liberalism argues that China simply benefits too much from the existing order to want to do much toward revising it.[15] My own expectations are closer to the pessimistic camp, yet from an entirely different reasoning.

The more pessimistic camp rejects the thesis that China will maintain the current liberal order and instead looks within Chinese society to determine what order preferences its leaders might advocate on the international stage.[16] The "main political impact of China on the world," argues the journalist Martin Jacques in a prime example of this tendency, "will be its Confucian tradition, its lack of a Western-style democracy or tradition, the centrality of the state and the relative weakness of any civil society that is likely to develop."[17]

As I have shown, however, the exporting motive has proven to be a surprisingly weak predictor of great powers' order preferences throughout history (see Table 9.1). While the past does not necessarily dictate the future, it is still significant that dominant actors have so rarely before advocated particular visions of order *because* of their domestic makeup, even in instances where their visions were consistent with these characteristics. Promoting liberal and democratic principles made sense for the United States during the Cold War, for instance, *not* because these principles matched American values but because doing so often advanced the strategic objective of further ostracizing the USSR. Conversely, when mirroring one's own characteristics doesn't serve strategic objectives, great powers are usually willing to abandon advocacy of these characteristics even if it means directly contradicting their domestic ideals. The United States and China today fit this pattern, each sometimes advocating international positions at odds with their domestic systems. Pu and Schweller nicely illustrate this point:

> In domestic politics, the U.S. government has applied checks and balances to protect democracy and the rule of law, whereas in international politics it seeks to preserve its dominant status so that it can act without constraints. In a supposedly "democratic" world order, Chinese intellectuals ask, how can the United States assume the roles of police, prosecutor, and judge?[18]

Yet just as ironic as the democratic United States advocating rigid hierarchy at the international level is the autocratic regime in China pressing for more democratic principles in the conduct of world politics. The larger point here is that both history and contemporary events advise against investing too much in the assumption that a rising power like China will look inward to find its inspiration for reimagining international order.

Instead, ordering-to-exclude theory predicts that China's order preferences will be externally motivated and strategic. In particular, my findings suggest that Chinese elites will advance new order principles for the purpose of excluding *their own* perceived threat. And for the foreseeable future, Chinese threat perceptions will likely revolve around the United States of America. Possibilities are thus ripe for China to use its future dominance to enact a set of principles distinct from the liberal order of the postwar era, and one specifically designed to weaken the United States.

Optimistic liberals on the other side of the China order debate argue that this is unnecessary alarmism. Specifically, they posit that this is too pessimistic regarding the contemporary order's capacity to accommodate and satisfy China, and too optimistic about the universal appeal of any Chinese vision of order. On the latter, they focus in particular on the viability of Chinese-style authoritarian capitalism as an imitable ideology and building block for a new world order.[19] It simply isn't a credible model, they claim, either as an alternative domestic ideology or as an alternative vision for international order. As two prominent liberals have argued,

> The fact that these autocracies [China, Russia, and smaller states in Central Asia, Africa, and Latin America that might seek to emulate them] are capitalist has profound implications for the nature of their international interests that point toward integration and accommodation in the future. The domestic viability of these regimes hinges on their ability to sustain high economic growth rates, which in turn is crucially dependent on international trade and investment; today's autocracies may be illiberal, but they remain fundamentally dependent on a liberal international capitalist system.[20]

This may well be true, and capitalism and the international behaviors associated with capitalist practices are likely to go unchallenged even when China surpasses the United States. Yet this critique assumes that because the autocratic capitalist model cannot challenge the prevailing order on *all* fronts, its proponents will be unwilling to challenge it on *any* front. It is no doubt true that China's leaders accept important components of the liberal order, namely its commitment to economic stability and openness (liberal order rule #1 from chapter 7). Yet it does not logically follow that agreement over these aspects of order automatically preclude China from challenging the liberal order on other fronts.[21]

The form of this remaking is unlikely to be total upheaval of the liberal order, but instead selective revisions whereby China accepts aspects of the order's behavioral principles but strongly rejects its rules of membership. Indeed, Chinese leaders' greatest fears about the American-led order are intimately connected to its membership principles. "Chinese officials contend that the United States uses the ideas of democracy and human rights to delegitimize and destabilize regimes that espouse alternative values, such as socialism and Asian-style developmental authoritarianism," note two prominent China scholars.[22]

Yet the most effective counter to an order with liberal membership principles isn't one with illiberal membership principles—as those looking to China's domestic traditions often assume—but instead an order with *no* rules of membership. In my view, China's rival vision therefore isn't as likely to be an "authoritarian capitalist" order as it is an "agnostic capitalist" one.[23]

In an agnostic capitalist order, *some* of the contemporary order's behavior rules—economic openness, great power supremacy, perhaps even some form of basic collective security to deter truly international threats—would continue. The big change would be the elimination of attempts to impose *any* form of domestic conditionality on order membership.[24] Such an order revision would not only meet the perceived threat of creeping liberal interventionism but would also more realistically appeal to states in the developing world that feel the ever-increasing burden of Western demands for greater political openness and stronger environmental and human rights protections. The fundamental choice thus wouldn't be between democratic or authoritarian principles of membership—a proposition the Soviets discovered to be a losing one during the Cold War—but between the Western imposition of membership principles or the freedom of all members to forge their own domestic paths.[25] China already believes this is a winning proposition, openly advertising its ambition to create an order where, in the words of a former premier, "the selection of whatever social system by a country is the affair of the people of that country" rather than powerful states or the larger international community.[26] Chinese leaders thus seem to believe that there is great appeal in returning to an order that, in the words of one analyst, "looks almost classically Westphalian."[27]

If the combination of international capitalism and domestic agnosticism appears too paltry an ordering vision to garner worldwide appeal, one need only look to two contemporary developments for corroborating evidence. First is China's network of rapidly expanding bilateral relationships with resource-rich countries in Africa, Asia, and Latin America.[28] Chinese investment is sky-rocketing in these regions, making observations that it is "only a matter of time before China becomes Africa's largest trading partner and its biggest source of foreign investment, probably by a wide margin" practically truisms.[29] The most pointed sign yet of their ambitions is the Belt and Road Initiative (BRI), sometimes described as China's twenty-first-century version of the Marshall Plan. Announced by President Xi Jinping in 2013, the BRI promises massive investment in infrastructure and development projects along ancient trading routes for the purpose of cementing and expanding Chinese interests in vital geopolitical areas.[30]

A prominent reason for developing world enthusiasm for China's economic engagement is the simple fact that it comes with few strings attached, no doubt an appealing sign of what could come from a larger Chinese-led order without membership principles. China puts little or no political conditionality on its aid, creating a stark but favorable contrast to the assistance that comes from Western states and the international institutions they control.[31] Aside from reaping the material benefits of these interactions, China also continues to make reputational and perhaps even ideological gains by demonstrating to regimes of the Global South that a capitalist but nonetheless state-directed model of development can achieve rapid and lasting economic success.[32] Other countries can feel free to emulate the Chinese model, its leaders say, but under a Chinese-led order would never be forced into adopting it.[33]

Second is China's increasing interest in building new international institutions. On the economic front, the China-led Asian Infrastructure Investment Bank (AIIB) has attracted widespread membership since its 2013 announcement. This is largely due to the aforementioned promises of aid without conditionality, and has come in spite of significant resistance from the United States.[34] On the security front, China played a leading role in the development of the Shanghai Cooperation Organization (SCO), an organization ostensibly founded to promote security cooperation in central Asia. Yet its ambitions are clearly greater than that.[35] Speeches at its annual summits are routinely used to decry Western interventionism and depict an alternative order vision whereby, in the words of one leader, "the outside world will accept the social system and path to development independently chosen by our members and observers and respect the domestic and foreign policies adopted by the SCO participants in line with their national conditions."[36] While its members claim that it is not an anti-Western alliance, it has denied the United States membership or observer status while its elites have openly referred to it as a counterweight to NATO.[37] It has the support of Russian and especially Chinese leaders and continues to expand its membership, with India and Pakistan having become full members just in 2017.

Whether or not these institutions will become prominent fora for sustained coordination against Western interests remains to be seen. Yet such developments should give pause to those skeptical about the supply of and demand for an alternative conception of order on the world stage today. In sum, while there are any number of possibilities for a China-led international order in the twenty-first century, I believe the "agnostic capitalist" vision should be considered foremost among them. It is a significant revision of the current order, a credible and appealing alternative to an American-led international system, and one that has a good chance of attracting increasingly powerful advocates around the globe.

If this long-term forecast rings true, what might the United States seek to do about it in the meantime? Perhaps surprisingly, I do not believe it means that American leaders should simply reject cooperation with China at every front, as some foreign policy hawks have advocated, and prepare for a protracted geopolitical struggle.[38] But they must escape the illusion that efforts to incorporate China into the existing order will necessarily bear the fruit of accommodation and assimilation. This, I have attempted to show in this book, is not the pattern of history. Above all, US officials must recognize that international order is not a safety net from power politics but is instead a product of those very politics. Rather than a repudiation of realpolitik, major components of international order have been built throughout history to serve as its instruments. Orders are shaped by the most powerful actors to deal with their most powerful threats.

With this in mind, I would advocate American leaders instituting a radically accommodative order strategy toward China in the near term and switching to a more confrontational order strategy in the long term only if it becomes clear that the near-term strategy has failed. Because this might appear counterintuitive, it requires some elaboration.

The goal of near-term accommodation would be to make China less fearful of the United States for whenever it engages in its own process of order building by exclusion. By downplaying differences and disagreements between the two countries over ideology, human rights, the responsibility of developed versus developing powers, and so on, American leaders could instead highlight areas of convergence where the United States and China share similar threat perceptions—over the dangers of extremism, weapons of mass destruction, armed non-state actors, and transnational threats like mass pandemics and climate change, for instance.[39] Adopting such a strategy would no doubt be difficult for American elites, as it would mean admitting that the United States does not control the future shape of order and can instead only push it in a "least bad" direction. But successfully doing so could forestall a new Cold War–like struggle.

This near-term strategy might sound indistinguishable from the policy prescriptions of the liberal order optimists, and there are indeed similarities. Yet they are also very different in two significant ways. First, such a strategy would be based on the recognition that the cycle of order building by exclusion—and competition between a rising state and a declining one more generally—very likely cannot be transcended. The goal would be influencing China's threat perceptions, not fully integrating China into the existing order. Second, this strategy would recognize near-term cooperative and accommodative Chinese behavior for what it really is—"hedging" until it amasses enough power to truly compete with the United States and implement its own order strategy—rather than evidence that China can be fully integrated into the existing order.[40]

In the event that this short-term strategy fails to bear fruit, however, US elites would need to consider a turn to order confrontation in the long term. This would entail taking off the rose-colored glasses through which Americans often view order and accepting the inevitable: China will likely reorder the international system against the United States of America. Absent a radical change of course in US choices or international developments, the narrative of this book suggests that this is the storm that is eventually coming. Should it come to pass, American statesmen would be wise to use their time left at the top of the system to batten down the hatches of the liberal order by reaffirming important alliances that marginalize China, doubling down on organizations where they hold institutional advantages over China, and finding new ways to attract uncommitted regimes in the developing world to join the US-led bloc before they are permanently pulled into the Chinese orbit.

At the most, such efforts might help to concretize some of America's most important order preferences at the regional level, allowing the United States to maintain a sphere of influence in the Western Hemisphere and perhaps even the North Atlantic. At the least, they could help make the transition to a much more Sino-centric international order a little less abrupt and painful for the declining American superpower in an increasingly post-American world.

Identifying the Great Powers

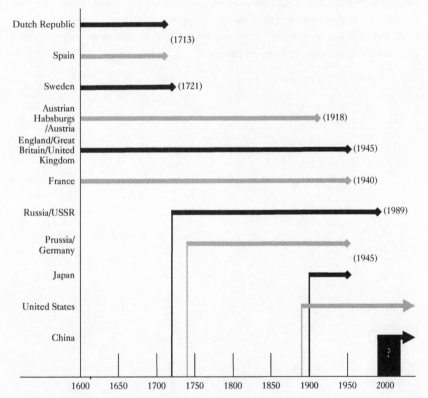

FIGURE A.1. Great powers in the modern international system, 1600–2000.

Source: Jack Levy, *War in the Modern Great Power System, 1475–1975* (Lexington: The University Press of Kentucky, 1983).

Figure A.1 tracks the presence of great powers (GPs) across the modern international system. In so doing, it adopts a majority of Jack Levy's estimations from his comprehensive study *War in the Modern Great Power System, 1475–1975*. I part ways with Levy on a number of cases, however. For starters, I exclude the Ottoman Empire and Italy from the GP category entirely. The former was neither strong enough nor recognized as such in Europe, and the latter simply never had the capabilities or clout to justify its inclusion.

On other cases I agree with Levy on GP inclusion but disagree with him on exit timing. I cut off Spain nearly one hundred years earlier, immediately following the War of the Spanish Succession, because she had much of her empire dismembered at that time and never again played a significant role in GP politics. Rather than keeping Britain, France, Germany, and Japan as GPs through to the present day, I cut them off in or after World War II. For Germany and Japan, I do this *not* because they were temporarily occupied, but because they each had significant limits placed on their militaries that continue to this day. Britain and France are cut off not only for the devastation they suffered in World War II but also because of the significant loss of power that came with the subsequent dismantling of their overseas empires.

Finally, I leave it to others to determine when China became or will become a GP.[1] Answering that question is above my pay grade.

Notes

CHAPTER I

1. *National Security Strategy of the United States*, May 2010, http://www.whitehouse. gov/sites/default/files/rss_viewer/national_security_strategy.pdf, esp. 12–13, 40–50; *National Security Strategy of the United States*, February 2015, https:// www.whitehouse.gov/sites/default/files/docs/2015_national_security_strategy. pdf, 23–28.

2. G. John Ikenberry, "The Future of the Liberal World Order: Internationalism After America," *Foreign Affairs* 90, No. 3 (2011), 1–14, 2.

3. Zachary Keck, "Why Did BRICS Back Russia on Crimea?" *The Diplomat*, March 31, 2014, http://thediplomat.com/2014/03/why-did-brics-back-russia-on-crimea/ ; Astrid Prange, "Quiet Revolution of Emerging Countries," *DW*, May 5, 2014, http://www.dw.de/quiet-revolution-of-the-emerging-countries/a-17615162.

4. Andrew Higgins, "Far-Right Fever for a Europe Tied to Russia," *The New York Times*, May 19, 2014, https://www.nytimes.com/2014/05/21/world/europe/ europes-far-right-looks-to-russia-as-a-guiding-force.html.

5. Jane Perlez, "China and Russia Reach 30-Year Gas Deal," *The New York Times*, May 20, 2014, https://www.nytimes.com/2014/05/22/world/asia/china-russia-gas-deal.html; Neil MacFarquhar, "Russia and 2 Neighbors Form Economic Union That Has a Ukraine-Size Hole," *The New York Times*, May 29, 2014, https://www. nytimes.com/2014/05/30/world/europe/putin-signs-economic-alliance-with-presidents-of-kazakhstan-and-belarus.html.

6. "The New World Order," *The Economist*, March 22, 2014, https://www.econo-mist.com/news/leaders/21599346-post-soviet-world-order-was-far-perfect-vladimir-putins-idea-replacing-it; Robert Kagan, "A Changing World Order?" *The Washington Post*, November 15, 2013, https://www.washingtonpost.com/opinions/ a-changing-world-order/2013/11/15/4ce39d1a-489a-11e3-b6f8-3782ff6cb769_ story.html?utm_term=.6d452edbc1e0.

7. Alarmist accounts since the rise of Trump include Stephen M. Walt, "The Collapse of the Liberal World Order," *Foreign Policy*, June 26, 2016, https://foreignpolicy.com/2016/ 06/26/the-collapse-of-the-liberal-world-order-european-union-brexit-donald-trump/; Robert Kagan, "The Twilight of the Liberal World Order," *Brookings*,

January 24, 2017, https://www.brookings.edu/research/the-twilight-of-the-liberal-world-order/; Stewart M. Patrick, "Trump and World Order," *Foreign Affairs* 96, No. 2 (2017); G. John Ikenberry, "The Plot Against American Foreign Policy: Can the Liberal Order Survive?" *Foreign Affairs* 96, No. 3 (2017); Jeff D. Colgan and Robert O. Keohane, "The Liberal Order Is Rigged: Fix It Now or Watch It Wither," *Foreign Affairs* 96, No. 3 (2017); Richard Haass, *A World in Disarray: American Foreign Policy and the Crisis of the Old Order* (New York: Penguin Press, 2017); and Thomas J. Wright, *All Measures Short of War: The Contest for the Twenty-First Century and the Future of American Power* (New Haven: Yale University Press, 2017). Alarmist accounts that predate Trump include Charles A. Kupchan, *No One's World: The West, the Rising Rest, and the Coming Global Turn* (Oxford: Oxford University Press, 2012); Randall L. Schweller, *Maxwell's Demon and the Golden Apple: Global Discord in the New Millennium* (Baltimore: Johns Hopkins University Press, 2014); and Paul D. Miller, *American Power and Liberal Order: A Conservative Internationalist Grand Strategy* (Washington, DC: Georgetown University Press, 2016).

8. John McCain, "Driving Back Chaos," *Medium*, December 7, 2017, https://medium.com/wordsthatmatter/driving-back-chaos-aadae9725824.

9. *National Security Strategy of the United States*, December 2017, https://www.whitehouse.gov/wp-content/uploads/2017/12/NSS-Final-12-18-2017-0905.pdf, 4, 38, 40.

10. Walter Russell Mead, "The Jacksonian Revolt: American Populism and the Liberal World Order," *Foreign Affairs* 96, No. 2 (2017), 2.

11. Francis Fukuyama, "US Against the World? Trump's America and the New Global Order," *Financial Times*, November 11, 2016, https://www.ft.com/content/6a43cf54-a75d-11e6-8b69-02899e8bd9d1.

12. One notable exception here is David A. Lake, *Hierarchy in International Relations* (Ithaca: Cornell University Press, 2009).

13. See, for instance, Max Weber, *The Theory of Social and Economic Organization*, ed. Talcott Parsons (New York: The Free Press), 324–386.

14. Samuel P. Huntington, *Political Order in Changing Societies* (New Haven: Yale University Press, 1969), 12.

15. Francis Fukuyama, *The Origins of Political Order: From Prehuman Times to the French Revolution* (New York: Farrar, Straus and Giroux, 2011).

16. Hedley Bull, *The Anarchical Society: A Study of Order in World Politics* (New York: Columbia University Press, 1977), 4.

17. Charles A. Kupchan, Emanuel Adler, Jean-Marc Coicaud, and Yuen Foong Khong, *Power in Transition: The Peaceful Change of International Order* (New York: United Nations University Press, 2001), 36.

18. *National Security Strategy of the United States*, May 2010, http://www.whitehouse.gov/sites/default/files/rss_viewer/national_security_strategy.pdf, 12.

19. Charles Tilly, "Reflections on the History of European State-Making," in *The Formation of National States in Western Europe*, ed. Charles Tilly (Princeton: Princeton University Press, 1975), 42.

20. Prominent studies that embrace this thesis include Charles Tilly, *Coercion, Capital, and European States*, AD 990–1992 (Malden, MA: Blackwell, 1992); Brian M. Downing, *The Military Revolution and Political Change: Origins of Democracy and Autocracy in Early Modern Europe* (Princeton: Princeton University Press, 1992); Bruce D. Porter, *War and the Rise of the State: The Military Foundations of Modern Politics* (New York: The Free Press, 1994); Hendrik Spruyt, *The Sovereign State and Its Competitors: An Analysis of Systems Change* (Princeton: Princeton University Press, 1994); Thomas Ertman, *Birth of the Leviathan: Building States and Regimes in Medieval and Early Modern Europe* (Cambridge: Cambridge University Press, 1997); and Carles Boix, *Political Order and Inequality: Their Foundations and Their Consequences for Human Welfare* (New York: Cambridge University Press, 2015).

21. Robert Gilpin, *War and Change in World Politics* (Cambridge: Cambridge University Press, 1981).

22. G. John Ikenberry, *Liberal Leviathan: The Origins, Crisis, and Transformation of the American World Order* (Princeton: Princeton University Press, 2011), 11.

23. Prominent neorealist treatises include Kenneth N. Waltz, *Theory of International Politics* (Reading: Addison-Wesley Publishing Company, 1979); and John J. Mearsheimer, *The Tragedy of Great Power Politics*, updated ed. (New York: W. W. Norton & Company, 2001/2014). Interestingly, Mearsheimer appears to have drastically changed his position on the importance of order in international relations in a recent article. See "Bound to Fail: The Rise and Fall of the Liberal International Order," *International Security* 43, No. 4 (2019).

24. Important examples of classical realist thinking include E. H. Carr, *The Twenty Years' Crisis: An Introduction to the Study of International Relations* (New York: Harper Perennial, 1964); Henry A. Kissinger, *A World Restored: Metternich, Castlereagh and the Problems of Peace, 1812–1822* (Boston: Houghton Mifflin Company, 1957); and Hans J. Morgenthau, *Politics Among Nations: The Struggle for Power and Peace*, 4th ed. (New York: Alfred A. Knopf, 1967). Newer studies that embrace a classical realist perspective on order as I have described it include Gilpin, *War and Change*; and Stephen D. Krasner, *Sovereignty: Organized Hypocrisy* (Princeton: Princeton University Press, 1999).

25. Gilpin admits, for instance, to having no general theory for the types of order rising powers will prefer. See *War and Change*, 47.

26. Though I have already articulated this critique of realism in this chapter, I develop the argument against constructivist studies more comprehensively in chapter 2.

CHAPTER 2

1. Hedley Bull, *The Anarchical Society: A Study of Order in World Politics* (New York: Columbia University Press, 1977), 9. See also Charles Tilly, *Coercion, Capital, and European States, AD 990–1992* (Cambridge, MA: Blackwell, 1992), 162.

2. Robert Jervis, *System Effects: Complexity in Political and Social Life* (Princeton: Princeton University Press, 1997), 6.

3. Gary Goertz, *Social Science Concepts: A User's Guide* (Princeton: Princeton University Press, 2006), 30.

4. Donald Black, "Crime as Social Control," *American Sociological Review* 48, No. 1 (1983).

5. On this topic, see Ian Hurd, "The International Rule of Law: Law and the Limits of Politics," *Ethics & International Affairs* 28, No. 1 (2014); and *How to Do Things with International Law* (Princeton: Princeton University Press, 2017).

6. Charles A. Kupchan, Emanuel Adler, Jean-Marc Coicaud, and Yuen Foong Khong, *Power in Transition: The Peaceful Change of International Order* (New York: United Nations University Press, 2001), 36.

7. Richard Ned Lebow, *A Cultural Theory of International Relations* (Cambridge: Cambridge University Press, 2008), 14, 558–560.

8. Janice Bially Mattern, *Ordering International Politics: Identity, Crisis, and Representational Force* (New York: Routledge University Press, 2005), 30–31.

9. For a recent representation of this view, see Charles L. Glaser, "A Flawed Framework: Why the Liberal International Order Concept Is Misguided," *International Security* 43, No. 4 (2019).

10. Kenneth N. Waltz, *Theory of International Politics* (Reading, MA: Addison-Wesley Publishing Company, 1979), 97–99; Robert Gilpin, *War and Change in World Politics* (Cambridge: Cambridge University Press, 1981), 9.

11. That said, realists fundamentally differ on which of these power configurations is ultimately more "orderly." See Michael Mastanduno, "A Realist View: Three Images of the Coming International Order," in *International Order and the Future of World Politics*, ed. T. V. Paul and John A. Hall (Cambridge: Cambridge University Press, 1999).

12. Lisa Martin, "An Institutionalist View: International Institutions and State Strategies," in *International Order and the Future of World Politics*, ed. T. V. Paul and John A. Hall (Cambridge: Cambridge University Press, 1999), 91. On institutionalism more generally, see Arthur Stein, "Coordination and Collaboration: Regimes in an Anarchic World," *International Organization* 36, No. 2 (1982); Robert O. Keohane, *After Hegemony: Cooperation and Discord in the World Political Economy* (Princeton: Princeton University Press, 1984); Robert Axelrod, *The Evolution of Cooperation* (New York: Basic Books, 1984); Charles Lipson, "International Cooperation in Economic and Security Affairs," *International Organization* 37, No. 1 (1984); and Kenneth A. Oye, ed., *Cooperation Under Anarchy* (Princeton: Princeton University Press, 1986.

13. See G. John Ikenberry, *After Victory: Institutions, Strategic Restraint, and the Rebuilding of Order after Major Wars* (Princeton: Princeton University Press, 2001), 62–63.

14. See Henry A. Kissinger, *A World Restored: Metternich, Castlereagh and the Problem of Peace, 1812–1822* (Boston: Houghton Mifflin Company, 1957); Bruce Cronin, *Community Under Anarchy: Transnational Identity and the Evolution*

of Cooperation (New York: Columbia University Press, 1999); Rodney Bruce Hall, *National Collective Identity: Social Constructs and International Systems* (New York: Columbia University Press, 1999); Mlada Bukovansky *Legitimacy and Power Politics: The American and French Revolutions in International Political Culture* (Princeton: Princeton University Press, 2002); Martha Finnemore, *The Purpose of Intervention: Changing Beliefs about the Use of Force* (Ithaca: Cornell University Press, 2003); and Andrew Phillips, *War, Religion and Empire: The Transformation of International Orders* (New York: Cambridge University Press, 2011).

15. Alexander Wendt, *Social Theory of International Politics* (Cambridge: Cambridge University Press, 1999), 249.

16. Wendt, *Social Theory*, 190.

17. See for instance John W. Meyer, John Boli, George M. Thomas, and Francisco O. Ramirez, "World Society and the Nation-State," *The American Journal of Sociology* 103, No. 1 (1997).

18. See Keohane, *After Hegemony*, 80–84.

19. See Robert O. Keohane, "The Demand for International Regimes," *International Organization* 36, No. 2 (1982), 339–341.

20. See, for instance, Wendt, *Social Theory*, 273.

21. Bull, *The Anarchical Society*, 52.

22. I thus reject Young's differentiation between spontaneous orders and negotiated or imposed orders. There must always be some level of negotiation or imposition for recognition to occur, and thus for order to emerge. See Oran R. Young, "Regime Dynamics: The Rise and Fall of International Regimes," in *International Regimes*, ed. Stephen D. Krasner (Ithaca: Cornell University Press, 1983), 98–101.

23. This is the approach Stephen D. Krasner takes toward sovereignty throughout history in *Sovereignty: Organized Hypocrisy* (Princeton: Princeton University Press, 1999).

24. Bull, *The Anarchical Society*, 53.

25. Jutta Brunnee and Stephen J. Toope, *Legitimacy and Legality in International Law: An Interactional Account* (Cambridge: Cambridge University Press, 2010), 35.

26. Muthiah Alagappa, "The Study of International Order: An Analytical Framework," in *Asian Security Order: Instrumental and Normative Features*, ed. Muthiah Alagappa (Stanford: Stanford University Press, 2003), 39–41.

27. At this broadest level my rules-based conception of order is closer to the so-called English School of international relations theory than any other paradigm. On English School rules-based conceptions of order, see especially Bull, *The Anarchical Society*; Martin Wight, *Systems of States* (Leicester: Leicester University Press, 1977).; Adam Watson, *The Evolution of International Society: A Comparative Historical Analysis* (New York: Routledge, 1992); Barry Buzan and Richard Little, *International Systems in World History: Remaking the Study of International Relations* (Oxford.: Oxford University Press, 2000); Alagappa, "The Study of International

Order"; Barry Buzan, *From International to World Society? English School Theory and the Social Structure of Globalisation* (Cambridge: Cambridge University Press, 2004); Ian Clark, *Legitimacy in International Society* (Oxford: Oxford University Press, 2005); Andrew Linklater and Hidemi Suganami, *The English School of International Relations: A Contemporary Reassessment* (Cambridge: Cambridge University Press, 2006); and Andrew Hurrell, *On Global Order: Power, Values, and the Constitution of International Society* (Oxford: Oxford University Press, 2007).

28. John Gerard Ruggie, "What Makes the World Hang Together? Neo-Utilitarianism and the Social Constructivist Challenge," *International Organization* 52, No. 4 (1998).

29. Alagappa, "The Study of International Order," 41–52.

30. Craig Murphy, *International Organization and Industrial Change: Global Governance since 1850* (New York: Oxford University Press, 1994); Judith L. Goldstein, Miles Kahler, Robert O. Keohane, and Anne-Marie Slaughter, eds., *Legalization and World Politics* (Cambridge, MA: MIT Press, 2001).

31. Ian Clark, "How Hierarchical Can International Society Be?" *International Relations* 23, No. 3 (2009).

32. Goertz, *Social Science Concepts*, 65.

33. This classification is similar but not identical to the regulative and constitutive rules discussed in John R. Searle, *Speech Acts: An Essay on the Philosophy of Language* (Cambridge: Cambridge University Press, 1969), 33–42. For more apt and recent comparisons, see the differentiations between different types of rules in Christian Reus-Smit, *The Moral Purpose of the State: Culture, Social Identity, and Institutional Rationality in International Relations* (Princeton: Princeton University Press, 1999); Daniel Philpott, *Revolutions in Sovereignty: How Ideas Shaped Modern International Relations* (Princeton: Princeton University Press, 2001); and Clark, *Legitimacy in International Society* .

34. By orders without membership rules, I mean those without strict principles prescribing or proscribing particular internal attributes of polities. That said, even orders without these kinds of principles typically still favor some kinds of actors over others—territorially discreet principalities over pirates, mercenaries, or chartered companies, for example. By my definition here, however, this favoritism does not constitute what I refer to as membership rules. Furthermore, and as is made clear in the Westphalia case study in chapter 4, the rule that would eventually result in the primacy of sovereign states over all other types of actors was actually a principle of behavior rather than one of membership.

35. In fact, at least one important study has argued that heterogeneous orders— those without membership principles—have actually been more historically prevalent than homogeneous ones. See Andrew Phillips and J. C. Sharman, *International Order in Diversity: War, Trade and Rule in the Indian Ocean* (Cambridge: Cambridge University Press, 2015).

36. See, for instance, Tanisha M. Fazal and Ryan D. Griffiths, "Membership Has Its Privileges: The Changing Benefits of Statehood," *International Studies Review* 16, No. 1 (2014).

37. John J. Mearsheimer has also recently discussed "depth" as a dimension of international order, though he and I employ the term differently. See "Bound to Fail: The Rise and Fall of the Liberal International Order," *International Security* 43, No. 4 (2019), 11–16.

38. See, for example, Clark, *Legitimacy in International Society*; Andreas Osiander, *The States System of Europe, 1640–1990: Peacemaking and the Conditions of International Stability* (New York: Oxford University Press, 1994); and Paul W. Schroeder, *The Transformation of European Politics, 1763–1848* (Oxford: Oxford University Press, 1994).

39. Examples include Hall, *National Collective Identity*; Reus-Smit, *The Moral Purpose of the State*; Philpott, *Revolutions in Sovereignty*; and Bukovansky, *Legitimacy and Power Politics*.

40. For variants of this critique, see John J. Mearsheimer, "The False Promise of International Institutions," *International Security* 19, No. 3 (1994/1995), 37–47; Vaughn P. Shannon, "Wendt's Violation of the Constructivist Project: Agency and Why a World State Is Not Inevitable," *European Journal of International Relations* 11, No. 4 (2005); Petr Drulak, "Reflexivity and Structural Change," in *Constructivism and International Relations: Alexander Wendt and His Critics*, ed. Stefano Guzzini and Anna Leander (New York: Routledge, 2006); and Brent J. Steele, "Liberal-Idealism: A Constructivist Critique," *International Studies Review* 9 (2007).

41. Stephen Brooks and William Wohlforth, *World Out of Balance: International Relations and the Challenge of American Primacy* (Princeton: Princeton University Press, 2008), 186.

42. Of his major works, this is most explicit in G. John Ikenberry, *Liberal Leviathan: The Origins, Crisis, and Transformation of the American World Order* (Princeton: Princeton University Press, 2011).

43. Stacie E. Goddard, *When Right Makes Might: Rising Powers and World Order* (Ithaca: Cornell University Press, 2018), 19.

44. What I call "vertical imposition" can be considered synonymous with what others from a variety of theoretical backgrounds have called "hegemonic order theory," a term notably employed most recently in G. John Ikenberry and Daniel H. Nexon, "Hegemony Studies 3.0: The Dynamics of Hegemonic Orders," *Security Studies* 28, No. 3 (2019); and Daniel H. Nexon and Iver B. Neumann, "Hegemonic-Order Theory: A Field-Theoretic Account," *European Journal of International Relations* 24, No. 3 (2018). For other recent examples of vertical imposition accounts, see John M. Hobson and J. C. Sharman, "The Enduring Place of Hierarchy in World Politics: Tracing the Social Logics of Hierarchy and Political Change," *European Journal of International Relations* 11, No. 1 (2005); Daniel H.

Nexon and Thomas Wright, "What's at Stake in the American Empire Debate?" *American Political Science Review* 101, No. 2 (2007); Julian Go, "Global Fields and Imperial Forms: Field Theory and the British and American Empires," *Sociological Theory* 26, No. 3 (2008); Ahsan I. Butt, "Anarchy and Hierarchy in International Relations: Examining South America's War-Prone Decade, 1932–41," *International Organization* 67, No. 3 (2013); Janice Bially Mattern and Ayse Zarakol, "Hierarchies in World Politics," *International Organization* 70, No. 3 (2016); and Paul Musgrave and Daniel H. Nexon, "Defending Hierarchy from the Moon to the Indian Ocean: Symbolic Capital and Political Dominance in Early Modern China and the Cold War," *International Organization* 72, No. 3 (2018).

45. See Gary King, Robert O. Keohane, and Sidney Verba, *Designing Social Inquiry: Scientific Inference in Qualitative Research* (Princeton: Princeton University Press, 1994), 129

46. On identifying great powers, see the Appendix of this book.

47. On major war as an agent of structural change, see Ikenberry, *After Victory*, 254; and Seva Gunitsky, *Aftershocks: Great Powers and Domestic Reforms in the Twentieth Century* (Princeton: Princeton University Press, 2017), 8–12. On defining major wars, see Dale C. Copeland, *The Origins of Major War* (Ithaca: Cornell University Press, 2000), 27–28.

48. "One hundred thousand battle deaths" is included because it disqualifies conflicts that did not necessitate full mobilization.

49. As Table 2.3 indicates, the 1848 French regime death induced a similar but only partial regime death in Austria.

50. C. William Walldorf, Jr., *To Shape Our World for Good: Master Narratives and Regime Change in U.S. Foreign Policy, 1900–2011* (Ithaca: Cornell University Press, 2019), 25, 27. Note that while Walldorf makes his argument at the domestic level, I am extrapolating his claims to the international level. Other accounts that similarly highlight external shocks as trauma-inducing catalysts for change include Peter Gourevitch, *Politics in Hard Times: Comparative Responses to International Economic Crises* (Ithaca: Cornell University Press, 1986); Judith Goldstein, *Ideas, Interests and American Trade Policy* (Ithaca: Cornell University Press, 1993); and especially Jeffrey W. Legro, *Rethinking the World: Great Power Strategies and International Order* (Ithaca: Cornell University Press, 2005).

CHAPTER 3

1. Charles A. Kupchan, *How Enemies Become Friends: The Sources of Stable Peace* (Princeton: Princeton University Press, 2010), 64–65.

2. Stephen Van Evera, *Causes of War: Power and the Roots of Conflict* (Ithaca: Cornell University Press, 1999); Charles Glaser, "Realists as Optimists: Cooperation as Self-Help," *International Security* 19, No. 3 (1994/1995).

3. Randall L. Schweller, *Deadly Imbalances: Tripolarity and Hitler's Strategy of World Conquest* (New York: Columbia University Press, 1997); David M. Edelstein, "Managing Uncertainty: Beliefs about Intentions and the Rise of Great Powers," *Security Studies* 12, No. 1 (2002); Charles L. Glaser, *Rational Theory of International Politics: The Logic of Competition and Cooperation* (Princeton: Princeton University Press, 2010); Karen Yarhi-Milo, *Knowing the Adversary: Leaders, Intelligence, and Assessment of Intentions in International Relations* (Princeton: Princeton University Press, 2014); Brandon K. Yoder, "Hedging for Better Bets: Power Shifts, Credible Signals, and Preventive Conflict," *Journal of Conflict Resolution* 63, No. 4 (2019); Kyle Haynes, "A Question of Costliness: Time Horizons and Interstate Signaling," *Journal of Conflict Resolution* 63, no. 8 (2019).

4. Robert Gilpin, *War and Change in World Politics* (Cambridge: Cambridge University Press, 1981); Dale C. Copeland, *The Origins of Major War* (Ithaca: Cornell University Press, 2000).

5. Stephen M. Walt, *The Origins of Alliances* (Ithaca: Cornell University Press, 1987).

6. While I discuss some of the benefits of primacy here, I am ultimately ambivalent as to the reasons why dominant actors want to maintain their dominance and do not see elaborating upon it as crucial to the core logic of ordering-to-exclude theory.

7. The following discussion of primacy's benefits has been most informed by Nuno P. Monteiro, *Theory of Unipolar Politics* (New York: Cambridge University Press, 2014), 73–77; and Carla Norrlof and William Wohlforth, "*Raison de l'Hégémonie* (The Hegemon's Interest): The Costs and Benefits of Hegemony," *Security Studies* 28, No. 3 (2019). For a related argument that the United States in particular benefits from both its primacy and its grand strategy of "deep engagement," see Stephen G. Brooks and William C. Wohlforth, *America Abroad: The United States' Global Role in the 21st Century* (New York: Oxford University Press, 2016).

8. See Lloyd Gruber, *Ruling the World: Power Politics and the Rise of Supranational Institutions* (Princeton: Princeton University Press, 2000); and Norrlof and Wohlforth, "*Raison de l'Hégémonie.*"

9. On primacy's economic benefits in particular, see Carla Norrlof, *America's Global Advantage: US Hegemony and International Cooperation* (Cambridge: Cambridge University Press, 2010).

10. David A. Lake, *Hierarchy in International Relations* (Ithaca: Cornell University Press, 2009), 34.

11. Stephen Brooks and William Wohlforth, *World Out of Balance: International Relations and the Challenge of American Primacy* (Princeton: Princeton University Press, 2008), 215–216.

12. Martha Finnemore, "Legitimacy, Hypocrisy, and the Social Structure of Unipolarity: Why Being a Unipole Isn't All It's Cracked Up to Be," *World Politics* 61, No. 1 (2009), 62–63.

13. On these points, see Monteiro, *Theory of Unipolar Politics*, 73–77.

14. Rodney Bruce Hall, "Moral Authority as a Power Resource," *International Organization* 51, No. 4 (1997); Stephen D. Krasner, "Westphalia and All That," in *Ideas and Foreign Policy: Beliefs, Institutions, and Political Change*, ed. Judith Goldstein and Robert O. Keohane (Ithaca: Cornell University Press, 1993).

15. Stacie E. Goddard, "Uncommon Ground: Indivisible Territory and the Politics of Legitimacy," *International Organization* 60, No. 1 (2006).

16. Stacie E. Goddard, *When Right Makes Might: Rising Powers and World Order* (Ithaca: Cornell University Press, 2018).

17. Ronald R. Krebs and Patrick Thaddeus Jackson, "Twisting Tongues and Twisting Arms: The Power of Political Rhetoric," *European Journal of International Relations* 13, No. 1 (2007).

18. For examples, see Frank Schimmelfenig, "The Community Trap: Liberal Norms, Rhetorical Action, and the Eastern Enlargement of the European Union," *International Organization* 55, No. 1 (2001); Ian Hurd, "The Strategic Use of Liberal Internationalism: Libya and the UN Sanctions, 1992–2003," *International Organization* 59, No. 3 (2005); and Eric Voeten, "The Political Origins of the UN Security Council's Ability to Legitimize the Use of Force," *International Organization* 59, No. 3 (2005).

19. Stephen D. Krasner, *Sovereignty: Organized Hypocrisy* (Princeton: Princeton University Press, 1999).

20. Daniel Nexon, *The Struggle for Power in Early Modern Europe: Religious Conflict, Dynastic Empires, and International Change* (Princeton: Princeton University Press, 2009), 131.

21. Goddard, *When Right Makes Might*, 22.

22. I thank Brandon Yoder for help in clarifying this point.

23. The underlying assumption here is that an actor's past statements can be used to generate international or domestic audience costs against it should its behavior deviate from that rhetoric. On rhetorical coercion, see Krebs and Jackson, "Twisting Tongues and Twisting Arms"; Janice Bially Mattern, *Ordering International Politics: Identity, Crisis, and Representational Force* (New York: Routledge University Press, 2005), 96; Patrick Thaddeus Jackson, *Civilizing the Enemy, German Reconstruction and the Invention of the West* (Ann Arbor: The University of Michigan Press, 2006), x, 44–45; and Goddard, *When Right Makes Might*, esp. 24–25. On audience costs, see, for example, James D. Fearon, "Domestic Political Audiences and the Escalation of International Disputes," *American Political Science Review* 88, No. 3 (1994); and Fearon, "Signaling Foreign Policy Interests: Tying Hands versus Sinking Costs," *Journal of Conflict Resolution* 41, No. 1(1997).

24. On this point see Bially Mattern, *Ordering International Politics*, 96; Jennifer Mitzen, "Ontological Security in World Politics: State Identity and the Security Dilemma," *European Journal of International Relations* 12, No. 3 (2006); and Goddard, *When Right Makes Might*, 25–27.

25. Hall, "Moral Authority as a Power Resource," 601–604.

26. In the interest of maintaining theoretical simplicity, I do not engage with the question of when dominant actors are more or less likely to be successful in employing these mechanisms. But for an intelligent discussion in this regard, yet one that is applied to what is nearly the opposite strategic scenario—a *rising* actor attempting to convince dominant actors that it *isn't* threatening—see Goddard, *When Right Makes Might*, 27–39. For interesting albeit more general hypotheses on these kinds of questions, see also Stacie E. Goddard and Ronald R. Krebs, "Rhetoric, Legitimation, and Grand Strategy," *Security Studies* 24, No. 1 (2015), esp. 18–30.

27. Hurd, "The Strategic Use of Liberal Internationalism," 500.

28. For a discussion of the more traditional options available to rational security-seeking actors as they anticipate emerging threats and/or their own relative decline, see Copeland, *The Origins of Major War*, chapter 2; and Paul K. MacDonald and Joseph M. Parent, *Twilight of the Titans: Great Power Decline and Retrenchment* (Ithaca: Cornell University Press, 2018), chapters 1–2.

29. See Waltz, *Theory of International Politics*; and Sebastian Rosato, "The Inscrutable Intentions of Great Powers," *International Security* 39, No. 3 (2014/2015).

30. See Copeland, *The Origins of Major War*, chapters 1–2.

31. On the importance of offensive military capabilities, see Walt, *The Origins of Alliances;* and Van Evera, *Causes of War*.

32. Walt, *The Origins of Alliances*.

33. Mark L. Haas, "Ideological Polarity and Balancing in Great Power Politics," *Security Studies* 23, No. 4 (2014), 717–719.

34. Mark L. Haas, *The Ideological Origins of Great Power Politics, 1789–1989* (Ithaca: Cornell University Press, 2005), 7. See also Stephen M. Walt, *Revolution and War* (Ithaca: Cornell University Press, 1996), 38–41; Fred Halliday, *Revolution and World Politics: The Rise and Fall of the Sixth Great Power* (Durham: Duke University Press, 1999), 203–205; and Owen, *The Clash of Ideas*, 39–40.

35. Halliday, *Revolution and World Politics*, 13–14, 18.

36. On the rationality of fearing contrary ideological movements, see Haas, *Ideological Origins of Great Power Politics*, 19–20; John M. Owen IV, "When Do Ideologies Produce Alliances? The Holy Roman Empire, 1517–1555," *International Studies Quarterly* 49, No. 1 (2005); "Transnational Liberalism and American Primacy; or, Benignity Is in the Eye of the Beholder," in *America Unrivaled: The Future of the Balance of Power*, ed. G. John Ikenberry (Ithaca: Cornell University Press, 2002); *The Clash of Ideas*, 59–60; and Haas, "Ideological Polarity," 722–724.

37. A "system" need not be global. If competition between a dominant actor and a threatening ideology is limited to a particular region, "universal appeal" would mean only appeal across that region.

38. These criteria are similar but not identical to Owen's in *The Clash of Ideas*, 64–65.

39. Yoav Gortzak, "How Great Powers Rule: Coercion and Positive Inducements in International Order Enforcement," *Security Studies* 14, No. 4 (2005), 671.

40. On these types of costs, see, for instance, Christian Reus-Smit, *American Power and World Order* (Cambridge: Polity Press, 2004); Finnemore, "Legitimacy, Hypocrisy," 73; Kelly Greenhill, *Weapons of Mass Migration: Forced Displacement, Coercion, and Foreign Policy* (Ithaca: Cornell University Press, 2011); Goddard and Krebs, "Rhetoric, Legitimation, and Grand Strategy," 20–21; and Goddard, *When Right Makes Might*, 16–21.

41. Krasner, *Sovereignty*, 66.

42. See, for instance, Andrew Moravcsik, "Taking Preferences Seriously: A Liberal Theory of International Politics," *International Organization* 51, No. 4 (1997); Daniel Deudney and G. John Ikenberry, "The Nature and Sources of Liberal International Order," *Review of International Studies* 25, No. 2 (1999); Daniel H. Deudney, *Bounding Power: Republican Security Theory from the Polis to the Global Village* (Princeton: Princeton University Press, 2007); Deborah Boucoyannis, "The International Wanderings of a Liberal Idea, or Why Liberals Can Learn to Stop Worrying and Love the Balance of Power," *Perspectives on Politics* 5, No. 4 (2007); Anne-Marie Slaughter, "International Law in a World of Liberal States," *European Journal of International Law* 6 (1995); Christian Reus-Smit, "The Strange Death of Liberal International Theory," *European Journal of International Law* 12, No. 3 (2001); and Kevin Narizny, "On Systemic Paradigms and Domestic Politics: A Critique of the Newest Realism," *International Security* 42, No. 2 (2017).

43. These maxims are drawn from Michael W. Doyle, *Ways of War and Peace: Realism, Liberalism, and Socialism* (New York: W. W. Norton & Company, 1997), 210–211.

44. Due to considerations of length, I do not systematically examine hypotheses that begin from the premise that dominant actors focus more on things other than international order and thus do not care much about order in the first place. But I could foresee a larger project evaluating actors' preferences for pursuing "order-maximizing" goals (my assumption throughout this book) against hypotheses that they instead care much more about power-maximizing, wealth-maximizing, or ideology-maximizing goals.

45. Robert O. Keohane, *After Hegemony: Cooperation and Discord in the World Political Economy* (Princeton: Princeton University Press, 1984), chapter 6; G. John Ikenberry, *After Victory: Institutions, Strategic Restraint, and the Rebuilding of Order After Major Wars* (Princeton: Princeton University Press, 2001), 52–61.

46. *After Victory* remains the most theoretically rigorous version of the argument, and I focus on it here for this reason.

47. *After Victory*, 78. The degree to which this should *always* apply to *every* dominant actor is not clear in Ikenberry's logic, though my interpretation is as follows: *Power asymmetries* (a) should affect both capacity and willingness. They affect capacity to the extent that the leading state is in a position to forgo short-term gains as well as to sufficiently scare smaller states into fearing its domination. Yet they also affect willingness since the leading state shouldn't want to bind if it doesn't think it has this power capacity. But if we bracket cases examined only to those

where asymmetries are sufficiently large, as I do in this book, the power asymmetry threshold is satisfied. The presence of *democracy* (b), on the other hand, only affects capacity, not willingness. Its presence in Ikenberry's argument is not about norm externalization, but instead about the ability of states to credibly commit to a mutually binding settlement through transparent domestic processes. Democracy thus shouldn't affect order preferences. See *After Victory*, 51–79. Yet for a critique of Ikenberry's logic connecting democracy to constitutional order production and maintenance, see Paul Musgrave, "International Hegemony Meets Domestic Politics: Why Liberals Can Be Pessimists," *Security Studies* 28, No. 3 (2019).

48. It is for this reason that adopting the simple dichotomy of "excluding vs. including" doesn't quite work when pitting these theories against one another.

49. Moravcsik, "Taking Preferences Seriously," 517–518.

50. For example, Martin Jacques, *When China Rules the World: The End of the Western World and the Birth of a New Global Order*, 2nd ed. (New York: Penguin Books, 2009/2012).

51. For example, Tony Smith, *America's Mission: The United States and the Worldwide Struggle for Democracy*, updated ed. (Princeton: Princeton University Press, 2012).

52. Charles A. Kupchan, "The Normative Foundations of Hegemony and the Coming Challenge to Pax Americana," *Security Studies* 23, No. 2 (2014), 225; Colin Dueck, *Reluctant Crusaders: Power, Culture, and Change in American Grand Strategy* (Princeton: Princeton University Press, 2007).

53. Haas, *The Ideological Origins*; Owen, *The Clash of Ideas*.

54. For one such example, see Elizabeth Borgwardt, *A New Deal for the World: America's Vision for Human Rights* (Cambridge, MA: Harvard University Press, 2006).

55. See Ernest May, *"Lessons" of the Past: The Use and Misuse of History in American Foreign Policy* (New York: Oxford University Press, 1975); Robert Jervis, *Perception and Misperception in International Politics* (Princeton: Princeton University Press, 1976), 217–282; Yuen Foong Khong, *Analogies at War: Korea, Munich, Dien Bien Phu, and the Vietnam Decisions of 1965* (Princeton: Princeton University Press, 1992); Jack S. Levy, "Learning and Foreign Policy: Sweeping a Conceptual Minefield," *International Organization* 48, No. 2 (1994); Dan Reiter, *Crucible of Beliefs: Learning, Alliances, and World Wars* (Ithaca: Cornell University Press, 1996); 490–526; Christopher Hemmer, *Which Lessons Matter? American Foreign Policy Decision Making in the Middle East, 1979–1987* (Albany: State University of New York Press, 2000); and Jeffrey W. Legro, *Rethinking the World: Great Powers Strategies and International Order* (Ithaca: Cornell University Press, 2005).

56. See, for example, Deudney, *Bounding Power*; and Boucoyannis, "The International Wanderings of a Liberal Idea." Classical liberal works that highlight learning from the past include Norman Angell, *The Great Illusion, 1933* (New York: Putnam Press, 1933) and Richard Rosecrance, *The Rise of the Trading State: Commerce and Conquest in the Modern World* (New York: Basic Books, 1986).

57. Alexander L. George and Andrew Bennett, *Case Studies and Theory Development in the Social Sciences* (Cambridge, MA: MIT Press, 2004), chapter 3.
58. Ann Swidler, "Culture in Action: Symbols and Strategies," *American Sociological Review* 51, No. 2 (1996); David A. Lake, *Entangling Relations: American Foreign Policy in Its Century* (Princeton: Princeton University Press, 1999), 73.
59. For a similar point, see Bially Mattern, *Ordering International Politics*, 57.
60. On congruence testing and process tracing, see George and Bennett, *Case Studies*, chapters 8–10.
61. George and Bennett, *Case Studies*, 181.
62. Lake, *Entangling Relations*, 75.

CHAPTER 4

1. Daniel Philpott, *Revolutions in Sovereignty: How Ideas Shaped Modern International Relations* (Princeton: Princeton University Press, 2001), chapters 5–7; Christian Reus-Smit, *Individual Rights and the Making of the International System* (New York: Cambridge University Press, 2013), chapter 3.
2. Stephen D. Krasner, "Westphalia and All That," in *Ideas and Foreign Policy: Beliefs, Institutions, and Political Change.* ed. Judith Goldstein and Robert O. Keohane (Ithaca: Cornell University Press, 1993); and *Sovereignty: Organized Hypocrisy* (Princeton: Princeton University Press, 1999).
3. For background, see Richard Bonney, *The European Dynastic States, 1494–1660* (New York: Oxford University Press, 1991), chapter 4.
4. Bonney, *The European Dynastic States*, 189–190.
5. For an account of these events through the lens of transnational religious polarization, see John M. Owen IV, *The Clash of Ideas in World Politics: Transnational Networks, States, and Regime Change, 1510–2010* (Princeton: Princeton University Press, 2010), 111–114.
6. The best account of the negotiations is Derek Croxton, *Westphalia: The Last Christian Peace* (New York: Palgrave Macmillan, 2013).
7. See C. V. Wedgwood, *The Thirty Years War* (New York: The New York Review of Books, 1938/2005), chapter 11, esp. 458–462.
8. On the complex nature of the conferences, see Croxton, *Westphalia*, chapter 5.
9. Derek Croxton and Geoffrey Parker. "'A Swift and Sure Peace': The Congress of Westphalia, 1643–1648," in *The Making of Peace: Rulers, States, and the Aftermath of War*, ed. Williamson Murray and Jim Lacey (New York: Cambridge University Press, 2009), 72.
10. The negotiations are well summarized in Andreas Osiander, *The States System of Europe, 1640–1990: Peacemaking and the Conditions of International Stability* (New York: Oxford University Press, 1994), 17–20.
11. For this argument see, for example, Wedgwood, *The Thirty Years War*, 500–502; Kalevi Holsti, *Peace and War: Armed Conflicts and International Order, 1648–1989*

(New York: Cambridge University Press, 1991), chapter 2; Bonney, *The Thirty Years' War*, 18, 86; and Tim Blanning, *The Pursuit of Glory: The Five Revolutions That Made Modern Europe, 1648–1815* (New York: Penguin Books, 2008), 535.

12. On this position see, for instance, Andreas Osiander, "Sovereignty, International Relations, and the Westphalia Myth," *International Organization* 55, No. 1 (2001); Benno Teschke, *The Myth of 1648: Class, Geopolitics, and the Making of Modern International Relations* (London: Verso, 2003), chapter 7; and Daniel Nexon, *The Struggle for Power in Early Modern Europe: Religious Conflict, Dynastic Empires, and International Change* (Princeton: Princeton University Press, 2009), 279.

13. For a nice articulation of this point, see Peter H. Wilson, *The Thirty Years War: Europe's Tragedy* (Cambridge, MA: Harvard University Press, 2011), 778.

14. IPM, Article LXV. IPM can be found in Fred L. Israel, ed., *Major Peace Treaties of Modern History, 1648–1967*, Vol. 1 (New York: Chelsea House Publishers, 1967), 27–28.

15. This quote comes from IPO, Article VIII, para 2. The corresponding text in IPM can also be found in Article LXV.

16. Wilson, *The Thirty Years War*, 755.

17. On both points see Osiander, "Sovereignty, International Relations"; and Peter H. Wilson, *Heart of Europe: A History of the Holy Roman Empire* (Cambridge, MA: The Belknap Press of Harvard University Press, 2016), e.g., 174–175, 441–442. On religious limits compared with Augsburg, see Reus-Smit, *Individual Rights*, chapter 3.

18. Heinhard Steiger, "Concrete Peace and General Order: The Legal Meaning of the Treaties of 24 October 1648," in *1648: War and Peace in Europe*, ed. Klaus Bussmann and Heinz Schilling (Münster: Westfalisches Landesmuseum, 1998), 440.

19. John Gerard Ruggie, "Territoriality and Beyond: Problematizing Modernity in International Relations, *International Organization* 47, No. 1 (1993).

20. Reus-Smit, *Individual Rights*, 77; 102–103. For a similar sentiment, see Wilson, *The Thirty Years War*, 774.

21. Hendrik Spruyt, *The Sovereign State and Its Competitors: An Analysis of Systems Change* (Princeton: Princeton University Press, 1994), 35.

22. Quoted in Peter H. Wilson, ed., *The Thirty Years War: A Sourcebook* (London: Palgrave Macmillan, 2010), 122.

23. See Holsti, *Peace and War*, 29–30.

24. Quoted in Klaus Malettke, "France's Imperial Policy during the Thirty Years' War and the Peace of Westphalia," in *1648: War and Peace in Europe*, ed. Klaus Bussmann and Heinz Schilling (Münster: Westfalisches Landesmuseum, 1998), 181.

25. On the evolution of Richelieu's strategic thinking, see William F. Church, *Richelieu and Reason of State* (Princeton: Princeton University Press, 1972), 283–302; Malettke, "France's Imperial Policy," especially 180–183; and Hermann Weber, "'Une Bonne Paix': Richelieu's Foreign Policy and the Peace of Christendom," in *Richelieu and His Age*, ed. Joseph Bergin and Laurence Brockliss (Oxford: Clarendon Press, 1992).

26. There is some disagreement over whether France and Sweden intervened in the HRE defensively, as I have argued, or opportunistically, seeing a chance to go on the offensive to weaken the Holy Roman Emperor. For this dissenting view, see Osiander, "Sovereignty, International Relations."

27. Different parts of this passage are quoted in Osiander, *The States System of Europe*, 79; and Brendan Simms, *Europe: The Struggle for Supremacy, from 1453 to the Present* (New York: Basic Books, 2013), 7.

28. Both are quoted in Osiander, *The States System of Europe*, 79.

29. On this point, see Derek Croxton, *Peacemaking in Early Modern Europe: Cardinal Mazarin and the Congress of Westphalia, 1643–1648* (Selinsgrove: Susquehanna University Press, 1999), 261; Malettke, "France's Imperial Policy," 184.

30. Weber, "'Une Bonne Paix,'" 47–48.

31. Holsti, *Peace and War*, 32. The peace directive is reprinted in Fritz Dickmann et al., *Acta Pacis Westphalicae, Serie I: Instruktionen.* Vol. 1: *Frankreich, Schweden, Kaiser* (Münster Westfalen: Aschendorffsche Verlagsbuchhandlung, 1962), 58–123.

32. Malettke, "France's Imperial Policy," 183.

33. Croxton and Parker, "'A Swift and Sure Peace,'" 79–81.

34. For their specific territorial gains, see A.W. Ward, "The Peace of Westphalia," in *The Cambridge Modern History*, Vol. 4: *The Thirty Years' War*, ed. A. W. Ward, G. W. Prothero and Stanley Leathes (Cambridge: Cambridge University Press, 1906).

35. Derek Croxton, "The Peace of Westphalia of 1648 and the Origins of Sovereignty," *The International History Review* 21, No. 3 (1999), 571.

36. Ward, "The Peace of Westphalia," 413; Weber, "'Une Bonne Paix,'" 58.

37. See Wedgwood, *The Thirty Years War*, 447–448; Croxton, *Westphalia*, 76–81.

38. Croxton, *Westphalia*, 87.

39. E.A. Beller, "The Thirty Years War," in *The New Cambridge Modern History*, Vol. 4, *The Decline of Spain and the Thirty Years' War, 1609–48/59*, ed. J. P. Cooper (Cambridge: Cambridge University Press, 1970), 356–357; Holsti, *Peace and War*, 34–35; Croxton and Parker, "'A Swift and Sure Peace,'" 84–85.

40. Krasner, "Westphalia and All That," 246.

41. Wilson, *Heart of Europe*, 175.

42. Wedgwood, *The Thirty Years War*, 453.

43. On these three examples, respectively, see Croxton, *Westphalia*, chapters 7, 8, and 5.

44. Croxton and Parker, "'A Swift and Sure Peace,'" 76.

45. See Holsti, *Peace and War*, 32; Weber, "'Une Bonne Paix,'"; Osiander, *The States System of Europe*, 27, 58–59; Croxton, "The Peace of Westphalia," 584.

46. Croxton and Parker, "'A Swift and Sure Peace,'" 80, 97.

47. G. John Ikenberry, *After Victory: Institutions, Strategic Restraint, and the Rebuilding of Order after Major Wars* (Princeton: Princeton University Press, 2001), 38.

48. Henry A. Kissinger, *Diplomacy* (New York: Simon and Schuster, 1994), 59.

49. Quoted in Henry A. Kissinger, *World Order* (New York: Penguin, 2014), 23.

50. Ward, "The Peace of Westphalia," 410.

51. Quoted in Osiander, *The States System of Europe*, 28.

52. Philpott, *Revolutions in Sovereignty*, chapters 5–7; Reus-Smit, *Individual Rights*, chapter 3.
53. See Philpott, *Revolutions in Sovereignty*, chapter 6, especially the chart on p. 111.
54. *Revolutions in Sovereignty*, 118.
55. Wilson, *The Thirty Years War*, 554–565. After crushing the Swedes and German Protestants at Nördlingen, the Emperor was able to negotiate the Peace of Prague from a position of strength, bringing numerous estates back into the HRE while gaining unprecedented powers for himself. Croxton, *Westphalia*, 46–47.
56. A series of military setbacks in the war's early years and Imperial troops pushing into French territory by 1636 only emphasized that his long-held fears had become reality. See Paul Kennedy, *The Rise and Fall of the Great Powers* (New York: Vintage Books, 1987), 39–40; and Bonney, *The Thirty Years' War*, 56.
57. This is a major theme of Krasner, "Westphalia and All That."
58. Osiander, *The States System of Europe*, 34; Reus-Smit, *Individual Rights*.
59. Croxton and Parker, "'A Swift and Sure Peace,'" 79.
60. Volker Gerhardt, "On the Historical Significance of the Peace of Westphalia: Twelve Theses," in *1648: War and Peace in Europe*, ed. Klaus Bussmann and Heinz Schilling (Münster: Westfalisches Landesmuseum, 1998), 485.
61. Krasner, "Westphalia and All That," 246.
62. Ward, "The Peace of Westphalia," 415.
63. The Dutch and League of Augsburg Wars were major ones. Yet in terms of longevity and destruction, both paled in comparison to the War of the Spanish Succession. For comparisons, see Table 2.2.
64. See, for instance, John B. Wolf, *Louis XIV* (New York: W. W. Norton & Company, 1968), 498.
65. For a good overview of the war's most immediate causes in 1702, see Jeremy Black, *European International Relations: 1648–1815* (New York: Palgrave, 2002), 128.
66. The Grand Alliance had succeeded in rolling back French/Bourbon offensive gains. Yet numerous attempts to invade France and Spain had failed, a brutal winter in 1708–1709 had sapped resources, and all parties were beset by financial problems by 1709–1710. See Black, *European International Relations*, 129–131.
67. See M. S. Anderson, *Europe in the Eighteenth Century, 1713–1789* (New York: Holt, Rinehart and Winston, Inc., 1961), 217–219; Holsti, *Peace and War*, 77–78; Osiander, *The States System of Europe*, 160–165, and the Appendix of this book.
68. J. H. Shennan, *International Relations in Europe, 1689–1789* (New York: Routledge, 1995), 16, 24. On the divide between Britain and its allies in the war's endgame see, for instance, Charles F. Doran, *The Politics of Assimilation: Hegemony and Its Aftermath* (Baltimore: The Johns Hopkins Press, 1971), chapter 11.
69. On the complicated diplomacy of Britain arranging a separate peace with France behind the backs of its allies, see B. W. Hill, "Oxford, Bolingbroke, and the Peace of Utrecht," *The Historical Journal* 16, No. 2 (1973).
70. Britain technically had multiple foreign secretaries, but Bolingbroke was the most powerful throughout the settlement negotiations.

71. For analysis of the more specific (non-ordering) elements of the Utrecht settlement, see W. F. Reddaway, "Rivalry for Colonial Power, 1660–1713," in *The Cambridge History of the British Empire*, Vol. 1: *The Old Empire*, ed. J. Holland Rose, A. P. Newton and E. A. Benians (Cambridge: Cambridge University Press, 1929), 328–329; A. W. Ward, "The War of the Spanish Succession. (2) The Peace of Utrecht and the Supplementary Pacifications," in *The Cambridge Modern History*, Vol. 5: *The Age of Louis XIV*, ed. A. W. Ward, G. W. Prothero, and Stanley Leathes (Cambridge: Cambridge University Press, 1908); Penfield Roberts, *The Quest for Security, 1715–1740* (New York: Harper & Brothers Publishers, 1947), 11; John B. Wolf, *The Emergence of the Great Powers, 1685–1713* (New York: Harper & Row, 1951), 90; Ragnhild Hatton, *Europe in the Age of Louis XIV* (Great Britain: Harcourt, Brace & World, Inc, 1969), 107–108; Hill, "Oxford, Bolingbroke, and the Peace of Utrecht," 247; J. R. Jones, *Britain and the World, 1649–1815* (Sussex: The Harvester Press, 1980), 177; and Shennan, *International Relations in Europe*, 17.

72. See Osiander, *The States System of Europe*, 120–121.

73. Secondary literature confirming this first rule change includes H. F. Hinsley, *Power and the Pursuit of Peace: Theory and Practice in the History of Relations between States* (London: Cambridge University Press, 1963), 178; Holsti, *Peace and War*, 76–77; Evan Luard, *The Balance of Power: The System of International Relations, 1648–1815* (New York: St. Martin's Press, 1992), chapter 6; Osiander, *The States System of Europe*, 120–147; Christian Reus-Smit, *The Moral Purpose of the State: Culture, Social Identity, and Institutional Rationality in International Relations* (Princeton: Princeton University Press, 1999), 117; and Ian Clark, *Legitimacy and International Society* (Oxford: Oxford University Press, 2005), 77–78.

74. See the heart of the treaty on this point, reprinted in George Chalmers, ed., *A Collection of Treaties between Great Britain and Other Powers* (London: J. Stockdale, 1790), 344–345.

75. Secondary sources agreeing on this second rule change include Wolf, *The Emergence of the Great Powers*, 90; Hinsley, *Power and the Pursuit of Peace*, 171; Holsti, *Peace and War*, 81; Luard, *The Balance of Power*, 12; Osiander, *The States System of Europe*, 123–138; Reus-Smit, *The Moral Purpose of the State*, 118; and Clark, *Legitimacy and International Society*, 80–83.

76. See Chalmers, *A Collection of Treaties*, 365.

77. Chalmers, *A Collection of Treaties*, 363–364.

78. Chalmers, *A Collection of Treaties*, 364–365.

79. This recognition was important for Britain because (a) Louis XIV had previously recognized James' son as King in 1701; and (b) Queen Anne was believed incapable of producing an heir, forecasting a potential succession crisis with the ousted Stuarts whenever she died.

80. See Chalmers, *A Collection of Treaties*, 369.

81. Holsti, *Peace and War*, 77.

82. See Holsti's data on the causes of eighteenth-century conflicts in *Peace and War*, 88–89, 92. This claim might seem a dubious one in the face of numerous wars named for dynastic successions in the decades following Utrecht. But the titles of these wars are misnomers compared to the War of the Spanish Succession, as this was the only conflict that began explicitly *because* of competing dynastic claims.

83. See, for instance, Philip Bobbitt, *The Shield of Achilles: War, Peace, and the Course of History* (New York: Alfred A. Knopf, 2002), 527–537.

84. Anderson, *Europe in the Eighteenth Century*, 166.

85. On the logical connection between these rules, see Reus-Smit, *The Moral Purpose of the State*, 119.

86. This link was in fact the one that Louis XIV most feared, and it may have even motivated him into a series of preventive wars (rather than offensive ones, as they are commonly portrayed) to forestall this possibility. See Dale C. Copeland, *The Origins of Major War* (Ithaca: Cornell University Press, 2000), 220–225.

87. Doran, *The Politics of Assimilation*, 112. On the enormity of the French challenge throughout the reign of Louis XIV, see Jones, *Britain and the World*, 119–123.

88. Doran, *The Politics of Assimilation*, 113–114; *The Shield of Achilles*, 520–521.

89. This point is perhaps best summed up by Bolingbroke himself in his reflections on the period. See Henry St. John, Viscount Bolingbroke, "Letter VIII," in *The Works of Lord Bolingbroke, II* (London: Frank Cass, 1967, reprint of the 1844 edition), 294.

90. On Louis's *réunions* policy, see Hatton, *Europe in the Age of Louis XIV*, 97; and J. H. Shennan, *Louis XIV* (London: Methuen & Co. Ltd, 1986), 37.

91. The prior English Kings Charles II and James II had been close allies of Louis. By contrast, William, already the longtime leader of the Dutch Republic, was one of the Sun King's greatest adversaries.

92. On the Sun King's foreign policy throughout this period, see Hatton, *Europe in the Age of Louis XIV*, 92–108; Shennan, *Louis XIV*, 33–45; and Jeremy Black, *The Rise of the European Powers, 1679–1793* (London: Edward Arnold, 1990), 31–45.

93. Bolingbroke, "Letter VIII," *The Works of Lord Bolingbroke, II*, 278.

94. Quoted in Osiander, *The States System of Europe*, 124.

95. Quoted in Osiander, *The States System of Europe*, 125.

96. Paul W. Schroeder, "Power and Order in the Early Modern Era," in *History and Neorealism*, ed. Ernest R. May, Richard Rosecrance, and Zara Steiner (New York: Cambridge University Press, 2010), 93.

97. See, for instance, Osiander, *The States System of Europe*, 152–153.

98. See the relevant quotation in Osiander, *The States System of Europe*, 153.

99. See Bolingbroke to Torcy, October 2, 1711, Henry St. John, Viscount Bolingbroke, *Letters and Correspondence, Public and Private of the Right Honourable Henry St John, Lord Viscount Bolingbroke, During the Time He Was Secretary of State to Queen Anne*, ed. Gilbert Parke (London: G. G. & J. Robinson, 1798), Vol. 1, 507.

100. John C. Rule, "King and Minister: Louis XIV and Colbert de Torcy," in *William III and Louis XIV: Essays 1689–1720 by and for Mark A. Thomson*, ed. Ragnhild Hatton and J. S. Bromley (England: Liverpool University Press, 1968), 234–235.

101. Torcy to Bolingbroke, March 23 and March 28, 1712, Henry St. John, Viscount Bolingbroke, *Letters and Correspondence*, Vol. 2, 532, 534.

102. Bolingbroke to Torcy, March 23, 1712, Bolingbroke, *Letters and Correspondence*, Vol. 2, 536.

103. Bolingbroke, *Letters and Correspondence*, Vol. 2, 536. On Bolingbroke's recognition that the issue of succession was paramount to the peace before British troops could leave the battlefield, see George Macaulay Trevelyan, *England under Queen Anne*, Vol. 3: *The Peace and the Protestant Succession* (London: Longmans, Green and Co., 1934), 212–215.

104. Torcy to Bolingbroke, April 11, 1712, Bolingbroke, *Letters and Correspondence*, Vol. 2, 546.

105. Bolingbroke to Torcy, April 29, 1712, Bolingbroke, *Letters and Correspondence*, Vol. 2, 548–550.

106. Aspects of these negotiations are traced in Wolf, *Louis XIV*, chapter 33.

107. Bolingbroke to Torcy, June 6, 1712, Bolingbroke, *Letters and Correspondence*, Vol. 2, 583. Emphasis added.

108. Quoted in Osiander, *The States System of Europe*, 157.

109. See Ikenberry, *After Victory*, 40.

110. Ward, "The Peace of Utrecht and the Supplementary Pacifications," 458; Mark A. Thomson, "Parliament and Foreign Policy, 1689–1714," in *William III and Louis XIV: Essays 1689–1720 by and for Mark A. Thomson*, ed. Ragnhild Hatton and J. S. Bromley (England: Liverpool University Press, 1968), 134–135; Doran, *The Politics of Assimilation*, 136; Osiander, *The States System of Europe*, 143–144.

111. On the Dutch Republic's ill treatment and subsequent exit from the ranks of great powers, see Hatton, *Europe in the Age of Louis XIV*, 107; Derek McKay and H. M. Scott, *The Rise of the Great Powers, 1648–1815* (New York: Longman Group Limited, 1983), 100; and this book's appendix.

112. See, for instance, Black, *Rise of the European Powers*, 32; and Doran, *The Politics of Assimilation*, 114.

113. See, for instance, Clark, *Legitimacy in International Society*, 72–73.

114. McKay and Scott, *The Rise of the Great Powers*, 64.

115. McKay and Scott, *The Rise of the Great Powers*, 63–64. On these expanding war aims, see 60–63.

116. Hatton, *Europe in the Age of Louis XIV*, 107; Kennedy, *The Rise and Fall of the Great Powers*, 105; Osiander, *The States System of Europe*, 97.

117. On this point see Bobbitt, *The Sword of Achilles*, 521.

118. *Peace and War*, 81. Simms also articulates a version of this thesis in *Europe*, 78.

119. Schroeder, "Power and Order in the Early Modern Era," 92.

120. See Holsti, *Peace and War*, chapter 4; Clark, *Legitimacy in International Society*, chapter 4.

121. See, for instance, Mark A. Thomson, "Self-Determination and Collective Security as Factors in English and French Foreign Policy, 1689–1718," in *William III and Louis XIV: Essays 1689–1720 by and for Mark A. Thomson*, ed. Ragnhild Hatton and J. S. Bromley (England: Liverpool University Press, 1968), 283–284; and J. M. Roberts, *A History of Europe* (New York: Allen Lane The Penguin Press, 1996), 262.

122. Blanning, *The Pursuit of Glory*, 556.

123. See McKay and Scott, *The Rise of the Great Powers*, 94–101; and this book's appendix.

124. On Britain's specific territorial gains, see Wolf, *The Emergence of the Great Powers*, 90; Lindsay, "International Relations," 192–193; Hatton, *Europe in the Age of Louis XIV*, 107; Doran, *The Politics of Assimilation*, 136; William Doyle, *The Old European Order, 1600–1800* (Oxford: Oxford University Press, 1978), 274–277; Jones, *Britain and the World*, 177; McKay and Scott, *The Rise of the Great Powers*, 95–96; and Shennan, *International Relations of Europe*, 17.

125. McKay and Scott, *The Rise of the Great Powers*, 110; Kennedy, *The Rise and Fall of the Great Powers*, 105–106.

126. Black, *Rise of the European Powers*, 96–97.

127. Anderson, *Europe in the Eighteenth Century*, 243–246; Doyle, *The Old European Order*, 283, 286.

128. Fred Anderson, *Crucible of War: The Seven Years' War and the Fate of Empire in British North America, 1754–1766* (Westminster: Alfred A. Knopf, 2000), 36–37.

129. Black, *Rise of the European Powers*, 106–107; Simms, *Europe*, 103.

130. For excellent summaries of the events that led to war, see Black, *European International Relations, 1648–1815*, 158–176; and Daniel Marston, *The Seven Years' War* (Great Britain: Osprey Publishing, 2001), 10–15.

131. On this last point see James Riley, *The Seven Years' War and the Old Regime in France: The Economic and Financial Toll* (Princeton: Princeton University Press, 1986).

132. The classic account is Zenab Esmat Rashed, *The Peace of Paris 1763* (Liverpool: University Press of Liverpool, 1951).

133. See Chalmers, *Major Peace Treaties in Modern History*, 307–308.

134. To be clear, *all* of the peace settlements examined in this book dealt with case-specific issues. The difference is that while others, like Westphalia and Utrecht, also included general order principle changes that reached beyond the specific issues of the day, the 1763 settlement dealt only with these kinds of immediate grievances.

135. Fred Anderson, "The Peace of Paris, 1763," in *The Making of Peace: Rulers, States, and the Aftermath of War*, ed. Williamson Murray and Jim Lacey (New York: Cambridge University Press, 2009), 127.

136. On this possibility and Pitt's desire for it, see Anderson, "The Peace of Paris, 1763," 106–108.

137. On these details, see Anderson, *Crucible of War*, 503.

138. H. W. V. Temperley, "The Peace of Paris," in *The Cambridge History of the British Empire*, Vol. 1: *The Old Empire*, ed. J. Holland Rose, A. P. Newton, and E. A. Benians (Cambridge: Cambridge University Press, 1929), 501.

139. Rodney Bruce Hall, *National Collective Identity: Social Constructs and International Systems* (New York: Columbia University Press, 1999), 111.

140. On the breakdown between Britain and Prussia during the war's endgame, see Matt Schumann and Karl Schweizer, *The Seven Years War: A Transatlantic History* (New York: Routledge, 2008), chapter 6.

141. McKay and Scott, *The Rise of the Great Powers*, 215–216.

142. Daniel Baugh, *The Global Seven Years War, 1754–1763: Britain and France in a Great Power Contest* (London: Pearson Education Limited, 2011), 646.

143. See Paul W. Schroeder, *The Transformation of European Politics, 1763–1848* (New York: Oxford University Press, 1994), 35–36.

144. Schroeder, *The Transformation of European Politics*, 39.

145. McKay and Scott, *The Rise of the Great Powers*, 198.

146. See William M. Fowler, Jr., *Empires at War: The French and Indian War and the Struggle for North America, 1754–1763* (New York: Walker & Company, 2005), 269.

147. Quoted in Sir Julian S. Corbett, *England in the Seven Years' War: A Study in Combined Strategy*, Vol. 2 (London: Longmans, Green and Co., 1918), 172.

148. Bedford to Bute, July 9, 1761, in John Russell, Lord Bedford, *Correspondence of John, Fourth Duke of Bedford*, Vol. 3 (London: Brown, Green, and Longmans, 1846), 26.

149. Bute to Bedford, July 12, 1761, *Correspondence of Bedford*, Vol. 3, 30, 33. Emphasis in original.

150. Bute to Bedford, July 12, 1761, *Correspondence of Bedford*, Vol. 3, 30.

151. See Temperley, "The Peace of Paris," 500.

152. Anderson, "The Peace of Paris, 1763," 112.

153. See, for instance, his extensive correspondence with his mentor reprinted in Romney Sedgwick, ed. *Letters From George III to Lord Bute, 1756–1766* (London: Macmillan, 1939).

154. For this domestic politics variant of the exporting thesis, see Blanning, *The Pursuit of Glory*, 586; and Lindsay, "International Relations," 213.

155. See relevant quotes in Temperley, "The Peace of Paris," 502; and Baugh, *The Global Seven Years War*, 638.

156. McKay and Scott, *The Rise of the Great Powers*, 199.

157. Fowler, *Empires at War*, 271.

158. Fowler, *Empires at War*, 270–272.

159. On the broad societal and parliamentary support for the lenient treaty terms, see Andersen, "The Peace of Paris, 1763," 116–119; and Fowler, *Empires at War*, 273.

160. Baugh, *The Global Seven Years War*, 654.

161. Blanning, *The Pursuit of Glory*, 588–589.

CHAPTER 5

1. Henry A. Kissinger, *A World Restored: Metternich, Castlereagh and the Problems of Peace, 1812–1822* (Boston: Houghton Mifflin Company, 1957), 5.

2. For examples, see Mark Mazower, *Governing the World: The History of an Idea* (New York: The Penguin Press, 2012), 123–125, 195–197.

3. See, for instance, Philip Zelikow, "The New Concert of Europe," *Survival* 34, No. 2 (1992); Richard Rosecrance, "A New Concert of Powers," *Foreign Affairs* 71, No. 2 (1992); Charles A. Kupchan and Adam Mount, "The Autonomy Rule," *Democracy* 12 (2009); The 21st Century Concert Study Group, *A Twenty-First Century Concert of Powers—Promoting Great Power Multilateralism for the Post-Transatlantic Era* (Frankfurt: Peace Research Institute Frankfurt, 2014); and Thomas Wright, "The Rise and Fall of the Unipolar Concert," *The Washington Quarterly* 37, No. 4 (2015).

4. See, for instance, Korina Kagan, "The Myth of the European Concert: The Realist–Institutionalist Debate and Great Power Behavior in the Eastern Question, 1821–41," *Security Studies* 7, No. 2 (1997/1998); Matthew Rendall, "Russia, the Concert of Europe, and Greece 1821–29: A Test of Hypotheses about the Vienna System," *Security Studies* 9, No. 4 (2000); and Branislav L. Slantchev, "Territory and Commitment: The Concert of Europe as Self-Enforcing Equilibrium," *Security Studies* 14, No. 4 (2005).

5. Robert Jervis, "Security Regimes," in *International Regimes*, ed. Stephen D. Krasner (Ithaca: Cornell University Press, 1983) and "From Balance to Concert: A Study of International Security Cooperation," *World Politics* 38, No. 1 (1985); Charles A. Kupchan and Clifford A. Kupchan, "Concerts, Collective Security, and the Future of Europe," *International Security* 16, No. 1 (1991); G. John Ikenberry, *After Victory: Institutions, Strategic Restraint and the Rebuilding of Order after Major Wars* (Princeton: Princeton University Press, 2001), chapter 4; Dan Lindley, "Avoiding Tragedy in Power Politics: The Concert of Europe, Transparency, and Crisis Management," *Security Studies* 13, No. 2 (2003); and Jennifer Mitzen, *Power in Concert: The Nineteenth-Century Origins of Global Governance* (Chicago: University of Chicago Press, 2013).

6. On the former, see Charles A. Kupchan, *How Enemies Become Friends: The Sources of Stable Peace* (Princeton: Princeton University Press, 2010), chapter 5. On the latter, see Bruce Cronin, *Community under Anarchy: Transnational Identity and the Evolution of Cooperation* (New York: Columbia University Press, 1999), chapter 3; Mark L. Haas, *The Ideological Origins of Great Power Politics, 1789–1989*

(Ithaca: Cornell University Press, 2005), chapter 3; and Paul W. Schroeder, *The Transformation of European Politics, 1763–1848* (New York: Oxford University Press, 1994).

7. On the demonstrable differences the Concert of Europe produced for behavior and outcomes across the continent, see Kyle Lascurettes, "The Concert of Europe and Great-Power Governance Today: What Can the Order of 19th-Century Europe Teach Policymakers About International Order in the 21st Century?" *RAND National Defense Research Institute/ISDP Report* (2017).

8. For example, Richard B. Elrod, "The Concert of Europe: A Fresh Look at the International System," *World Politics* 28, No. 2 (1976), 161–162; Paul W. Schroeder, "The 19th-Century International System: Changes in the Structure," *World Politics* 39, No. 1 (1986) and "Did the Vienna Settlement Rest on a Balance of Power?" *The American Historical Review*, 97, No. 2 (1992); and Slantchev, "Territory and Commitment," 577–580.

9. Elrod, "The Concert of Europe,"; Slantchev, "Territory and Commitment," esp. 591 and 606; Kupchan, *How Enemies Become Friends*, 196–200.

10. Lindley, "Avoiding Tragedy."

11. The Concert case studies in Cronin, *Community under Anarchy*; Haas, *The Ideological Origins*; and Kupchan, *How Enemies Become Friends*, 200, 238–239 all endorse elements of this argument.

12. For a discussion of these systemic outcomes, see Lascurettes, "The Concert of Europe."

13. For an excellent summary of the Vienna Settlement and its significance, see Mitzen, *Power in Concert*, chapter 3.

14. See, for example, Elrod, "The Concert of Europe," 163–165; David King, *Vienna, 1814: How the Conquerors of Napoleon Made Love, War, and Peace at the Congress of Vienna* (New York: Three Rivers Press, 2008), 50. This principle was consecrated in a secret clause of the First Treaty of Paris (May 1814). See Edward Hertslet, ed., *The Map of Europe by Treaty: Political and Territorial Changes since the General Peace of 1814*, Vol. 1 (London: Butterworths, 1875), 18.

15. See Andreas Osiander, *The States System of Europe, 1640–1990: Peacemaking and the Conditions of International Stability* (New York: Oxford University Press, 1994), 236.

16. Ikenberry, *After Victory*, 93–96; King, *Vienna, 1814*, 247.

17. Mitzen, *Power in Concert*, 95.

18. Kissinger, *A World Restored*, 186; King, *Vienna, 1814*, 309–310.

19. Hertslet, *The Map of Europe*, 375.

20. See Elrod, "The Concert of Europe," 163–168; Schroeder, "Did the Vienna Settlement Rest . . . ?"

21. The relevant parts of the text are quoted in Cronin, *Community under Anarchy*, 60–61.

22. Hertslet, *The Map of Europe*, 573; see also F. R. Bridge and Roger Bullen, *The Great Powers and the European States System, 1814–1914*, 2nd ed. (Great Britain: Pearson Education Limited, 1980/2005), 4–11.

23. Kissinger convincingly argues that Alexander's articulation of the Holy Alliance was unintelligible; it was Metternich who later gave the pact tangible meaning by connecting it to liberal revolutions. See *A World Restored*, 189; and *Diplomacy* (New York: Simon and Schuster, 1994), 83.

24. Quoted in René Albrecht-Carrié, *The Concert of Europe* (New York: Walker & Company, 1968), 48. Emphasis added.

25. Osiander, *The States System of Europe*, 223.

26. King, *Vienna, 1814*, 317.

27. See Martha Finnemore, *The Purpose of Intervention: Changing Beliefs about the Use of Force* (Ithaca: Cornell University Press, 2003), 117–121.

28. See Tim Blanning, *The Pursuit of Glory: The Five Revolutions That Made Modern Europe, 1648–1815* (New York: Penguin Books, 2008), chapters 5 and 6.

29. This narrative draws from Stephen M. Walt, *Revolution and War* (Ithaca: Cornell University Press), 74–89; Haas, *The Ideological Origins*, 53–66; and John M. Owen IV, *The Clash of Ideas in World Politics: Transnational Networks, States, and Regime Change, 1510–2010* (Princeton: Princeton University Press, 2010), 135–141.

30. Kissinger, *A World Restored*, 226.

31. Quoted in Albrecht-Carrié, *The Concert of Europe*, 30–31.

32. Quoted in Sir Charles Webster, *The Congress of Vienna, 1814–1815* (Great Britain: The Camelot Press Limited, 1919/1963), 189.

33. Hertslet, *The Map of Europe*, 374.

34. Hertslet, *The Map of Europe*, 342–343.

35. Quoted in John M. Sherwig, "Lord Grenville's Plan for a Concert of Europe, 1797–99," *Journal of Modern History* 34, No. 3 (1962), 286.

36. The full text of Pitt's 1805 memorandum can be found in Webster, *British Diplomacy*, 389–394.

37. On the collapse of the former, see Sherwig, "Lord Grenville's Plan." On the latter, see Adam Zamoyski, *Rites of Peace: The Fall of Napoleon and the Congress of Vienna* (New York: HarperCollins, 2007), 17–19.

38. For an excellent account of this kind of threat-driven learning, see Richard Langhorne, "The Development of International Conferences, 1648–1830," *Studies in History and Politics* 2, No. 2 (1981–82), 76–85.

39. See, for instance, Webster, *British Diplomacy*, 1. On the evolution and importance of Castlereagh's project, see Edward Vose Gulick, *Europe's Classical Balance of Power* (New York: W. W. Norton & Company, 1955/1967), chapter 5.

40. Webster, *British Diplomacy*, 104.

41. See Webster, *The Congress of Vienna*, 28–39.

42. Webster, *British Diplomacy*, 20.

43. Schroeder, *The Transformation of European Politics*, 501.

44. This proposal and Castlereagh's thoughts about it can be found in Webster, *British Diplomacy*, 19–27.

45. Quoted in C. K. Webster, *The Foreign Policy of Castlereagh, 1812–1815: Britain and the Reconstruction of Europe* (London: G. Bell and Sons, Ltd., 1931), 226–227.

46. Quoted in Osiander, *The States System of Europe*, 201.

47. See, for instance, Kissinger, *A World Restored*, 213.

48. Quoted in Alan Sked, "The Metternich System, 1815–48," in *Europe's Balance of Power 1815–1848*, ed. Alan Sked (Great Britain: The Macmillan Press Ltd, 1979), 112.

49. Kissinger, *A World Restored*, 123.

50. Quoted in Alan Sked, "Metternich's Enemies or the Threat from Below," in *Europe's Balance of Power 1815–1848*, ed. Alan Sked (Great Britain: The Macmillan Press Ltd, 1979), 164–165.

51. Quoted in King, *Vienna, 1814*, 164.

52. Webster, *British Diplomacy*, p. 105.

53. See for instance Kissinger, *A World Restored*, 184–185; 188–190; 217–218.

54. On these revolutions and reactions, see Owen, *The Clash of Ideas*, 147–148.

55. Kissinger, *A World Restored*, 227.

56. See document 5 in Albrecht-Carrié, *The Concert of Europe*, 49–52.

57. See Kissinger, *A World Restored*, 217–218, 318; Jervis, "From Balance to Concert," 65.

58. The full text of Castlereagh's 1820 State Paper can be found in Adolphus William Ward and George Peabody Gooch, eds., *The Cambridge History of British Foreign Policy, 1783–1919*, Vol. 2: 1815–1866 (Cambridge: Cambridge University Press, 1927), 627.

59. See Kissinger, *Diplomacy*, 83–89, as well as *A World Restored*, 266.

60. Quoted in Kissinger, *A World Restored*, 203.

61. Henry Kissinger and Dan Lindley fit in this camp, as do classic works like Harold George Nicolson, *The Congress of Vienna: A Study in Allied Unity: 1812–1822* (London: Constable & Co ltd., 1946); Carsten Holbraad, *The Concert of Europe: A Study in German and British International Theory* (New York: Barnes & Noble, Inc., 1970); and Roy Bridge, "Allied Diplomacy in Peacetime: The Failure of the Congress 'System,' 1815–23," in *Europe's Balance of Power 1815–1848*, ed. Alan Sked (Great Britain: The Macmillan Press Ltd, 1979).

62. The exceptions came only in 1856 and 1878, at the conclusion of two particularly important wars.

63. Elrod, "The Concert of Europe," 171–172.

64. Kissinger, *A World Restored*, p. 285.

65. Ikenberry, *After Victory*, 81.

66. Both are quoted in Webster, *British Diplomacy*, 93, 24. Emphasis added.

67. Ikenberry, *After Victory*, 107–114.

68. Ikenberry, *After Victory*, 83.

69. See Ikenberry, *After Victory*, 90–98.

70. Ikenberry, *After Victory*, 116. See also 82, n 4.

71. Indeed, there is enough support that it passes both congruence and process tracing tests for this rule.

72. Quoted in Ward and Gooch, *The Cambridge History of British Foreign Policy*, 631.

73. See A. J. P. Taylor, *The Struggle for Mastery in Europe, 1848–1918* (Oxford: Oxford University Press, 1954), 2.

74. Quoted in Kissinger, *A World Restored*, 196.

75. See Kissinger, *A World Restored*, chapters 14 and 15.

76. Langhorne, "The Development of International Conferences," 67.

77. Paul W. Schroeder, "The Transformation of Political Thinking, 1787–1848," in *Coping with Complexity in the International System*, ed. Jack Snyder and Robert Jervis (Boulder: Westview Press, 1993), 68.

78. Quoted in Richard Langhorne, "Reflections on the Significance of the Congress of Vienna," *Review of International Studies* 12, No. 4 (1986), 319.

79. Langhorne, "The Development of International Conferences," 65.

80. Jervis, "From Balance to Concert," 66–68.

81. See King, *Vienna, 1814*, 240–242.

82. Quoted in Osiander, *The States System of Europe*, 202.

83. Kalevi J. Holsti, *Peace and War: Armed Conflicts and International Order, 1648–1989* (New York: Cambridge University Press, 1991), 138–145.

84. See Matthew Rendall, "A Qualified Success for Collective Security: The Concert of Europe and the Belgian Crisis, 1831," *Diplomacy and Statecraft* 18, No. 2 (2007).

85. On the development of these dueling ideological camps, see Haas, *The Ideological Origins*, chapter 3.

86. See Owen, *The Clash of Ideas*, 149–151.

87. Quoted in Taylor, *The Struggle for Mastery in Europe*, 5.

88. For an overview of these ideologies, see Michael Broers, *Europe After Napoleon: Revolution, Reaction and Romanticism, 1814–1848* (New York: Manchester University Press, 1996).

89. See Kurt Weyland, "The Diffusion of Revolution: '1848' in Europe and Latin America," *International Organization* 63, No. 3 (2009).

90. E. J. Hobsbawm, *The Age of Revolution, 1789–1848* (New York: The World Publishing Company, 1962), 302. See also Schroeder, *The Transformation of European Politics*, 791.

91. These structural preconditions are effectively detailed by Hobsbawm, *The Age of Revolution*, 301–308.

92. Mike Rapport, *1848: Year of Revolution* (New York: Basic Books, 2008), 5.

93. See Schroeder, *The Transformation of European Politics*, 799–804.

94. Quoted in Rapport, *1848*, p. 14.

95. See Rapport, *1848*, 21–23.

96. See Rapport, *1848*, 30–36.

97. On some of these complicated dynamics, see Schroeder, *The Transformation of European Politics*, 785.

98. Quoted in Sked, "Metternich's Enemies or the Threat from Below," 175.

99. See John Saville, *1848: The British State and the Chartist Movement* (New York: Cambridge University Press, 1987).

100. See Haas, *The Ideological Origins*, 99–104.

101. Henry Weisser, "Chartism in 1848: Reflections on a Non-Revolution," *Albion: A Quarterly Journal Concerned with British Studies* 13, No. 1 (1981), 25.

102. Charles Pouthas, "The Revolutions of 1848," in *The New Cambridge Modern History*, Vol. 10, *The Zenith of European Power 1830–70*, ed. J. P. T. Bury (New York: Cambridge University Press, 1960), 392–395.

103. Pouthas, "The Revolutions of 1848," 403–405.

104. See Owen, *The Clash of Ideas*, 151–153.

105. Broers, *Europe after Napoleon*, 80–87; 114–118.

106. Rapport, *1848*, 405–406.

107. Owen, *The Clash of Ideas*, 154.

108. Owen, *The Clash of Ideas*, 156.

109. Quoted in Klari Kingston, "Gunboat Liberalism? Palmerston, Europe and 1848," *History Today* (August 1997), 39.

110. Quoted in R. W. Seton-Watson, *Britain in Europe, 1789–1914: A Survey of Foreign Policy* (New York: The Macmillan Company, 1937), 258.

111. Quoted in Kingston, "Gunboat Liberalism?" 40.

112. Frank G. Weber, "Palmerston and Prussian Liberalism, 1848," *Journal of Modern History* 35, No. 2 (1963).

113. Weber, "Palmerston and Prussian Liberalism," 135. On the bipartisan nature of Palmerston's continental policies throughout the revolution, see Schroeder, *The Transformation of European Politics*, 790.

114. Quoted in Kingston, "Gunboat Liberalism?" 41.

115. See Eugene Horváth, "Kossuth and Palmerston (1848–1849)," *The Slavonic and East European Review* 9, No. 27 (1931), 618.

116. See Seton-Watson, *Britain in Europe*, 265–271.

117. Horváth, "Kossuth and Palmerston," 625.

118. For such an interpretation, see Christopher Bartlett, "Britain and the European Balance, 1815–48," in *Europe's Balance of Power 1815–1848*, ed. Alan Sked (Great Britain: The Macmillan Press Ltd, 1979).

119. Palmerston's speech is reprinted in Kenneth Bourne, *The Foreign Policy of Victorian England, 1830–1902* (Great Britain: Oxford University Press, 1970), 296. For Palmerston's similar pro-Austrian position on Wallachia's attempted revolution against the Ottoman Empire, see Radu R. Florescu, "Stratford Canning, Palmerston, and the Wallachian Revolution of 1848," *Journal of Modern History* 35, No. 3 (1963), especially 240–242.

120. See, for instance, Kissinger, *Diplomacy*, chapter 5.

121. See Orlando Figes, *The Crimean War: A New History* (New York: Metropolitan Books, 2011), xxiii.

122. The issue had been intentionally left out of the Final Act of the Congress of Vienna, but not because the powers ignored it. Instead, they recognized that it was an intractable issue that could kill the entire settlement. See Schroeder, "The 19th-Century International System."

123. Like the statesmen of the time, I use "Turkey" and "Ottoman Empire" interchangeably throughout this section.

124. Figes, *The Crimean War*, 36–37.

125. Bridge and Bullen, *The Great Powers and the European States System*, 114–117.

126. Figes, *The Crimean War*, 158.

127. Mitzen, *Power in Concert*, 198–199.

128. John Sweetman, *Essential Histories: The Crimean War* (Great Britain: Osprey Publishing, 2001), 87.

129. The best account of these terms is Norman Rich, *Why the Crimean War? A Cautionary Tale* (Hanover: University Press of New England, 1985), chapter 11.

130. Known as "counterpoise," this policy would have allowed Britain and France to send in half the total number of warships as Russia if she were to violate this policy.

131. On these complex negotiations, see Harold Temperley, "The Treaty of Paris of 1856 and Its Execution," *Journal of Modern History* 4, No. 3 (1932), 390.

132. See Figes, *The Crimean War*, 432–433.

133. Once again, *all* of the peace settlements examined in this book dealt with case-specific issues. The difference is that while others, like Westphalia and Utrecht, also included general order principle changes that reached beyond the specific issues of the day, the 1856 settlement (like that in 1763) dealt only with these kinds of immediate grievances. A number of such rules—governing general principles of behavior—were debated in the negotiations but ultimately dismissed. The first was great power agreement to accept as maritime law the principle that "the neutral flag covers the enemy's goods." The second was a British proposal to transform an existing treaty statute calling for impartial mediation of future Turkish–European power disputes into a more general principle for the mediation of *all* future disputes. See Temperley, "The Treaty of Paris," 412–413. For documents on these negotiations, see Albrecht-Carrié, *The Concert of Europe*, 191–196.

134. Rich, *Why the Crimean War?* 196.

135. Quoted in Paul Kennedy, *The Rise and Fall of the Great Powers* (New York: Vintage Books, 1987), 177.

136. Quoted in Rich, *Why the Crimean War?* 157–158.

137. See Figes, *The Crimean War*, 435–436.

138. Quoted in Herbert C. F. Bell, *Lord Palmerston*, Vol. 2 (Hamden: Archon Books, 1966), 149. Emphasis added.

139. See Rich, *Why the Crimean War?* 160–161; and Winfried Baumgart, *The Crimean War, 1853–1856* (New York: Oxford University Press, 1999), 206.

140. See, for instance, the French Foreign Minister admitting as much in Kupchan, *How Enemies Become Friends*, 246.

141. Quoted in Rich, *Why the Crimean War?* 183.

142. David Wetzel, *The Crimean War: A Diplomatic History* (New York: Columbia University Press, 1985), 172–174; Andrew D. Lambert, *The Crimean War: British Grand Strategy, 1853–56* (New York: Manchester University Press, 1990), 336–338. On Poland, see Jasper Ridley, *Lord Palmerston* (New York: E. P. Dutton & Company, Inc.,1971), chapter 31. On Italy and Romania, see Bell, *Lord Palmerston*, chapter 25.

143. This comment, by French Ambassador Morny, is quoted in Taylor, *The Struggle for Mastery in Europe*, 93.

144. See, for instance, Winfried Baumgart, *The Peace of Paris, 1856* (Santa Barbara: ABC-Clio, Inc., 1981), 31–37.

145. Figes, *The Crimean War*, 434.

146. Quoted in Ridley, *Lord Palmerston*, 448.

147. Quoted in Bell, *Lord Palmerston*, 149. See also Ridley, *Lord Palmerston*, 452–453.

148. On elite stoking of Russophobia in Britain, see Jack Snyder, *Myths of Empire: Domestic Politics and International Ambition* (Ithaca: Cornell University Press, 1991), chapter 5.

149. Paul W. Schroeder, *Austria, Great Britain, and the Crimean War: The Destruction of the European Concert* (Ithaca: Cornell University Press, 1974), 422.

150. Temperley, "The Treaty of Paris of 1856," 390.

151. Quoted in Bell, *Lord Palmerston*, 149. See also Ridley, *Lord Palmerston*, 452–453.

152. For an argument that Palmerston's "social imperialist" foreign policy was domestically motived, see Snyder, *Myths of Empire*, chapter 5. For a dissenting view, see Dale C. Copeland, *Economic Interdependence and War* (Princeton: Princeton University Press, 2014), 347–372.

153. Perspectives that fit in this camp include René Albrecht-Carrié's classic study; Richard Langhorne's various works; R. J. Crampton, "The Decline of the Concert of Europe in the Balkans, 1913–1914," *Slavonic and East European Review* 52, No. 128 (1974); and Georges-Henri Soutou, "Was There a European Order in the Twentieth Century? From the Concert of Europe to the End of the Cold War," *Contemporary European History* 9, No. 3 (2000).

154. Great power negotiations may have prevented the scramble from resulting in war, but they could not stop the rise of mutual suspicions and mistrust that this new wave of imperialism unleashed.

155. These examples are taken from Matthias Schulz, "Did Norms Matter in Nineteenth-Century International Relations? Progress and Decline in the 'Culture of Peace'; before World War I," in *An Improbable War: The Outbreak of World War I and European Culture before 1914*, ed. Holger Afflerbach and David Steffenson (New York: Berghan Books, 2007), 49–50.

156. Notable scholars in this camp include Bruce Cronin, Richard Elrod, Mark Haas, Charles Kupchan, Paul Schroeder, and Branislav Slantchev.

157. Gordon A. Craig, *Europe, 1815–1914,* 2nd ed. (New York: Holt, Rinehart and Winston, 1961), 165.

158. Kupchan, *How Enemies Become Friends,* 239–240.

159. Schroeder, *Austria, Great Britain, and the Crimean War,* 409.

160. Kissinger, *Diplomacy,* 94.

161. For an effective contrast of the post-1856 and pre–Crimean War dynamics in Europe, see Bridge and Bullen, *The Great Powers and the European States System,* 126–134.

CHAPTER 6

1. On the utility of studying "least likely" cases, see Alexander L. George and Andrew Bennett, *Case Studies and Theory Development in the Social Sciences* (Cambridge, MA: MIT Press, 2004), 120–123.

2. Thomas J. Knock, *To End All Wars: Woodrow Wilson and the Quest for a New World Order* (Princeton: Princeton University Press, 1992), 20.

3. Margaret Macmillan, *Paris 1919: Six Months That Changed the World* (New York: Random House, 2001), 61.

4. On the limits of US opportunities in 1919, see also G. John Ikenberry, *After Victory: Institutions, Strategic Restraint, and the Rebuilding of Order after Major Wars* (Princeton: Princeton University Press, 2001), 119–123.

5. The final text of the Covenant as it appears in the Treaty of Versailles is available in Ray Stannard Baker, ed., *Woodrow Wilson and World Settlement,* Vol. 3 [hereafter *WW&WS*] (New York: Doubleday, Page & Company, 1927), 175–188.

6. Technically, League members could still legally declare war, but only in very limited circumstances where all sanctioned processes had been exhausted. See Article 15 in *WW&WS,* Vol. 3, 108.

7. See the relevant parts of Article 8 in *WW&WS,* Vol. 3, 178–179.

8. See Article 12 in *WW&WS,* Vol. 3, 179. Articles 13 through 15 set up the rules for such deliberations and called for the creation of a Permanent Court of International Justice.

9. *WW&WS,* Vol. 3, 182–183.

10. *WW&WS,* Vol. 3, 179.

11. The term "self-determination" was not actually used in the Covenant.

12. See Article 22 in particular. *WW&WS,* Vol. 3, 184–185.

13. On this point, see Wilson's War Address to Congress, April 2, 1917, *The Public Papers of Woodrow Wilson* [hereafter *PPWW*], Vol. 6, ed. Ray Stannard Baker and William Dodd (New York: Harper & Brothers Publishers, 1927), 12.

14. Third meeting of the League of Nations Commission, February 4, 1919, quoted in David Hunter Miller, *The Drafting of the Covenant,* Vol. 1 (New York: G. P. Putnam's Sons, 1928). 165–166.

15. Ikenberry, *After Victory*, 117.

16. See Ikenberry, *After Victory*, 160.

17. Ikenberry, *After Victory*, 169.

18. See *After Victory*, 144–160.

19. Quoted in Macmillan, *Paris 1919*, 97.

20. For concurring opinions, see Lloyd E. Ambrosius, *Woodrow Wilson and the American Diplomatic Tradition: The Treaty Fight in Perspective* (Cambridge: Cambridge University Press, 1990), x; Colin Dueck, *Reluctant Crusaders: Power, Culture, and Change in American Grand Strategy* (Princeton: Princeton University Press, 2007), 48.

21. Quoted in Dueck, *Reluctant Crusaders*, 53.

22. The democracy/autocracy narrative was pushed on Wilson largely by Secretary of State Robert Lansing and Colonel House. Ironically, Wilson eventually accepted the narrative because of the *first* Russian Revolution in March 1917. Her (temporary) transition to democratic institutions allowed the Allies to claim ideological consistency in their cause. See N. Gordon Levin, Jr., *Woodrow Wilson and World Politics: America's Response to War and Revolution* (London: Oxford University Press, 1968), 43; Knock, *To End All Wars*, 138.

23. This is a theme of Ross A. Kennedy, *The Will to Believe: Woodrow Wilson, World War I, and America's Strategy for Peace and Security* (Kent, OH: Kent University State Press, 2009).

24. While they certainly noted the empowerment of leftist groups, this caused more fear of radical Bolshevik-like revolutions than hope that they would soon become consolidated democracies. Nonetheless, Wilson *did* believe that he could help induce more liberal outcomes for the international settlement by appealing directly to the European people over the heads of their conservative rulers. See, for instance, Knock, *To End All Wars*, 162.

25. Ikenberry, *After Victory*, 53.

26. *After Victory*, 118, 160.

27. *WW&WS*, Vol. 3, 179.

28. For example, Jeffrey W. Legro, *Rethinking the World: Great Powers Strategies and International Order* (Ithaca: Cornell University Press, 2005), chapter 3; and A. Scott Berg, *Wilson* (New York: The Berkeley Publishing Group, 2013), 538–539.

29. Quoted in Melvyn P. Leffler, *The Elusive Quest: America's Pursuit of European Stability and French Security, 1919–1933* (Chapel Hill: The University of North Carolina Press, 1979), 11.

30. Address at the University of Paris, December, 21 1918, *The Papers of Woodrow Wilson* [hereafter *PWW*], ed. Arthur S. Link et al. (Princeton: Princeton University Press, 1966–1994), Vol. 53, 462.

31. Eighth meeting of the League of Nations Commission, February 11, 1919, *PWW*, Vol. 55, 79.

32. Ambrosius, *Woodrow Wilson and the American Diplomatic Tradition*, 74–75. Curiously, Ikenberry himself seems to agree with Cecil's view here; see *After Victory*, 145–146.

33. On this point, see Lloyd E. Ambrosius, "Democracy, Peace, and World Order," in *Reconsidering Woodrow Wilson: Progressivism, Internationalism, War, and Peace*, ed. John Milton Cooper, Jr. (Baltimore: The Johns Hopkins University Press, 2008), 228–230; and especially Stephen Wertheim, "The League That Wasn't: American Designs for a Legalist-Sanctionist League of Nations and the Intellectual Origins of International Organization, 1914–1920," *Diplomatic History* 35, No. 5 (2011); as well as Trygve Throntveit, *Power Without Victory: Woodrow Wilson and the American Internationalist Experiment* (Chicago: The University of Chicago Press, 2017).

34. Kalevi J. Holsti, *Peace and War: Armed Conflicts and International Order, 1648–1989* (Cambridge: Cambridge University Press, 1991), 181, 187. Similar points are made in Daniel H. Deudney, *Bounding Power: Republican Security Theory from the Polis to the Global Village* (Princeton: Princeton University Press, 2007), 186–188.

35. Andreas Osiander, *The States System of Europe, 1640–1990: Peacemaking and the Conditions of International Stability* (New York: Oxford University Press, 1994), 261.

36. Dueck, *Reluctant Crusaders*, 81.

37. See, for instance, Knock, *To End All Wars*, 14.

38. Throntveit, *Power without Victory*, 11.

39. This line of argument draws heavily from Wertheim, "The League That Wasn't," as well as Benjamin Allen Coates, *Legalist Empire: International Law and American Foreign Relations in the Early Twentieth Century* (New York: Oxford University Press, 2016), chapter 7.

40. Wertheim, "The League That Wasn't," 814.

41. A similar definition is provided in Coates, *Legalist Empire*, 3.

42. Quoted in Wertheim, "The League That Wasn't," 824.

43. Quoted in Coates, *Legalist Empire*, 166.

44. Address to Third Plenary Session of the Peace Conference, February 14, 1919, *PPWW*, Vol. 5, 426.

45. Seventh meeting of the League of Nations Commission, February 10, 1919, *PWW*, Vol. 55, 44.

46. This is a theme of Kurt Wimer, "Woodrow Wilson and World Order," in *Woodrow Wilson and a Revolutionary World, 1913–1921*, ed. Arthur S. Link (Chapel Hill: The University of North Carolina Press, 1982).

47. Wilson made a comment of this sort while meeting with the Inquiry in transit to Paris in December, 1918. See *PWW*, Vol. 53, 354.

48. For summaries of British and French postwar visions and their discrepancies with Wilson's, see Ikenberry, *After Victory*, 128–134.

49. On Republicans' competing fears and corresponding visions of postwar order, see Dueck, *Reluctant Crusaders*, chapter 3.

50. Quoted in John Milton Cooper, Jr., *Woodrow Wilson: A Biography* (New York: Alfred A. Knopf, 2009), 446–448; 460–466.

51. Cooper, *Woodrow Wilson*, 446–448.

52. Quoted in Levin, *Woodrow Wilson and World Politics*, 133.

53. Stephen M. Walt, *Revolution and War* (Ithaca: Cornell University Press), 202.

54. These include Arno J. Mayer, *Wilson vs. Lenin: Political Origins of the New Diplomacy, 1917–1918* (Cleveland: Meridan Books, The World Publishing Company, 1964); John M. Thompson, *Russia, Bolshevism, and the Versailles Peace* (Princeton: Princeton University Press, 1966); Levin, *Woodrow Wilson and World Politics*; and David S. Foglesong, *America's Secret War Against Bolshevism: U.S. Intervention in the Russian Civil War, 1917–1920* (Chapel Hill: The University of North Carolina Press, 1995).

55. On this thesis, see Walter LaFeber, *The New Empire: An Interpretation of American Expansion, 1860–1898* (Ithaca: Cornell University Press, 1963).

56. See Levin, *Woodrow Wilson and World Politics*, 18, 245.

57. Odd Arne Westad, *The Global Cold War: Third World Interventions and the Making of Our Times* (New York: Cambridge University Press, 2005), 49.

58. Quoted in Westad, *The Global Cold War*, 46.

59. Knock, *To End All Wars*, 140.

60. Quoted in Walt, *Revolution and War*, 131.

61. Walt, *Revolution and War*, 138.

62. Melvyn P. Leffler, *The Specter of Communism: The United States and the Origins of the Cold War, 1917–1953* (New York: Hill and Wang, 1994), 7.

63. *PWW*, Vol. 45, 428.

64. See Levin, *Woodrow Wilson and World Politics*, 193.

65. On this point, see Macmillan, *Paris 1919*, 94–96; and Anthony Read, *The World On Fire: 1919 and the Battle with Bolshevism* (New York: W. W. Norton & Company, 2008), chapter 3.

66. Hoover's address to the Heads of Delegations of the Five Powers, July 5, 1919, quoted in Levin, *Woodrow Wilson and World Politics*, 194.

67. Hoover to Wilson, November 11, 1918, in Francis William O'Brien, ed., *The Hoover-Wilson Wartime Correspondence: September 24, 1914, to November 11, 1918* (Ames: The Iowa State University Press, 1974), 289–290.

68. For a comprehensive look at the fear of radicalism in America in 1919, see Read, *The World on Fire*, especially chapter 2.

69. Leffler, *The Specter of Communism*, 14–15. See also Knock, *To End All Wars*, 134–137.

70. Address in Seattle, Washington, September 13, 1919, *PPWW*, Vol. 6, 193.

71. See Levin, *Woodrow Wilson and World Politics*, 135; and Klaus Schwabe, *Woodrow Wilson, Revolutionary Germany, and Peacemaking, 1918–1919* (Chapel Hill: The University of North Carolina Press, 1985), 118–120.

72. Wilson to Wiseman, October 16, 1918, quoted in Levin, *Woodrow Wilson and World Politics*, 131.

73. Council of Four meeting, March 26, 1919, Paul Mantoux, *The Deliberations of the Council of Four (March 24–June 28, 1919)*, Vol. 1, ed. Arthur S. Link (Princeton: Princeton University Press, 1992), 20.

74. Jon Jacobson, "The Soviet Union and Versailles," in *The Treaty of Versailles: A Reassessment After 75 Years*, ed. Manfred F. Boemeke, Gerald D. Feldman, and Elisabeth Glaser (New York: Cambridge University Press, 1998).

75. Mayer, *Wilson vs. Lenin*, 382.

76. Council of Four meeting, March 27, 1919, Mantoux, *The Deliberations of the Council of Four*, Vol. 1, 47.

77. Remarks to Members of the Democratic National Committee, February 28, 1919, *PWW*, Vol. 55, 314.

78. Quoted in Leffler, *The Specter of Communism*, 12.

79. See, for instance, Betty Miller Unterberger, "Woodrow Wilson and the Bolsheviks: The 'Acid Test' of Soviet–American Relations," *Diplomatic History* 11, No. 2 (1987); "Wilson vs. the Bolsheviks," *Diplomatic History* 21, No. 1 (1997).

80. See William Appleman Williams, *The Tragedy of American Diplomacy* (New York: W. W. Norton & Company, 1959), 115–117; Leffler, *The Specter of Communism*, chapter 1.

81. On this point, see Knock, *To End All Wars*, 156–157; Walt, *Revolution and War*, 145–156; and Cooper, *Woodrow Wilson*, 438–439.

82. These January 1919 comments are quoted in Levin, *Woodrow Wilson and World Politics*, 208–209. For Wilson expressing similar sentiments elsewhere, see Georg Schild, *Between Ideology and Realpolitik: Woodrow Wilson and the Russian Revolution, 1917–1921* (Westport: Greenwood Press, 1995), 99. This adjacent conference was subsequently tabled due to opposition from non-Bolshevik groups in Russia.

83. Knock, *To End All Wars*, 142.

84. These observations come from House's diary. See Charles Seymour, ed., *The Intimate Papers of Colonel House*, Vol, 3 (New York: Houghton Mifflin Company, 1928), 322.

85. Wilson to Sir Cecil Spring Rice, retiring British Ambassador, January 3, 1918, Ray Stannard Baker, ed., *Woodrow Wilson: Life and Letters* [hereafter *WWLL*], Vol. 6 (New York: Charles Scribner's Sons, 1946), 448. This document/quote also appears in *PWW*, Vol. 45, 456.

86. See House's diary notes about the Russia portion of the speech in Seymour, *The Intimate Papers of Colonel House*, Vol. 3, 331.

87. See Seymour, *The Intimate Papers of Colonel House*, Vol. 3, 330–331; and Lloyd C. Gardner, "The Geopolitics of Revolution," *Diplomatic History* 38, No. 4 (2014), 746.

88. Fourteen Points Address, January 8, 1918, *PPWW*, Vol. 5, 158. Emphasis added.

89. See, for instance, Mayer, *Wilson vs. Lenin*, 334–342.

90. Prominent examples include William R. Keylor, "Versailles and International Diplomacy," in *The Treaty of Versailles: A Reassessment after 75 Years*, ed. Manfred F. Boemeke, Gerald D. Feldman, and Elisabeth Glaser (New York: Cambridge University Press, 1998); Erez Manela, *The Wilsonian Moment: Self-Determination and the International Origins of Anticolonial Nationalism* (London: Oxford University Press, 2007); Ambrosius, "Democracy, Peace, and World Order"; and Throntveit, *Power Without Victory*.

91. Wilson to Sir Cecil Spring Rice, retiring British Ambassador, January 3, 1918, *WWLL*, Vol. 6, 448.

92. Quoted in Manela, *The Wilsonian Moment*, 28–30.

93. Quoted in Robert David Johnson, "Article XI in the Debate on the United States' Rejection of the League of Nations," *The International History Review* 15, No. 3 (1993), 506.

94. This is the paramount theme of Trygve Throntveit, "The Fable of the Fourteen Points: Woodrow Wilson and National Self-Determination," *Diplomatic History* 35, No. 3 (2011).

95. Quoted in Mayer, *Wilson vs. Lenin*, 299. Emphasis in original. See also Derek Heater, *National Self-Determination: Woodrow Wilson and his Legacy* (New York: St. Martin's, 1994), 32–36.

96. Quoted in Heater, *National Self-Determination*, 35.

97. Quoted in Adam Tooze, *The Deluge: The Great War and the Remaking of Global Order* (Great Britain: Penguin Press, 2015), 126.

98. Mayer, *Wilson vs. Lenin*, 296–298.

99. Quoted in Heater, *National Self-Determination*, 39.

100. On the regional specificity and inconsistent application of Wilson's calls for self-determination, see Osiander, *The States System of Europe*, 289; Keylor, "Versailles and International Diplomacy," 475; Allen Lynch, "Woodrow Wilson and the Principle of 'Self-Determination': A Reconsideration," *Review of International Studies* 28, No. 2 (2002); Philip Bobbitt, *The Shield of Achilles: War, Peace, and the Course of History* (New York: Alfred A. Knopf, 2002), 576; and Stephen Schuker, "The 1919 Peace Settlement: A Subaltern View," *Reviews in American History* 36, No. 4 (2008).

101. This is a theme of Arno J. Mayer, *Politics and Diplomacy of Peacemaking: Containment and Counterrevolution at Versailles, 1918–1919* (New York: Alfred A. Knopf, 1967), chapter 10.

102. Manela, *The Wilsonian Moment*, 43.

103. "War Aims of Germany and Austria," February 11, 1918, *PPWW*, Vol. 5, 183.

104. Address to the International Law Society in Paris, France, May 9, 1919, *PPWW*, Vol. 5, 478–479.

105. See, for instance, his comments to members of the Inquiry while in transit to Paris in *PWW*, Vol. 53, 351.

106. See George Curry, "Woodrow Wilson, Jan Smuts, and the Versailles Settlement," *The American Historical Review* 66, No. 4 (1961).

107. Jan Christiaan Smuts, *The League of Nations: A Practical Suggestion* (London: Hodder and Stoughton, 1918), 9.

108. This argument is advanced in Susan Pedersen, *The Guardians: The League of Nations and the Crisis of Empire* (New York: Oxford University Press, 2015), 23–24.

109. See Pedersen, *The Guardians*, 29–32.

110. This is a point made in Mayer, *Wilson vs. Lenin*, 302–303; 361; and in Levin, *Woodrow Wilson and World Politics*, 129.

111. Quoted in Fogelsong, *America's Secret War against Bolshevism*, 39.

112. See Fogelsong, *America's Secret War against Bolshevism*, 25–30.

113. Thompson, *Russia, Bolshevism, and the Versailles Peace*, 41, 43.

114. Quoted in Fogelsong, *America's Secret War against Bolshevism*, 38.

115. Armistice Address to Congress, November 11, 1918, *PPWW*, Vol. 5, 301–302.

116. Quoted in Schild, *Between Ideology and Realpolitik*, 4.

117. See this "Magnolia" draft in *WW&WS*, Vol. 3, 88.

118. Address in Billings, Montana, September 11, 1919, *PPWW*, Vol. 6, 109.

119. Address in Minneapolis, Minnesota, September 9, 1919, *PPWW*, Vol. 6, 70.

120. Address in Des Moines, Iowa, September 6, 1919, *PPWW*, Vol. 6, 15.

121. Address in Tacoma, Washington, September 13, 1919, *PPWW*, Vol. 6, 168.

122. Address in St. Paul, Minnesota, September 9, 1919, *PPWW*, Vol. 6, 109.

123. See Levin, *Woodrow Wilson and World Politics*, 159–160, 168–169. Though some of Wilson's closest advisers articulated the view that Germany should be integrated into the League, Wilson remained consistently opposed.

124. Address in Tacoma, Washington, September 13, 1919, *PPWW*, Vol. 6, 167.

125. *WW&WS*, Vol. 3, 166.

126. Johnson, "Article XI in the Debate on the United States' Rejection of the League of Nations," 514.

127. Johnson, "Article XI in the Debate on the United States' Rejection of the League of Nations," 508–509.

128. Address in Bismarck, North Dakota, September 10, 1919, *PPWW*, Vol. 6, 101.

129. See, for instance, a crucial note the president wrote to Colonel House on the early idea of the League in 1916, discussed in Godfrey Hodgson, *Woodrow Wilson's Right Hand: The Life of Colonel Edward M. House* (New Haven: Yale University Press, 2006), 199.

130. For a brief but comprehensive narrative of the Covenant's evolution from the Hurst-Miller draft to its final form in the Versailles Treaty, see David Hunter Miller, "The Making of the League of Nations," in *What Really Happened at Paris: The Story of the Peace Conference, 1918–1919*, ed. Edward Mandell House and Charles Seymour (New York: Charles Scribner's Sons, 1921).

131. Specifically, compare Wilson's Magnolia draft with his first Paris draft in *WW&WS*, Vol. 3.

132. Thompson, *Russia, Bolshevism, and the Versailles Peace*, 43.

133. British Imperial War Cabinet Meeting, December 30, 1918, *PWW*, Vol. 53, 568.

134. Ikenberry, *After Victory*, 119.

135. Dueck, *Reluctant Crusaders*, chapter 3; Holsti, *Peace and War*, chapter 8; Ambrosius, *Woodrow Wilson and the American Diplomatic Tradition*; Cooper, *Woodrow Wilson*; Knock, *To End All Wars*; Alexander L. George and Juliette L. George, *Woodrow Wilson and Colonel House: A Personality Study* (New York: Dover Publications, 1956); and Stephen Walker, "Psychodynamic Processes and Framing Effects in Foreign Policy Decision-Making: Woodrow Wilson's Operational Code," *Political Psychology* 16, No. 4 (1995).

136. Wilson is also faulted for sending Colonel House to negotiate a pre-Armistice agreement with the Allies in late 1918. By some accounts, House had already given the game away on everything aside from the League before Wilson even set sail for Paris. See Knock, *To End All Wars*, 183.

137. Leffler, *The Elusive Quest*, 5. See also Cooper, *Woodrow Wilson*, 497–498.

138. Eighth meeting of the League of Nations Commission, February 11, 1919, *PWW*, Vol. 55, 75–76. On this debate, see also Cooper, *Breaking the Heart of the World*, 52; and Berg, *Wilson*, 538–539.

139. On the negotiation of these changes in the League Commission, see Miller, "The Making of the League," 415–420; Cooper, *Woodrow Wilson*, 484–485, 494; Knock, *To End All Wars*, 247–248; and Ikenberry, *After Victory*, 151.

140. For an argument that it could have made a difference, see Cooper, *Woodrow Wilson*, 511–514. On the varied, complex, and nuanced positions of Lodge and the Senate's "irreconcilables," see Ralph A. Stone, *The Irreconcilables: The Fight against the League of Nations* (Lexington: The University of Kentucky Press, 1970); and William C. Widenor, *Henry Cabot Lodge and the Search for American Foreign Policy* (Berkeley: University of California Press, 1980).

141. On Clemenceau in particular as an advocate for the "old" system, see Osiander, *The States System of Europe*, 264.

142. Recent evidence has made it more difficult to conclude that Lodge and his allies were motived by allegiance to any particular or sizable constituency in the United States. See Throntveit, *Power without Victory*, 295.

143. This helps put into context, for example, Wilson's disagreements with Taft's League to Enforce Peace, a Republican-leaning group championing a more traditional anti-German order. See Knock, *To End All Wars*, 55–57.

144. Wilson to Raymond Blaine Fosdick, December 11, 1918, *PWW*, Vol. 53, 366.

145. These profound disagreements can also shed light on the often-contradictory ways in which the Allies dealt with Germany, vacillating as they did between punishing and reintegrating impulses.

146. Thompson, *Russia, Bolshevism, and the Versailles Peace*, 320.

CHAPTER 7

1. G. John Ikenberry, *Liberal Leviathan: The Origins, Crisis, and Transformation of the American World Order* (Princeton: Princeton University Press, 2011), 6,–7.

2. See for instance, the signatories to G. John Ikenberry and Anne-Marie Slaughter, "Forging a World of Liberty under Law: U.S. National Security in the 21st Century," *Final Report of the Princeton Project on National Security* (Princeton: The Woodrow Wilson School of Public and International Affairs, 2006), 79–89.

3. Ikenberry, *Liberal Leviathan*, 161.

4. In this way, my analysis aligns with David M. Edelstein's insightful recent treatment of the same period in *Over the Horizon: Time, Uncertainty, and the Rise of Great Powers* (Ithaca: Cornell University Press, 2017), chapter 5.

5. See Alexander L. George and Andrew Bennett, *Case Studies and Theory Development in the Social Sciences* (Cambridge, MA: MIT Press, 2004), 120–123; as well as John Gerring, *Case Study Research: Principles and Practices* (New York: Cambridge University Press, 2007), chapter 5.

6. Recent policy commentary that fits in this camp includes Daniel Deudney and G. John Ikenberry, "Liberal World: The Resilient Order," *Foreign Affairs* 97, No. 4 (2018); Rebecca Friedman Lissner and Mira Rapp-Hooper, "The Liberal Order Is More than a Myth," *Foreign Affairs* (2018); and Michael J. Mazarr, "The Real History of the Liberal Order," *Foreign Affairs* (2018).

7. For recent policy commentary that is closer to the argument I develop in this chapter, see Graham Allison, "The Myth of the Liberal Order: From Historical Accident to Conventional Wisdom," *Foreign Affairs* 97, No. 4 (2018).

8. Paul Kennedy, *The Rise and Fall of the Great Powers: Economic and Military Conflict from 1500 to 2000* (New York: Random House, Inc., 1987), 357–361.

9. Kennedy, *The Rise and Fall of the Great Powers*, 366, 367.

10. See Kennedy, *The Rise and Fall of the Great Powers*, 361–365.

11. See David Reynolds, *From Munich to Pearl Harbor: Roosevelt's America and the Origins of the Second World War* (Chicago: Ivan R. Dee, 2001), 108.

12. Quoted in Lloyd Gardner, "The Atlantic Charter: Idea and Reality, 1942,1945," in *The Atlantic Charter*, ed. Douglas Brinkley and David R. Facey-Crowther (New York: St. Martin's Press, 1994), 58.

13. Reynolds, *From Munich to Pearl Harbor*, 144–145.

14. See Reynolds, *From Munich to Pearl Harbor*, 54–55.

15. Elizabeth Borgwardt, *A New Deal for the World: America's Vision for Human Rights* (Cambridge, MA: Harvard University Press, 2006), 29.

16. On Dumbarton Oaks, see Robert C. Hilderbrand, *Dumbarton Oaks: The Origins of the United Nations and the Search for Postwar Security* (Chapel Hill: The University of North Carolina Press, 1990). On San Francisco, see Stephen C. Schlesinger, *Act of Creation: The Founding of the United Nations* (Boulder: Westview Press, 2003). On these events more generally, see Townsend Hoopes and Douglas Brinkley, *FDR*

and the Creation of the U.N. (New Haven: Yale University Press, 1997); and Ilya V. Gaiduk, *Divided Together: The United States and the Soviet Union in the United Nations, 1945–1965* (Washington, DC: Woodrow Wilson Center Press, 2012), chapter 1.

17. See Paul Kennedy, *The Parliament of Man: The Past, Present, and Future of the United Nations* (New York: Random House, 2006), 27–28.

18. See Chapter V, Article 27 of the UN Charter.

19. See Chapter IV, Article 12, and Chapter V, Article 24 of the UN Charter.

20. See, for instance, discussion over the League's Assembly and Council in the Eleventh meeting of the League of Nations Commission, March 22, 1919, in David Hunter Miller, *The Drafting of the Covenant*, Vol. 1 (New York: G. P. Putnam's Sons, 1928), 315.

21. Chapter VII, Article 39 (9) of the UN Charter. Emphasis added.

22. In fact, the mandate system was seen as one of the League's few successes worth emulating in the UN Charter. See Mark Mazower, *No Enchanted Palace: The End of Empire and the Ideological Origins of the United Nations* (Princeton: Princeton University Press, 2009).

23. The Charter had established a joint Military Staff Committee for the five permanent GPs with the understanding that it would work out the necessary logistics for creating a UN military force. Yet it quickly fell victim to great power tensions and eventually disbanded. See Kennedy, *The Parliament of Man*, 37–39; Adam Roberts, "Proposals for UN Standing Forces: A Critical History," in *The United Nations Security Council and War: The Evolution of Thought and Practice Since 1945*, ed. Vaughan Lowe et al. (New York: Oxford University Press, 2008), 99–103; and John Gerard Ruggie, *Winning the Peace: America and World Order in the New Era*. (New York: Columbia University Press, 1998), 52–55.

24. The World Bank (IBRD) received far less attention at the conference than the IMF, which was seen as both more consequential and more controversial, and I thus focus most upon the IMF here. But for a dissenting view that the Bank was not tangential to these negotiations, see Eric Helleiner, *Forgotten Foundations of Bretton Woods: International Development and the Making of the Postwar Order* (Ithaca: Cornell University Press, 2014).

25. This view is also well described in Ikenberry, *Liberal Leviathan*, 169–174.

26. G. John Ikenberry, "A World Economy Restored: Expert Consensus and the Anglo-American Postwar Settlement," *International Organization* 46, No. 1 (1992); and *Liberal Leviathan*, 174–179.

27. IMF Charter, Article 1 (emphasis added).

28. Borgwardt, *A New Deal*, 93. "Embedded liberalism" comes from John Gerard Ruggie, "International Regimes, Transactions and Change: Embedded Liberalism in the Postwar Economic Order," *International Organization* 36, No. 2 (1982).

29. George Marshall's famous Harvard University speech is reprinted in Department of State, *Foreign Relations of the United States* [hereafter *FRUS*], *1947* (Washington, DC: Government Printing Office), Vol. 3, 237–239.

30. The treaty is reprinted in *FRUS, 1949*, Vol. 4, 281–285.

31. *FRUS, 1949*, Vol. 4, 281–282.

32. "Radio Address by Secretary Acheson," September 18, 1951, quoted in Patrick Thaddeus Jackson, "Defending the West: Occidentalism and the Formation of NATO," *Journal of Political Philosophy* 11, No. 3 (2003), 224.

33. See *FRUS, 1949*, Vol. 4, 282. On the origins and impact of Article 5, see Lawrence S. Kaplan, *NATO Divided, NATO United: The Evolution of an Alliance* (Westport: Praeger Press, 2004), chapter 1.

34. While the North Atlantic Treaty's preamble pledged to defend democratic values, Article 2 explicitly obligated members to "strengthening their free institutions" as well as "bringing about a better understanding of the principles upon which these institutions are founded." *FRUS, 1949*, Vol. 4, 281–283.

35. On the distinct cultural identity of NATO, see Thomas Risse-Kappen, *Cooperation among Democracies: The European Influence on U.S. Foreign Policy* (Princeton: Princeton University Press, 1995), chapter 2; and Andrew M. Johnston, *Hegemony and Culture in the Origins of NATO Nuclear First Use, 1945–1955* (New York: Palgrave Macmillan, 2005), 9–15.

36. For another recent account that similarly highlights the tensions rather than complementarities between these two visions of order, see John J. Mearsheimer, "Bound to Fail: The Rise and Fall of the Liberal International Order," *International Security* 43, No. 4 (2019), 18–21.

37. "The Great Arsenal of Democracy," December 29, 1940, quoted in Reynolds, *From Munich to Pearl Harbor*, 107.

38. On the Nazi "New Order" in Europe (*Neuordnung Europas*), see Mark Mazower, "Hitler's New Order, 1939–1945," *Diplomacy & Statecraft* 7, No. 1 (1996); and Benjamin G. Martin, *The Nazi-Fascist New Order for European Culture* (Cambridge, MA: Harvard University Press, 2016).

39. He voiced his fear of such a battle in his first meeting with Molotov in 1942. See *FRUS, 1942*, Vol. 3, 578–583. On FDR's anti-colonialism more generally, see Warren F. Kimball, *The Juggler: Franklin Roosevelt as Wartime Statesman* (Princeton: Princeton University Press, 1991), chapter 7; and "The Sheriffs: FDR's Postwar World," in *FDR's World: War, Peace, and Legacies*, ed. David B. Woolner, Warren F. Kimball, and David Reynolds (New York: Palgrave Macmillan, 2008), 106–107.

40. Ruggie, *Winning the Peace*, 35. On Nazi Germany's economic practices, see Adam Tooze, *The Wages of Destruction: The Making and Breaking of the Nazi Economy* (New York: Penguin Group, 2006).

41. Charles S. Maier, "Conditions for Stability Western Europe," in Charles S. Maier, *In Search of Stability: Explorations in Historical Political Economy* (New York: Cambridge University Press, 1987), 182.

42. "Message to Congress on the Concentration of Economic Power," April 29, 1938, quoted in Charles S. Maier, "The Politics of Productivity: Foundations of American International Economic Policy After World War II," in Charles S. Maier, *In Search*

of Stability: Explorations in Historical Political Economy (New York: Cambridge University Press, 1987), 131.

43. John Lamberton Harper, *American Visions of Europe: Franklin D. Roosevelt, George F. Kennan, and Dean G. Acheson* (Cambridge: Cambridge University Press, 1994), 88; Frank Costigliola, *Roosevelt's Lost Alliances: How Personal Politics Helped Start the Cold War* (Princeton: Princeton University Press, 2012), 179.

44. Roosevelt to Queen Wilhelmina, August 26, 1944, quoted in Harper, *American Visions of Europe*, 91.

45. Reynolds, *From Munich to Pearl Harbor*, 138; Costigliola, *Roosevelt's Lost Alliances*, 121–127.

46. The "family circle" quote comes from Roosevelt's opening remarks at the First Plenary Meeting of the Tehran Conference, November 28, 1943, *FRUS, Cairo and Tehran*, 487.

47. As evidence for the importance of cooperating with the Soviet Union in his plans, Roosevelt's first explicit discussion of the "Four Policemen" appears to have come in his first meeting with Molotov in 1942. See Memoranda of Conversations by Samuel H. Cross and Harry Hopkins, May 29, 1942, *FRUS, 1942*, Vol. 3, 569, 573.

48. Stalin's comment here comes from *FRUS, Malta and Yalta*, 668.

49. See, for example, the sharp differences between Churchill on one side and Stalin and Roosevelt on the other over Germany's fate. Tripartite Political Meeting at the Tehran Conference, December 1, 1943, *FRUS, Cairo and Tehran*, 600–603.

50. On the former, see Kimball, *The Juggler*, 101, 183; Costigliola, *Roosevelt's Lost Alliances*, 191, 212, 220, 228–229, 247–248. On the latter, see Harper, *American Visions of Europe*, 98–99; James McAllister, *No Exit: America and the German Problem, 1943–1954* (Ithaca: Cornell University Press, 2002), chapter 2, especially 44–45.

51. On Roosevelt's optimism regarding the USSR, see David Reynolds, *From World War to Cold War: Churchill, Roosevelt, and the International History of the 1940s* (New York: Oxford University Press, 2006), chapter 13.

52. This paper, originally dated March 8, was circulated as JCS Memo for Information no. 382, "A Security Policy for Post-War America," March 29, 1945, CCS 092 (7-27-44), RG 165, National Archives. It is also discussed in Mark A. Stoler, *Allies and Adversaries: The Joint Chiefs of Staff, the Grand Alliance, and U.S. Strategy in World War II* (Chapel Hill: The University of North Carolina Press, 2000), 227–229.

53. This report, JCS 838/1, was the basis for a shorter memo quoted here from Leahy to Hull, May 16, 1944, *FRUS, Malta and Yalta*, 106–107. JCS 838/1 is summarized and discussed in Walter S. Poole, "From Conciliation to Containment: The Joint Chiefs of Staff and the Coming of the Cold War, 1945–1946," *Military Affairs* 42, No. 1 (1978), 12; and Mark A. Stoler, "From Continentalism to Globalism: General Stanley D. Embick, the Joint Strategic Survey Committee, and the Military View of American National Security Policy during the Second World War," *Diplomatic History* 6, No. 3 (1981), 312–315.

54. OSS, "Capabilities and Intentions of the USSR in the Postwar Period," January 5, 1945, in *State Department Intelligence and Research Reports: The Soviet Union*, Part 6, reel 4. It is discussed in more detail in McAllister, *No Exit*, 40–42.

55. See McAllister, *No Exit*, 63–73.

56. See Benn Steil, *The Battle of Bretton Woods: John Maynard Keynes, Harry Dexter White, and the Making of a New World Order* (Princeton: Princeton University Press, 2013), 40–42; 136–137.

57. Both are quoted in Cass R. Sunstein, *The Second Bill of Rights: FDR's Unfinished Revolution and Why We Need It More than Ever* (New York: Basic Books, 2004), 83.

58. Alfred E. Eckes, Jr., *A Search for Solvency: Bretton Woods and the International Monetary System, 1941–1971* (Austin: University of Texas Press, 1975), 38.

59. On these points, see Sunstein, *The Second Bill of Rights*, chapter 4; and Borgwardt, *A New Deal*, 46–56.

60. Roosevelt Press Conference, July 5, 1940, quoted in Sunstein, *The Second Bill of Rights*, 80. On the threat and potency of fascism in the United States, see Seva Gunitsky, *Aftershocks: Great Powers and Domestic Reforms in the Twentieth Century* (Princeton: Princeton University Press, 2017), 135–142.

61. Borgwardt, *A New Deal*, 53.

62. Robert Pollard, "Economic Security and the Origins of the Cold War: Bretton Woods, the Marshall Plan, and American Rearmament, 1944–50," *Diplomatic History* 9, No. 3 (1985); Ruggie, *Winning the Peace*, 35; and Patrick, *The Best Laid Plans*, 123.

63. The entire draft plan is available as an enclosure of Henry Morgenthau (Treasury Secretary) to Roosevelt, May 15, 1942, *FRUS, 1942*, Vol 1, 171–190. The quote comes from 174.

64. See Fred L. Block, *The Origins of Economic Disorder: A Study of United States International Monetary Policy from World War II to the Present* (Berkeley: University of California Press, 1977), chapter 3.

65. Lloyd C. Gardner, *Architects of Illusion: Men and Ideas in American Foreign Policy, 1941–1949* (Chicago: Quadrangle Books, 1970), 114.

66. See Ikenberry, "A World Economy Restored," 318–321.

67. Ikenberry advances aspects of this argument in "A World Economy Restored"; "Creating Yesterday's New World Order: Keynesian 'New Thinking' and the Anglo-American Postwar Settlement," in *Ideas and Foreign Policy: Beliefs, Institutions, and Political Change*, ed. Judith Goldstein and Robert O. Keohane (Ithaca: Cornell University Press, 1993); and *After Victory: Institutions, Strategic Restraint, and the Rebuilding of Orders after Major Wars* (Princeton: Princeton University Press, 2001), chapter 6.

68. Ikenberry, "A World Economy Restored," 318–319.

69. See, for instance, a 1938 letter Morgenthau had White draft for Roosevelt on the international economic situation, discussed in Steil, *The Battle of Bretton Woods*, 50–53.

70. See, for instance, Block, *Origins of Economic Disorder*, 45–46.

71. On the divides between Treasury and State and the former's victory over the latter for control of monetary and financial planning, see Richard N. Gardner, *Sterling-Dollar Diplomacy: Anglo-American Collaboration in the Reconstruction of Multilateral Trade* (Oxford: Clarendon Press, 1956), 72–73; Eckes, *A Search for Solvency*, 41–43; 59–63; Block, *Origins of Economic Disorder*, 38–42; and Steil, *The Battle of Bretton Woods*, 169–170.

72. Steil, *The Battle of Bretton Woods*, 149.

73. Patrick, *The Best Laid Plans*, 141. On the differences between the White and Keynes plans, see E. F. Penrose, *Economic Planning for the Peace* (Princeton: Princeton University Press, 1953), chapters 2 and 3; Gardner, *Sterling-Dollar Diplomacy*, chapter 5; Eckes, *A Search for Solvency*, chapter 4; Armand Van Dormael, *Bretton Woods: Birth of a Monetary System* (New York: Holmes & Meier Publishers, Inc., 1978), chapters 4 and 5; Ngaire Woods, *The Globalizers: The IMF, the World Bank and Their Borrowers* (Ithaca: Cornell University Press, 2006), 22–27; and Steil, *The Battle of Bretton Woods*, chapter 6.

74. On these issues, see Gardner, *Sterling-Dollar Diplomacy*, 110–121; Block, *Origins of Economic Disorder*, 48–55; Randall B. Woods, "The Trials of Multilateralism: America, Britain, and the New Economic Order, 1941–1947," in *From War to Peace: Altered Strategic Landscapes in the Twentieth Century*, ed. Paul Kennedy and William I. Hitchcock (New Haven: Yale University Press, 2000), 126–130; and Patrick, *The Best Laid Plans*, 144–147.

75. FDR's instructions to Morgenthau reinforce the point that the conference itself was not designed to actually create new policy. See Georg Schild, *Bretton Woods and Dumbarton Oaks: American Economic and Postwar Planning in the Summer of 1944* (New York: St. Martin's Press, 1995), 112.

76. The episodes referenced in this paragraph are all vividly recounted in Steil, *The Battle of Bretton Woods*, 182–184; 190; 197–199; 205–206; 210–211; 214–216; 222–224.

77. See Block, *Origins of Economic Disorder*, 50–55; Ruggie, *Winning the Peace*, 35–38; and Borgwardt, *A New Deal for the World*, chapters 3 and 4. Whether or not the "scarce currency" clause was another American concession is a matter of debate. See Gardner, *Sterling-Dollar Diplomacy*, 114–117.

78. Both are quoted in Gardner, *Sterling-Dollar Diplomacy*, 226. On the loan negotiations, see Gardner, *Architects of Illusion*, chapter 5, especially 123–126; Block, *Origins of Economic Disorder*, 55–68; Woods, "The Trials of Multilateralism," 132–134; and Steil, *The Battle of Bretton Woods*, chapter 9.

79. Borgwardt, *A New Deal*, 96–97; Gardner, *Sterling-Dollar Diplomacy*, 76.

80. Jeffry A. Frieden, *Global Capitalism, Its Fall and Rise in the Twentieth Century* (New York: W. W. Norton & Company, 2006), 259.

81. Quoted in Gardner, *Architects of Illusion*, 133.

82. See Willard Range, *Franklin D. Roosevelt's World Order* (Athens, GA: University of Georgia Press, 1959), chapter 5; Kimball, *The Juggler*, chapter 6; and Kimball, "The Sheriffs: FDR's Postwar World," 96.

83. Patrick, *The Best Laid Plans*, 110.

84. Melvyn P. Leffler, *A Preponderance of Power: National Security, the Truman Administration, and the Cold War* (Stanford: Stanford University Press, 1992), 23.

85. Borgwardt, *A New Deal*, 93, 95.

86. Steil, *The Battle of Bretton Woods*, 194.

87. Block, *Origins of Economic Disorder*, 32–42; Frieden, *Global Capitalism*, 261–262.

88. See, for instance, Judith Goldstein, "Creating the GATT Rules: Politics, Institutions, and American Policy," in *Multilateralism Matters: The Theory and Praxis of an Institutional Form*, ed. John Gerard Ruggie (New York: Columbia University Press, 1993).

89. For an account of the disagreements over Eastern Europe favoring the US side, see Eduard Mark, "American Policy toward Eastern Europe and the Origins of the Cold War, 1941–1946: An Alternative Interpretation," *Journal of American History* 68, No. 2 (1981). For one more sympathetic to the Soviet position, see Melvyn P. Leffler, "Adherence to Agreements: Yalta and the Experiences of the Early Cold War," *International Security* 11, No. 1 (1986).

90. Leffler, *Preponderance of Power*, 79–80; 110–111; Bruce R. Kuniholm, *The Origins of the Cold War in the Near East: Great Power Conflict and Diplomacy in Iran, Turkey, and Greece* (Princeton: Princeton University Press, 1980), 304–342; Trachtenberg, *A Constructed Peace*, 34–38.

91. Quoted in Melvyn P. Leffler, *The Specter of Communism: The United States and the Origins of the Cold War, 1917–1953* (New York: Hill and Wang, 1994), 41. This was in stark contrast to Charles Bohlen's view in 1940 that Marxist ideology had by "all evidence ceased to be a factor" in Soviet foreign policy. Quoted in Eduard Mark, "October or Thermidor? Interpretations of Stalinism and the Perception of Soviet Foreign Policy in the United States, 1927–1947," *The American Historical Review* 94, No. 4 (1989), 944–945.

92. On the Turkish Straits crisis, see Kuniholm, *Cold War in the Near East*, 359–378; Robert L. Beisner, "Patterns of Peril: Dean Acheson Joins the Cold Warriors, 1945–46," *Diplomatic History* 20, No. 3 (1996); and Eduard Mark, "The War Scare of 1946 and Its Consequences," *Diplomatic History* 21, 3 (1997). For a dissenting view that the United States wasn't threatened by Soviet incursions and acted instead out of its own offensive ambitions in Turkey, see Melvyn P. Leffler, "Strategy, Diplomacy, and the Cold War: The United States, Turkey, and NATO, 1945–1952," *Journal of American History* 71, No. 4 (1985).

93. On the marked shift in US perceptions of Soviet intentions in late 1945 and 1946, see Robert L. Messer, "Paths Not Taken: The United States Department of State and Alternatives to Containment, 1945–1946," *Diplomatic History* 1, No. 4 (1977); Melvyn P. Leffler, "The American Conception of National Security and the Beginnings of the Cold War, 1945–48," *The American Historical Review* 89, No. 2 (1984), 366–378; Mark, "October or Thermidor?" 951–962; Stoler, *Allies and Adversaries*, chapters 11–13; and Edelstein, *Over the Horizon*, chapter 5.

94. The long telegram is reprinted in George Kennan (Chargé in the Soviet Union) to James Byrnes (Secretary of State), February 22, 1946, *FRUS, 1946*, Vol. 6, 696–709. For analysis, see John Lewis Gaddis, *Strategies of Containment: A Critical Appraisal of American National Security Policy during the Cold War*, rev. and exp. ed. (New York: Oxford University Press, 2005), chapter 2. The Clifford-Elsey report is reprinted in Arthur Krock, *Memoirs: Sixty Years on the Firing Line* (New York: Funk and Wagnalls, 1968), 417–482. For analysis, see Leffler, *Preponderance of Power*, 130–138.

95. On the effects of technological changes on American threat perceptions in the 1940s, see David A. Lake, *Entangling Relations: American Foreign Policy in Its Century* (Princeton: Princeton University Press, 1999), 152–156; and Aaron L. Friedberg, *In the Shadow of the Garrison State: America's Anti-Statism and Its Cold War Grand Strategy* (Princeton: Princeton University Press. 2000), 36–39.

96. "Address before a Joint Session of the Congress on Universal Military Training," October 23, 1945, quoted in Friedberg, *Garrison State*, 37.

97. The quote comes from J. H. Burns (Executive of President's Soviet Protocol Committee) to Harry Hopkins (President's Special Assistant), August 10, 1943, *FRUS, Washington and Quebec*, 625. For many others like it, see Stoler, *Allies and Adversaries*, chapters 7 and 9. On the accuracy of American estimates of Soviet military strength in Europe after World War II, see Matthew A. Evangelista, "Stalin's Postwar Army Reappraised," *International Security* 7, No. 3 (1982); and Phillip A. Karber and Jerald A. Combs, "The United States, NATO, and the Soviet Threat to Western Europe: Military Estimates and Policy Options, 1945–1963," *Diplomatic History* 22, No. 3 (1998).

98. Leffler, "The American Conception," 365.

99. Acheson Senate Testimony, March 13, 1946, quoted in Leffler, *Preponderance of Power*, 101.

100. See Leffler, "Adherence to Agreements," 103–106; and *Preponderance of Power*, 63–71; Trachtenberg, *A Constructed Peace*, 15–33; Hitchcock, *The Struggle for Europe*, 25–26.

101. Kennan, "Russia's National Objectives," April 10, 1947, quoted in Melvyn P. Leffler, *For the Soul of Mankind: The United States, the Soviet Union, and the Cold War* (New York: Hill and Wang, 2007), 64.

102. On the former, see McAllister, *No Exit*, 108. On the latter, see Carolyn Woods Eisenberg, *Drawing the Line: The American Decision to Divide Germany, 1945–1949* (New York: Cambridge University Press, 1996), 234–248.

103. George Marshall (Secretary of State) to Jefferson Caffery (Ambassador to France), February 19, 1948, *FRUS, 1948*, Vol. 2, 71. See also Marshall to Lewis Douglas (Ambassador to the United Kingdom), February 20, 1948, *FRUS, 1948*, Vol. 2, 72.

104. Leffler, *The Specter of Communism*, 59.

105. "Address on Foreign Economic Policy," March 6, 1947, https://www.trumanlibrary.org/publicpapers/index.php?pid=2193&st=&st1=.

106. President's Committee on Foreign Aid, *A Report on European Recovery and American Aid* (Washington, DC, November 7, 1947), 27–28; 32.

107. US Congress, Senate, Committee on Foreign Relations, *Hearings, Interim Aid for Europe*, 80th Cong., 1st sess., 1947, 10.

108. See Gunitsky, *Aftershocks*, 72–73.

109. William J. Donovan to Truman, "Problems and Objectives of United States Policy," May 5, 1945, quoted in Leffler, *Preponderance of Power*, 60.

110. Acheson Senate testimony, March 8, 1945, quoted in Leffler, *For the Soul of Mankind*, 59.

111. "U.S. Policy with Respect to Russia," April, 1946, quoted in Leffler, "The American Conception," 370.

112. John M. Owen IV, *The Clash of Ideas in World Politics: Transnational Networks, States, and Regime Change, 1510–2010* (Princeton: Princeton University Press, 2010), 190–196; Odd Arne Westad, *The Global Cold War: Third World Interventions and the Making of Our Times* (New York: Cambridge University Press, 2005), 54–55.

113. Leffler, "Adherence to Agreements," 107–110.

114. On the latter, see Leffler, *Preponderance of Power*, 195–197; 206, 213–214.

115. On the profound effects of the Czechoslovak coup on American threat perceptions of the USSR, see Daniel Yergin, *Shattered Peace: The Origins of the Cold War and the National Security State* (Boston: Houghton Mifflin Company, 1977), 336–365; and Leffler, *Preponderance of Power*, 203–206.

116. Quoted in Marc Selverstone, *Constructing the Monolith: The United States, Great Britain, and International Communism, 1945–1950* (Cambridge, MA: Harvard University Press, 2009), 75.

117. For an argument that this unified bloc view was essentially correct, see Douglas J. Macdonald, "Communist Bloc Expansion in the Early Cold War: Challenging Realism, Refuting Revisionism," *International Security* 20, No. 3 (1995/1996).

118. The preceding discussion draws from Owen, *The Clash of Ideas*, 180–188; and John Lewis Gaddis, *The Cold War: A New History* (New York: Penguin Press, 2005), 20–25.

119. This was close to Roosevelt's vision, first described to Stalin in Tehran, of a big four consortium, a slightly larger executive committee, and a general assembly for all members. See Roosevelt-Stalin Meeting, November 29, 1943, *FRUS, Cairo and Tehran*, 530–532, as well as FDR's drawing on 622.

120. See Gaiduk, *Divided Together*, chapter 2.

121. Joseph E. Johnson (Chief of the Division of International Security Affairs) to George Kennan (Head of Policy Planning), August 6, 1947, *FRUS, 1947*, Vol. 1, 16.

122. Important documents on the origins of this Interim Committee include Dean Rusk (Office of Special Affairs Director) to Robert Lovett (Under Secretary of State) in which the idea was perhaps first proposed, July 23, 1947; G. Hayden Raynor's Memorandum of Conversation in which a British official questions

whether it would be legal under the UN Charter, September 17, 1947; and a meeting of the American and British UN delegations in which John Foster Dulles explains how its purpose would be to either change Soviet UNSC behavior or get around the UNSC altogether, September 24, 1947. These documents are all available in *FRUS, 1947*, Vol. 1, 16–17, 173–174, 191, 194–195, 212, 213, 568. For context and discussion, see Gaiduk, *Divided Together*, chapter 3.

123. The first is quoting Edward Stettinius quoting Truman in Gaiduk, *Divided Together*, 46. The second is quoting Truman in William C. Widenor, "American Planning for the United Nations: Have We Been Asking the Right Questions?" *Diplomatic History* 6, No. 4 (1982), 248.

124. Alexander Cadogan to Ernest Bevin (UK Foreign Minister), April 27, 1946, quoted in Gaiduk, *Divided Together*, 86.

125. See Schild, *Bretton Woods and Dumbarton Oaks*, 109.

126. Steil nicely illustrates this point in *The Battle of Bretton Woods*, 136–137.

127. Specifically, they wanted special exemptions on the amount of gold they would contribute, the amount of information they would have to provide, and, most notably, the size of their quota relative to their voting power. See Raymond F. Mikesell, "Negotiating at Bretton Woods, 1944," in *Negotiating with the Russians*, ed. Raymond Dennett and Joseph E. Johnson (USA: World Peace Foundation, 1951); and Steil, *The Battle of Bretton Woods*, 233–244.

128. Mikesell, "Negotiating at Bretton Woods, 1944."

129. Quoted in Schild, *Bretton Woods and Dumbarton Oaks*, 112.

130. Mikesell, "Negotiating at Bretton Woods, 1944," 116.

131. This meant that they would have to report to the IMF on sensitive subjects like their annual imports, exports, levels of production, and gold reserves. See Thomas G. Paterson, *Soviet-American Confrontation: Postwar Reconstruction and the Origins of the Cold War* (Baltimore: The Johns Hopkins University Press, 1973), 155.

132. Gabriel Kolko, *The Politics of War: The World and United States Foreign Policy, 1943–1945* (New York: Random House, 1968), 258.

133. Leffler, *Preponderance of Power*, 50.

134. Leffler, "Adherence to Agreements," 101–102. On similar American duplicity outside of Europe, see Leffler, *Preponderance of Power*, 136.

135. Vladimir O. Pechatnov, "The Soviet Union and the World, 1944–1953," in *The Cambridge History of the Cold War, Volume 1: Origins*, ed. Melvyn P. Leffler and Odd Arne Westad (New York: Cambridge University Press, 2010), 100–104.

136. Quoted in Vladislav M. Zubok, *A Failed Empire: The Soviet Union in the Cold War from Stalin to Gorbachev* (Chapel Hill: The University of North Carolina Press, 2007), 51–52.

137. The first IBRD President abruptly resigned in part because of the pressure placed on him by US officials to politicize the loan process. Meanwhile, the Bank only granted four loans in this period, all to American allies in Western Europe. See

Paterson, *Soviet-American Confrontation*, 156–158; Robert A. Pollard, *Economic Security and the Origins of the Cold War, 1945–1950* (New York: Columbia University Press 1985), 45–47.

138. Leading the way on this front were the ambassadors to Eastern European countries, as cables from Harriman (USSR), H. F. Arthur Schoenfeld (Hungary), and Laurence A. Steinhardt (Czechoslovakia) were strikingly critical of further economic aid to countries in the Soviet sphere. See Harriman to Byrnes, December 15, 1945, *FRUS, 1945*, Vol. 2, 1350–1351; Harriman to Byrnes, January 19, 1946; Schoenfeld to Byrnes, February 15, 1946; and Steinhardt to Byrnes, February 26, 1946, all in *FRUS, 1946*, Vol. 6, 187, 259–260, 820. See also Pollard, *Economic Security*, chapter 3.

139. Byrnes to Acheson (Under Secretary of State) and William Clayton (Under Secretary for Economic Affairs), September 24, 1946, *FRUS, 1946*, Vol. 7, 223.

140. On these points, see John Lewis Gaddis, *The United States and the Origins of the Cold War, 1941–1947* (New York: Columbia University Press, 1972), chapter 6; Pollard, *Economic Security*, 27–53.

141. Mark, "American Policy toward Eastern Europe," 332.

142. On CoCom's origins, see Michael Mastanduno, "Trade as a Strategic Weapon: American and Alliance Export Control Policy in the Early Postwar Period," *International Organization* 42, No. 1 (1988), 126–142; and, more broadly, Mastanduno, *Economic Containment: CoCom and the Politics of East-West Trade* (Ithaca: Cornell University Press, 1992).

143. See, for instance, Frieden, *Global Capitalism*, 270; and Patrick, *The Best Laid Plans*, 254–257.

144. Thomas W. Zeiler, *Free Trade, Free World: The Advent of GATT* (Chapel Hill: The University of North Carolina Press, 1999), 150, 151, 159, 163.

145. Goldstein, "Creating the GATT Rules," 223–225.

146. Zeiler, *Free Trade, Free World*, 161–162; Kerry Chase, "Multilateralism Compromised: The Mysterious Origins of GATT Article XXIV," *World Trade Review* 5, No. 1 (2006).

147. For a provocative account broadly consistent with my arguments in this subsection, see Michael Cox and Caroline Kennedy-Pipe, "The Tragedy of American Diplomacy? Rethinking the Marshall Plan," *Journal of Cold War Studies* 7, No. 1 (2005).

148. Quoted in Benn Steil, *The Marshall Plan: Dawn of the Cold War* (New York: Simon & Schuster, 2018), 85. On the importance of this moment for Marshall himself, see Philip Zelikow, "George C. Marshall and the Moscow CFM Meeting of 1947," *Diplomacy and Statecraft* 8, No. 3 (1997); and McAllister, *No Exit*, 126–129.

149. JCS 1769/1, "United States Assistance to Other Countries From the Standpoint of National Security, Report by the Joint Strategic Survey Committee," April 29, 1947, *FRUS, 1947*, Vol. 1, 736, 740.

150. See Maier, "The Politics of Productivity," 141–144, 184.

151. See Kennan Memorandum, May 16, 1947, *FRUS, 1947*, Vol. 3, 221; and Caffery to Marshall, October 2, 1948, *FRUS 1948*, Vol. 3, 661; and James Dunn (Ambassador to Italy) to Marshall, March 20 and 22, 1948, *FRUS, 1948*, Vol. 3, 857–858; as well as Melvyn P. Leffler, "The United States and the Strategic Elements of the Marshall Plan," *Diplomatic History* 12, No. 3 (1988), 281.

152. See, for instance, Leffler, *Preponderance of Power*, 182–184.

153. Kennan to Acheson (PPS/1), May 23, 1947, *FRUS, 1947*, Vol. 3, 228.

154. Quoted in Steil, *The Marshall Plan*, 109. On the American advantages to be gained either way, see Selverstone, *Constructing the Monolith*, 63–64.

155. This sentiment was also expressed in an important meeting between Clayton and Bevin in London. See Peterson Memoranda of Conversations, June 24–26, 1947, *FRUS, 1947*, Vol. 3, 268–270, 291.

156. Kennan to Acheson (PPS/1), May 23, 1947, *FRUS, 1947*, Vol. 3, 228.

157. Walter Isaacson and Evan Thomas, *The Wise Men: Six Friends and the World They Made* (New York: Simon & Schuster, 1986), 413–416.

158. Quoted in William C. Cromwell, "The Marshall Plan, Britain and the Cold War," *Review of International Studies* 8, No. 4 (1982), 238; and Steil, *The Marshall Plan*, 108.

159. Cromwell, "The Marshall Plan, Britain and the Cold War," 237.

160. See Caffery to Marshall, June 17, 1947, *FRUS, 1947*, Vol. 3, 258.

161. For Western accounts of these meetings with Molotov, see the Caffery and Douglas cables to Marshall, June 28–July 3, 1947, *FRUS, 1947*, Vol. 3, 297–307.

162. Kennan Notes for Marshall, July 21, 1947, *FRUS, 1947*, Vol. 3, 335.

163. "Summary of Discussion on Problems of Relief, Rehabilitation and Reconstruction of Europe," May 29, 1947, *FRUS, 1947*, Vol. 3, 235. See also Kennan to Acheson (PPS/1) and Clayton to Acheson, May 23 and 27, 1947, *FRUS, 1947*, Vol. 3, 228, 232.

164. Patrick, *The Best Laid Plans*, 260.

165. On this prior support, see Scott Jackson, "Prologue to the Marshall Plan: The Origins of the American Commitment for a European Recovery Program," *Journal of American History* 65, No. 4 (1979); Armin Rappaport, "The United States and European Integration: The First Phase," *Diplomatic History* 5, No. 2 (1981); Michael J. Hogan, "The Search for a 'Creative Peace': The United States, European Unity, and the Origins of the Marshall Plan," *Diplomatic History* 6, No. 3 (1982); and Klaus Schwabe, "The United States and European Integration: 1947–1957," in *Western Europe and Germany: The Beginnings of European Integration, 1945–1960*, ed. Clemens Wurm (Oxford: Berg Publishers Ltd, 1995), 115–135.

166. Specifically, the first concrete planning for the ERP, by the State-War-Navy Coordinating Committee (SWNCC), proposed that such aid should be used to combat Soviet influence, while Acheson's Mississippi speech highlighted the importance of overcoming divisions in Europe and getting it "working together in a harmonious whole." It was Kennan's first report that fused these ideas,

recommending a much more interdependent Europe for the purpose of combatting Soviet influence. See "Report of the Special 'Ad Hoc' Committee of the State-War-Navy Coordinating Committee," April 21, 1947, *FRUS, 1947*, Vol. 3, 217; Dean Acheson, "The Requirements of Reconstruction," May 8, 1947, *Department of State Bulletin* (May 18, 1947), 994; and Kennan to Acheson (PPS/1), May 23, 1947, *FRUS, 1947*, Vol. 3, 224–225. Also instructive are Dean Acheson, *Present at the Creation: My Years at the State Department* (New York: W. W. Norton & Company, 1969), 226–235; and Harry S. Truman, *Memoirs, Volume 2: Years of Trial and Hope* (Garden City: Doubleday & Company, 1956), chapter 8.

167. George F. Kennan, *Memoirs, 1925–1950* (Boston: Little, Brown and Company, 1967), 347, 340.

168. See Clayton's comments in "Summary of Discussion on Problems of Relief, Rehabilitation and Reconstruction of Europe," May 29, 1947, *FRUS, 1947*, Vol. 3, 236; as well as Michael J. Hogan, *The Marshall Plan: America, Britain, and the Reconstruction of Western Europe, 1947–1952* (Cambridge: Cambridge University Press, 1987), 52–53.

169. Important documents reflecting this point include Lovett to Clayton and Caffery (August 14), Lovett to Douglas (August 20), Lovett to Marshall (August 24), Clayton to Marshall (August 31), Kennan's "Situation with Respect to European Recovery Program" (September 4), Lovett to CEEC Representatives (September 7), and Marshall to Douglas (September 8), all in *FRUS, 1947*, Vol. 3, 346, 358, 367–368, 372–375, 395, 397–404, 413, 418–419. See also Hogan, *The Marshall Plan*, chapter 2; McAllister, *No Exit*, 134–135; Timothy Healey, "Will Clayton, Negotiating the Marshall Plan, and European Integration," *Diplomatic History* 35, No. 2 (2011); and Steil, *The Marshall Plan*, chapter 6.

170. Hogan, *The Marshall Plan*, 101–109. See also Kennan's complaints about proposals that the State Department relinquish control of the ERP in George F. Kennan, *The Kennan Diaries*, ed. Frank Costigliola (New York: W. W. Norton & Company, 2014), 208.

171. Hogan, *The Marshall Plan*, 123–128. On jockeying between the United States and Britain over the integrative aspects of the Marshall Plan, see also Robin Edmonds, *Setting the Mould: The United States and Britain, 1945–1950* (Oxford: Oxford University Press, 1986), 165–168; 182–194.

172. Hogan, *The Marshall Plan*, 123–128; McAllister, *No Exit*, 141–156.

173. See Hogan, *The Marshall Plan*, chapter 3; Selverstone, *Constructing the Monolith*, 80–95; Steil, *The Marshall Plan*, chapter 7.

174. "Special Address to Congress on the Marshall Plan," December 19, 1947, https://www.trumanlibrary.org/publicpapers/index.php?pid=1849&st=marshall+plan&st1=.

175. US Congress, Senate, Committee on Foreign Relations, *Hearings, European Recovery Program*, 80th Cong., 2nd sess., 1948, 70, 69. For Marshall speaking to the Soviet menace as impetus for cooperation, see 4, 9, 10, 33.

176. This is the main theme of Steil, *The Marshall Plan*, chapter 7.

177. November 2, 1947, quoted in Steil, *The Marshall Plan*, 193.

178. Acheson, *Present at the Creation*, 233.

179. This theme is emphasized by Truman himself in his *Memoirs, Volume 2*, chapter 17; as well as in Peter Foot, "America and the Origins of the Atlantic Alliance: A Reappraisal," in *The Origins of NATO*, ed. Joseph Smith (Exeter: University of Exeter Press, 1990).

180. This memorandum was enclosed in a message from Lord Inverchapel (UK Ambassador to the United States) to Marshall, January 13, 1948, *FRUS, 1948*, Vol. 3, 5

181. For a review of the different historiographical camps on the origins of the Cold War as applied to the origins of NATO, see Peter G. Boyle, "America's Hesitant Road to NATO, 1945–49," in *The Origins of NATO*, ed. Joseph Smith (Exeter: University of Exeter Press, 1990).

182. Trachtenberg, *A Constructed Peace*, 61–65; Steil, *The Marshall Plan*, 202–206.

183. See Memorandum of Conversation between Bevin and Marshall, December, 1947, *FRUS, 1947*, Vol. 2, 815–817.

184. "Summary of a Memorandum Representing Mr. Bevin's Views on the Formation of a Western Union," January 13, 1948, *FRUS, 1948*, Vol. 3, 4–6. On the preceding developments, see Martin H. Folly, "Breaking the Vicious Circle: Britain, the United States, and the Genesis of the North Atlantic Treaty," *Diplomatic History* 12, No. 1 (1988), 61–62.

185. See, for instance, Marshall to Douglas, February 27, 1948, *FRUS, 1948*, Vol. 3, 34.

186. See *FRUS, 1948*, Vol. 3, 49–50, 54–55.

187. On the importance of these events for threat perceptions, see John Hickerson (Director for European Affairs) to Marshall, March 8, 1948, Inverchapel to Lovett, March 11, 1948, and Marshall to Charles Bay (Ambassador to Norway), March 12, 1948, all in *FRUS, 1948*, Vol. 3, 40–41, 47, 52. On the American shift in response to these events, see the messages between Marshall and Inverchapel, March 11–12, 1948, *FRUS, 1948*, Vol. 3, 46–48; as well as Folly, "Breaking the Vicious Circle," 67–68. These negotiations produced the so-called "Pentagon Paper" of April 1, 1948, reprinted in *FRUS, 1948*, Vol. 3, 71–75. Finally, for a brief but clear narrative of these threatening developments and their direct connection to the origins of NATO, see Timothy Andrews Sayle, *Enduring Alliance: A History of NATO and the Postwar Global Order* (Ithaca: Cornell University Press, 2019) 11–17.

188. Timothy P. Ireland, *Creating the Entangling Alliance: The Origins of the North Atlantic Treaty Organization* (Westport, CT: Greenwood Press, 1981), 81, 91–92, 96–100; Trachtenberg, *A Constructed Peace*, 74–78, 84–85. On the necessity of reassuring France throughout this period, see Bevin's messages to Marshall, April 9 and June 1, 1948, *FRUS, 1948*, Vol. 3, 79–80, 138; as well as Eisenberg, *Drawing the Line*, 398–404, 469–474.

189. Ireland, *Creating the Entangling Alliance*, 101–102; Leffler, "Strategic Dimensions of the Marshall Plan," 292–298; McAllister, *No Exit*, 152–169.

190. Marshall to Caffery, June 23, 1948, *FRUS, 1948*, Vol. 3, 139; NSC 9/3, June 28, 1948, *FRUS, 1948*, Vol. 3, 140–141. On these developments, see Folly, "Breaking the Vicious Circle," 74–75; and Leffler, *Preponderance of Power*, 217–218.

191. "Memorandum by the Participants in the Washington Security Talks" (hereafter the "Washington Paper"), September 9, 1948, *FRUS, 1948*, Vol. 3, 237–248.

192. For a comprehensive description of these developments in the first half of 1948, see Leffler, *Preponderance of Power*, 199–218. On the talks that ultimately produced the NAT, see Edmonds, *Setting the Mould*, 174–178.

193. Lake, *Entangling Relations*, 150.

194. Steve Weber, "Shaping the Postwar Balance of Power: Multilateralism in NATO," in *Multilateralism Matters: The Theory and Praxis of an Institutional Form*, ed. John Gerard Ruggie (New York: Columbia University Press, 1993), 267.

195. Mary N. Hampton, "NATO at the Creation: US Foreign Policy, West Germany, and the Wilsonian Impulse," *Security Studies* 4, No. 3 (1995), 623. See also Thomas Risse-Kappen, "Collective Identity in a Democratic Community: The Case of NATO," in *The Culture of National Security: Norms and Identity in World Politics*, ed. Peter J. Katzenstein (New York: Columbia University Press, 1996), 372–379.

196. Weber, "Shaping the Postwar Balance of Power," 236.

197. "Minutes of Second Meeting of Washington Exploratory Talks on Security" [hereafter "Washington talks"], July 6, 1948, *FRUS, 1948*, Vol. 3, 154.

198. This was perhaps most clearly articulated by Hickerson in an important MemCon, January 21, 1948, *FRUS, 1948*, Vol. 3, 10–11, and by Lovett in the fifth meeting of the Washington talks, *FRUS, 1948*, Vol. 3, 172–173. See also Geir Lundestad, "Empire by Invitation? The United States and Western Europe, 1945–1952," *Journal of Peace Research* 23, No. 3 (1986), 269–273.

199. "Washington Paper," *FRUS, 1948*, Vol. 3, 244.

200. This was perhaps most emphatically stated by John Foster Dulles in a conversation with Marshall, Lovett, and Vandenberg. See Lovett MemCon, April 27, 1948, *FRUS, 1948*, Vol. 3, 108.

201. Kennan to Marshall and Lovett, November 24, 1948, *FRUS 1948*, Vol. 3, 285.

202. Harriman to Caffery, December 3, 1948, *FRUS 1948*, Vol. 3, 301–305.

203. Acheson to Douglas, February 16, 1949, *FRUS, 1949*, Vol. 4, 111. The importance of the ERP is also highlighted in the State Department's official reaction to the North Atlantic Treaty on March 20 (240–241).

204. A similar argument is made in Patrick Thaddeus Jackson, *Civilizing the Enemy: German Reconstruction and the Invention of the West* (Ann Arbor: The University of Michigan Press, 2006), 216–220.

205. Hickerson to Marshall, March 8, 1948, *FRUS, 1948*, Vol. 3, 40–41. Similar sentiments are expressed by Lovett, Kennan, and Bohlen (State Department

Counselor) in the third meeting of the Washington talks, July 7, 1948, *FRUS, 1948*, Vol. 3, 156–160.

206. This quote comes from the third meeting of the Washington talks, July 7, 1948, *FRUS, 1948*, Vol. 3, 156–160.

207. For examples of these concerns, see Kennan to Marshall, January 20, 1948, Bay to Marshall, February 25, 1948, and Inverchapel to Lovett, March 11, 1948, all in *FRUS, 1948*, Vol. 3, 30–32, 46–47.

208. A discussion about how Norway should decline a non-aggression pact with the Soviets and sign the NATO compact is particularly instructive. See the seventeenth meeting of the Washington talks, March 11, 1949, *FRUS, 1949*, Vol. 4, 187–191, and particularly Acheson's comments on 191.

209. On fears of resurgent German nationalism, see Acheson to George W. Perkins (Assistant Secretary of State for European Affairs), October 19, 1949, *FRUS, 1949*, Vol. 4, 469–470; as well as quotes from various officials in Leffler, *Preponderance of Power*, 319. On fears of the Soviets luring the Germans eastward with a conciliatory offer on reunification, see Trachtenberg, *A Constructed Peace*, 128–131.

210. On the importance of bringing West Germany in on equal footing, see, for instance, Harriman to Caffery, December 3, 1948, *FRUS, 1948*, Vol. 3, 303, 308–310, as well as an important meeting of the American Ambassadors to European states, October 21–22, 1949, *FRUS, 1949*, Vol. 4, 486–488; and Gustav Schmidt, "'Tying' (West) Germany into the West—But to What? NATO? WEU? The European Community?" in *Western Europe and Germany: The Beginnings of European Integration, 1945–1960*, ed. Clemens Wurm (Oxford: Berg Publishers Ltd, 1995).

211. Adenauer's strategic use of NATO principles in this way is highlighted in Mary Hampton, "NATO at the Creation"; and "NATO, Germany, and the United States: Creating Positive Identity in Trans-Atlantia," *Security Studies* 8, No. 2–3 (1998); as well as in Jackson, *Civilizing the Enemy*, 192–194.

212. House of Commons, January 22, 1948, http://hansard.millbanksystems.com/commons/1948/jan/22/foreign-affairs, col. 407–408.

213. Tenth Meeting of the Washington talks, December 22, 1948, *FRUS, 1948*, Vol. 3, 325.

214. A similar point is made in Patrick, *Best Laid Plans*, 283.

215. That term comes from Lundestad, "Empire by Invitation?"

216. See G. John Ikenberry, "The Myth of Post–Cold War Chaos," *Foreign Affairs* 75, No. 3 (1996); and *After Victory*, chapters 6 and 7.

217. For the portions of Ikenberry's work most germane to the genesis of these rules (via the origins of the Marshall Plan and NATO), see *After Victory*, 191–199, 205–210; and *Liberal Leviathan*, 183–190, 200–207, 215–216.

218. Ikenberry, *After Victory*, 165. Emphasis added.

219. Ikenberry, *Liberal Leviathan*, 165.

220. Ikenberry, *Liberal Leviathan*, 207.

221. Maier, "The Politics of Productivity," especially 123, 125.

222. See Maier, "The Politics of Productivity."

223. For evidence, contrast Hogan, *The Marshall Plan*, chapters 1–3 with his claims in the introduction and evidence he supplies in the rest of the book.

224. Patrick, *The Best Laid Plans*, 292.

225. Ruggie, *Winning the Peace*, 24.

226. On this point, see, for instance, Lake, *Entangling Relations*, chapter 5; Christopher J. Hemmer and Peter Katzenstein, "Why Is There No NATO in Asia? Collective Identity, Regionalism, and the Origins of Multilateralism," *International Organization* 56, No. 3 (2002); Galia Press-Barnathan, *Organizing the World: The United States and Regional Cooperation in Asia and Europe* (New York: Routledge, 2003); and Ikenberry, *Liberal Leviathan*, 89–90.

227. Leffler, *Preponderance of Power*, 52.

228. Quoted in Walter LaFeber, *Inevitable Revolutions: The United States in Central America*, 2nd ed. (New York: W. W. Norton & Company, 1983/1993), 109.

229. Ruggie, *Winning the Peace*, 19; 30–34; Harper, *American Visions of Europe*, 120; Robert Dallek, *Franklin D. Roosevelt and American Foreign Policy, 1932–1945*, 2nd ed. (New York: Oxford University Press, 1995), 482–483; Hoopes and Brinkley, *FDR and the Creation of the U.N.*, chapter 10; and especially Kimball, "The Sheriffs: FDR's Postwar World," 99–101.

230. This agreement is detailed in Trachtenberg, *A Constructed Peace*, chapter 1; and McAllister, *No Exit*, chapter 3.

231. Trachtenberg, *A Constructed Peace*, 42–43.

232. Colin Dueck, *Reluctant Crusaders: Power, Culture, and Change in American Grand Strategy* (Princeton: Princeton University Press, 2007), 98–99.

233. This is indeed a central theme of Timothy Andrews Sayle's recent history of NATO. See *Enduring Alliance*, esp. 5–7.

234. Jeffrey W. Legro, *Rethinking the World: Great Powers Strategies and International Order* (Ithaca: Cornell University Press, 2005), 75. The classic historical account embodying this narrative is Robert A. Divine, *Second Chance: The Triumph of Internationalism in America During World War II* (New York: Atheneum, 1967).

235. This data is most comprehensively presented in Jeffrey W. Legro, "Whence American Internationalism," *International Organization* 54, No. 2 (2000).

236. This is most thoroughly and convincingly demonstrated in McAllister, *No Exit*, chapters 2–3.

237. This argument has been advanced in Mark S. Sheetz, "Exit Strategies: American Grand Designs for European Postwar Security," *Security Studies* 8, No. 4 (1999); McAllister, *No Exit*; Johnston, *Hegemony and Culture*, 61–68; and Sebastian Rosato, "Stylized Narratives and Security Studies: The Case of America's European Policy," Manuscript, University of Notre Dame: American Political Science Association annual meeting, 2010.

238. For an overview of all of these negotiations, see Trachtenberg, *A Constructed Peace*, chapters 3–5. On the EDC in particular, see Thomas Alan Schwartz, *America's Germany: John J. McCloy and the Federal Republic of Germany* (Cambridge, MA: Harvard University Press, 1991), chapter 8; Sheetz, "Exit Strategies," 26–36; McAllister, *No Exit*, chapter 5; and Sebastian Rosato, *Europe United: Power Politics and the Making of the European Community* (Ithaca: Cornell University Press, 2011), chapter 4.

CHAPTER 8

1. Mary Elise Sarotte, *The Collapse: The Accidental Opening of the Berlin Wall* (New York: Basic Books, 2014), 121.

2. On the momentous nature of these developments, see Jacques Lévesque, "The East European Revolutions of 1989," in *The Cambridge History of the Cold War, Volume 3: Endings*, ed. Melvyn P. Leffler and Odd Arne Westad (New York: Cambridge University Press, 2010).

3. James Graham Wilson, *The Triumph of Improvisation: Gorbachev's Adaptability, Reagan's Engagement, and the End of the Cold War* (Ithaca: Cornell University Press, 2014), 174.

4. For accounts that effectively detail the continuity of economic order preferences and principles through this transition, see Andrew J. Bacevich, *American Empire: The Realities and Consequences of U.S. Diplomacy* (Cambridge, MA: Harvard University Press, 2002), chapters 1–4; and Robert B. Zoellick, "An Architecture of U.S. Strategy after the Cold War," in *In Uncertain Times: American Foreign Policy after the Berlin Wall and 9/11*, ed. Melvyn P. Leffler and Jeffrey W. Legro (Ithaca: Cornell University Press, 2011).

5. Bartholomew H. Sparrow, "Realism's Practitioner: Brent Scowcroft and the Making of the New World Order, 1989–1993," *Diplomatic History* 34, No. 1 (2010), 154.

6. Sparrow, "Realism's Practitioner," 147.

7. Quoted in Philip Zelikow and Condoleezza Rice, *Germany United and Europe Transformed: A Study in Diplomacy* (Cambridge, MA: Harvard University Press, 1995), 272.

8. Timothy Naftali, *George H. W. Bush: The American Presidents Series: The 41st President, 1989–1993* (New York: Times Press, 2007), 110.

9. Quoted in Hal Brands, *Making the Unipolar Moment: U.S. Foreign Policy and the Rise of the Post–Cold War Order* (Ithaca: Cornell University Press, 2016), 281.

10. The most comprehensive account of the diplomatic contestation over Germany is Mary Elise Sarotte, *1989: The Struggle to Create Post–Cold War Europe* (Princeton: Princeton University Press, 2009).

11. G. John Ikenberry, *After Victory: Institutions, Strategic Restraint, and the Rebuilding of Order after Major Wars* (Princeton: Princeton University Press, 2001), 222–233.

12. George Bush and Brent Scowcroft, *A World Transformed* (New York: Alfred A. Knopf, 1998), 300.

13. For a well-documented recent account of the developments I focus upon here (along with an argument compatible with my own), see Joshua R. Itzkowitz Shifrinson, *Rising Titans, Falling Giants: How Great Powers Exploit Power Shifts* (Ithaca: Cornell University Press, 2018), 140–152.

14. On Gorbachev's vision, see Sarotte, *1989*, chapter 3; and Marie-Pierre Rey, "'Europe Is Our Common Home': A Study of Gorbachev's Diplomatic Concept," *Cold War History* 4, No. 2 (2004).

15. Quoted in Jeffrey A. Engel, *When the World Seemed New: George H. W. Bush and the End of the Cold War* (New York: Houghton Mifflin Harcourt, 2017), 302. See also the Soviet transcripts of these meetings/passages in Svetlana Savranskaya, Thomas Blanton, and Vladislav Zubok, eds. *Masterpieces of History: The Peaceful End of the Cold War in Europe, 1989* (Budapest: Central European University Press, 2010), 634, 643.

16. Quoted in Michael R. Beschloss and Strobe Talbott, *At the Highest Levels: The Inside Story of the End of the Cold War* (Boston: Little, Brown and Company, 1993), 219.

17. Mikhail Gorbachev, *Memoirs* (London: Doubleday, 1996), 529.

18. See Sarotte, *1989*, 106–107.

19. Gorbachev, *Memoirs*, 428–429.

20. Rey, "Europe Is Our Common Home," 57–59.

21. See Kristina Spohr, "Germany, America and the Shaping of Post–Cold War Europe: A Story of German International Emancipation through Political Unification, 1989–90," *Cold War History* 15, No. 2 (2015), 235–242.

22. This was point six of Kohl's Ten-Point Program for Germany, announced in late November, 1989. See Savranskaya et al., *Masterpieces of History*, 617–618.

23. Quoted in William Taubman, *Gorbachev: His Life and Times* (New York: W. W. Norton & Company, 2017), 543–544.

24. Bush and Scowcroft, *A World Transformed*, 299.

25. Sarotte, *1989*, 206.

26. Quoted in Jon Meacham, *Destiny and Power: The American Odyssey of George Herbert Walker Bush* (New York: Random House, 2015), 402.

27. See Engel, *When the World Seemed New*, 320, 342–344, 346, 348, 353; and Timothy Andrews Sayle, *Enduring Alliance: A History of NATO and the Postwar Global Order* (Ithaca: Cornell University Press, 2019), 232.

28. On the momentous structural changes of the 1980s, see Stephen G. Brooks and William C. Wohlforth, "Power, Globalization, and the End of the Cold War: Reevaluating a Landmark Case for Ideas," *International Security* 25, No. 3 (2000–2001); Odd Arne Westad, *The Cold War: A World History* (New York: Basic Books, 2017), chapters 20–21; and especially Brands, *Making the Unipolar Moment*.

29. Quoted in Bush and Scowcroft, *A World Transformed*, 267.

30. Zelikow and Rice, *Germany United and Europe Transformed*, 169.

31. Quoted in Engel, *When the World Seemed New*, 314.

32. Quoted in Bush and Scowcroft, *A World Transformed*, 240–241; see also Wilson, *The Triumph of Improvisation*, 155; and Sayle, *Enduring Alliance*, 218–219. On Soviet capabilities during this period, see Shifrinson, *Rising Titans, Falling Giants*, chapter 4.

33. Quoted in Melvyn P. Leffler, *For the Soul of Mankind: The United States, the Soviet Union, and the Cold War* (New York: Hill and Wang, 2007), 425.

34. While they had both used these respective slogans before, each pointedly highlighted them again in notable speeches in 1989, Bush in Germany in May and Gorbachev before the Council of Europe in July. See Wilson, *The Triumph of Improvisation*, 156, 164.

35. Zelikow and Rice, *Germany United and Europe Transformed*, 254–255; Brands, *Making the Unipolar Moment*, 290.

36. The Bush administration's insistence on these points is a central theme of Sayle, *Enduring Alliance*, chapter 10. Yet it does not appear that there was a systematic attempt to evaluate the veracity of either position, at least until a European Strategy Steering Group (ESSG) meeting in March of 1991, after the formative period of potential transformation that I focus upon in this chapter had already ended. On this particular meeting, see Sayle, *Enduring Alliance*, 233–234.

37. Quoted in Mary Elise Sarotte, "Perpetuating U.S. Preeminence: The 1990 Deals to 'Bribe the Soviets Out' and Move NATO In," *International Security* 35, No. 1 (2010), 113.

38. Quoted in Bush and Scowcroft, *A World Transformed*, 243.

39. Bush and Scowcroft, *A World Transformed*, 231.

40. Quoted in Engel, *When the World Seemed New*, 350.

41. Quoted in Sarotte, "Perpetuating U.S. Preeminence," 113.

42. Quoted in Brands, *Making the Unipolar Moment*, 289.

43. Quoted in Bartholomew Sparrow, *The Strategist: Brent Scowcroft and the Call of National Security* (New York: PublicAffairs, 2015), 371.

44. Bush and Scowcroft, *A World Transformed*, 253.

45. Quoted in Wilson, *The Triumph of Improvisation*, 178–179.

46. James A. Baker, III, with Thomas M. DeFrank, *The Politics of Diplomacy: Revolution, War, and Peace, 1989–1992* (New York: Putnam Press, 1995), 196.

47. Bush and Scowcroft, *A World Transformed*, 236.

48. Bush and Scowcroft, *A World Transformed*, 249.

49. Quoted in Sparrow, *The Strategist*, 371.

50. On the ambiguous origins of the American position here, see Zelikow and Rice, *Germany United and Europe Transformed*, chapter 5.

51. Quoted in Bush and Scowcroft, *A World Transformed*, 272.

52. George H. W. Bush, *All the Best, George Bush: My Life in Letters and Other Writings* (New York: Scribner, 2013), 460–461.

53. Perhaps Scowcroft fit this model more than any of the other principals. See Wilson, *The Triumph of Improvisation*, 149–150.

54. Quoted in Brands, *Making the Unipolar Moment*, 281.

55. Baker with DeFrank, *The Politics of Diplomacy*, 198–199.

56. Zoellick, "An Architecture of U.S. Strategy after the Cold War," 31. In the same passage, Zoellick also quickly dismisses arguments that "a 'Third Way' should have eliminated the Cold War institutions and started anew," yet without providing justification for this dismissal.

57. Quoted in Bush and Scowcroft, *A World Transformed*, 253, as well as in Sarotte, *1989*, 128; Brands, *Making the Unipolar Moment*, 293; and Engel, *When the World Seemed New*, 350. Scowcroft writes that he "was pleased at the promptness and firmness with which the President knocked down the notion of a French-like German role in NATO." *A World Transformed*, 255.

58. For example, compare Havel's earlier and later statements on the appropriate security architecture for Europe in Engel, *When the World Seemed New*, 318, 342, 356.

59. For this very reason, Shevardnadze was not at all in favor of 2 + 4 when it was first proposed. See William C. Wohlforth, ed., *Cold War Endgame: Oral History, Analysis, Debates* (University Park: The Pennsylvania State University Press, 2003), 55–56. Indeed, the Soviets had hoped to push at least for a 4 + 2 structure where it would be clear that the occupying powers would have the most say. This was quickly rejected by the Americans and turned back to 2 + 4. See the February 9 conversation between Bush and Gorbachev in Savranskaya et al., *Masterpieces of History*, 679; and Taubman, *Gorbachev*, 548.

60. Quoted in Sarotte, *1989*, 126.

61. Both are quoted in Engel, *When the World Seemed New*, 337.

62. Robert Gates, *From the Shadows: The Ultimate Insider's Story of Five Presidents and How They Won the Cold War* (New York: Simon & Schuster, 1996), 485.

63. Quoted in Sparrow, *The Strategist*, 373.

64. Quoted in Engel, *When the World Seemed New*, 333.

65. Gorbachev himself has described the structure of the negotiations in this way in his *Memoirs*, 532.

66. Quoted in Engel, *When the World Seemed New*, 349–350.

67. Quoted from Genscher's Tutzing speech on January 31, 1990, in Sarotte, *1989*, 326. For his own perspective on his speech and approach, see Hans Dietrich Genscher, *Rebuilding a House Divided: A Memoir by the Architect of Germany's Reunification* (New York: Broadway Books, 1998), 335–338. On the seeming agreement by multiple sides to the Genscher formula, including Baker's infamous and contested pledges on no NATO expansion eastward, see Sarotte, *1989*, 104–115; and Spohr, "Germany, America, and the Shaping of Post–Cold War Europe," 237–238. On Baker's seeming acquiescence in particular, see Joshua R. Itzkowitz Shifrinson, "Deal or No Deal? The End of the Cold War and the U.S. Offer to Limit NATO Expansion," *International Security* 40, No. 4 (2016).

68. Quoted in Engel, *When the World Seemed New*, 351. Emphasis added. On this feat, see also Sarotte, *1989*, 126–129.

69. Quoted in Spohr, "Germany, America, and the Shaping of Post–Cold War Europe," 239. Emphasis in original.

70. On the events discussed in this paragraph, see Shifrinson, *Rising Titans, Falling Giants*, 141–152; and Sayle, *Enduring Alliance*, 224–229.

71. See Anatoly S. Chernyaev, *My Six Years with Gorbachev* (University Park: The Pennsylvania State University Press, 2000), 272; Robert Service, *The End of the Cold War, 1985–1991* (New York: Public Affairs, 2015), 437–438; Engel, *When the World Seemed New*, 372–373; and especially Taubman, *Gorbachev*, 548–549.

72. Quoted in Brands, *Making the Unipolar Moment*, 282.

73. Baker with DeFrank, *The Politics of Diplomacy*, 254.

74. Zelikow and Rice, *Germany United and Europe Transformed*, 279.

75. Quoted in Meacham, *Destiny and Power*, 403. See also Sarotte, *1989*, 167.

76. Quoted in Engel, *When the World Seemed New*, 372. See also Leffler, *For the Soul of Mankind*, 445–446.

77. Both are quoted in Baker with DeFrank, *The Politics of Diplomacy*, 253.

78. Chernyaev, *My Six Years with Gorbachev*, 273.

79. Service, *The End of the Cold War*, 443–448. On the Gorbachev-Kohl Moscow summit, see Sarotte, *1989*, 177–186.

80. For the most convincing account that material factors alone can explain these developments, see Stephen G. Brooks and William C. Wohlforth, "Economic Constraints and the End of the Cold War," in *Cold War Endgame: Oral History, Analysis, Debates*, ed. William C. Wohlforth (University Park: The Pennsylvania State University Press, 2003).

81. Engel, *When the World Seemed New*, 373.

82. Quoted in Taubman, *Gorbachev*, 553.

83. On these general trends, see Jeffrey A. Engel, "A Better World . . . but Don't Get Carried Away: The Foreign Policy of George H. W. Bush Twenty Years On," *Diplomatic History* 34, No. 1 (2010).

84. See, for instance, Wilson, *The Triumph of Improvisation*, 158–159; 172; 183–184; Engel, *When the World Seemed New*, 323.

85. William Safire, "Essay; Ukraine Marches Out," *The New York Times*, November 18, 1991.

86. Quoted in Melvyn P. Leffler, "Dreams of Freedom, Temptations of Power," in *The Fall of the Berlin Wall: The Revolutionary Legacy of 1989*, ed. Jeffrey A. Engel (New York: Oxford University Press, 2009), 143.

87. Quoted in Derek Chollet and James Goldgeier, *America between the Wars, From 11/9 to 9/11: The Misunderstood Years between the Fall of the Berlin Wall and the Start of the War on Terror* (New York: Public Affairs Press, 2008), 42.

88. Quoted in Brands, *Making the Unipolar Moment*, 286.

89. Ikenberry, *After Victory*, 232.

90. See Ikenberry, *After Victory*, 230–233.

91. For a concurring account from an IR perspective, see Thomas Risse, "'Let's Argue!': Communicative Action in World Politics," *International Organization* 54, No. 1 (2000), 23–28.

92. For both the quote and the larger point, see Sayle, *Enduring Alliance*, 229–230.

93. Zoellick admitted that the changes were designed above all not to fundamentally transform the alliance but instead to "give Gorb. some things to make him more comfortable with the process." Quoted in Brands, *Making the Unipolar Moment*, 297; and Shifrinson, "Deal or No Deal?" 40. On this reasoning, see Sarotte, *1989*, 174–177; Meacham, *Destiny and Power*, 408; and Service, *The End of the Cold War*, 445.

94. See, for instance, Sayle, *Enduring Alliance*, 228–229.

95. Quoted in Leffler, *For the Soul of Mankind*, 443.

96. Quoted in Wilson, *The Triumph of Improvisation*, 184–185.

97. Both are quoted in Shifrinson, "Deal or No Deal?" 31.

98. Shifrinson, "Deal or No Deal?" 39–40.

99. See Sparrow, *The Strategist*, 371.

100. See, for example, their conversation at Malta in Savranskaya et al., *Masterpieces of History*, 627.

101. See, for instance, data provided about Russian mass beliefs in William Zimmerman, *The Russian People and Foreign Policy: Russian Elite and Mass Perspectives, 1993–2000* (Princeton: Princeton University Press, 2002); as well as John J. Mearsheimer, "Why the Ukraine Crisis Is the West's Fault: The Liberal Delusions That Provoked Putin," *Foreign Affairs* 93, No. 5 (2014).

102. Sarotte, "Perpetuating U.S. Preeminence," 135–136.

103. Wilson, *The Triumph of Improvisation*, 171.

104. Chollet and Goldgeier, *America between the Wars*, xiv.

105. Both are quoted in Leffler, "Dreams of Freedom, Temptations of Power," 145.

106. For example, Robert Kagan, *The Return of History and the End of Dreams* (New York: Alfred A. Knopf, 2008).

CHAPTER 9

1. Council on Foreign Relations speech, July 15, 2009, https://www.cfr.org/event/conversation-us-secretary-state-hillary-rodham-clinton-1.

2. Evan A. Feigenbaum, "China and the World: Dealing with a Reluctant Power," *Foreign Affairs* 96, No. 1 (2017), 39.

3. For a study that *does* directly engage Ikenberry on order outcomes, however, see Randall L. Schweller, "The Problem of International Order Revisited: A Review Essay," *International Security* 26, No. 1 (2001).

4. John J. Mearsheimer, "Bound to Fail: The Rise and Fall of the Liberal International Order," *International Security* 43, No. 4 (2019), 7.

5. The dearth of these kinds of shocks in the twenty-first century and the possible consequences of an inability of the international system to "reboot" in this way are discussed in Randall L. Schweller, *Maxwell's Demon and the Golden Apple: Global Discord in the New Millennium* (Baltimore: Johns Hopkins University Press, 2014).

6. G. John. Ikenberry, *Liberal Leviathan: The Origins, Crisis, and Transformation of the American World Order* (Princeton: Princeton University Press, 2011), 348.

7. By most estimates China will surpass America in aggregate economic power at some point in the coming decade. For the purpose of this analysis, I assume that China is rising and will continue to do so. But for debates over this important issue, see Roger Cliff, *China's Military Power: Assessing Current and Future Capabilities* (New York: Cambridge University Press, 2015); Stephen G. Brooks and William C. Wohlforth, *America Abroad: The United States' Global Role in the 21st Century* (New York: Oxford University Press, 2016), chapters 2–3; and Michael Beckley, *Unrivaled: Why America Will Remain the World's Sole Superpower* (Ithaca: Cornell University Press, 2018).

8. On China defying predictions that it would democratize as it continued to grow, see Yuen Yuen Ang, "Autocracy with Chinese Characteristics: Beijing's Behind-the-Scenes Reforms," *Foreign Affairs* 97, No. 3 (2018).

9. G. John Ikenberry, "The Plot against American Foreign Policy: Can the Liberal Order Survive?" *Foreign Affairs* 96, No. 3 (2017), 2.

10. Other accounts that highlight these changes include Martha Finnemore, *The Purpose of Intervention: Changing Beliefs about the Use of Force* (Ithaca: Cornell University Press, 2003), chapters 3–4; Jeffrey W. Legro, *Rethinking the World: Great Power Strategies and International Order* (Ithaca: Cornell University Press, 2005), 178; and Thomas J. Christensen, *The China Challenge: Shaping the Choices of a Rising Power* (New York: W. W. Norton & Company, 2015), 59–62.

11. A similar point is made in David M. Edelstein, *Over the Horizon: Time, Uncertainty, and the Rise of Great Powers* (Ithaca: Cornell University Press, 2017), 157–161.

12. See, for instance, Barry R. Posen, "The Rise of Illiberal Hegemony: Trump's Surprising Grand Strategy," *Foreign Affairs* 97, No. 2 (2018).

13. For good summaries of the debate, see Shaun Breslin, "China and the Global Order: Signaling Threat or Friendship?" *International Affairs* 89, No. 3 (2013); and Christensen, *The China Challenge*, 53–62. For an excellent overview of official debates within China about their country's rise more generally, see David Shambaugh and Ren Xiao, "China: The Conflicted Rising Power," in *Worldviews of Aspiring Powers: Domestic Foreign Policy Debates in China, India, Iran, Japan, and Russia*, ed. Henry R. Nau and Deepa M. Ollapally (New York: Oxford University Press, 2012).

14. Examples include Martin Jacques, *When China Rules the World: The End of the Western World and the Birth of a New Global Order*, 2nd ed. (New York: The Penguin Press, 2009/2012); William A. Callahan, "Chinese Visions of World Order: Post-Hegemonic or a New Hegemony?" *International Studies Review* 10,

No. 4 (2008); Robert Kagan, "Ambition and Anxiety: America's Competition with China," in *The Rise of China: Essays on the Future Competition*, ed. Gary J. Schmitt (New York: Encounter Books, 2009); Xiaoyu Pu and Randall Schweller, "After Unipolarity: China's Visions of International Order in an Era of U.S. Decline," *International Security* 36, No. 1 (2011); Charles A. Kupchan, *No One's World: The West, the Rising Rest, and the Coming Global Turn* (Oxford: Oxford University Press, 2012); Henry Kissinger, *World Order* (New York: Penguin Books, 2014), chapter 6; Howard W. French, *Everything under the Heavens: How the Past Helps Shape China's Push for Global Power* (New York: Alfred A. Knopf, 2017); Graham Allison, "China vs. America: Managing the Next Clash of Civilizations," *Foreign Affairs* 96, No. 5 (2017); and Elizabeth C. Economy, "China's New Revolution: The Reign of Xi Jinping," *Foreign Affairs* 97, No. 3 (2018). For a collection of essays that explicitly adopts an exporting perspective but is not as negative on the prospects for a Sino-American order convergence, see G. John Ikenberry, Wang Jisi, and Zhu Feng, eds., *America, China, and the Struggle for World Order* (New York: Palgrave Macmillan, 2015).

15. See, for instance, Alastair Iain Johnston, *Social States: China in International Institutions, 1980–2000* (Princeton: Princeton University Press, 2007); G. John Ikenberry, "The Rise of China and the Future of the West: Can the Liberal System Survive?" *Foreign Affairs* 87, No. 1 (2008); Edward S. Steinfeld, *Playing Our Game: Why China's Rise Doesn't Threaten the West* (New York: Oxford University Press, 2010); Ikenberry, *Liberal Leviathan*, chapter 8; and Joseph S. Nye, Jr., "Will the Liberal Order Survive? The History of an Idea," *Foreign Affairs* 96, No. 1 (2017). For a more qualified version of this optimism, see Jeffrey W. Legro, "What China Will Want: The Future Intentions of a Rising Power," *Perspectives on Politics* 5, No. 3 (2007).

16. "Pessimism" here refers only to the likelihood of China embracing the rules of the existing liberal order, not to the likelihood of militarized conflict between the United States and China. For a pessimistic account more along those lines, see John J. Mearsheimer, *The Tragedy of Great Power Politics,* updated ed. (New York: W. W. Norton & Company, 2001/2014), chapter 10.

17. Jacques, *When China Rules the World*, 535.

18. Pu and Schweller, "After Unipolarity," 67.

19. For the standard argument about the viability of the authoritarian capitalist model, see Stefan Halper, *The Beijing Consensus: How China's Authoritarian Model Will Dominate the Twenty-First Century* (New York: Basic Books, 2010).

20. Daniel Deudney and G. John Ikenberry, "The Myth of the Autocratic Revival: Why Liberal Democracy Will Prevail," *Foreign Affairs* 88, No. 1 (2009), 90.

21. Economic openness and stability is, after all, only one out of five principles of the liberal order (chapter 7).

22. Andrew J. Nathan and Andrew Scobell, "How China Sees America: The Sum of Beijing's Fears," *Foreign Affairs* 91, No. 5 (2012), 39. See also Kagan, "Ambition and Anxiety," 14–22; and Christensen, *The China Challenge*, 162–165.

23. A similar prediction has been advanced in Robin Niblett, "Liberalism in Retreat: Demise of a Dream," *Foreign Affairs* 96, No. 1 (2017).

24. In the language of chapter 7, this would mean the elimination of liberal order rules # 2 (responsibility for general welfare) and #5 (liberal democracy), as well as the dilution or elimination of #3 (liberal security community).

25. This theme is emphasized in Gregory Chin and Ramesh Thakur, "Will China Change the Rules of Global Order?" *The Washington Quarterly* 33, No. 4 (2010); Liselotte Odgaard, *China and Coexistence: Beijing's National Security Strategy for the Twenty-First Century* (Baltimore: The Johns Hopkins University Press, 2012); and Ryan D. Griffiths, "States, Nations, and Territorial Stability: Why Chinese Hegemony Would Be Better for International Order," *Security Studies* 25, No. 3 (2016).

26. Quoted in Robert Kagan, *The Return of History and the End of Dreams* (New York: Knopf, 2008), 70.

27. Barry Buzan, "China in International Society: Is 'Peaceful Rise' Possible?" *The Chinese Journal of International Politics* 3 (2010), 31.

28. See, for instance, Breslin, "China and the Global Order," 626–628; and Christensen, *The China Challenge*, 74–81.

29. Jacques, *When China Rules the World*, 422.

30. "What Is China's Belt and Road Initiative?" *The Economist*, May 17, 2017, https://www.economist.com/blogs/economist-explains/2017/05/economist-explains-11; "Will China's Belt and Road Initiative Outdo the Marshall Plan?" *The Economist*, March 8, 2018, https://www.economist.com/news/finance-and-economics/21738370-how-chinas-infrastructure-projects-around-world-stack-up-against-americas-plan.

31. Jacques, *When China Rules the World*, 424–428.

32. Azar Gat, "The Return of the Authoritarian Great Powers," *Foreign Affairs* 86, No. 4 (2009).

33. Chin and Thakur, "Will China Change the Rules of Global Order?" 122–125.

34. See David Dollar, "China's Rise as a Regional and Global Power: The AIIB and the 'One Belt, One Road,'" *Horizons* No. 4 (Summer 2015), 162–174; and "Reversion to the Mean," *The Economist*, September 24, 2015, https://www.economist.com/news/asia/21667964-chinas-new-infrastructure-bank-has-gained-wide-support-lending-will-be-tougher-reversion.

35. "Pax Sinica," *The Economist*, September 20, 2014, https://www.economist.com/news/asia/21618866-china-trying-build-new-world-order-starting-asia-pax-sinica.

36. Breslin, "China and the Global Order," 628. Former President Hu Jintao is quoted in Dilip Hiro, "Shanghai Surprise: The Summit of the Shanghai Cooperation Organization Reveals How Power Is Shifting in the World," *The Guardian*, June 16, 2006, http://www.guardian.co.uk/commentisfree/2006/jun/16/shanghaisurprise.

37. Quoted in Kagan, *The Return of History*, 74.

38. This is the vision at the heart of Aaron L. Friedberg, *A Contest for Supremacy: China, America, and the Struggle for Mastery in Asia* (New York: W. W. Norton & Company, 2011).

39. See Christensen, *The China Challenge*, chapter 5; and Charles L. Glaser, "A U.S.-China Grand Bargain? The Hard Choice between Military Confrontation and Accommodation," *International Security* 39, No. 4 (2015).

40. For arguments that China has been hedging in this way, see Rosemary Foot, "Chinese Strategies in a US-Hegemonic Global Order: Accommodating and Hedging," *International Affairs* 82, No. 1 (2006); Men Honghua, "China: Security Dilemma and 'Win Win,'" in *Shaper Nations: Strategies for a Changing World*, ed. William I. Hitchcock, Melvyn P. Leffler, and Jeffrey W. Legro (Cambridge, MA: Harvard University Press, 2016); Jonathan D. Pollack, "Competing Visions: China, America, and the Asia-Pacific Security Order," in *China's Global Engagement: Cooperation, Competition, and Influence in the 21st Century*, ed. Jacques deLisle and Avery Goldstein (Washington, DC: The Brookings Institution, 2017); and Thomas J. Wright, *All Measures Short of War: The Contest for the Twenty-First Century and the Future of American Power* (New Haven: Yale University Press, 2017), chapter 3.

APPENDIX

1. But for intelligent analysis on this important issue, see Stephen G. Brooks and William C. Wohlforth, "The Rise and Fall of the Great Powers in the Twenty-First Century: China's Rise and the Fate of America's Global Position," *International Security* 40, No. 3 (2015/2016).

Index

For the benefit of digital users, indexed terms that span two pages (e.g., 52–53) may, on occasion, appear on only one of those pages.

Tables and figures are indicated by *t* and *f* following the page number